Nurarihyon's "past story" was first published as a one-shot in *Akamaru Jump*, and the rest was based on a story that I drew for my own pleasure.

It was a nine-page short story, but I didn't think it would turn out to be such a long episode! For both the work and for me it was definitely a lucky thing.

—HIROSHI SHIIBASHI, 2009

HIROSHI SHIIBASHI debuted in BUSINESS JUMP magazine with *Aratama*. NURA: RISE OF THE YOKAI CLAN is his breakout hit. He was an assistant to manga artist Hirohiko Araki, the creator of *Jojo's Bizarre Adventure*. *Steel Ball Run* by Araki is one of his favorite manga.

NURA: RISE OF THE YOKAI CLAN
VOLUME 8
SHONEN JUMP Manga Edition

Story and Art by HIROSHI SHIIBASHI

Translation — Yumi Okamoto
Adaptation — Mark Giambruno
Touch-up Art and Lettering — Annaliese Christman
Graphics and Cover Design — Fawn Lau
Editor — Joel Enos

NURARIHYON NO MAGO © 2008 by Hiroshi
Shiibashi. All rights reserved. First published in
Japan in 2008 by SHUEISHA Inc., Tokyo. English
translation rights arranged by SHUEISHA Inc.

The rights of the author(s) of the work(s) in this
publication to be so identified have been asserted
in accordance with the Copyright, Designs and
Patents Act 1988. A CIP catalogue record for this
book is available from the British Library.

Printed in the U.S.A.

Published by VIZ Media, LLC
P.O. Box 77010
San Francisco, CA 94107

10 9 8 7 6 5 4 3 2 1
First printing, April 2012

www.viz.com   www.shonenjump.com

NURA: RISE OF THE YOKAI CLAN

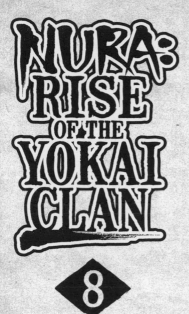

8

ECHOES OF THE PAST

STORY AND ART BY
HIROSHI SHIIBASHI

CHARACTERS

NURARIHYON

Rikuo's grandfather and the Lord of Pandemonium. He intends to pass leadership of the Nura clan—leaders of the yokai world—to Rikuo. He's mischievous and likes to dine and ditch.

RIKUO NURA

Though he appears to be a human boy, he's actually the grandson of Nurarihyon, a yokai. His grandfather's blood makes him one-quarter yokai, and he transforms into a yokai at times.

KIYOTSUGU

Rikuo's classmate. He has adored yokai ever since Rikuo saved him in his yokai form, leading him to form the Kiyojuji Paranormal Patrol.

KANA IENAGA

Rikuo's classmate and a childhood friend. Even though she hates scary things, she's a member of the Kiyojuji Paranormal Patrol for some reason.

YUKI-ONNA

A yokai of the Nura clan who is in charge of looking after Rikuo. She disguises herself as a human and attends the same school as Rikuo to protect him from danger. When in human form, she goes by the name Tsurara Oikawa.

YURA KEIKAIN

Rikuo's classmate and a descendant of the Keikain family of onmyoji. She transferred into Ukiyoe Middle School to do field training in yokai exorcism. She has the power to control her shikigami and uses them to destroy yokai.

PRINCESS YO

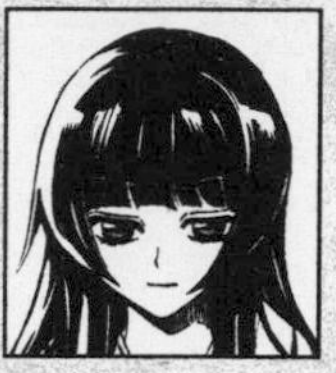

The daughter of a family of nobles in Kyoto. Said to be the most beautiful woman in all of Kyoto. She possesses a mysterious ability to heal injuries and illnesses, and has a very compassionate personality.

GYUKI

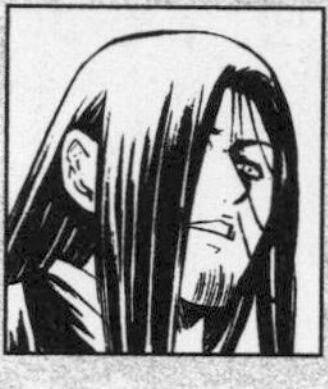

The leader of the Nura clan subgroup, the Gyuki clan. His headquarters are located at the top of Mt. Nejireme, in the westernmost region of Nura clan territory. He has a personality that is scholarly, calm and collected.

MAMIRU KEIKAIN

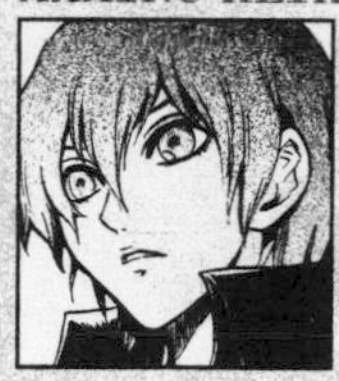

A Keikain family onmyoji. His talents were recognized and he was welcomed into the main house. His feelings about yokai are even stronger than Ryuji's. He controls a lightning shikigami.

RYUJI KEIKAIN

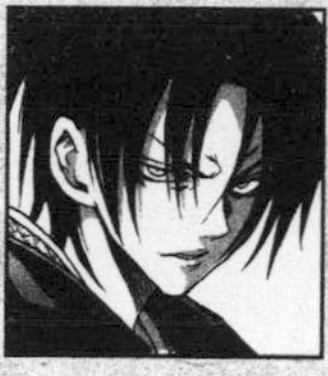

Yura's brother and himself a Keikain family onmyoji. A coolheaded man who views yokai as absolute evil. He controls a water shikigami and uses his smooth tongue to confuse enemies.

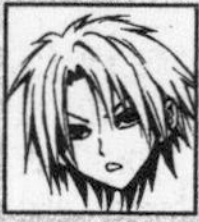

KUBINASHI

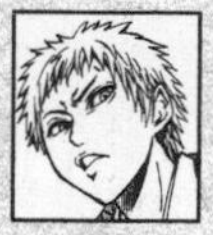

ZEN

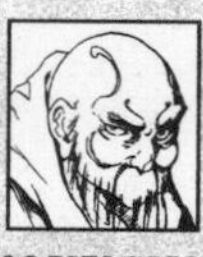

MOKUGYO-DARUMA

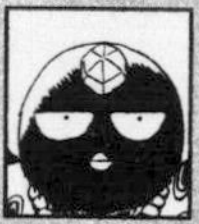

KARASU-TENGU

STORY SO FAR

Rikuo Nura appears to be just your average seventh-grader at Ukiyoe Middle School. But he's actually the grandson of the yokai Overlord Nurarihyon and has just been promoted to become the Underboss of the Nura clan, the Tokyo region's powerful yokai syndicate! For now, he lives his days as a human boy, but eventually, he is expected to take his grandfather's place as the leader of the clan.

The onmyoji Ryuji arrives in Ukiyoe Town. He attacks Rikuo, causing his sister Yura to be torn between her responsibilities as an onmyoji and her friendship with Rikuo. She comes to Rikuo's aid, infuriating her brother, who retaliates. After defeating her brother, Rikuo and his friends learn that the Keikain family's sworn enemy, the great yokai Hagoromo-Gitsune, is on the move. They return to their homeland to prepare for battle.

Four hundred years ago, the young Nurarihyon travels to Kyoto with his strongest clan members in his quest to become the Lord of Pandemonium. There, he is attracted to Princess Yo, who has a mysterious healing power. Some yokai want to capture her...and tear her apart to find out the source of her great power...

TABLE OF CONTENTS

NURA: RISE OF THE YOKAI CLAN

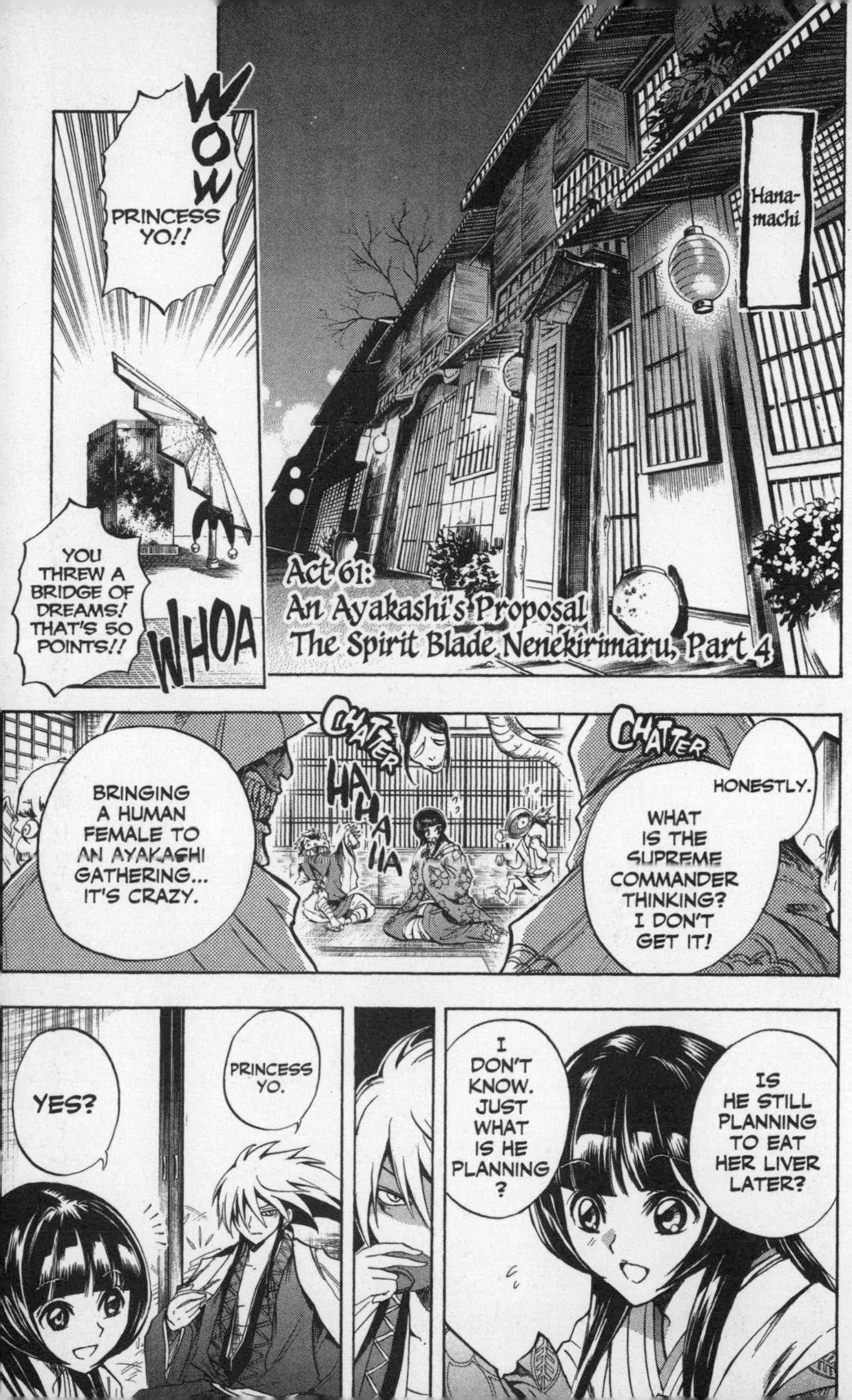
Hana-machi
Act 61: An Ayakashi's Proposal The Spirit Blade Nenekirimaru, Part 4
WOW
PRINCESS YO!!
YOU THREW A BRIDGE OF DREAMS! THAT'S 50 POINTS!!
WHOA
CHATTER
HONESTLY.
WHAT IS THE SUPREME COMMANDER THINKING? I DON'T GET IT!
CHATTER
HAHAHA
BRINGING A HUMAN FEMALE TO AN AYAKASHI GATHERING... IT'S CRAZY.
IS HE STILL PLANNING TO EAT HER LIVER LATER?
I DON'T KNOW. JUST WHAT IS HE PLANNING?
PRINCESS YO.
YES?

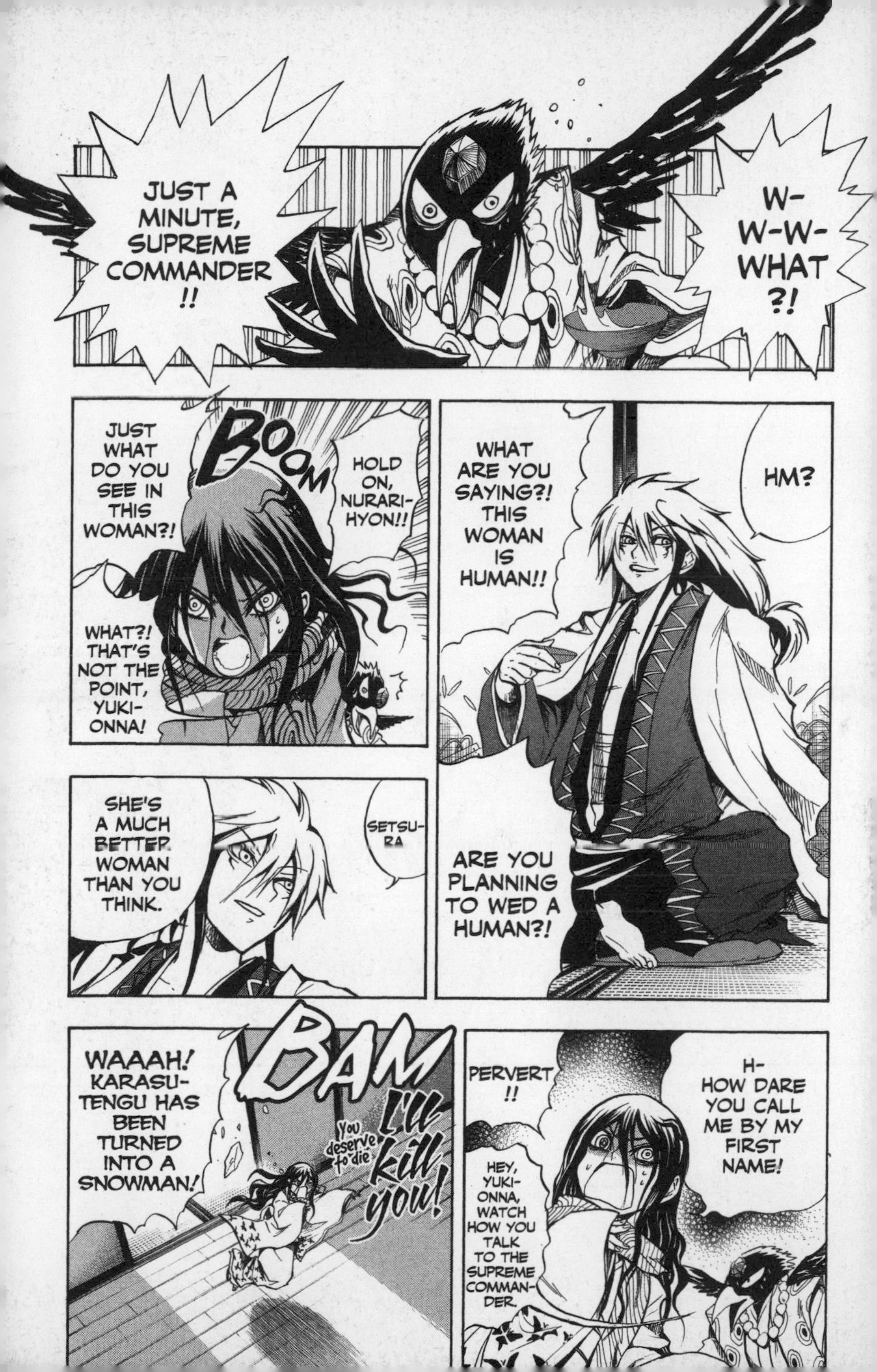
W-W-W-WHAT?!
JUST A MINUTE, SUPREME COMMANDER!!
HM?
WHAT ARE YOU SAYING?! THIS WOMAN IS HUMAN!!
ARE YOU PLANNING TO WED A HUMAN?!
HOLD ON, NURARI-HYON!!
BOOM
JUST WHAT DO YOU SEE IN THIS WOMAN?!
WHAT?! THAT'S NOT THE POINT, YUKI-ONNA!
SETSU-RA
SHE'S A MUCH BETTER WOMAN THAN YOU THINK.
H-HOW DARE YOU CALL ME BY MY FIRST NAME!
PERVERT!!
HEY, YUKI-ONNA, WATCH HOW YOU TALK TO THE SUPREME COMMAN-DER.
BAM
I'll kill you!
You deserve to die
WAAAH! KARASU-TENGU HAS BEEN TURNED INTO A SNOWMAN!

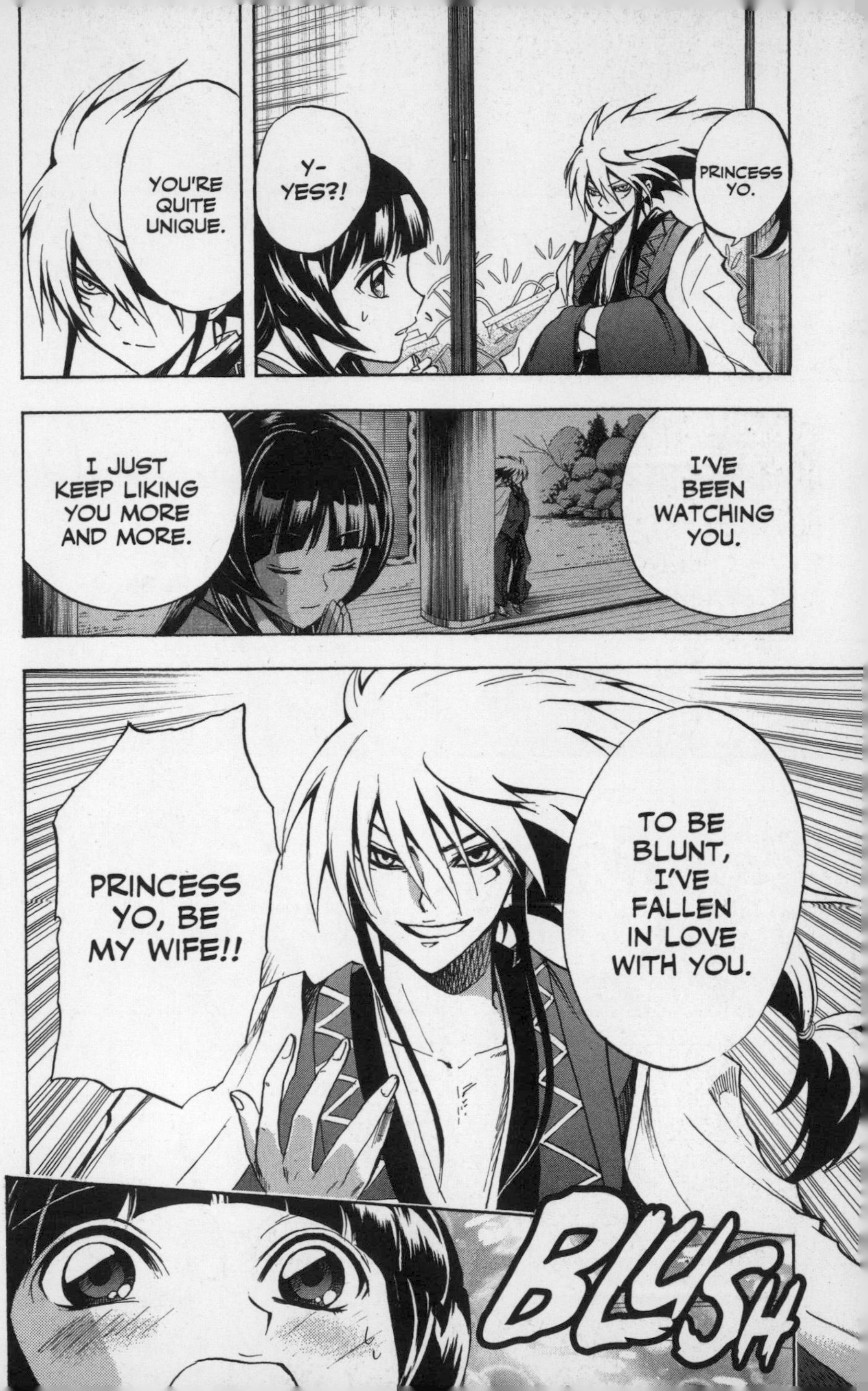
PRINCESS YO.
Y- YES?!
YOU'RE QUITE UNIQUE.
I'VE BEEN WATCHING YOU.
I JUST KEEP LIKING YOU MORE AND MORE.
TO BE BLUNT, I'VE FALLEN IN LOVE WITH YOU.
PRINCESS YO, BE MY WIFE!!
BLUSH

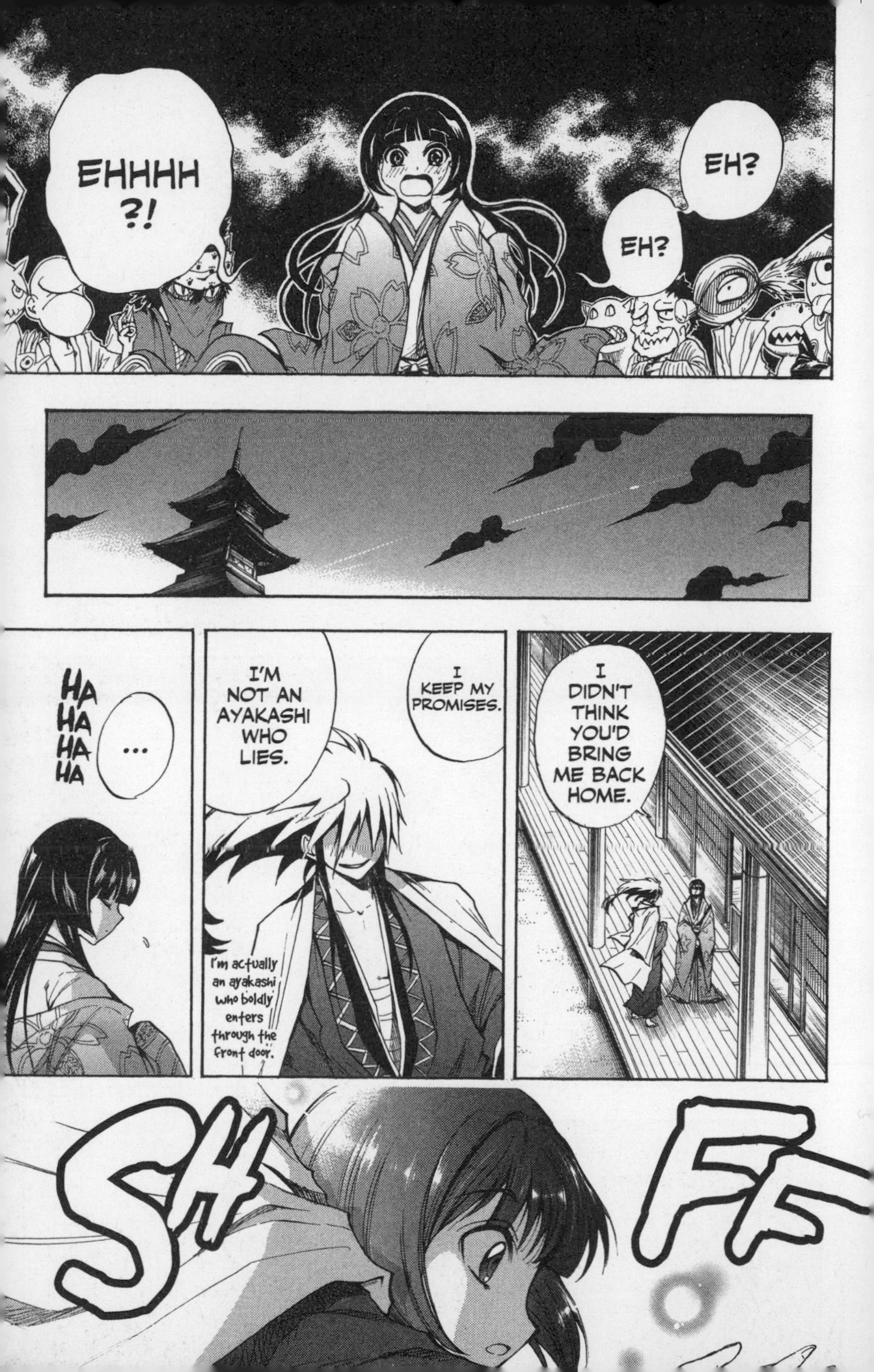
EH?
EH?
EHHHH ?!
I DIDN'T THINK YOU'D BRING ME BACK HOME.
I KEEP MY PROMISES.
I'M NOT AN AYAKASHI WHO LIES.
I'm actually an ayakashi who boldly enters through the front door.
HA HA HA HA
...
SHFF

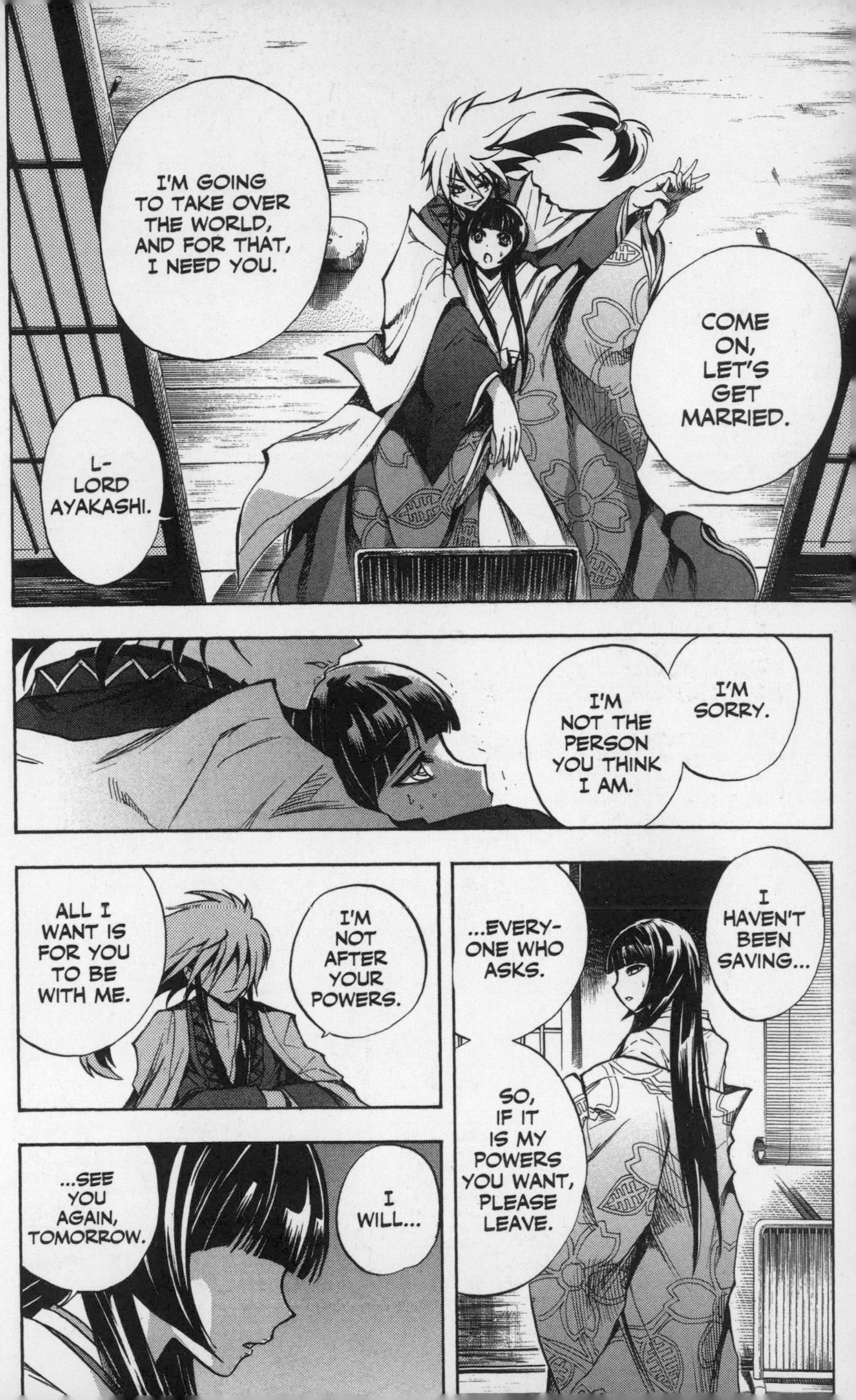
COME ON, LET'S GET MARRIED.
I'M GOING TO TAKE OVER THE WORLD, AND FOR THAT, I NEED YOU.
L- LORD AYAKASHI.
I'M SORRY.
I'M NOT THE PERSON YOU THINK I AM.
I HAVEN'T BEEN SAVING...
...EVERY-ONE WHO ASKS.
SO, IF IT IS MY POWERS YOU WANT, PLEASE LEAVE.
I'M NOT AFTER YOUR POWERS.
ALL I WANT IS FOR YOU TO BE WITH ME.
I WILL...
...SEE YOU AGAIN, TOMORROW.

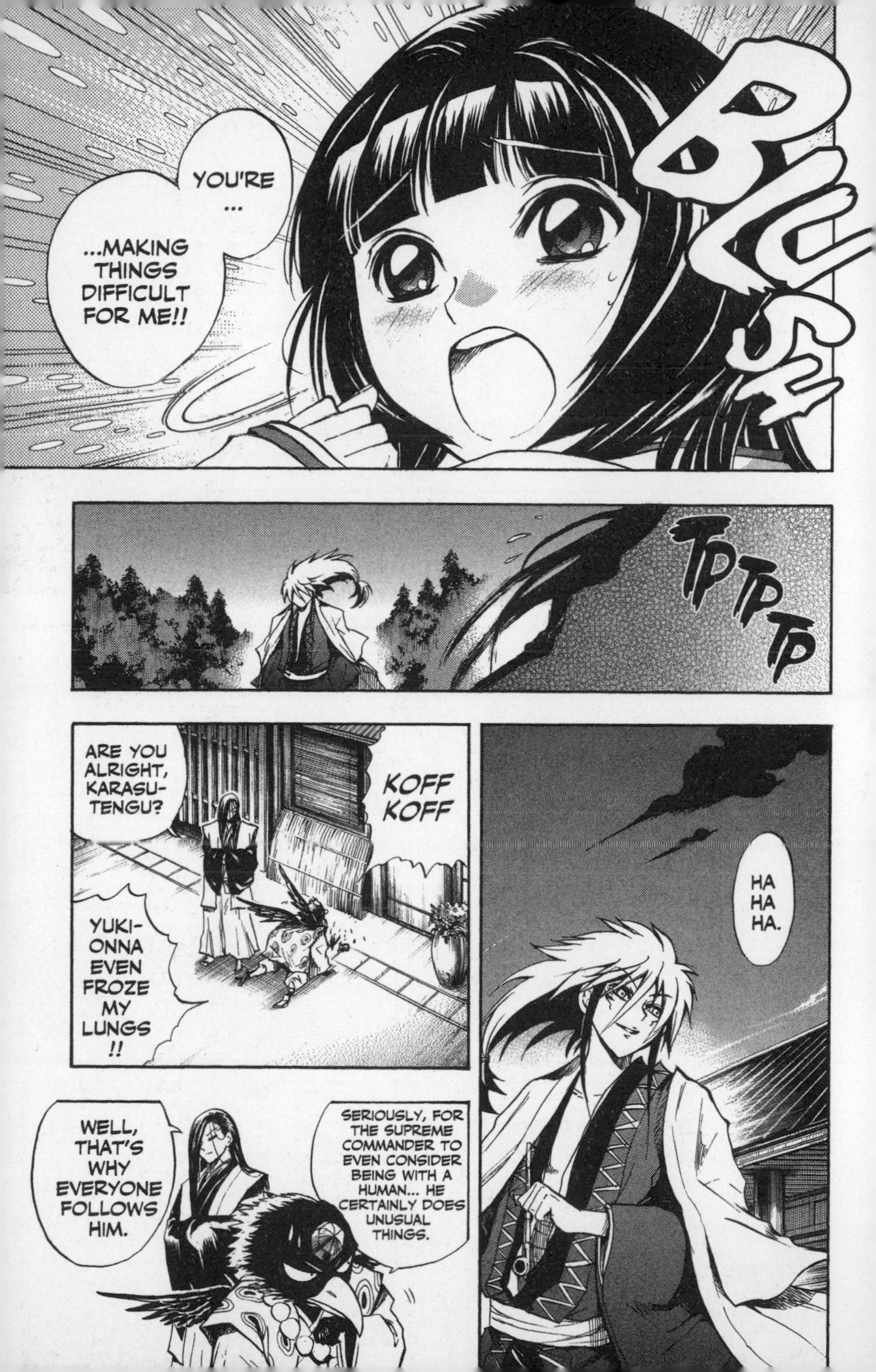
BYUSH
YOU'RE ...
...MAKING THINGS DIFFICULT FOR ME!!
TPTPTP
HA HA HA.
KOFF KOFF
ARE YOU ALRIGHT, KARASU-TENGU?
YUKI-ONNA EVEN FROZE MY LUNGS!!
SERIOUSLY, FOR THE SUPREME COMMANDER TO EVEN CONSIDER BEING WITH A HUMAN... HE CERTAINLY DOES UNUSUAL THINGS.
WELL, THAT'S WHY EVERYONE FOLLOWS HIM.

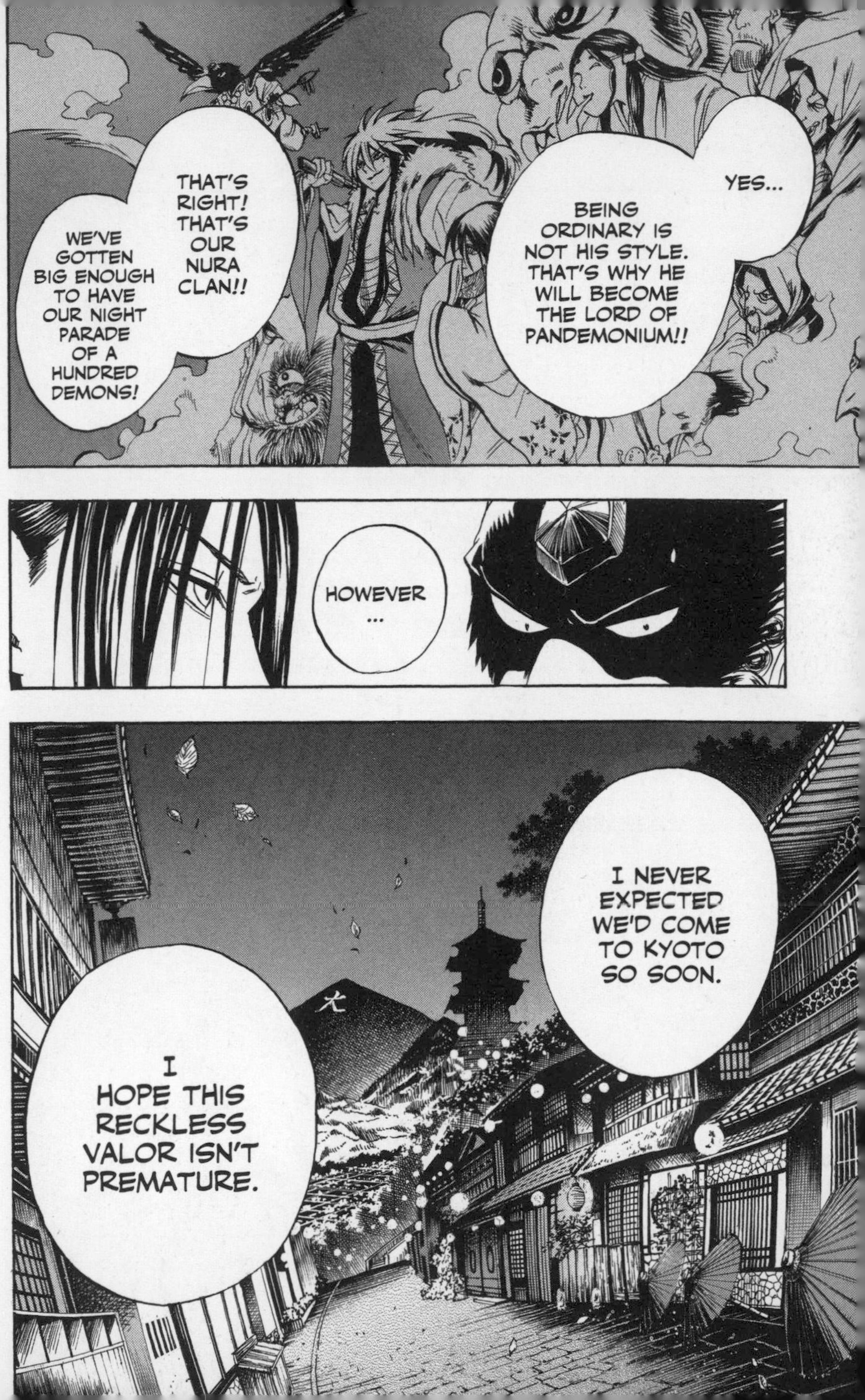
YES...
BEING ORDINARY IS NOT HIS STYLE. THAT'S WHY HE WILL BECOME THE LORD OF PANDEMONIUM!!
THAT'S RIGHT! THAT'S OUR NURA CLAN!!
WE'VE GOTTEN BIG ENOUGH TO HAVE OUR NIGHT PARADE OF A HUNDRED DEMONS!
HOWEVER ...
I NEVER EXPECTED WE'D COME TO KYOTO SO SOON.
I HOPE THIS RECKLESS VALOR ISN'T PREMATURE.

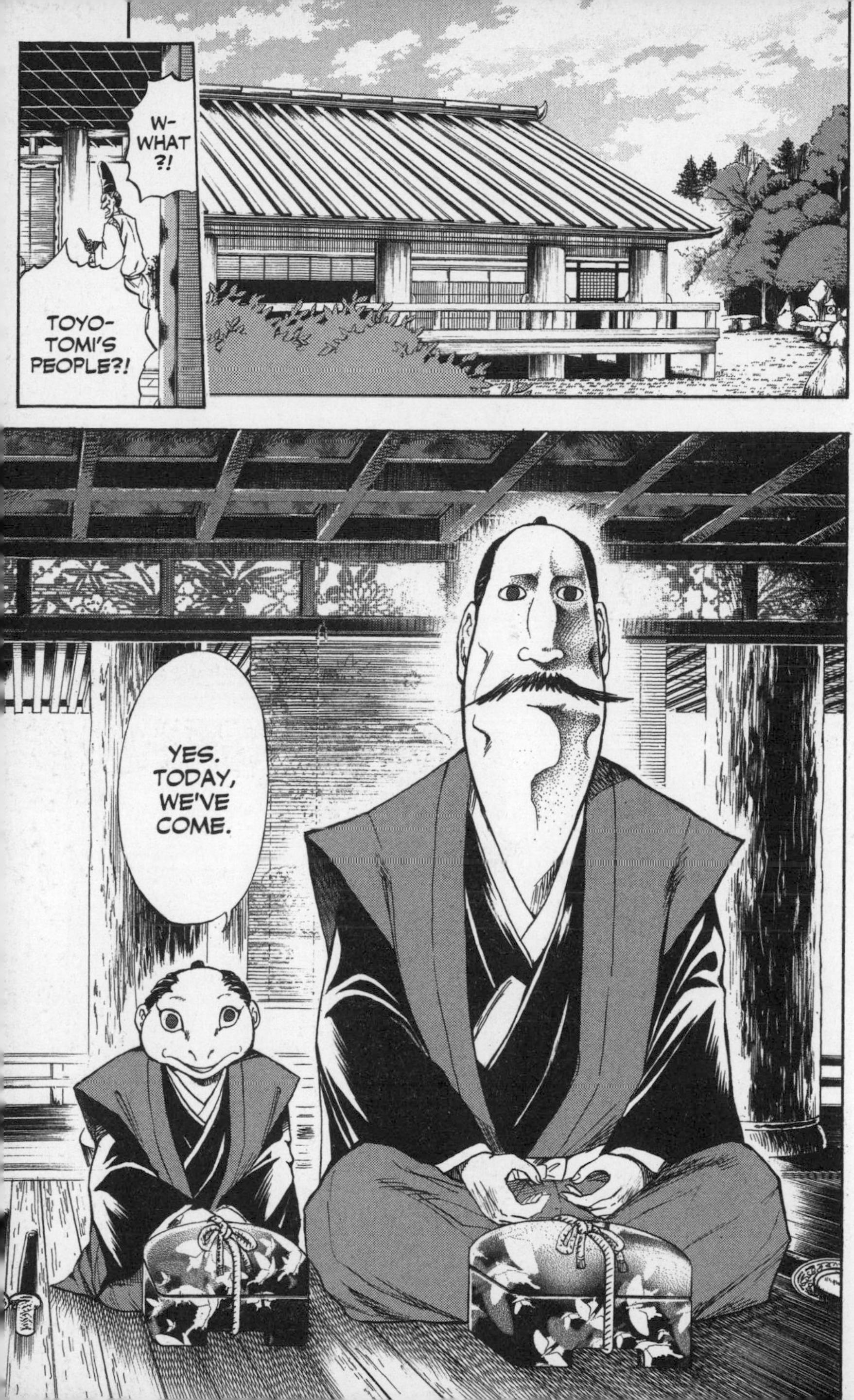
W-WHAT?!
TOYO-TOMI'S PEOPLE?!
YES. TODAY, WE'VE COME.

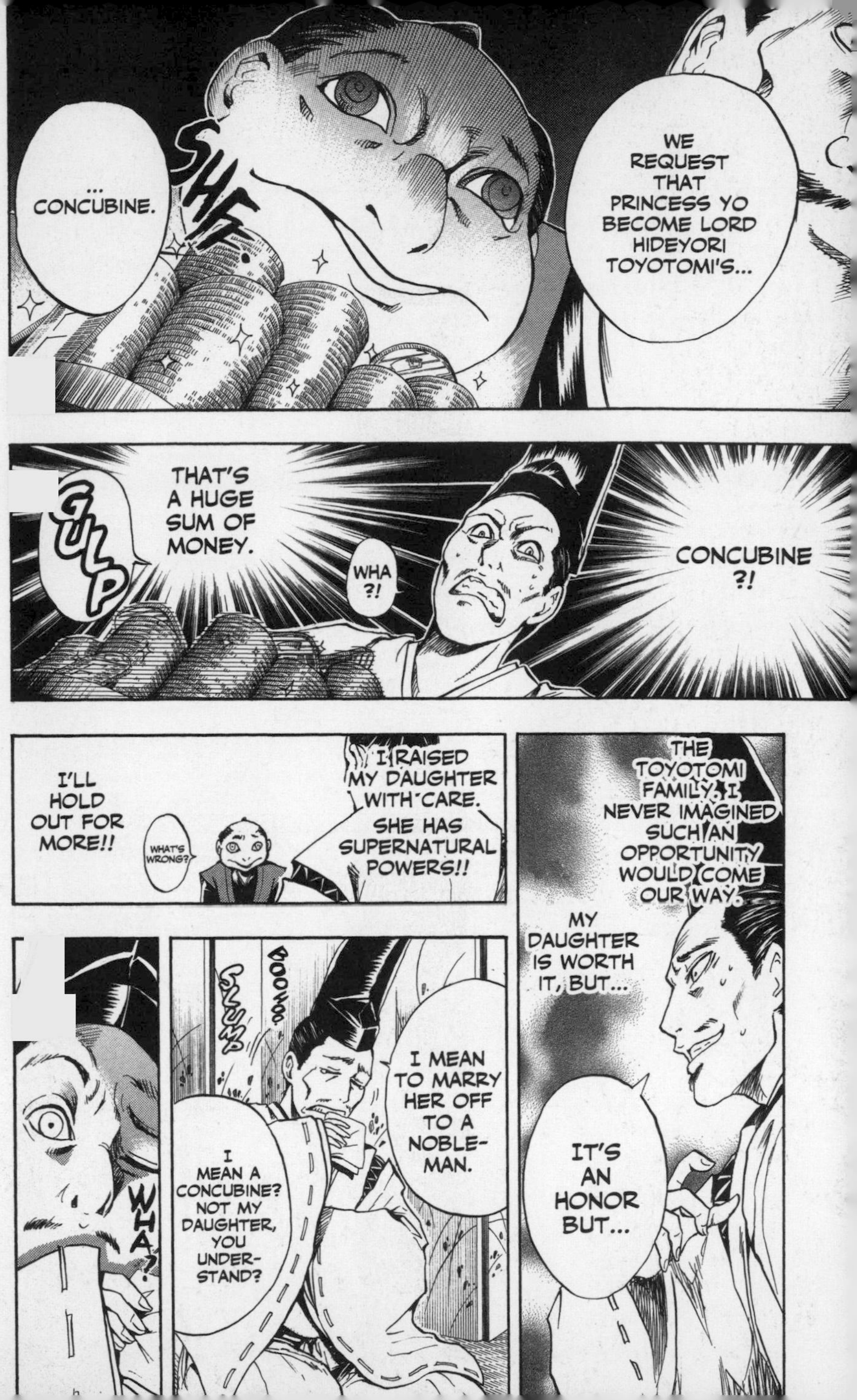
WE REQUEST THAT PRINCESS YO BECOME LORD HIDEYORI TOYOTOMI'S...
SHF
...CONCUBINE.
CONCUBINE?!
WHA?!
THAT'S A HUGE SUM OF MONEY.
GULP
THE TOYOTOMI FAMILY. I NEVER IMAGINED SUCH AN OPPORTUNITY WOULD COME OUR WAY.
MY DAUGHTER IS WORTH IT, BUT...
IT'S AN HONOR BUT...
I RAISED MY DAUGHTER WITH CARE.
SHE HAS SUPERNATURAL POWERS!!
WHAT'S WRONG?
I'LL HOLD OUT FOR MORE!!
BOOOOO
SLUMP
I MEAN TO MARRY HER OFF TO A NOBLE-MAN.
I MEAN A CONCUBINE? NOT MY DAUGHTER, YOU UNDER-STAND?
WHA?

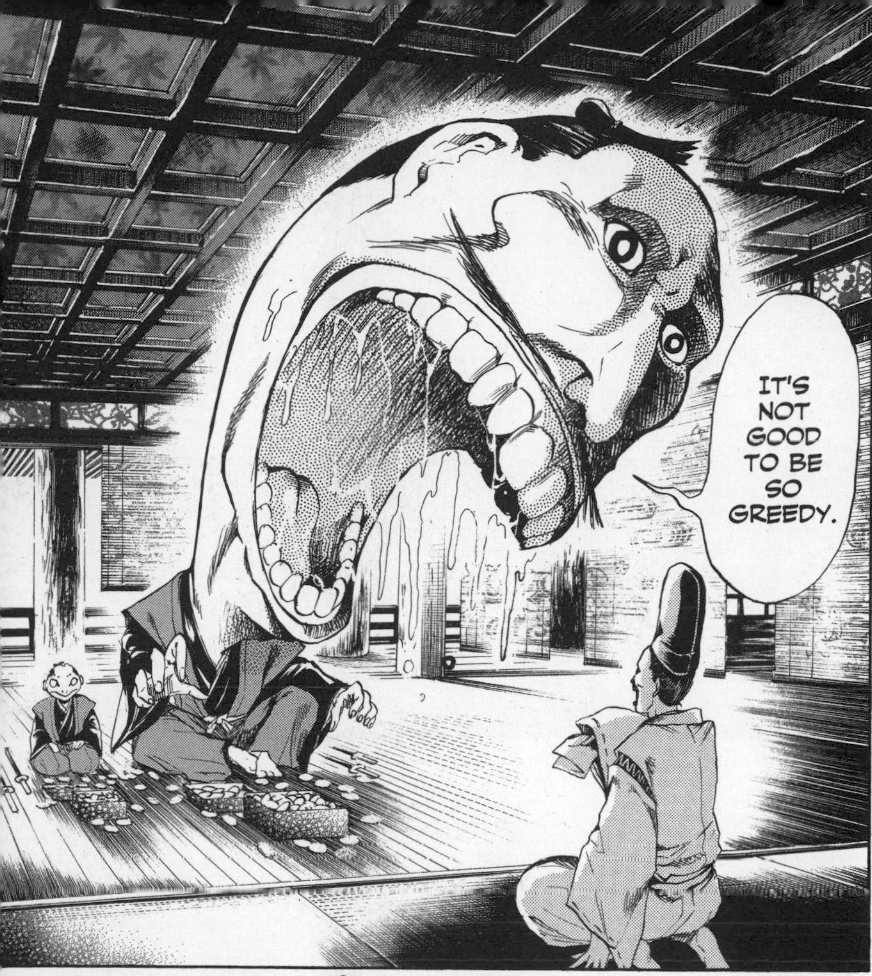
IT'S NOT GOOD TO BE SO GREEDY.

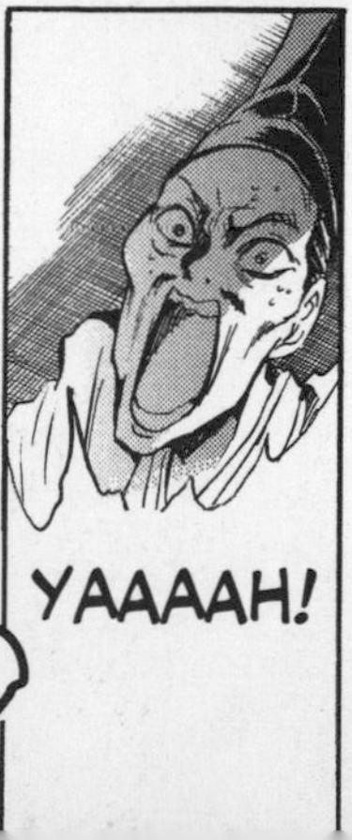
YAAAAH!

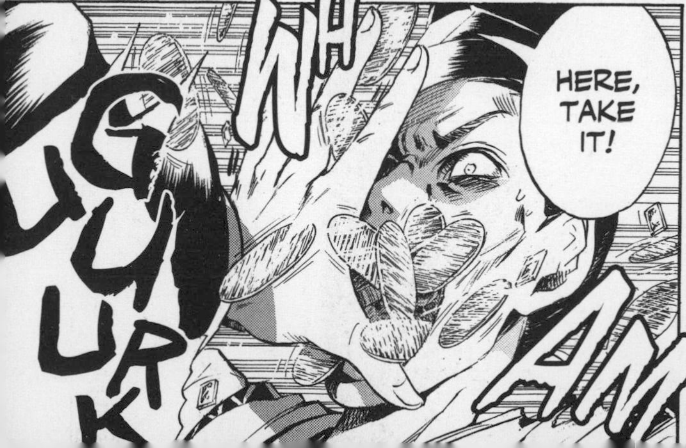
HERE, TAKE IT!
WHAM
GUUURK

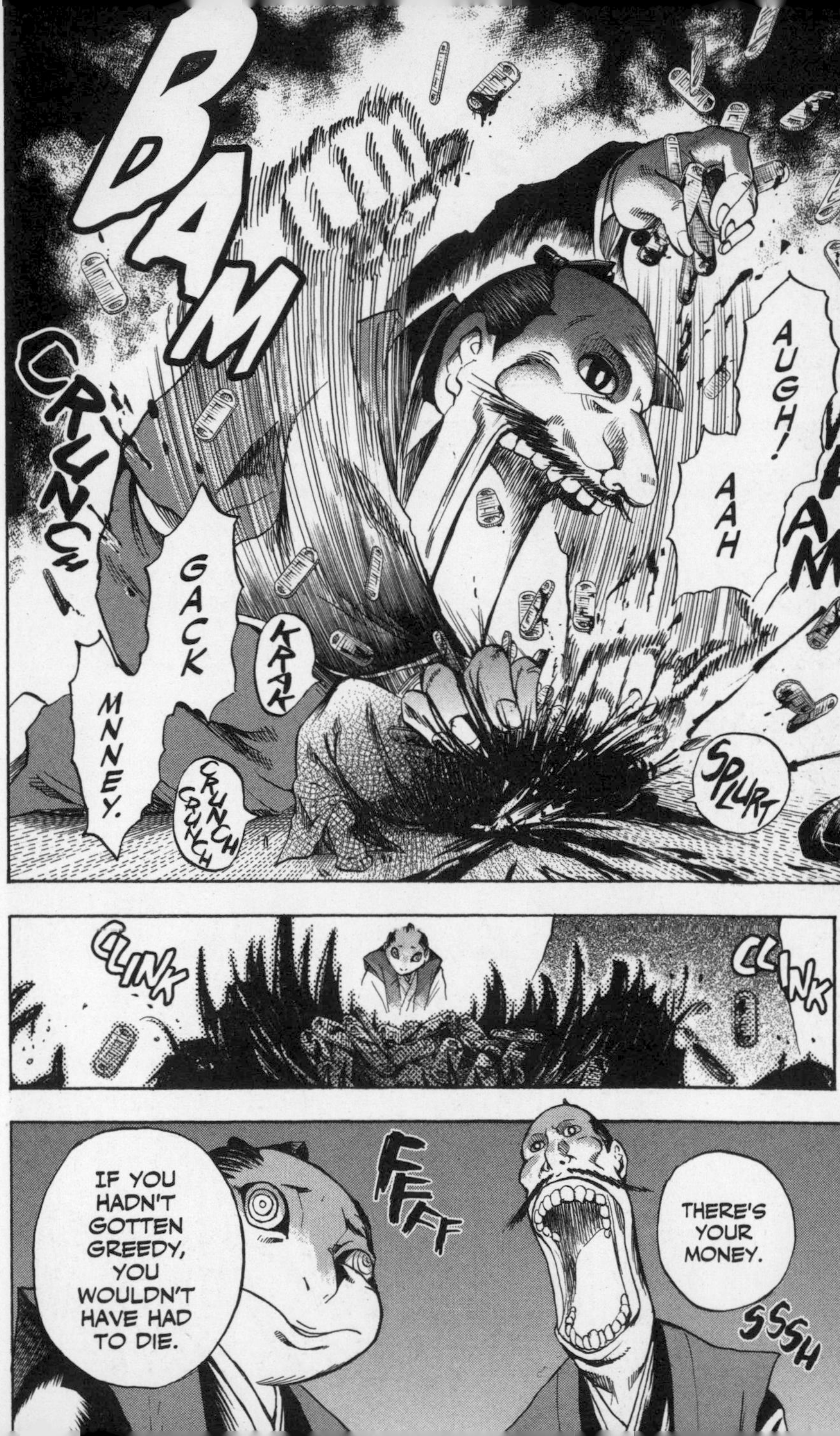
WHAM
AUGH! AAH
BAM
CRUNCH
SPLURT
KRAK
GACK
MNNEY.
CRUNCH CRUNCH
CLINK
CLINK
THERE'S YOUR MONEY.
SSSH
FFFF
IF YOU HADN'T GOTTEN GREEDY, YOU WOULDN'T HAVE HAD TO DIE.

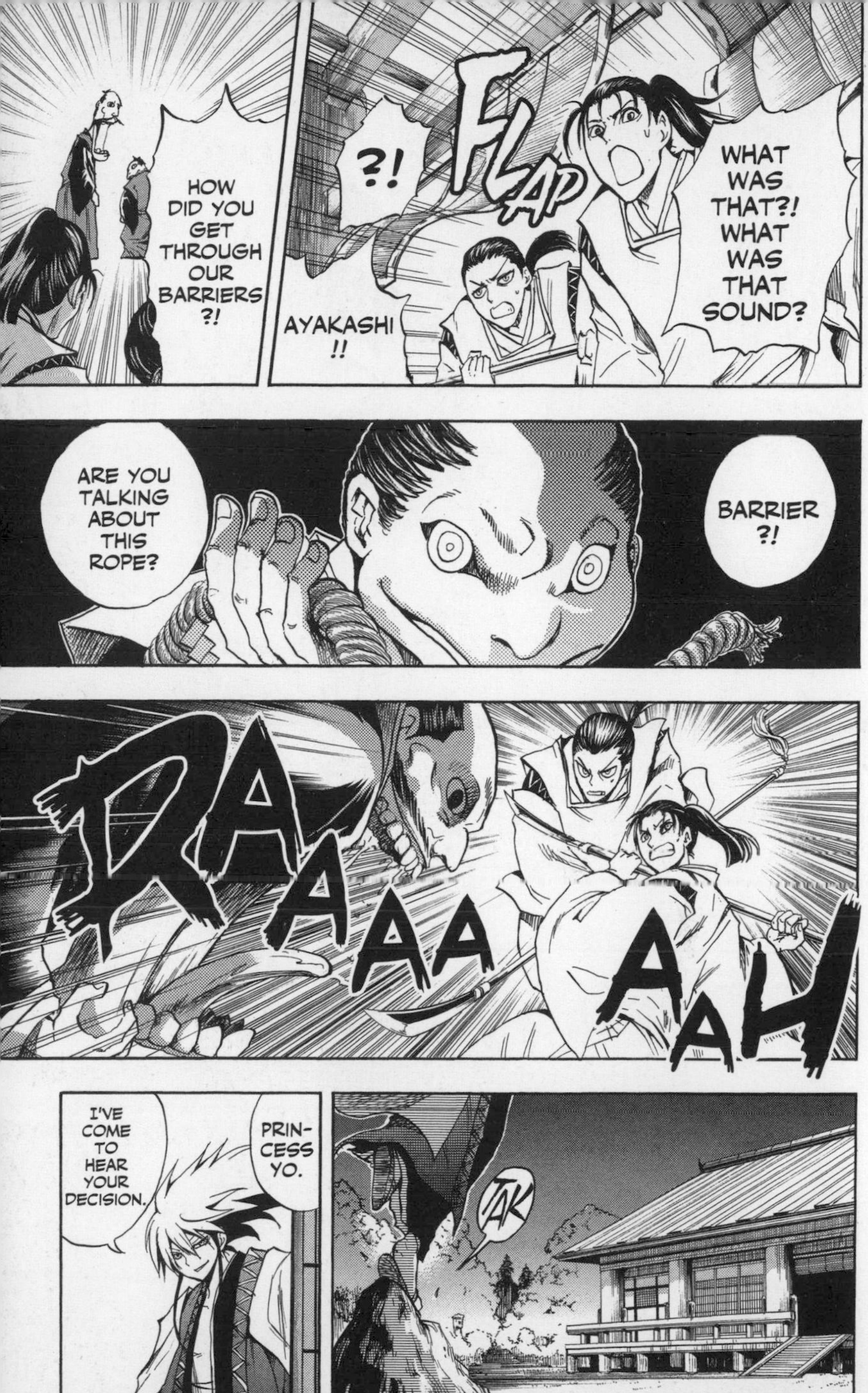
WHAT WAS THAT?! WHAT WAS THAT SOUND?
FLAP
?!
AYAKASHI !!
HOW DID YOU GET THROUGH OUR BARRIERS ?!
BARRIER ?!
ARE YOU TALKING ABOUT THIS ROPE?
RAAAAAAH
TAK
PRIN-CESS YO.
I'VE COME TO HEAR YOUR DECISION.

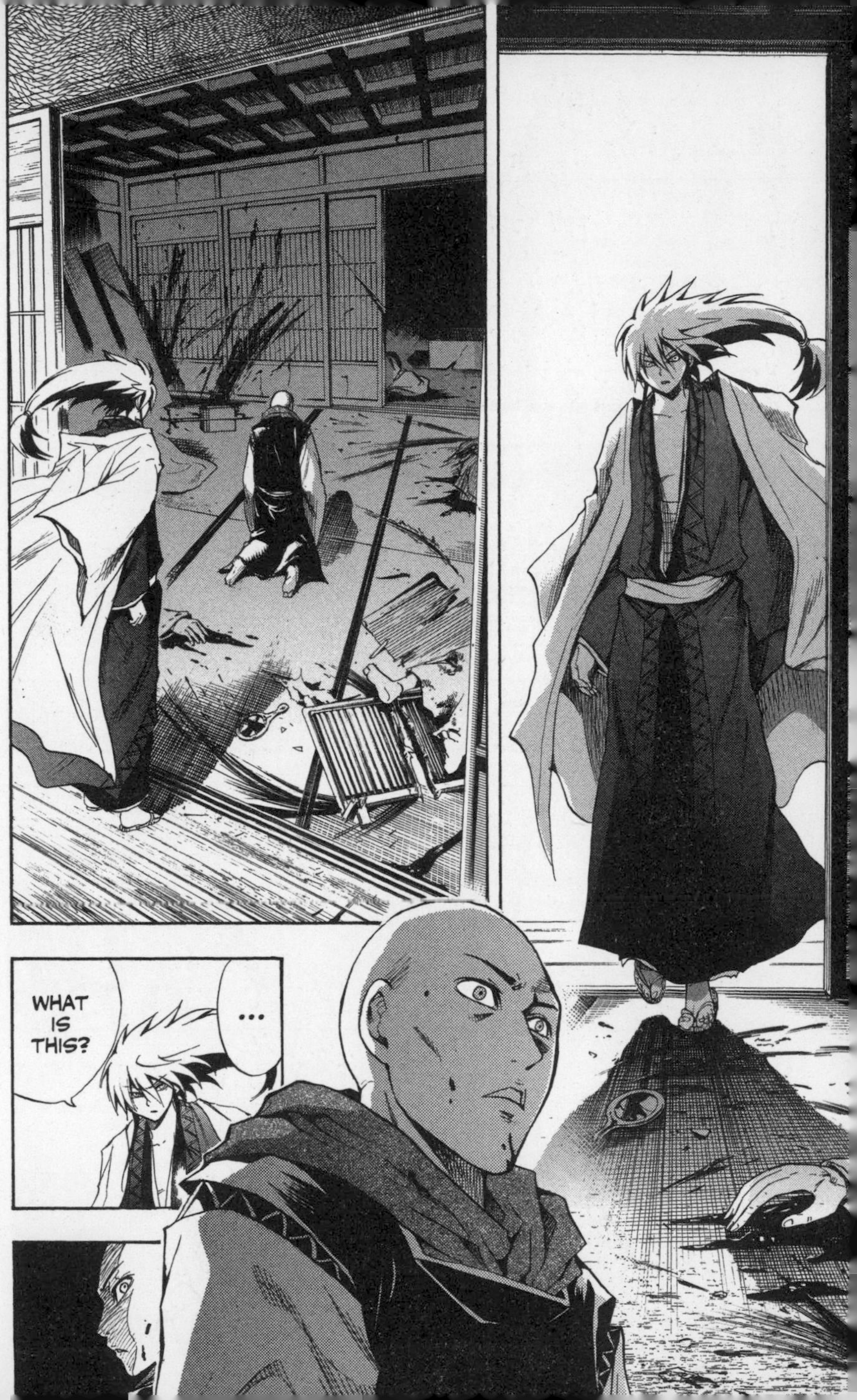
...
WHAT IS THIS?

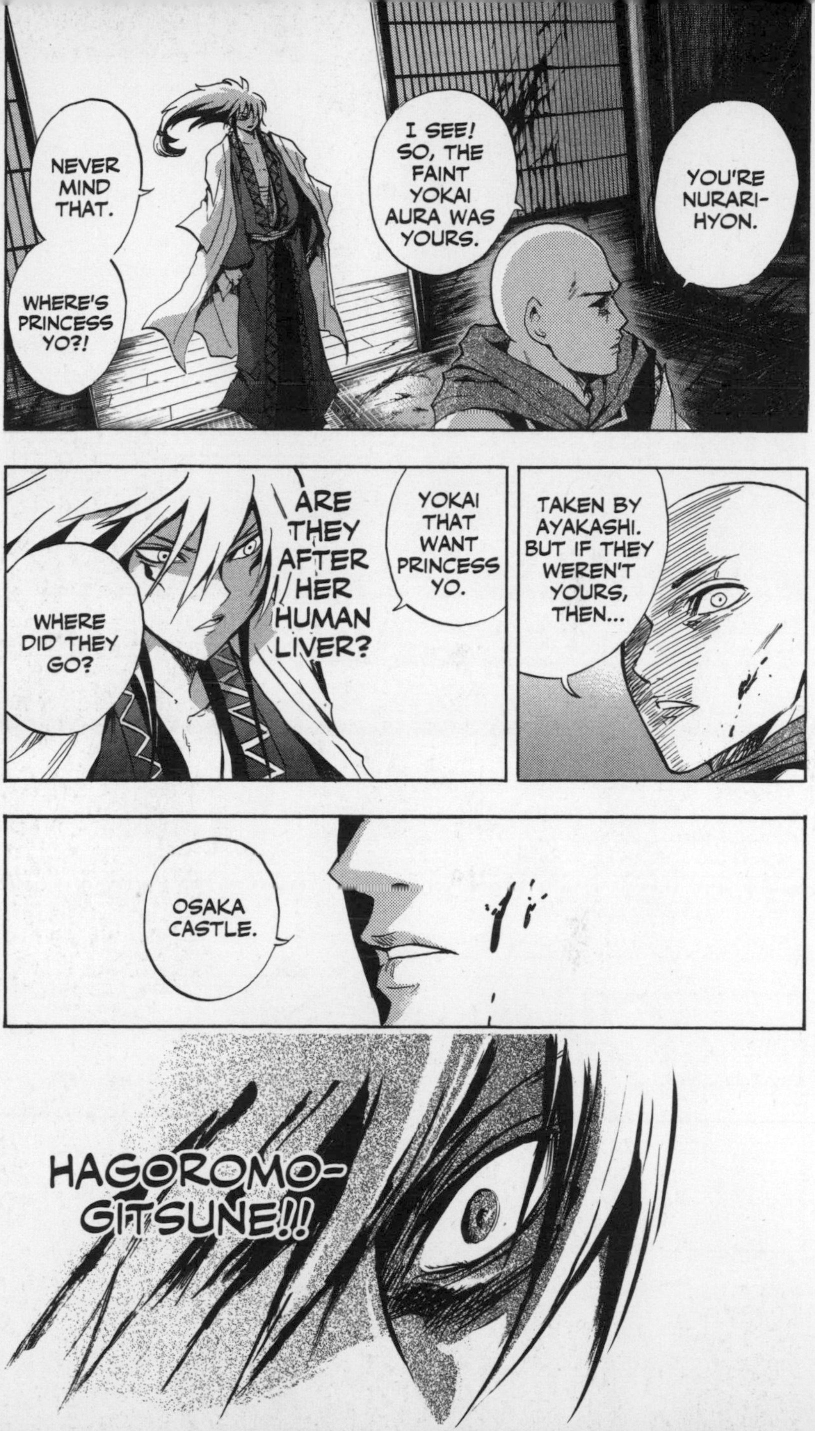
YOU'RE NURARI-HYON.
I SEE! SO, THE FAINT YOKAI AURA WAS YOURS.
NEVER MIND THAT.
WHERE'S PRINCESS YO?!
TAKEN BY AYAKASHI. BUT IF THEY WEREN'T YOURS, THEN...
YOKAI THAT WANT PRINCESS YO.
ARE THEY AFTER HER HUMAN LIVER?
WHERE DID THEY GO?
OSAKA CASTLE.
HAGOROMO-GITSUNE!!

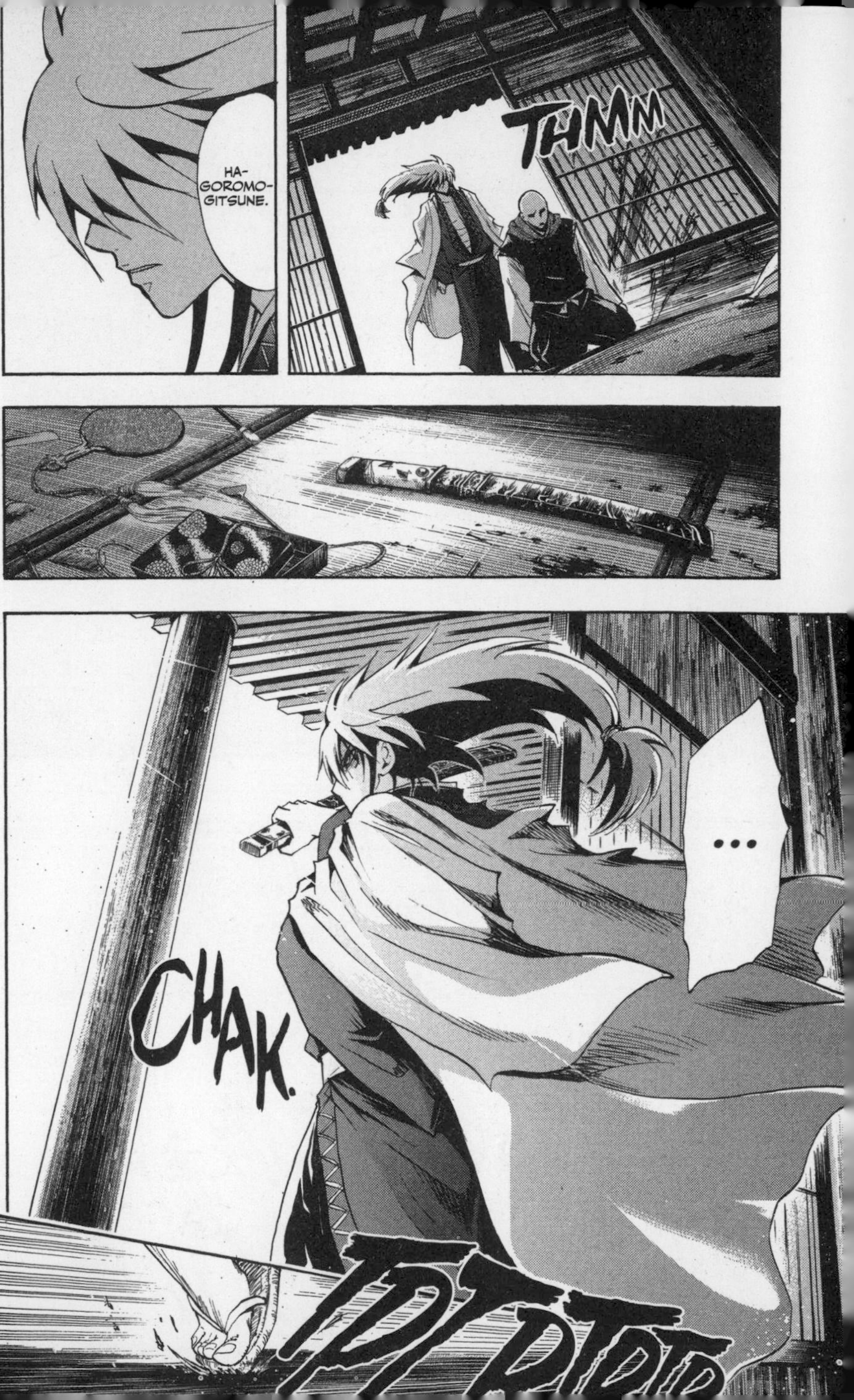
THMM
HA-
GOROMO-
GITSUNE.
...
CHAK.

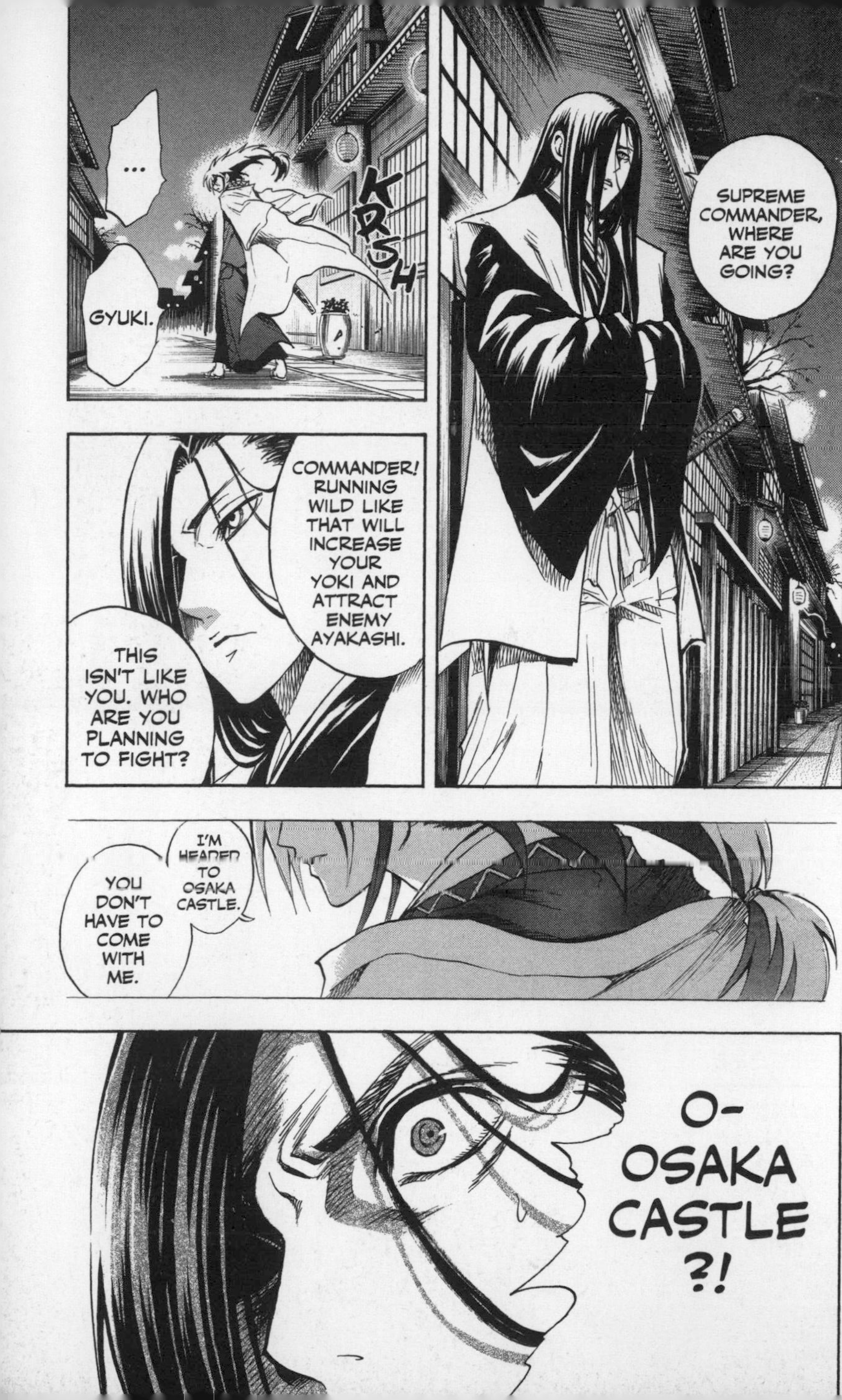
SUPREME COMMANDER, WHERE ARE YOU GOING?
KRSH
...
GYUKI.
COMMANDER! RUNNING WILD LIKE THAT WILL INCREASE YOUR YOKI AND ATTRACT ENEMY AYAKASHI.
THIS ISN'T LIKE YOU. WHO ARE YOU PLANNING TO FIGHT?
I'M HEADED TO OSAKA CASTLE.
YOU DON'T HAVE TO COME WITH ME.
O-OSAKA CASTLE ?!

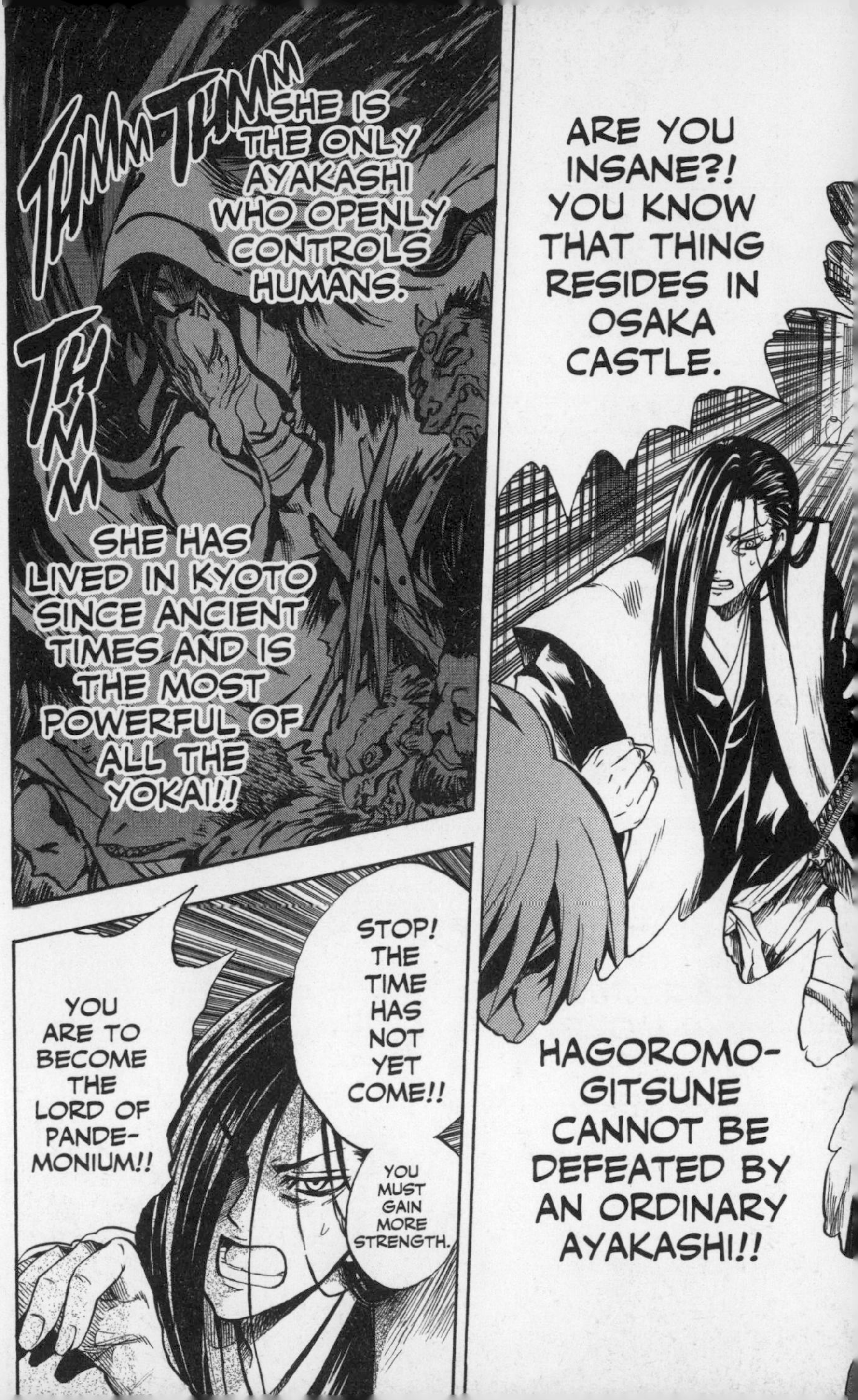
ARE YOU INSANE?! YOU KNOW THAT THING RESIDES IN OSAKA CASTLE.
HAGOROMO-GITSUNE CANNOT BE DEFEATED BY AN ORDINARY AYAKASHI!!
THMM THMM
SHE IS THE ONLY AYAKASHI WHO OPENLY CONTROLS HUMANS.
THMM
SHE HAS LIVED IN KYOTO SINCE ANCIENT TIMES AND IS THE MOST POWERFUL OF ALL THE YOKAI!!
STOP! THE TIME HAS NOT YET COME!!
YOU ARE TO BECOME THE LORD OF PANDE-MONIUM!!
YOU MUST GAIN MORE STRENGTH.

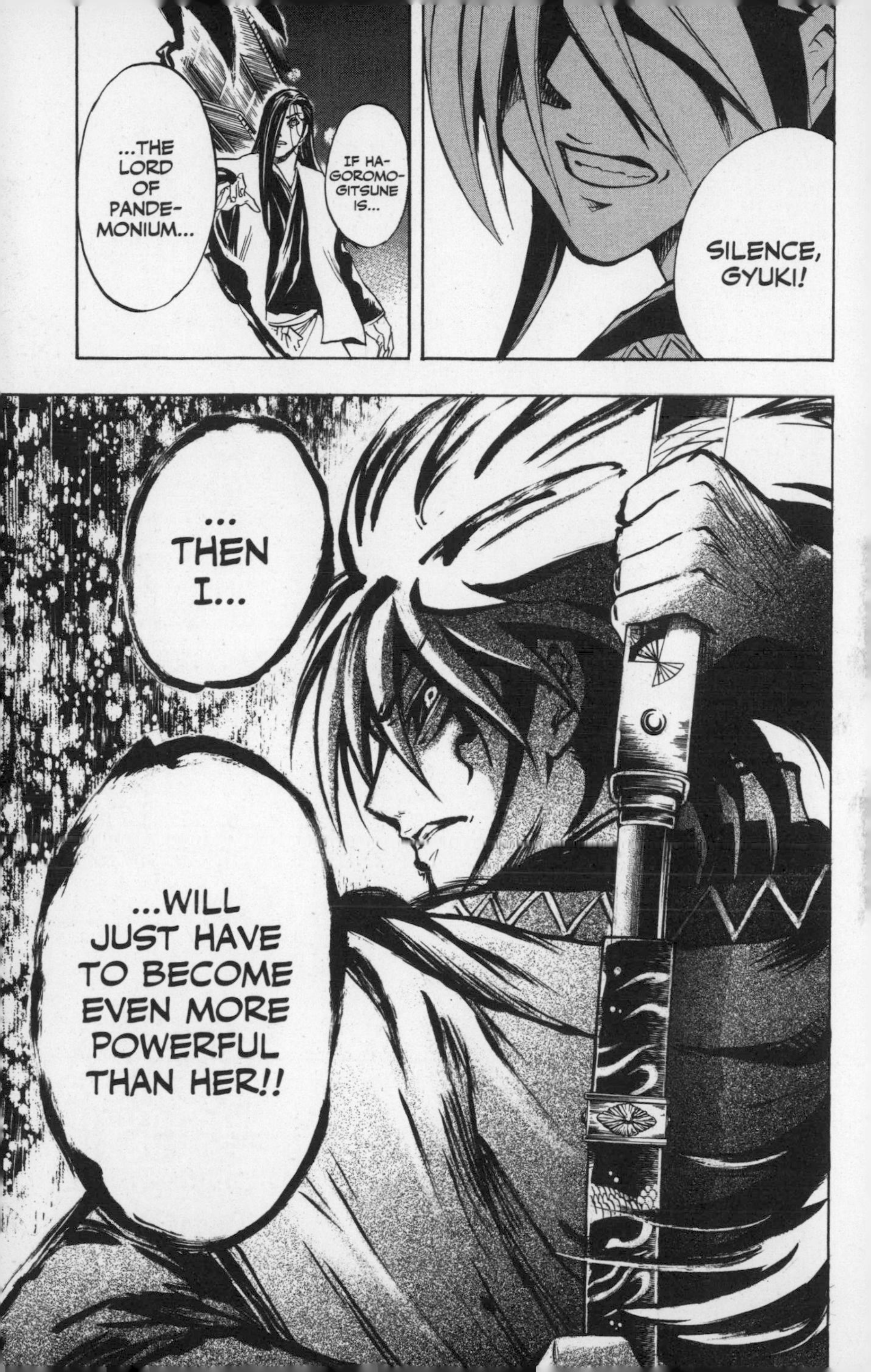
SILENCE, GYUKI!
IF HAGOROMO-GITSUNE IS...
...THE LORD OF PANDEMONIUM...
...THEN I...
...WILL JUST HAVE TO BECOME EVEN MORE POWERFUL THAN HER!!

NURA: RISE OF THE YOKAI CLAN

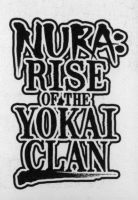

Act 62: Abducted Princess: The Spirit Blade Nenekirimaru, Part 5

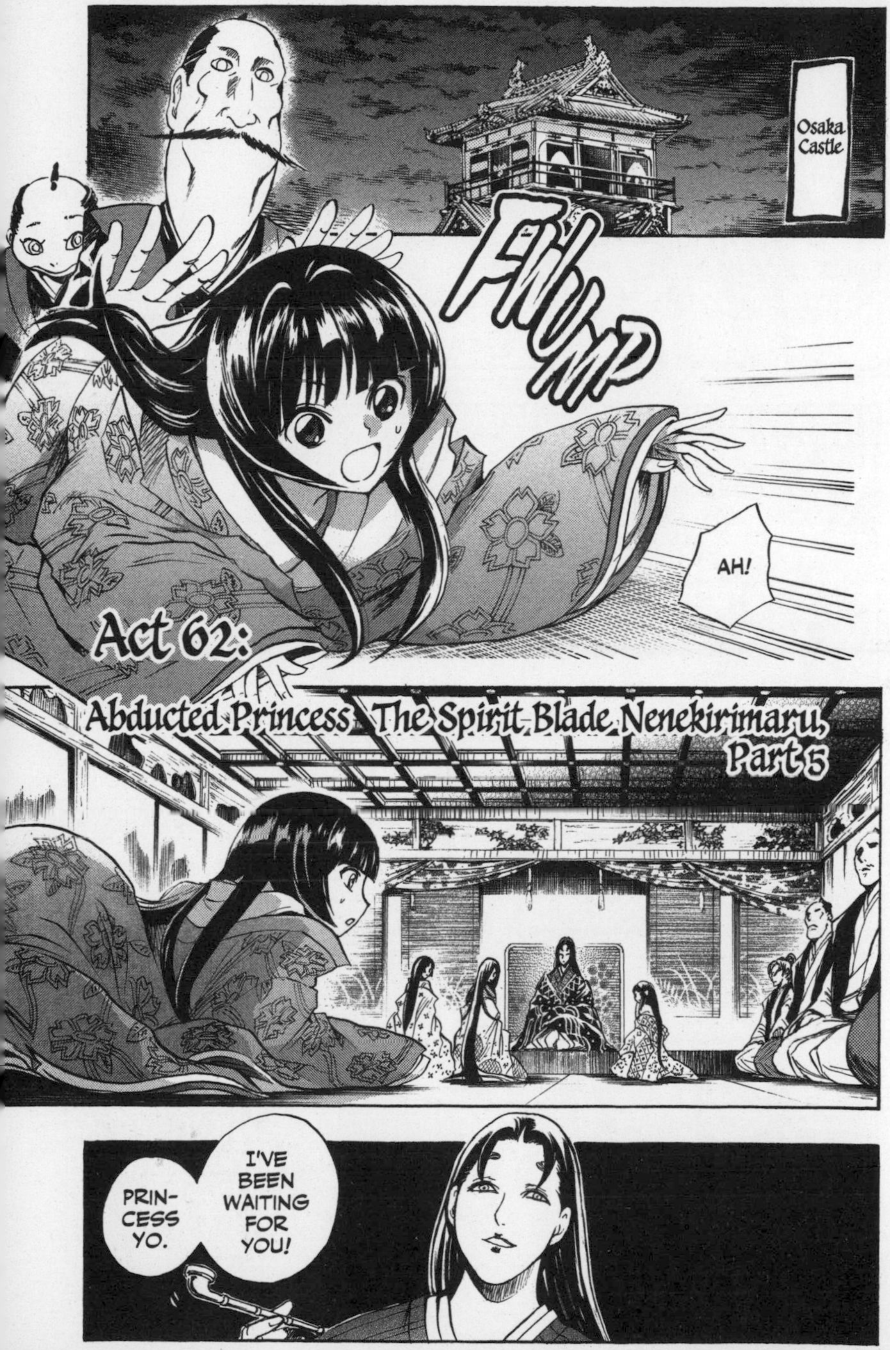
Osaka Castle
FLUMP
AH!
I'VE BEEN WAITING FOR YOU!
PRIN-CESS YO.

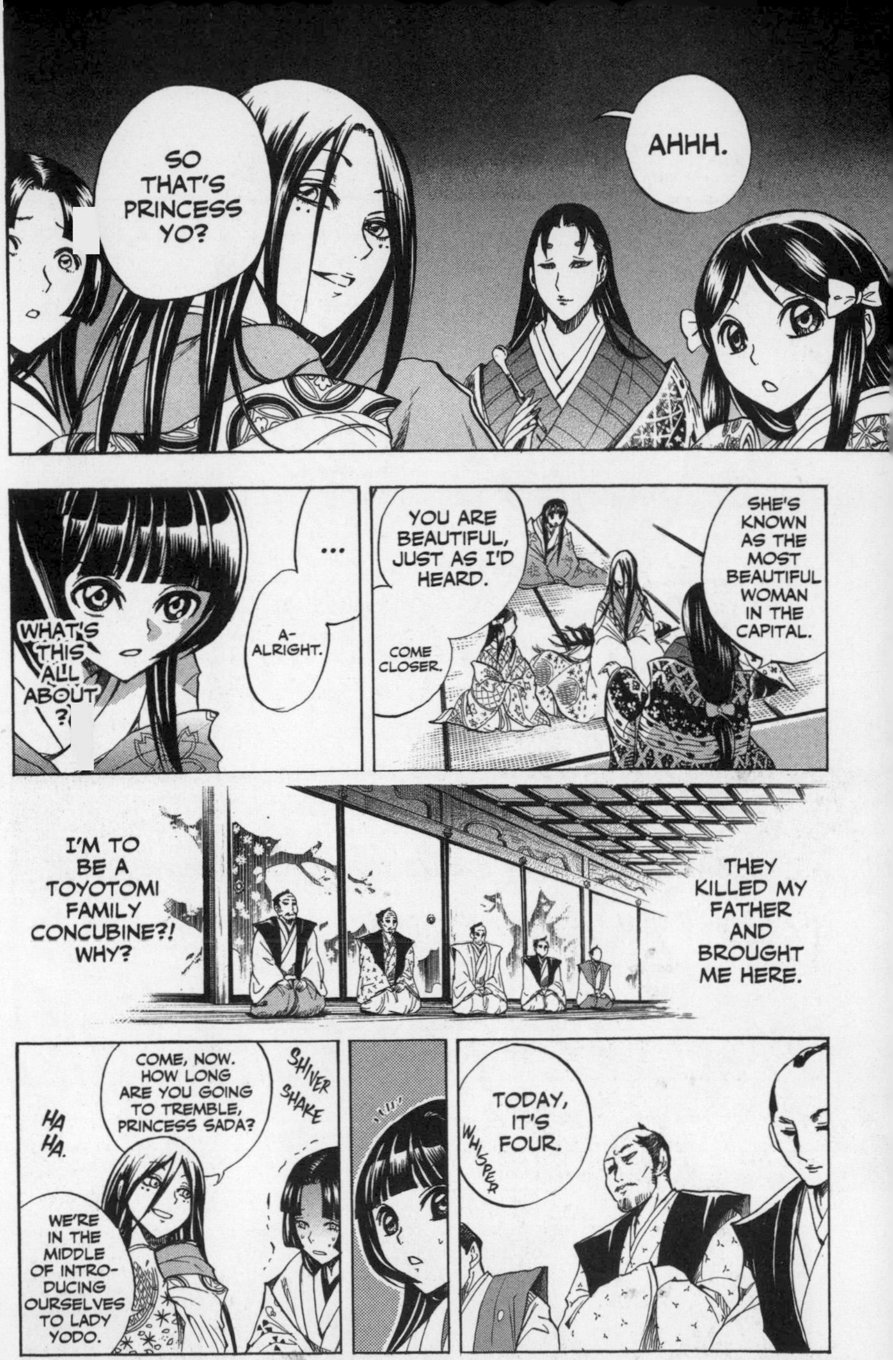
AHHH.
SO THAT'S PRINCESS YO?
SHE'S KNOWN AS THE MOST BEAUTIFUL WOMAN IN THE CAPITAL.
YOU ARE BEAUTIFUL, JUST AS I'D HEARD.
COME CLOSER.
...
A- ALRIGHT.
WHAT'S THIS ALL ABOUT?
THEY KILLED MY FATHER AND BROUGHT ME HERE.
I'M TO BE A TOYOTOMI FAMILY CONCUBINE?! WHY?
TODAY, IT'S FOUR.
WHISPER
SHIVER SHAKE
COME, NOW. HOW LONG ARE YOU GOING TO TREMBLE, PRINCESS SADA?
HA HA.
WE'RE IN THE MIDDLE OF INTRODUCING OURSELVES TO LADY YODO.

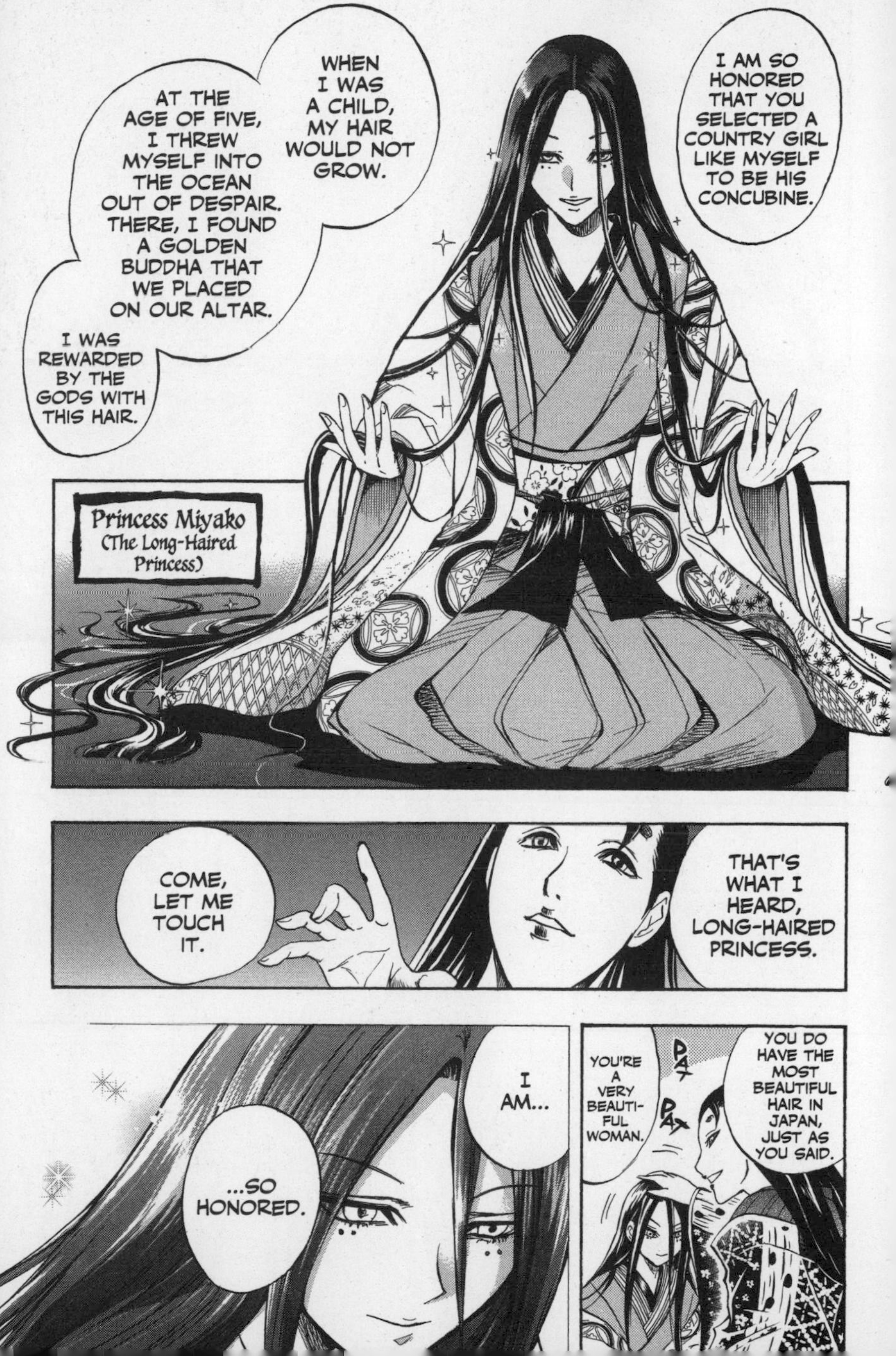
I AM SO HONORED THAT YOU SELECTED A COUNTRY GIRL LIKE MYSELF TO BE HIS CONCUBINE.
WHEN I WAS A CHILD, MY HAIR WOULD NOT GROW.
AT THE AGE OF FIVE, I THREW MYSELF INTO THE OCEAN OUT OF DESPAIR. THERE, I FOUND A GOLDEN BUDDHA THAT WE PLACED ON OUR ALTAR.
I WAS REWARDED BY THE GODS WITH THIS HAIR.
Princess Miyako (The Long-Haired Princess)
THAT'S WHAT I HEARD, LONG-HAIRED PRINCESS.
COME, LET ME TOUCH IT.
YOU DO HAVE THE MOST BEAUTIFUL HAIR IN JAPAN, JUST AS YOU SAID.
PAT
PAT
YOU'RE A VERY BEAUTIFUL WOMAN.
I AM...
...SO HONORED.

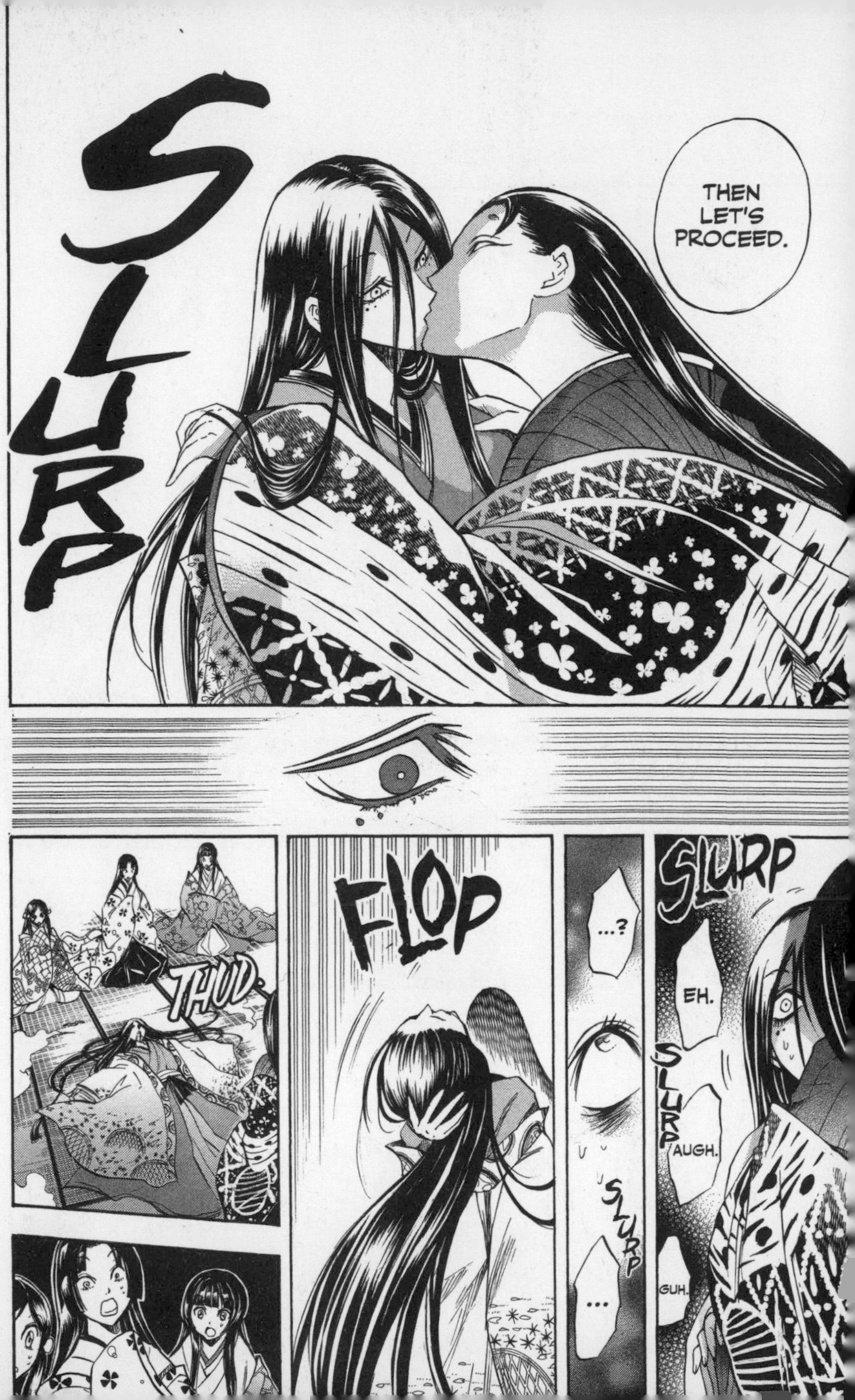
THEN LET'S PROCEED.
SLURP
SLURP
EH.
SLLURP
AUGH.
GUH.
...?
SLURP
...
FLOP
THUD

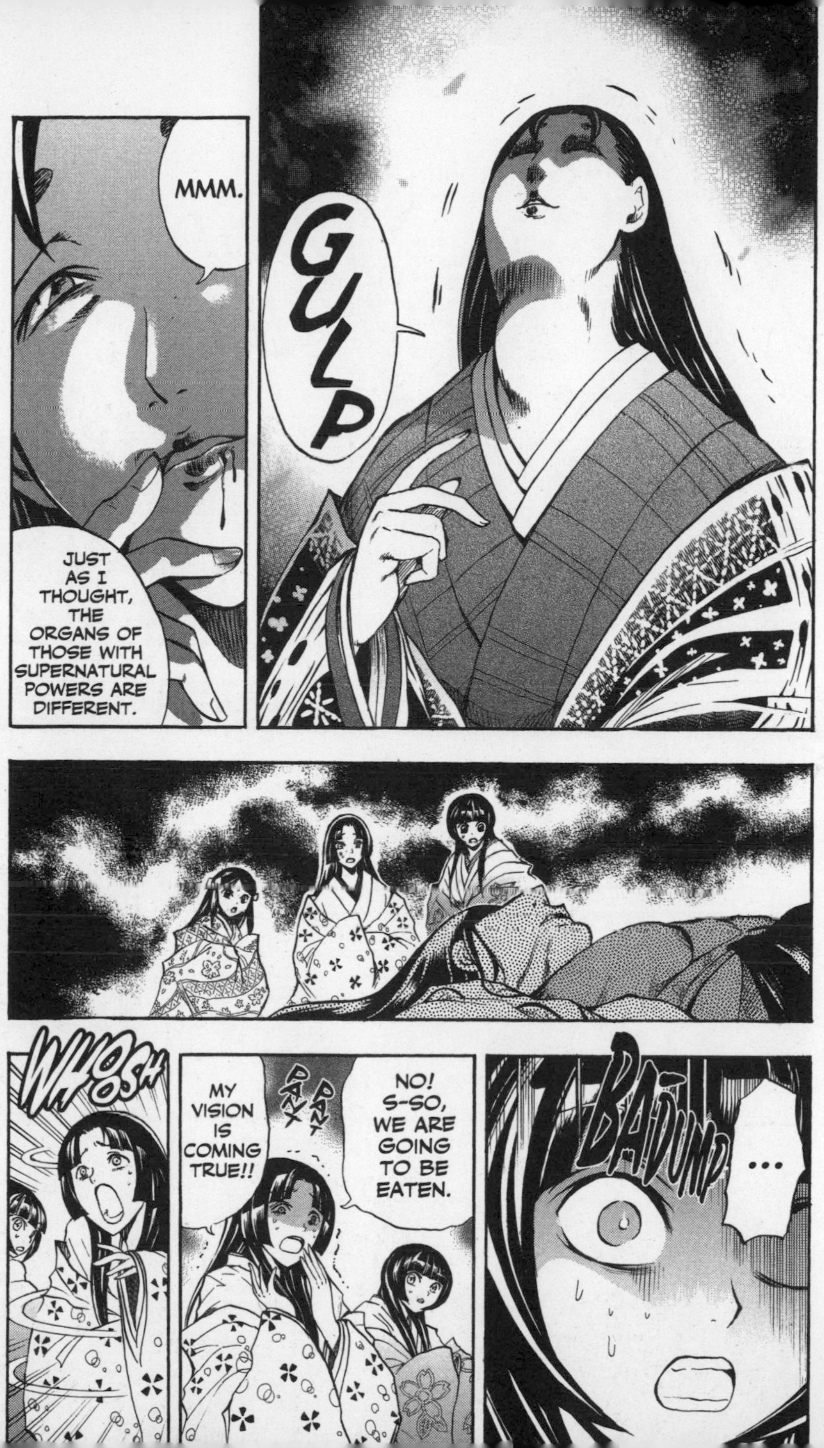
GULP
MMM.
JUST AS I THOUGHT, THE ORGANS OF THOSE WITH SUPERNATURAL POWERS ARE DIFFERENT.
BADUMP
...
NO! S-SO, WE ARE GOING TO BE EATEN.
PANT PANT
MY VISION IS COMING TRUE!!
WHOOSH

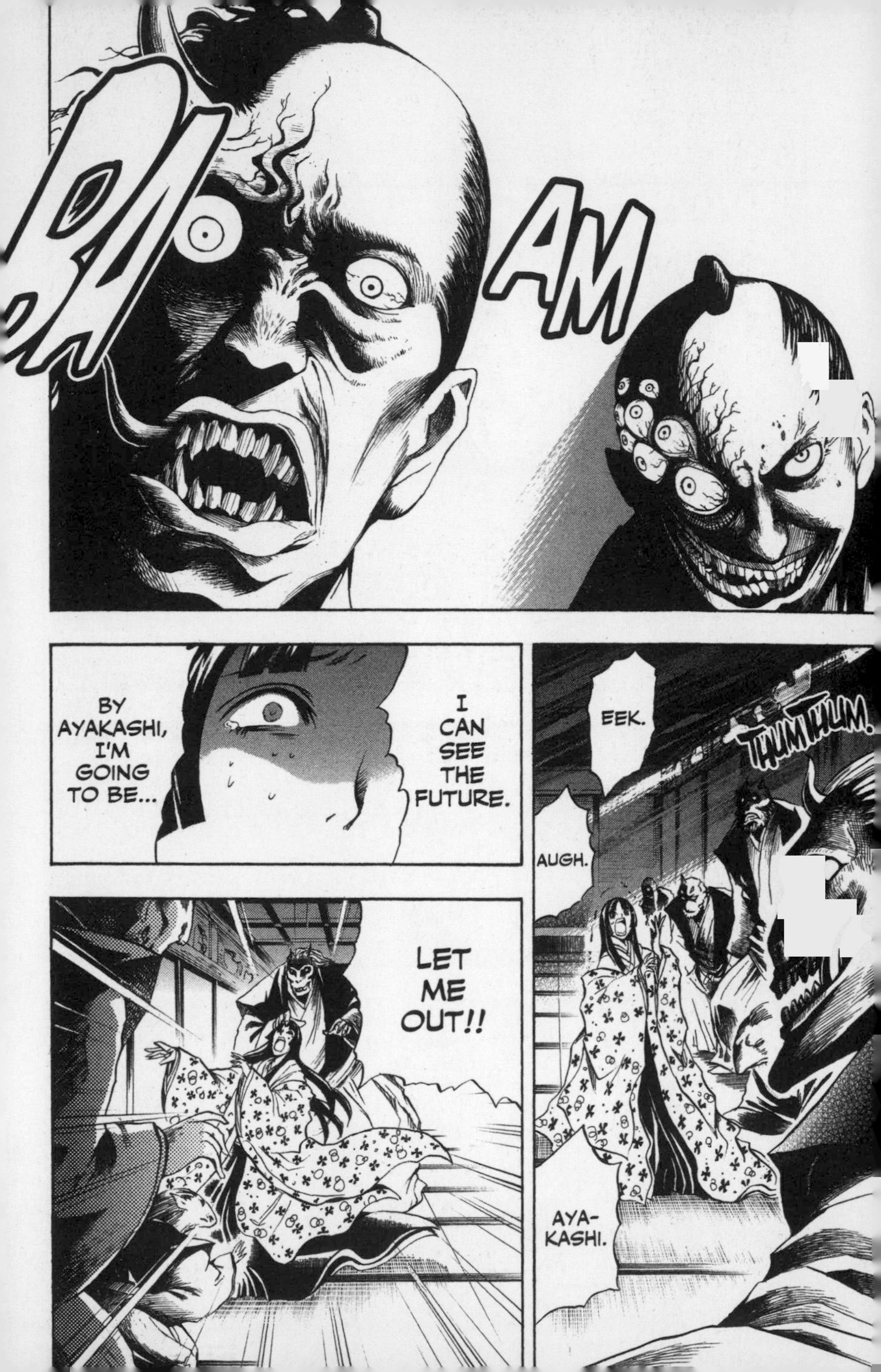
AM
EEK.
THUM THUM.
AUGH.
AYA-KASHI.
I CAN SEE THE FUTURE.
BY AYAKASHI, I'M GOING TO BE...
LET ME OUT!!

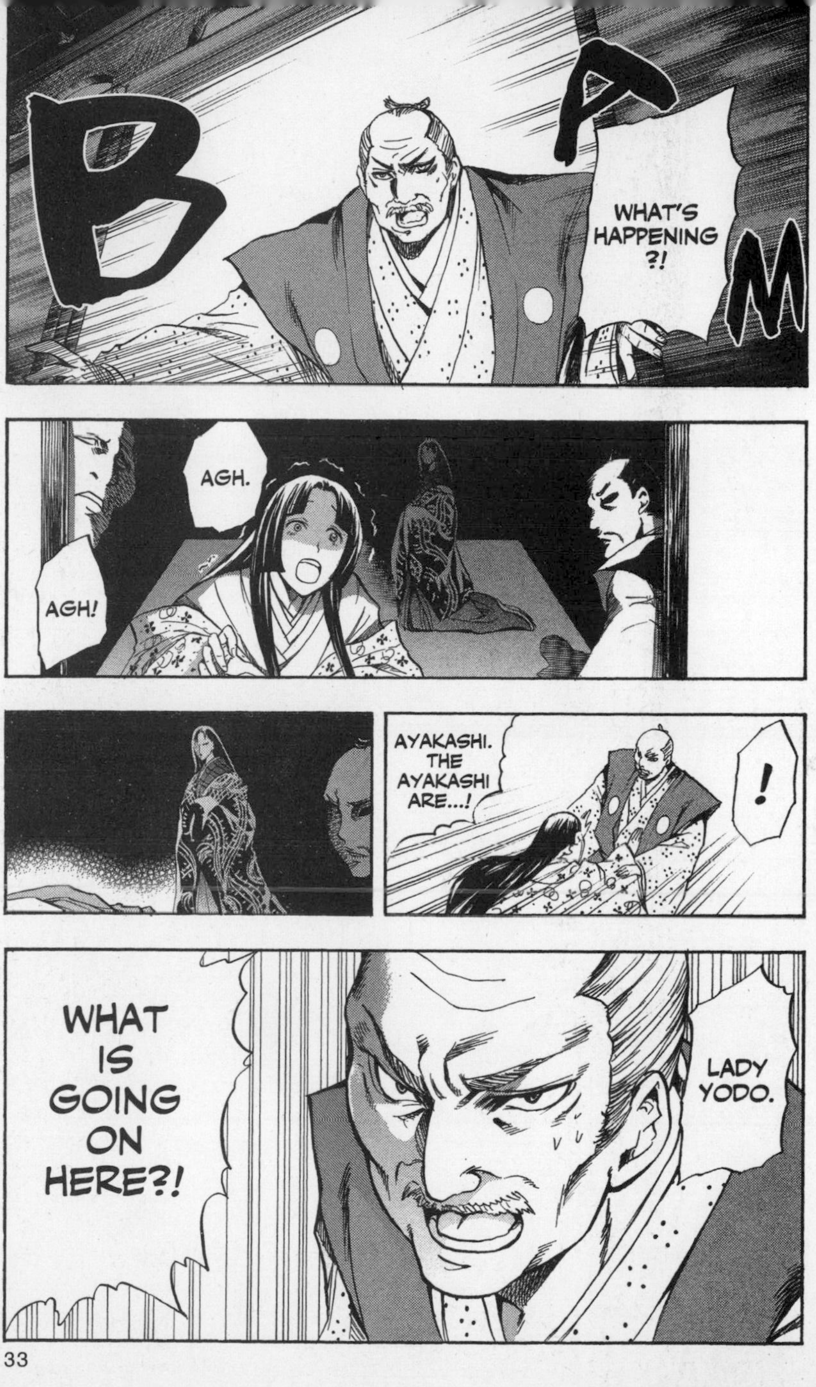
BAM
WHAT'S HAPPENING ?!
AGH.
AGH!
!
AYAKASHI. THE AYAKASHI ARE...!
LADY YODO.
WHAT IS GOING ON HERE?!

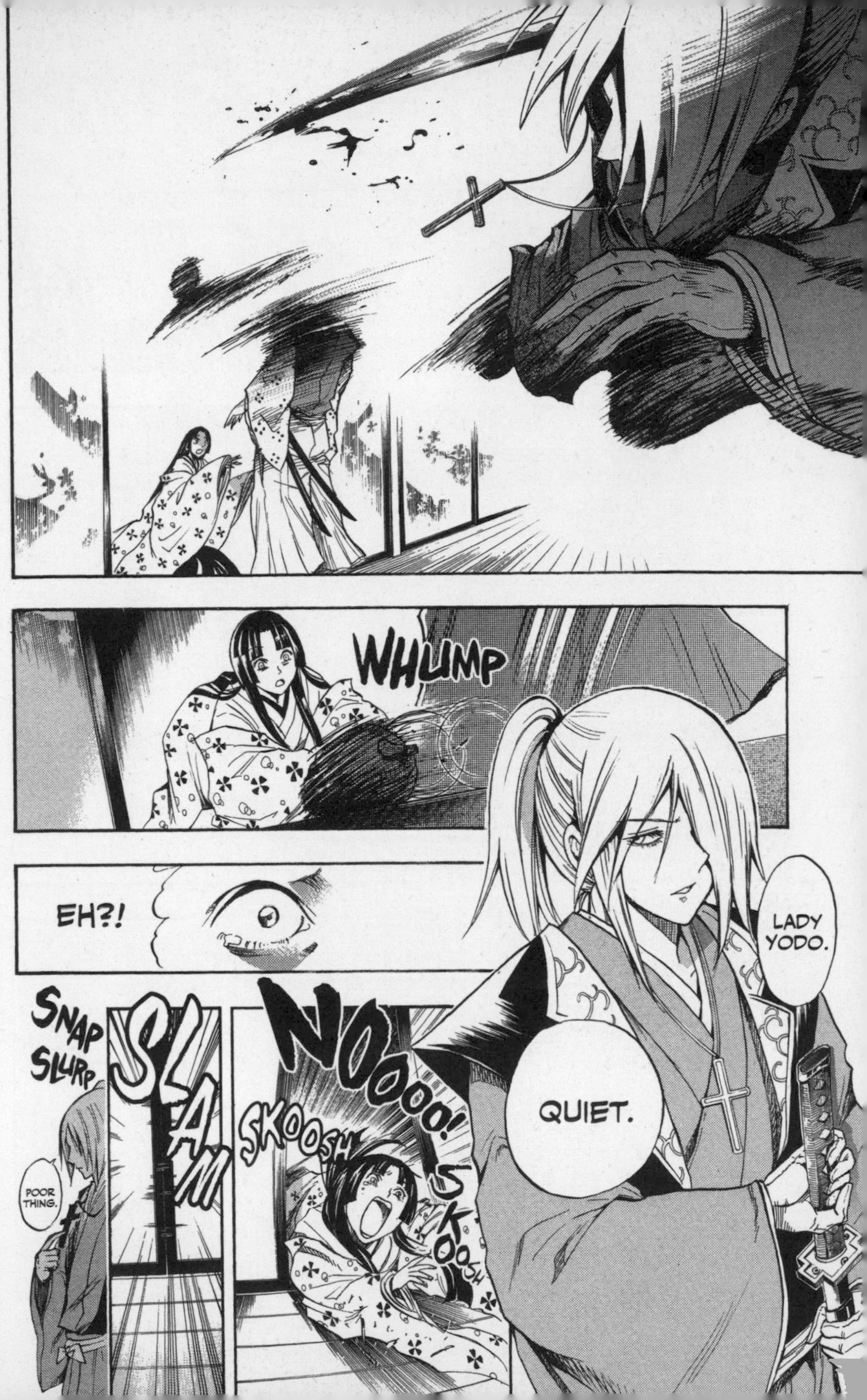
LADY YODO.
QUIET.
WHLUMP
EH?!
NOOOOO!
SKOOSH
SKOOSH
SLAM
SNAP
SLURP
POOR THING.

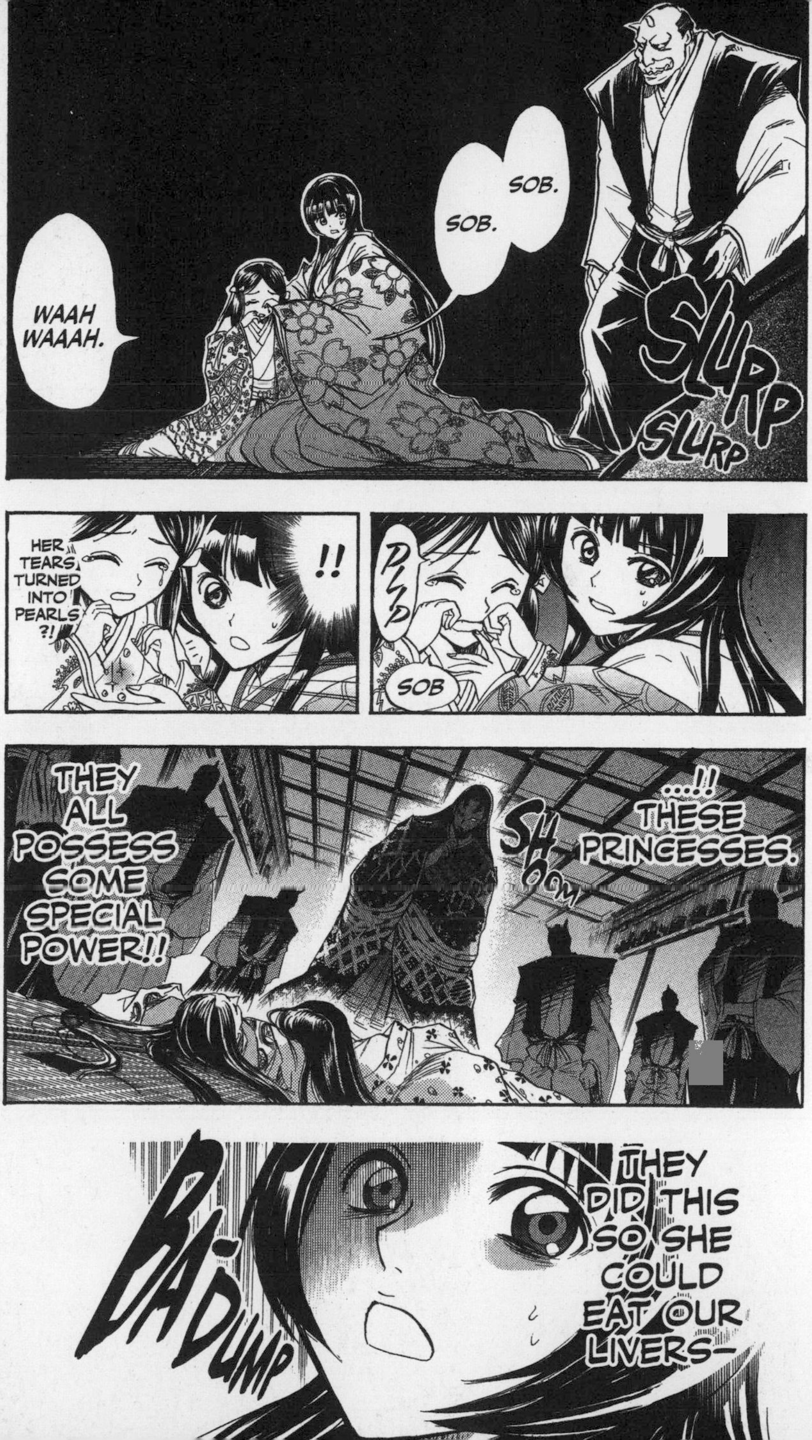
SLURP
SLURP
SOB.
SOB.
WAAH WAAAH.
DRIP
SOB
!!
HER TEARS TURNED INTO PEARLS?!
...!! THESE PRINCESSES.
SHOOM
THEY ALL POSSESS SOME SPECIAL POWER!!
THEY DID THIS SO SHE COULD EAT OUR LIVERS-
BA-DUMP

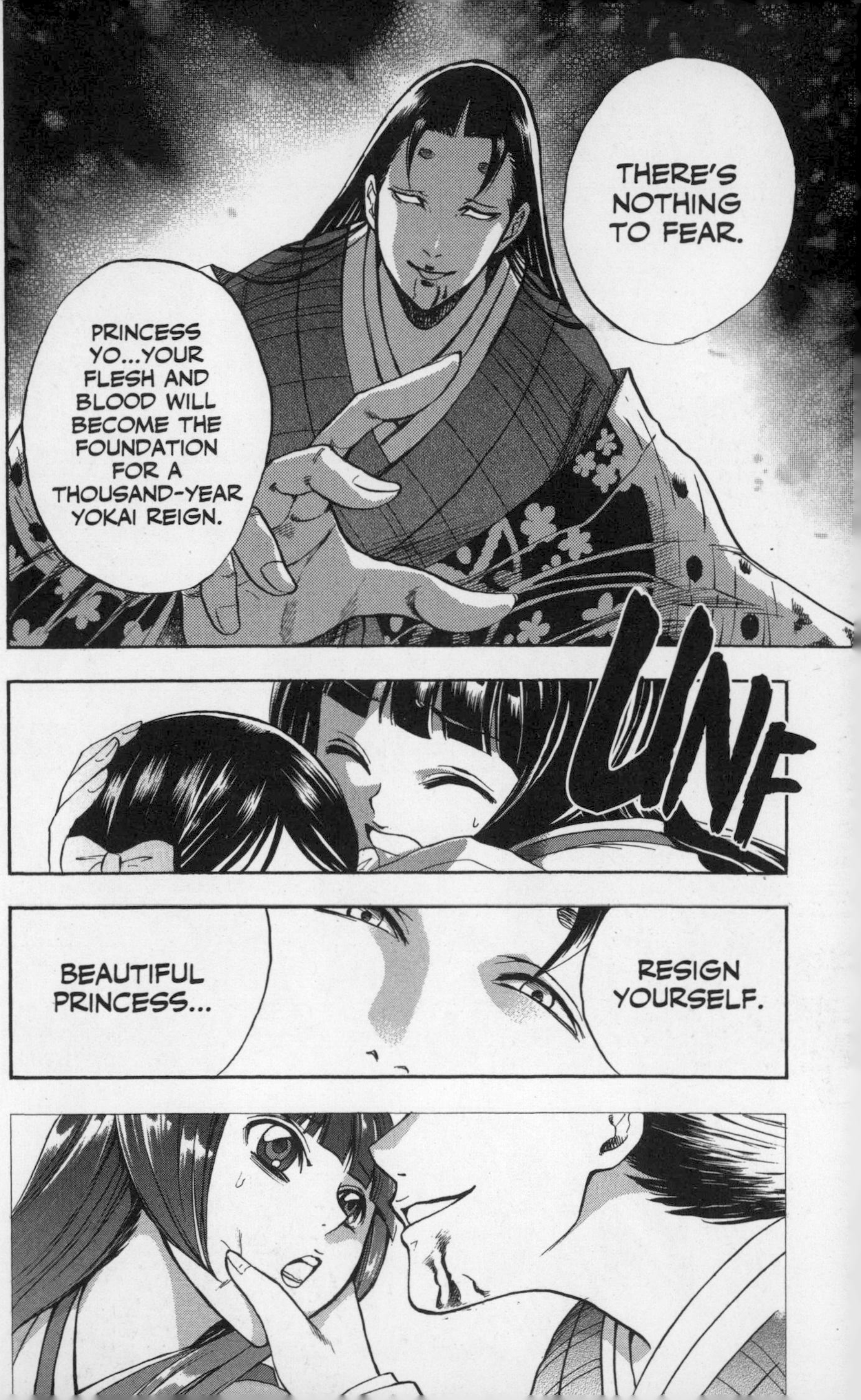
THERE'S NOTHING TO FEAR.
PRINCESS YO...YOUR FLESH AND BLOOD WILL BECOME THE FOUNDATION FOR A THOUSAND-YEAR YOKAI REIGN.
UNF
RESIGN YOURSELF.
BEAUTIFUL PRINCESS...

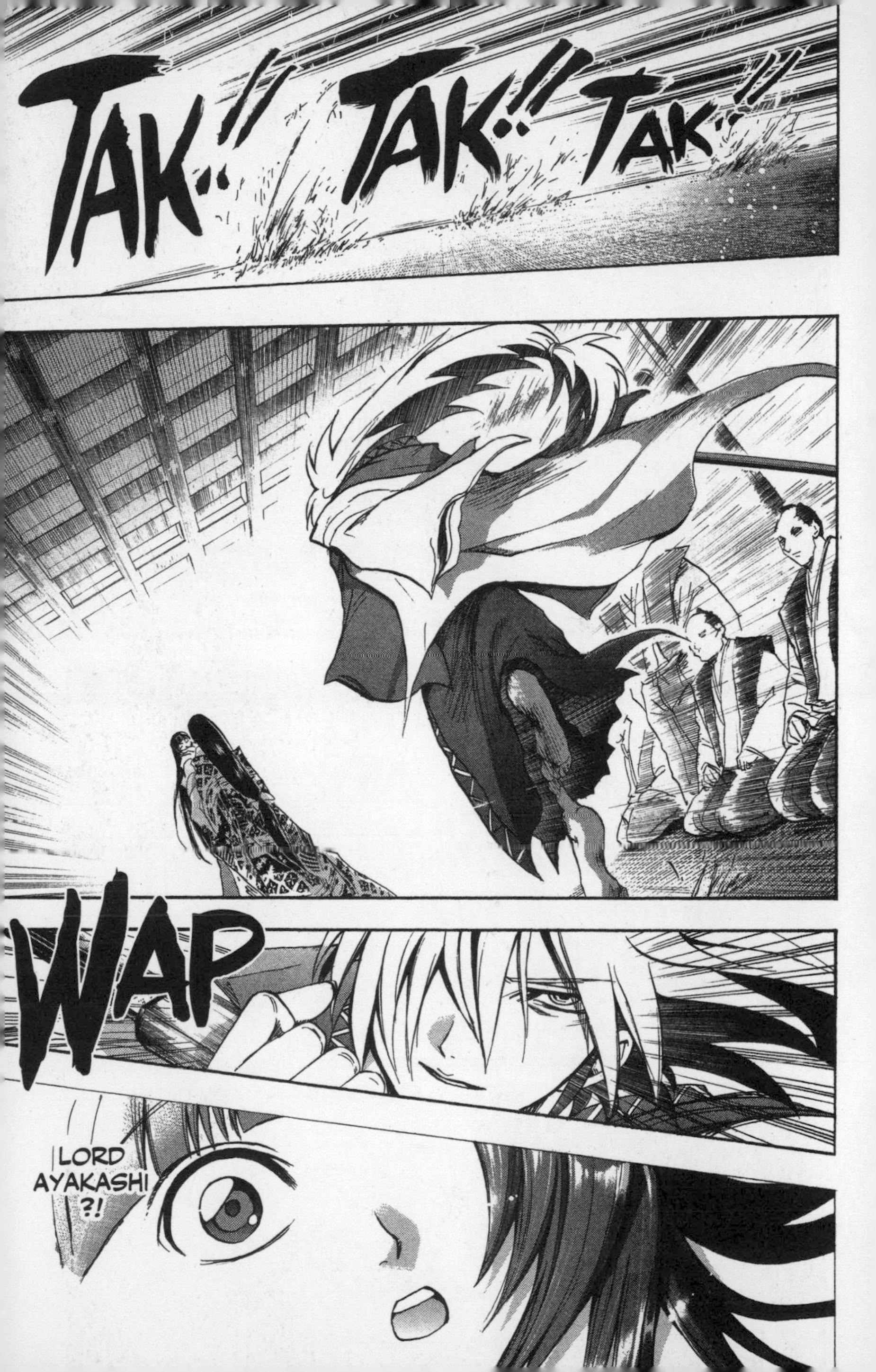
TAK!! TAK!! TAK!!
WAP
LORD AYAKASHI?!

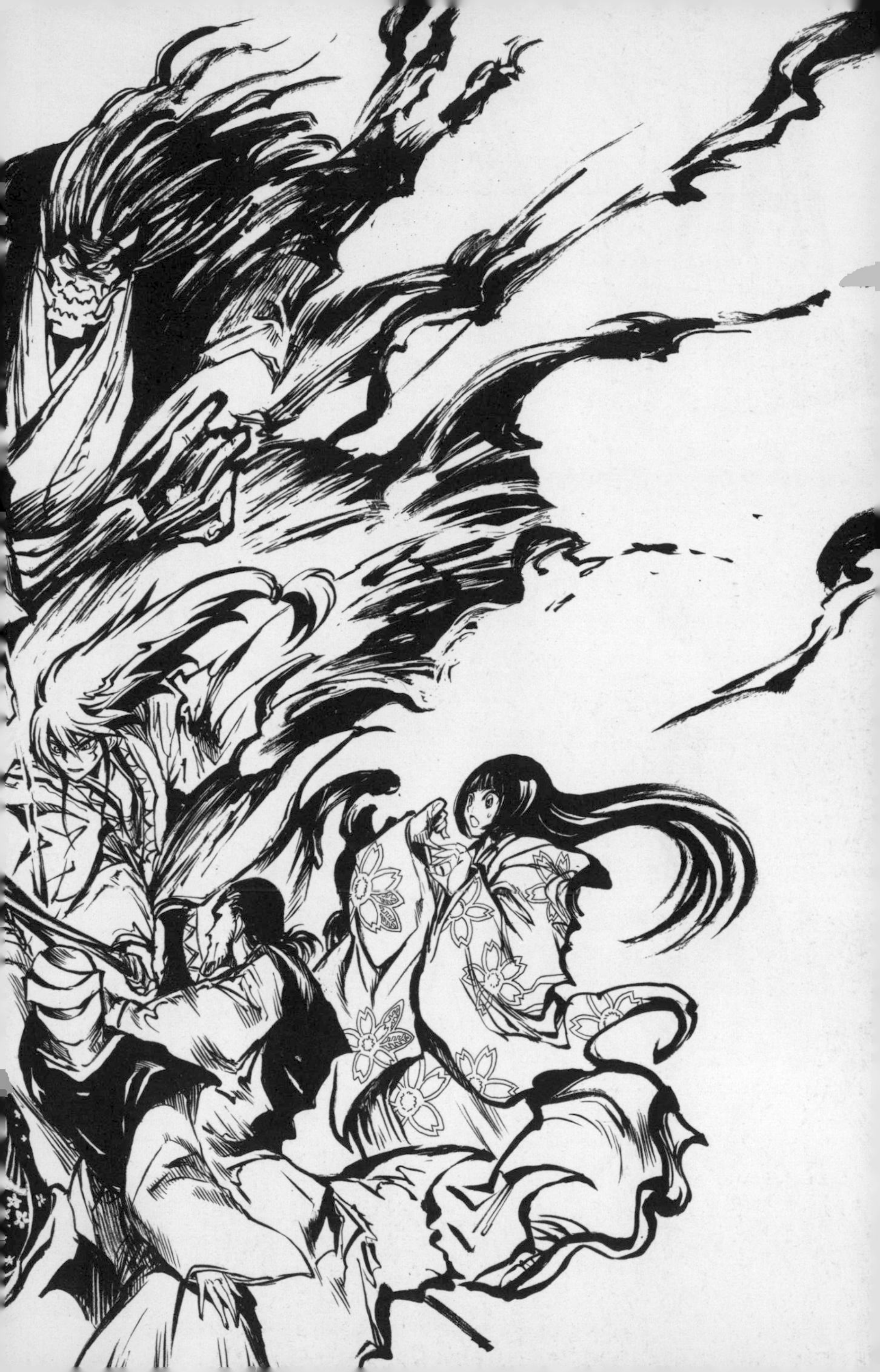

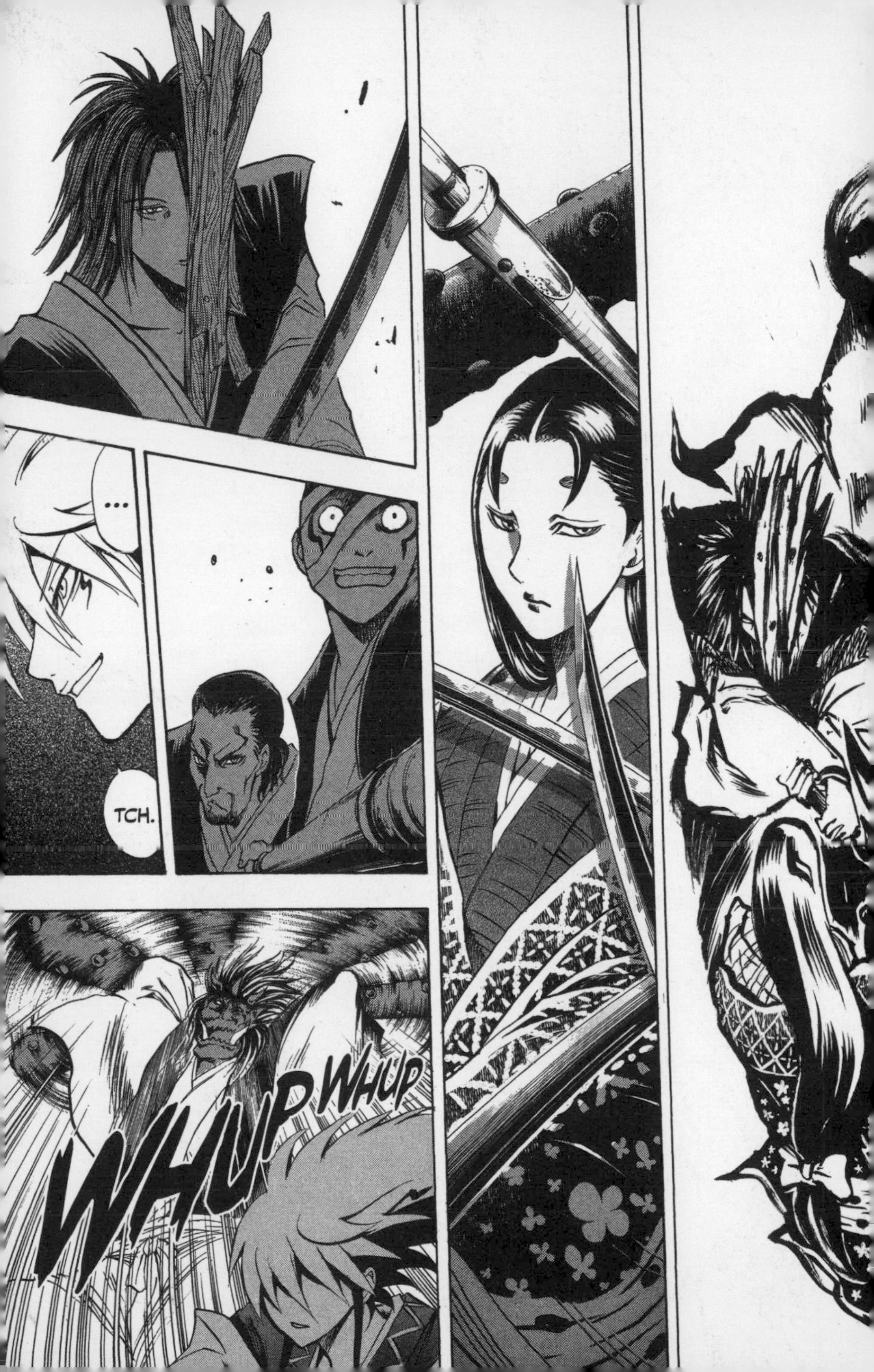
...
TCH.
WHUP WHUP

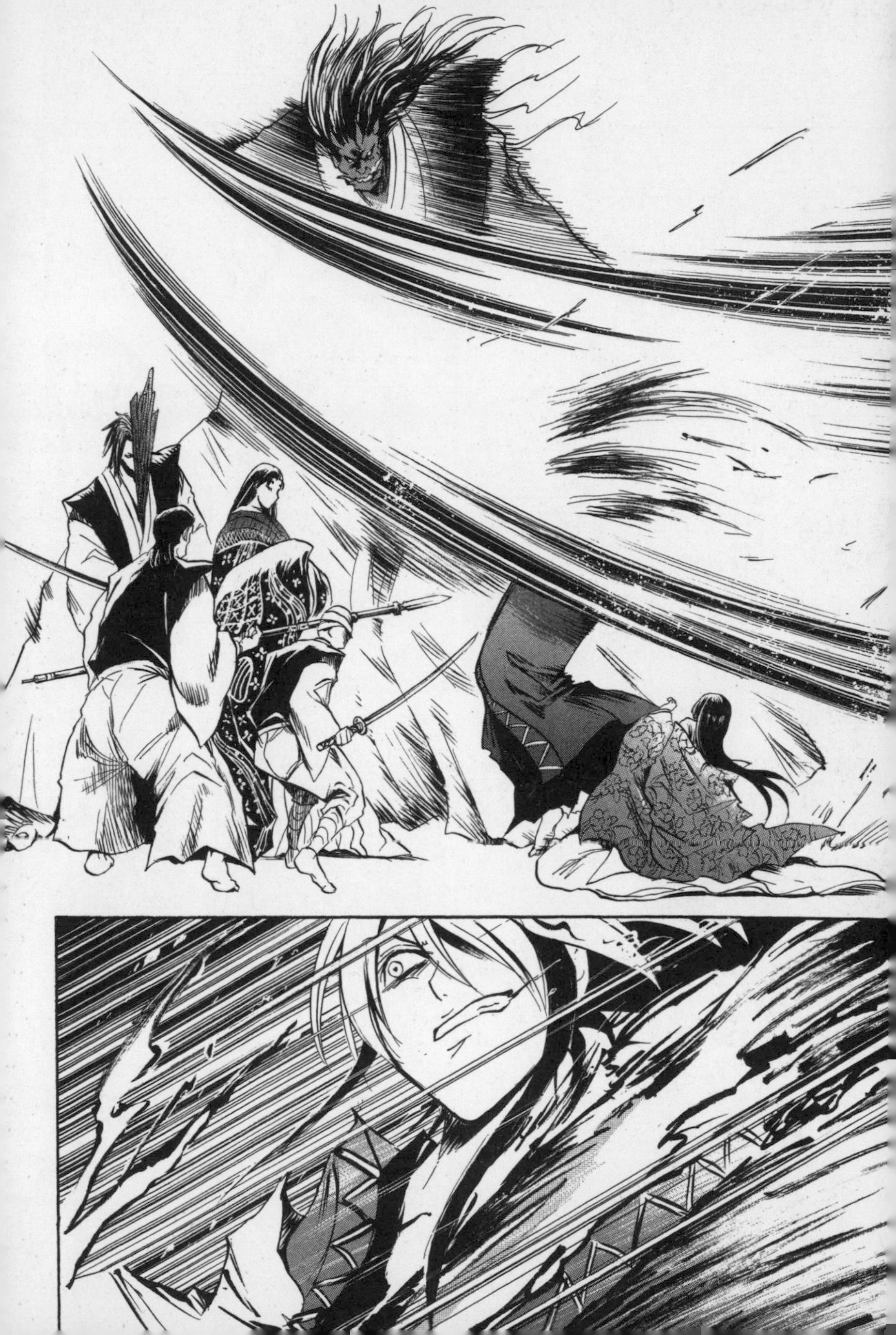

WHAT'S THIS?

AN INTRUDER?

WHO ARE YOU?!

A YAKUZA!

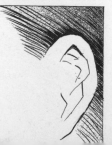

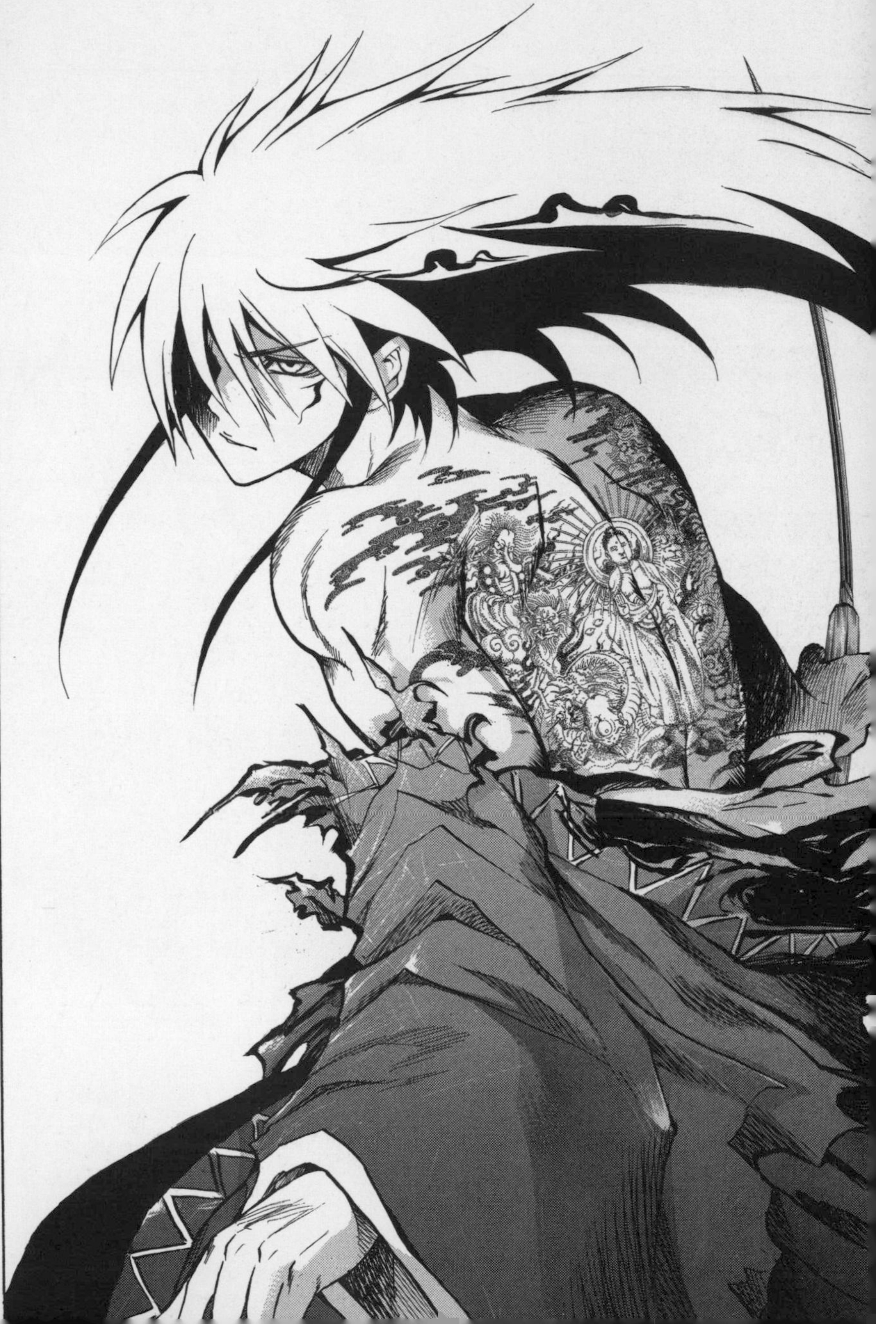

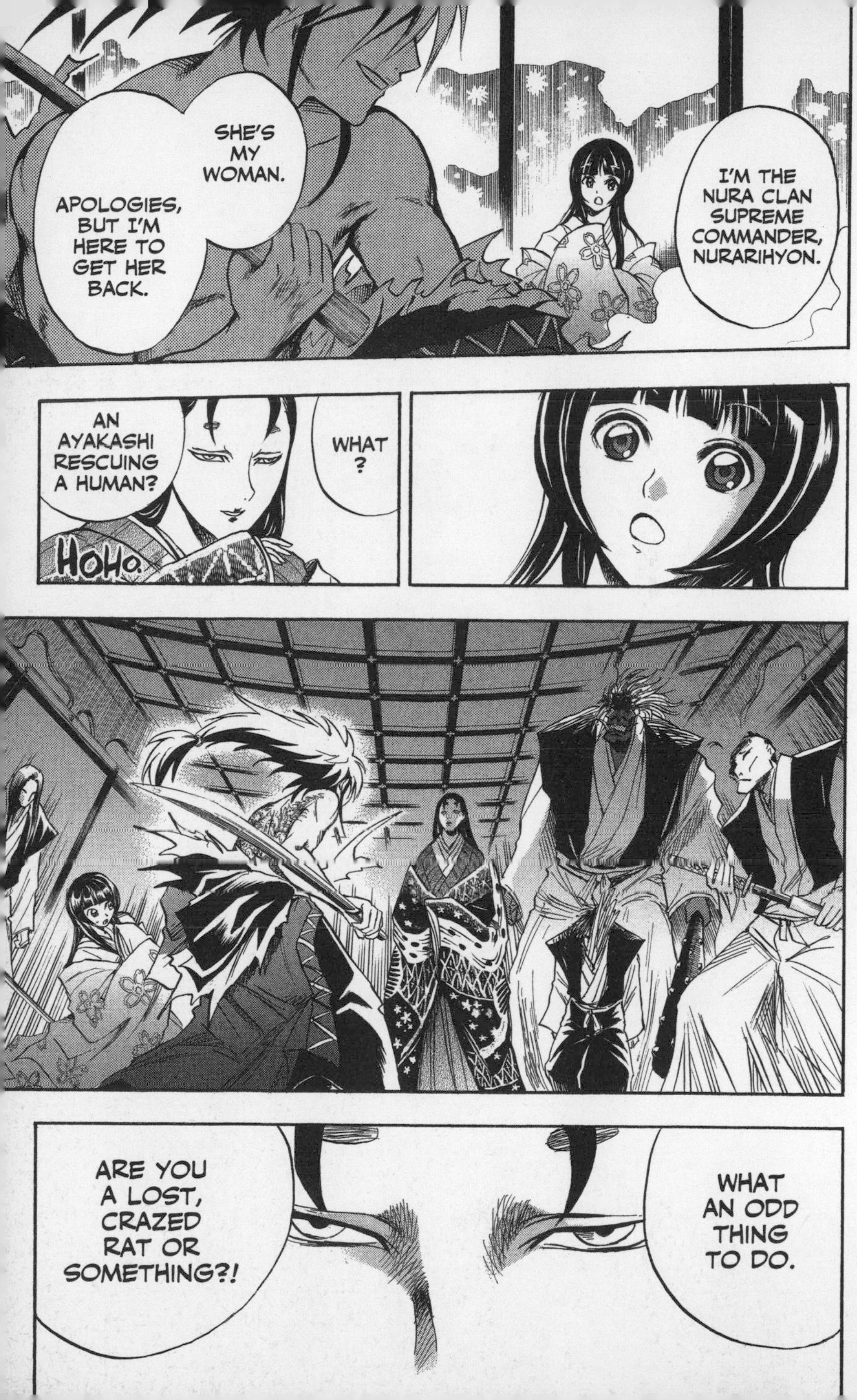
I'M THE NURA CLAN SUPREME COMMANDER, NURARIHYON.
SHE'S MY WOMAN.
APOLOGIES, BUT I'M HERE TO GET HER BACK.
WHAT?
AN AYAKASHI RESCUING A HUMAN?
HOHO.
WHAT AN ODD THING TO DO.
ARE YOU A LOST, CRAZED RAT OR SOMETHING?!

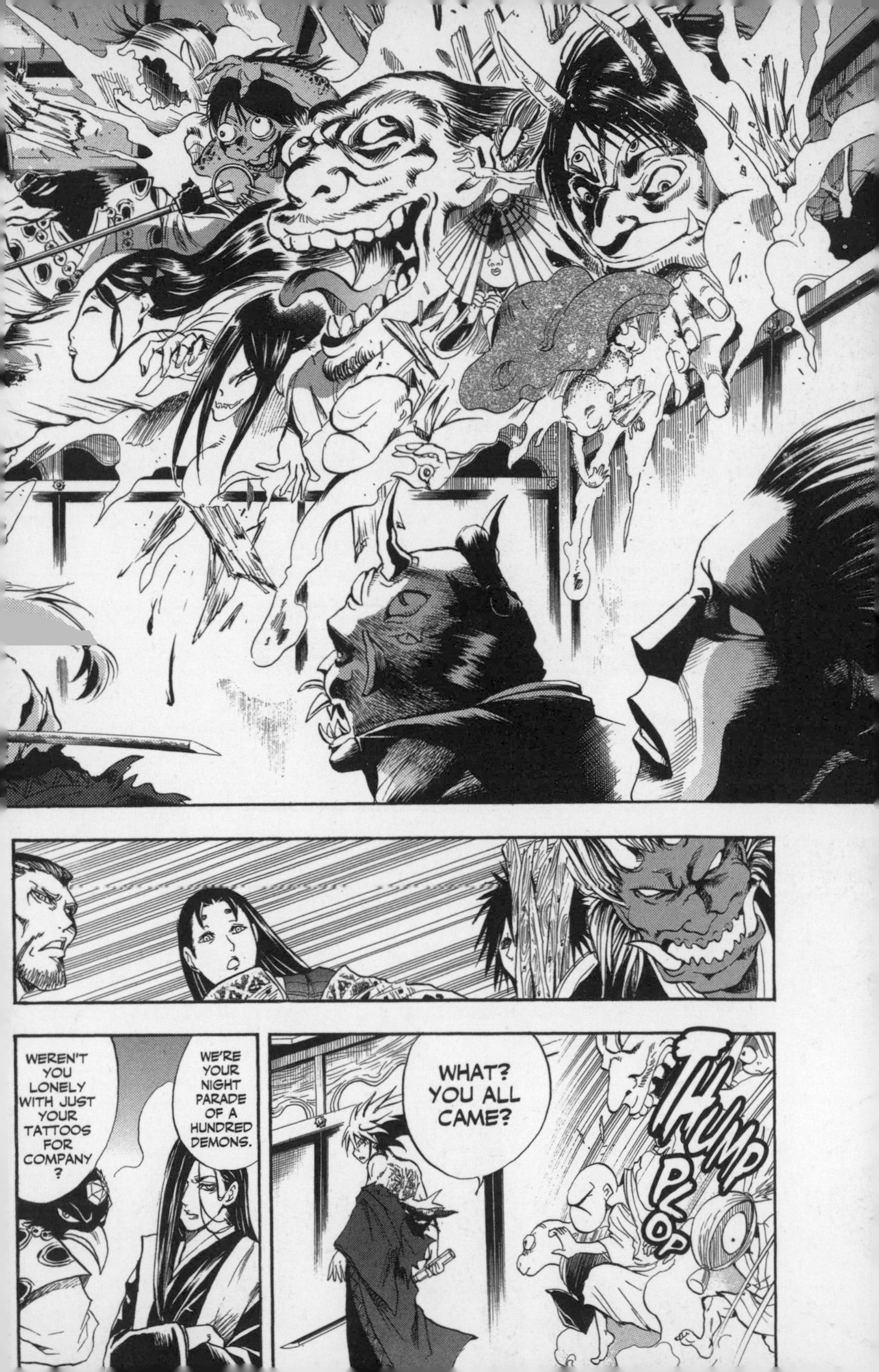
THUMP
PLOP
WHAT? YOU ALL CAME?
WE'RE YOUR NIGHT PARADE OF A HUNDRED DEMONS.
WEREN'T YOU LONELY WITH JUST YOUR TATTOOS FOR COMPANY?

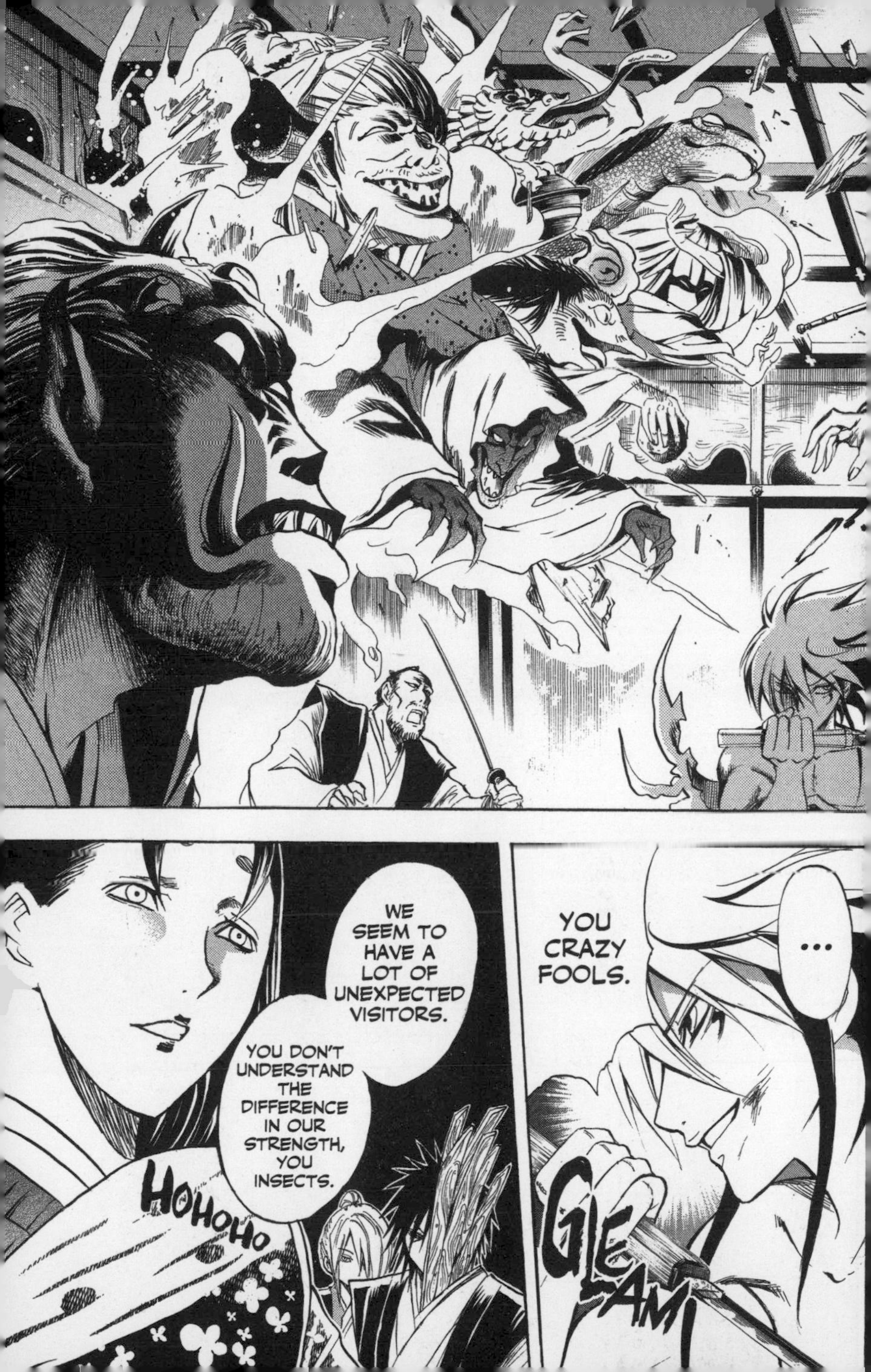
...
YOU CRAZY FOOLS.
GLEAM
WE SEEM TO HAVE A LOT OF UNEXPECTED VISITORS.
YOU DON'T UNDERSTAND THE DIFFERENCE IN OUR STRENGTH, YOU INSECTS.
HOHOHO

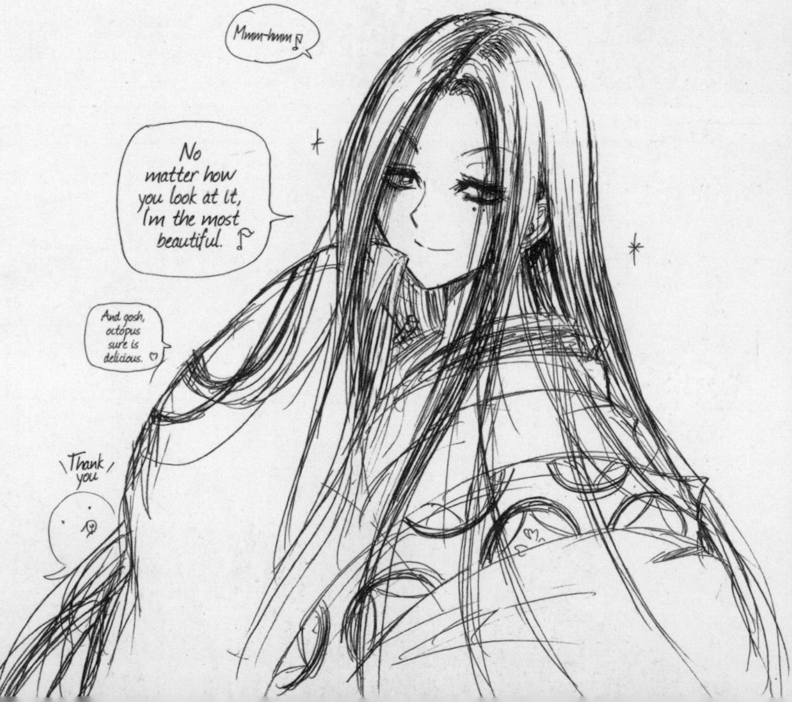
Mmm-hmm♪
No matter how you look at it, I'm the most beautiful. ♪
And gosh, octopus sure is delicious. ♡
Thank you

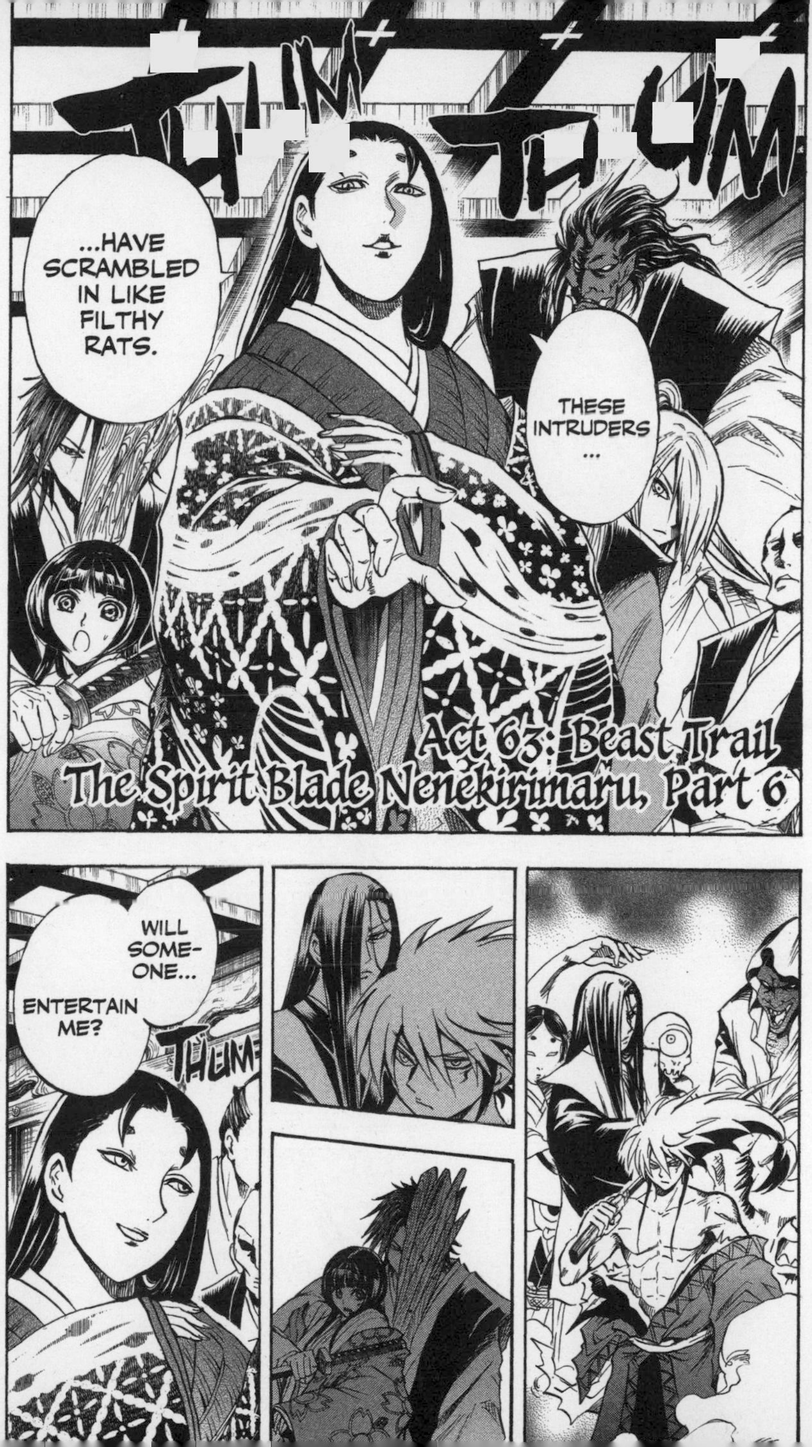
THUM
THUM
THESE INTRUDERS ...
...HAVE SCRAMBLED IN LIKE FILTHY RATS.
Act 63: Beast Trail
The Spirit Blade Nenekirimaru, Part 6
WILL SOME-ONE...
ENTERTAIN ME?
THUM

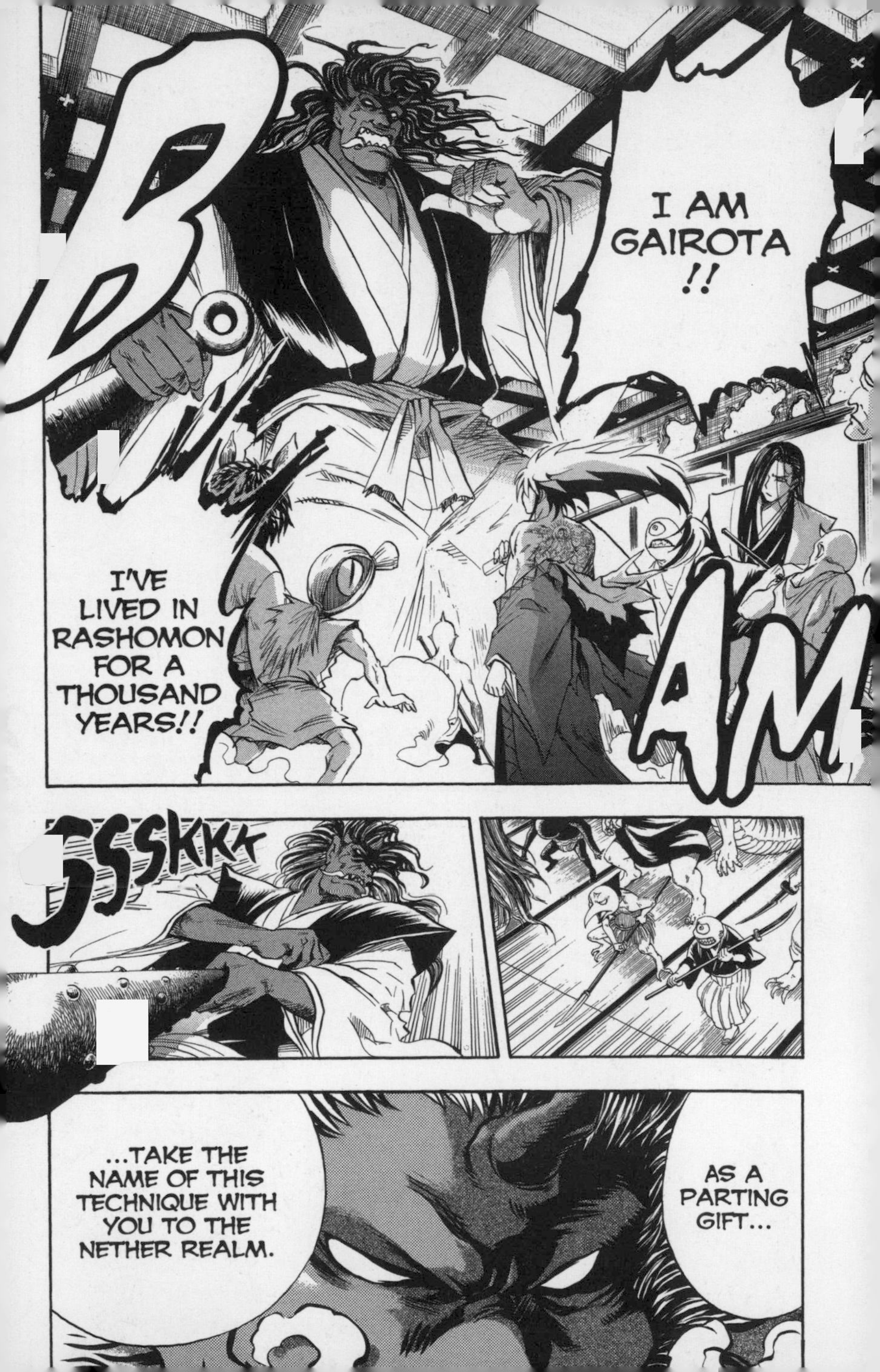
I AM GAIROTA!!
I'VE LIVED IN RASHOMON FOR A THOUSAND YEARS!!
SSSKKA
AS A PARTING GIFT...
...TAKE THE NAME OF THIS TECHNIQUE WITH YOU TO THE NETHER REALM.

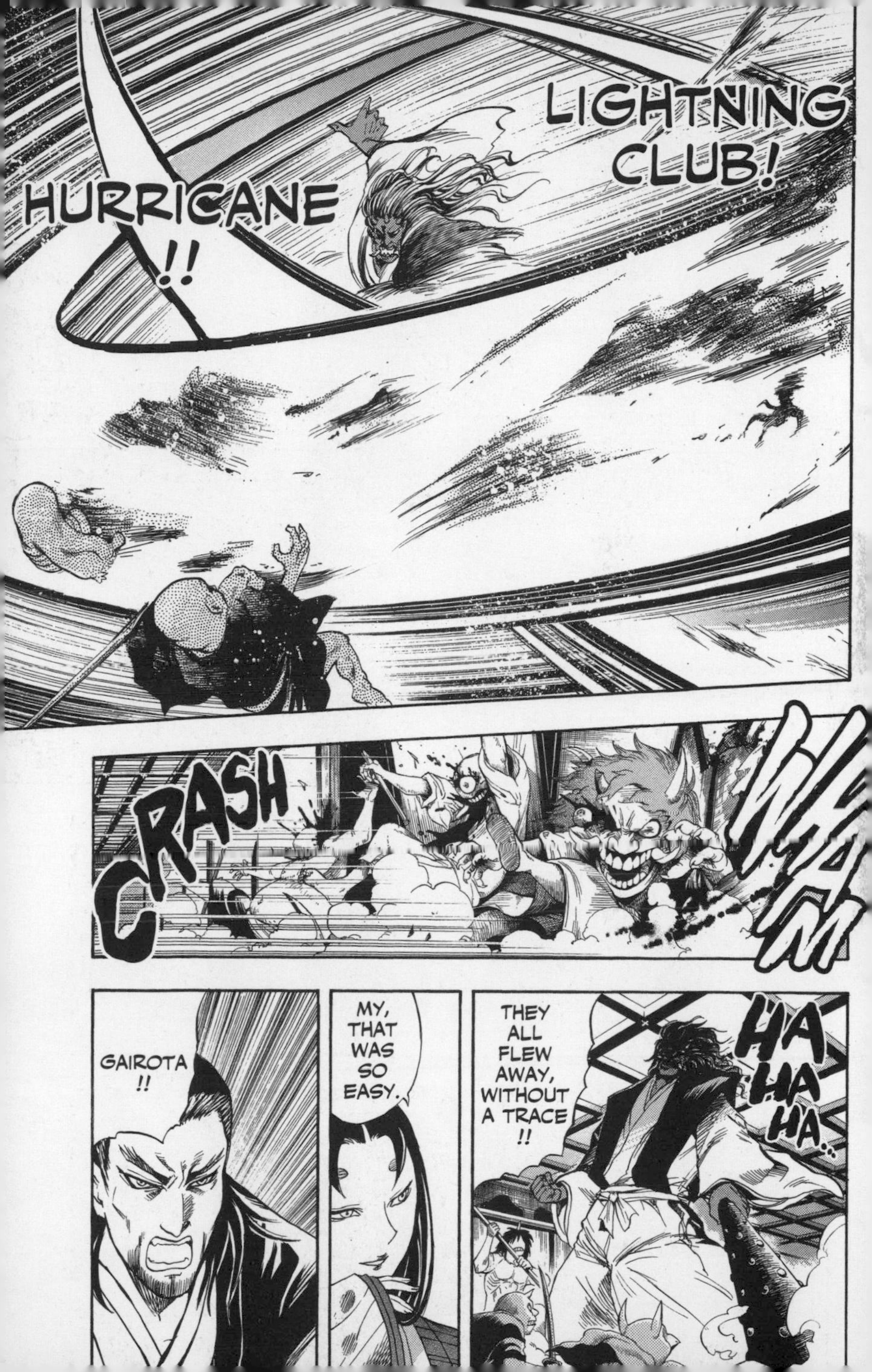
LIGHTNING CLUB!
HURRICANE !!
WHAM
CRASH
HA HA HA HA..
THEY ALL FLEW AWAY, WITHOUT A TRACE !!
MY, THAT WAS SO EASY.
GAIROTA !!

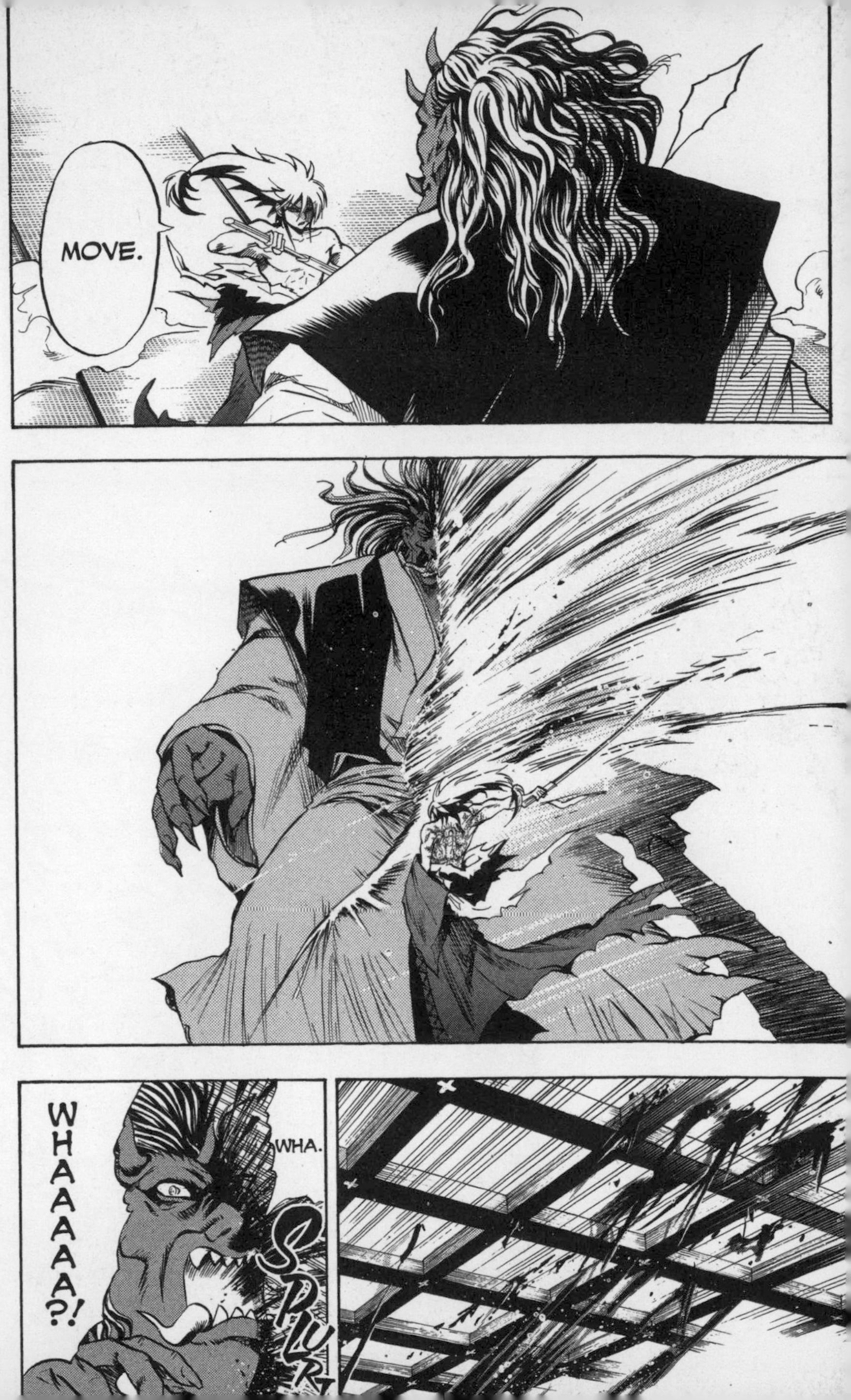
MOVE.
WHA.
WHAAAAA?!
SPLUR

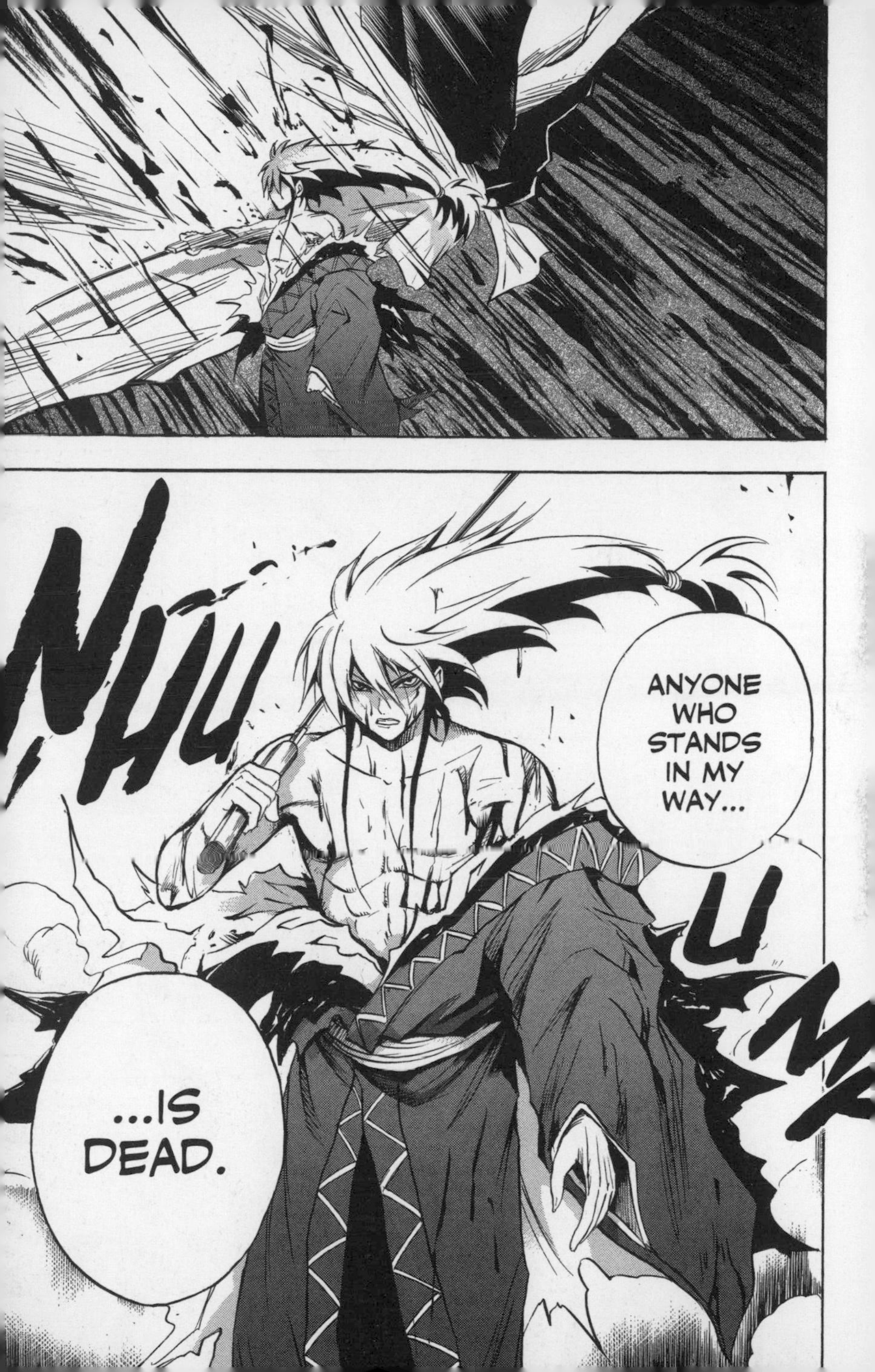
ANYONE WHO STANDS IN MY WAY...
NUU
UM
...IS DEAD.

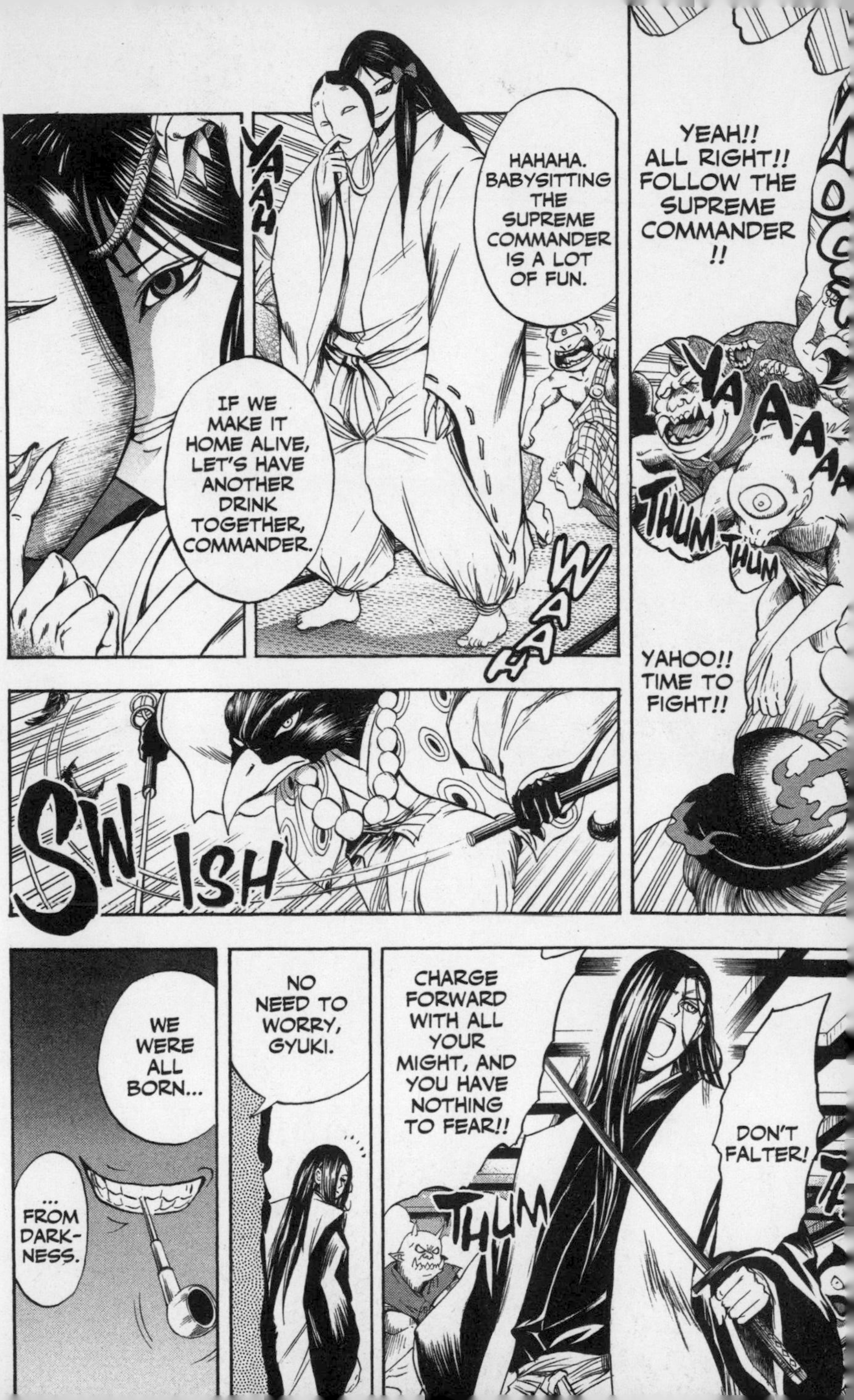
YEAH!! ALL RIGHT!! FOLLOW THE SUPREME COMMANDER!!
YAAAAA
THUM THUM
YAHOO!! TIME TO FIGHT!!
HAHAHA. BABYSITTING THE SUPREME COMMANDER IS A LOT OF FUN.
YAAH
WAAH
IF WE MAKE IT HOME ALIVE, LET'S HAVE ANOTHER DRINK TOGETHER, COMMANDER.
SWISH
DON'T FALTER!
CHARGE FORWARD WITH ALL YOUR MIGHT, AND YOU HAVE NOTHING TO FEAR!!
THUM
NO NEED TO WORRY, GYUKI.
WE WERE ALL BORN...
...FROM DARK-NESS.

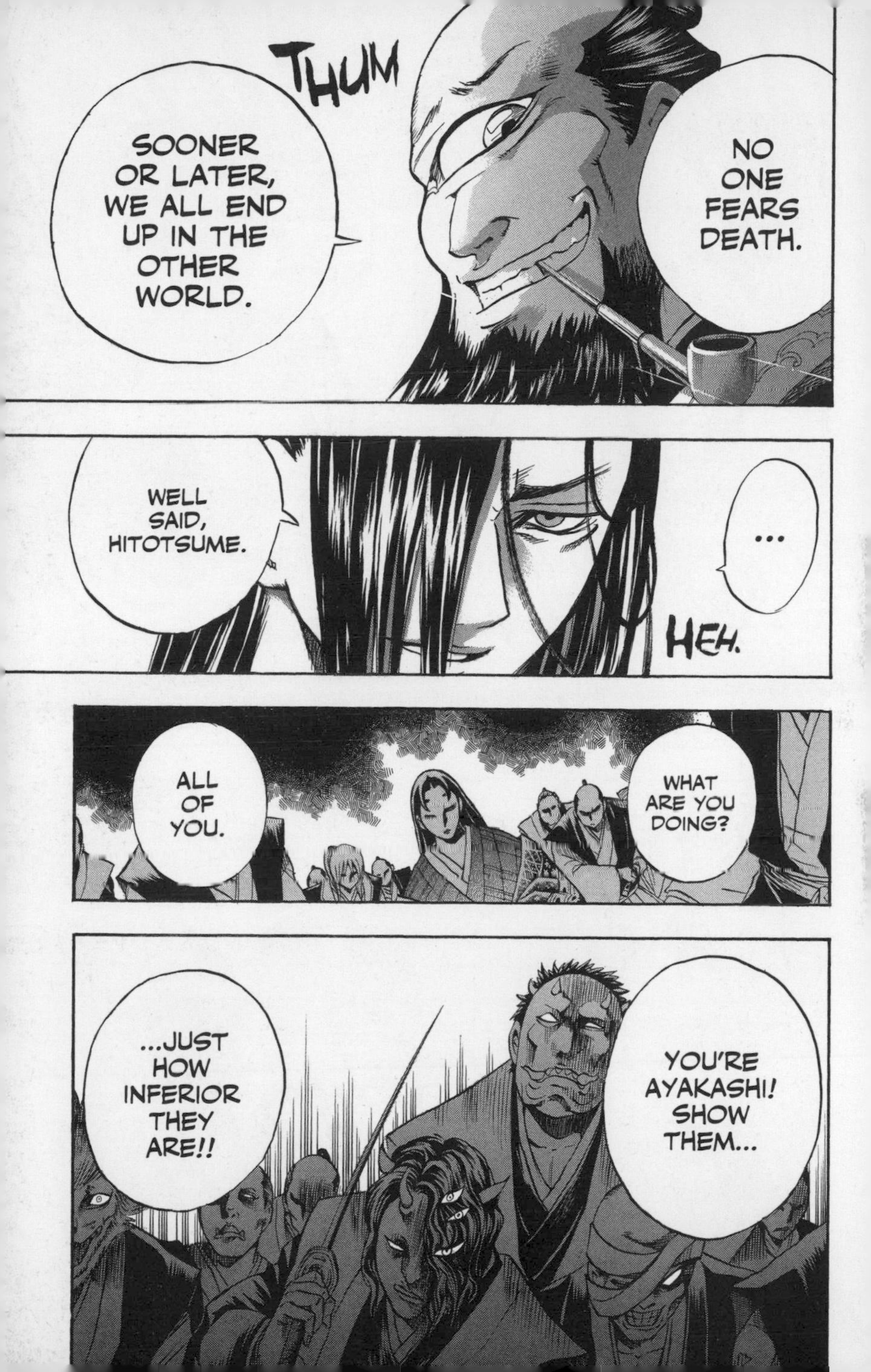
NO ONE FEARS DEATH.
THUM
SOONER OR LATER, WE ALL END UP IN THE OTHER WORLD.
...
HEH.
WELL SAID, HITOTSUME.
WHAT ARE YOU DOING?
ALL OF YOU.
YOU'RE AYAKASHI! SHOW THEM...
...JUST HOW INFERIOR THEY ARE!!

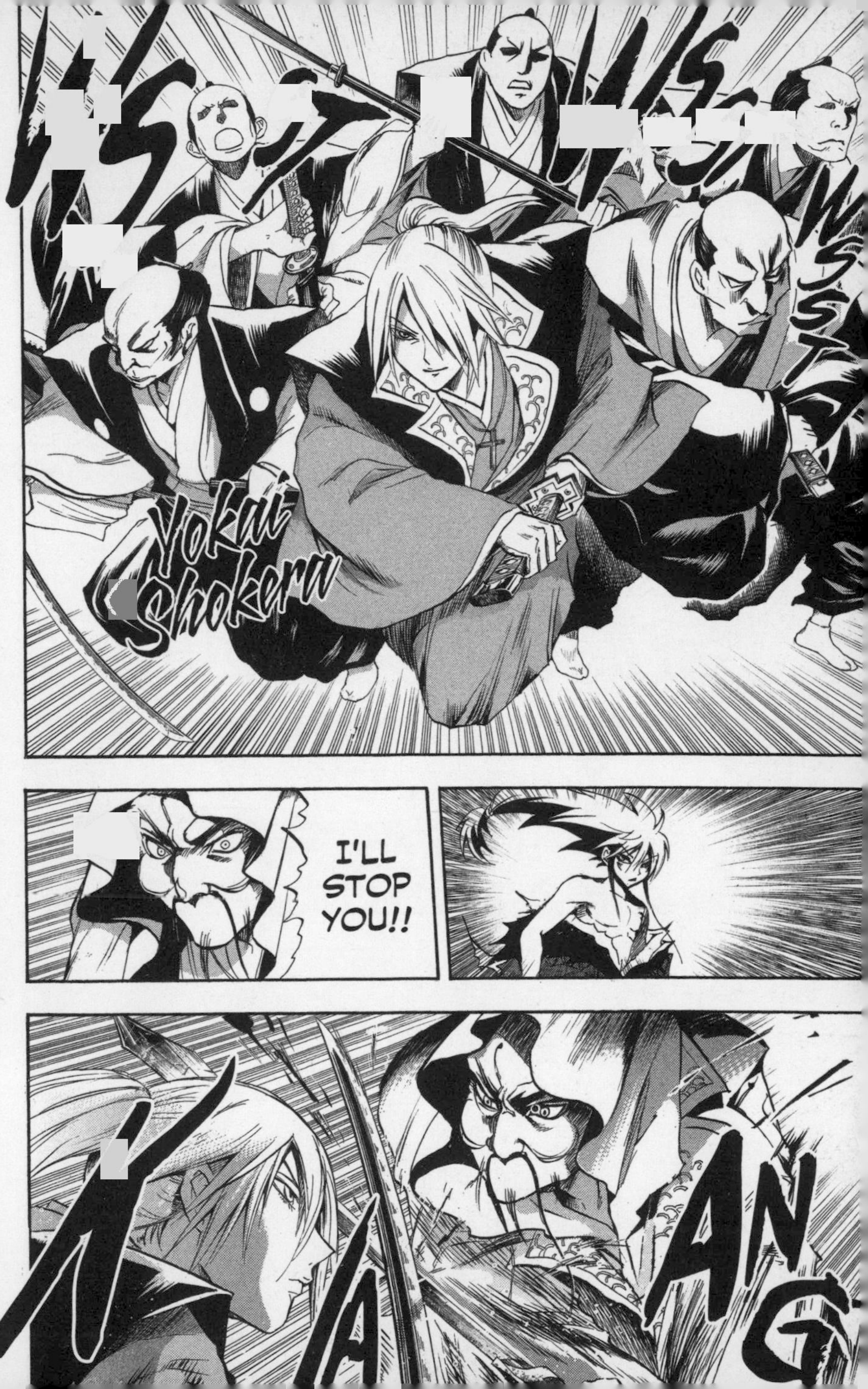
WSST
Yokai Shokera
I'LL STOP YOU!!

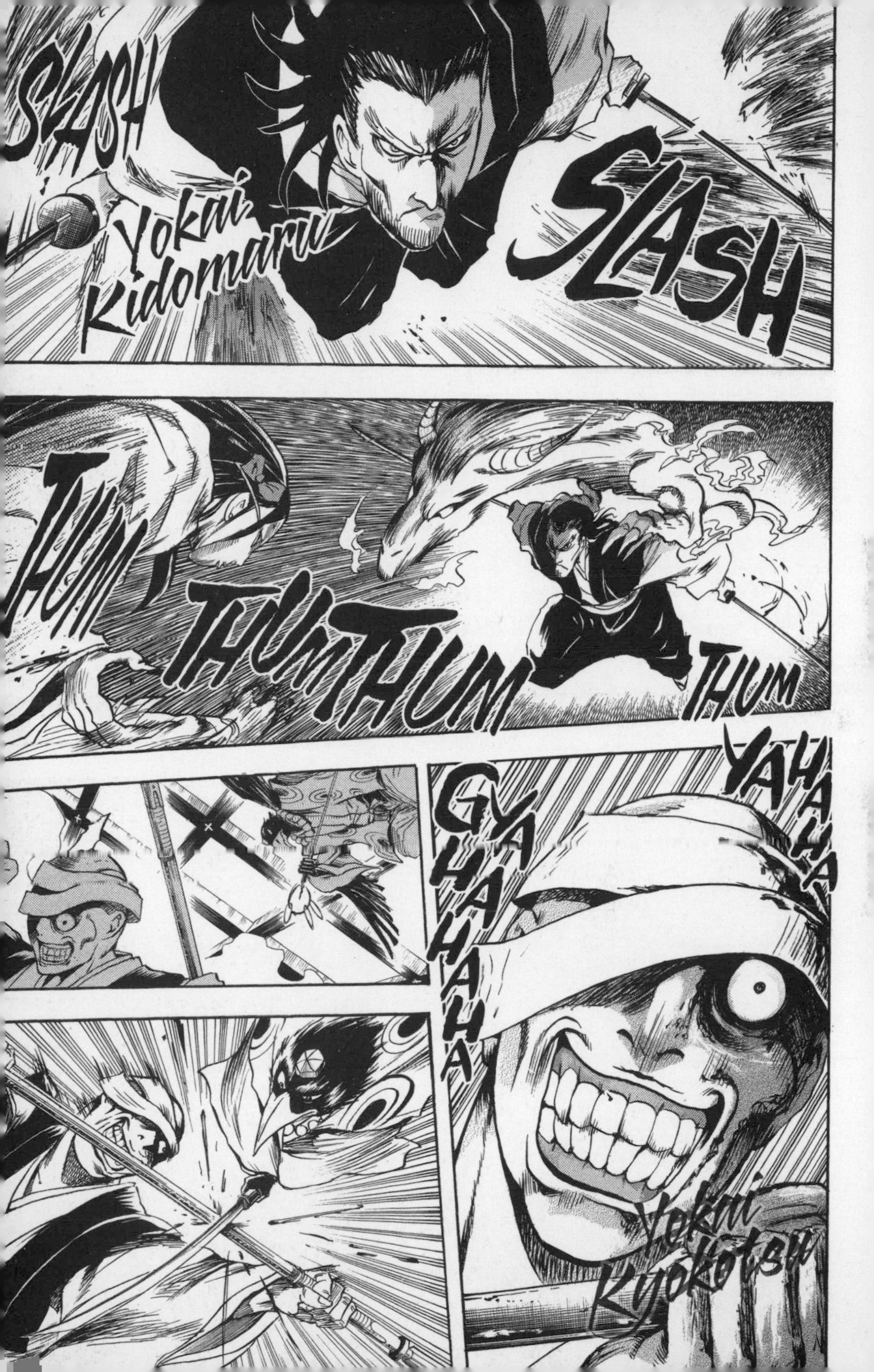
SLASH
Yokai Kidomaru
SLASH
THUM
THUM THUM
THUM
YAHAHAHA
GYAHAHAHAHAHA
Yokai Kyokotsu

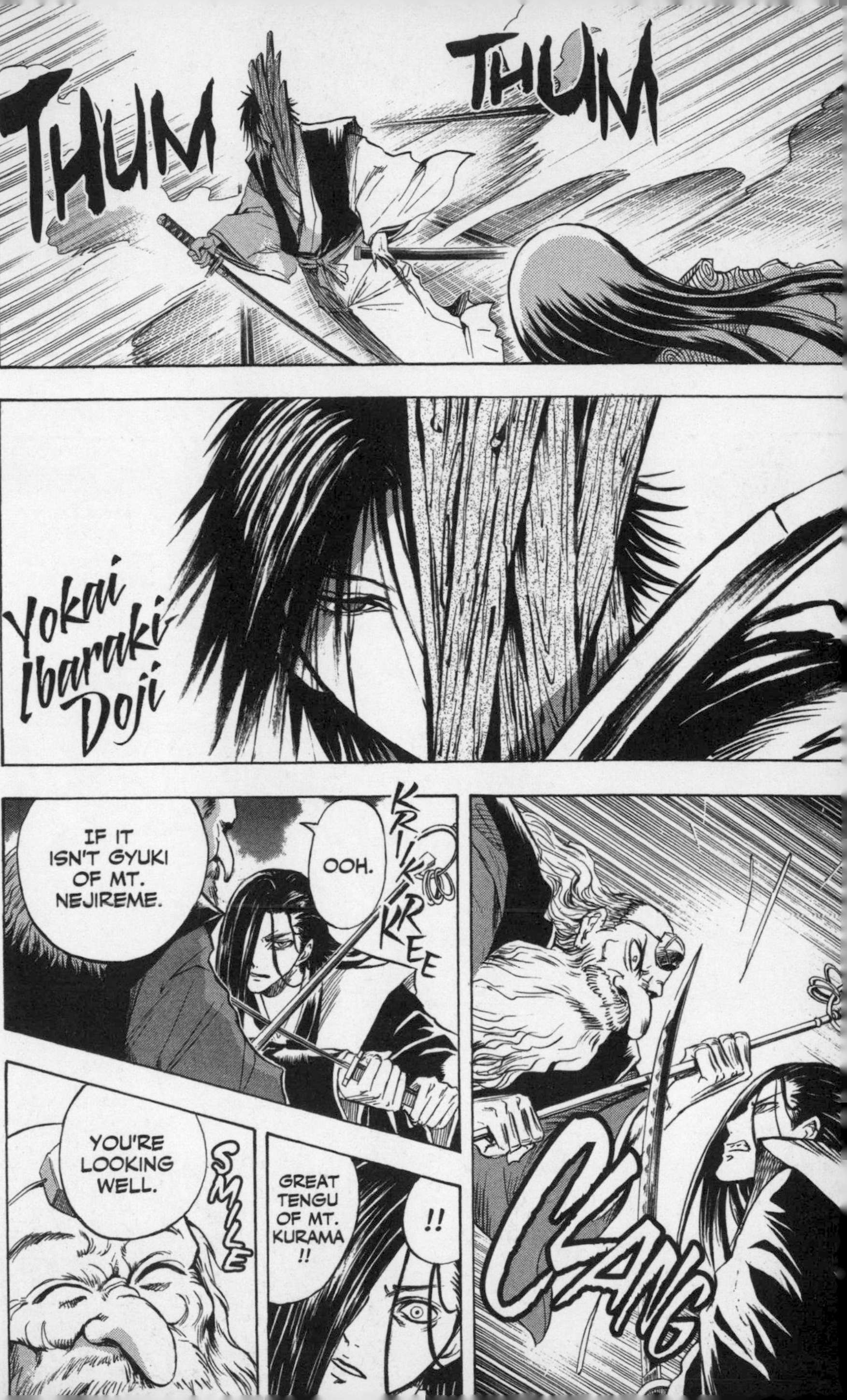
THUM
THUM
Yokai Ibaraki Doji
CLANG
OOH.
KRIKKREE
IF IT ISN'T GYUKI OF MT. NEJIREME.
!!
GREAT TENGU OF MT. KURAMA !!
SMILE
YOU'RE LOOKING WELL.

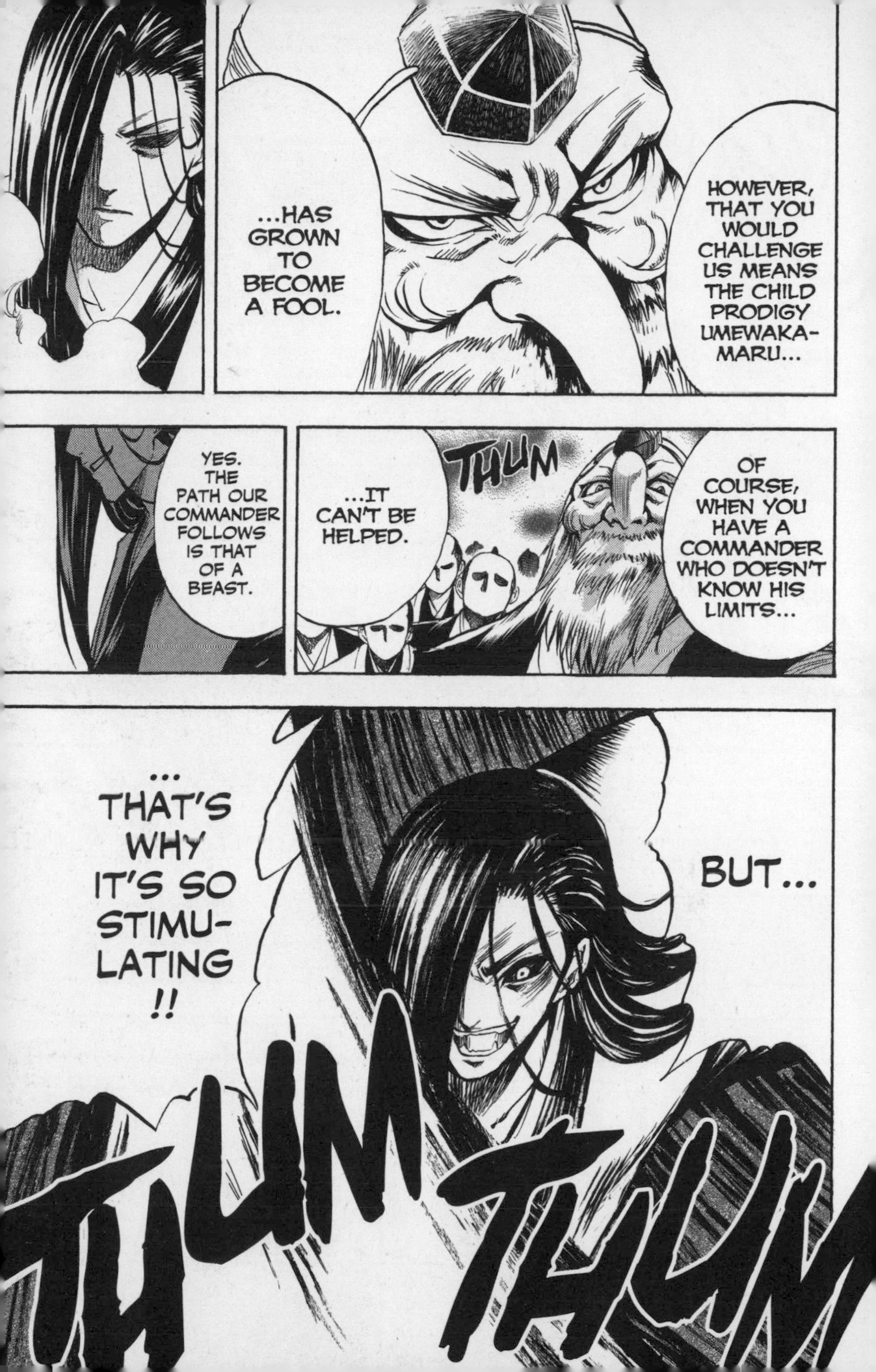
HOWEVER, THAT YOU WOULD CHALLENGE US MEANS THE CHILD PRODIGY UMEWAKA-MARU...
...HAS GROWN TO BECOME A FOOL.
OF COURSE, WHEN YOU HAVE A COMMANDER WHO DOESN'T KNOW HIS LIMITS...
THUM
...IT CAN'T BE HELPED.
YES. THE PATH OUR COMMANDER FOLLOWS IS THAT OF A BEAST.
BUT...
...THAT'S WHY IT'S SO STIMU-LATING!!
THUM THUM

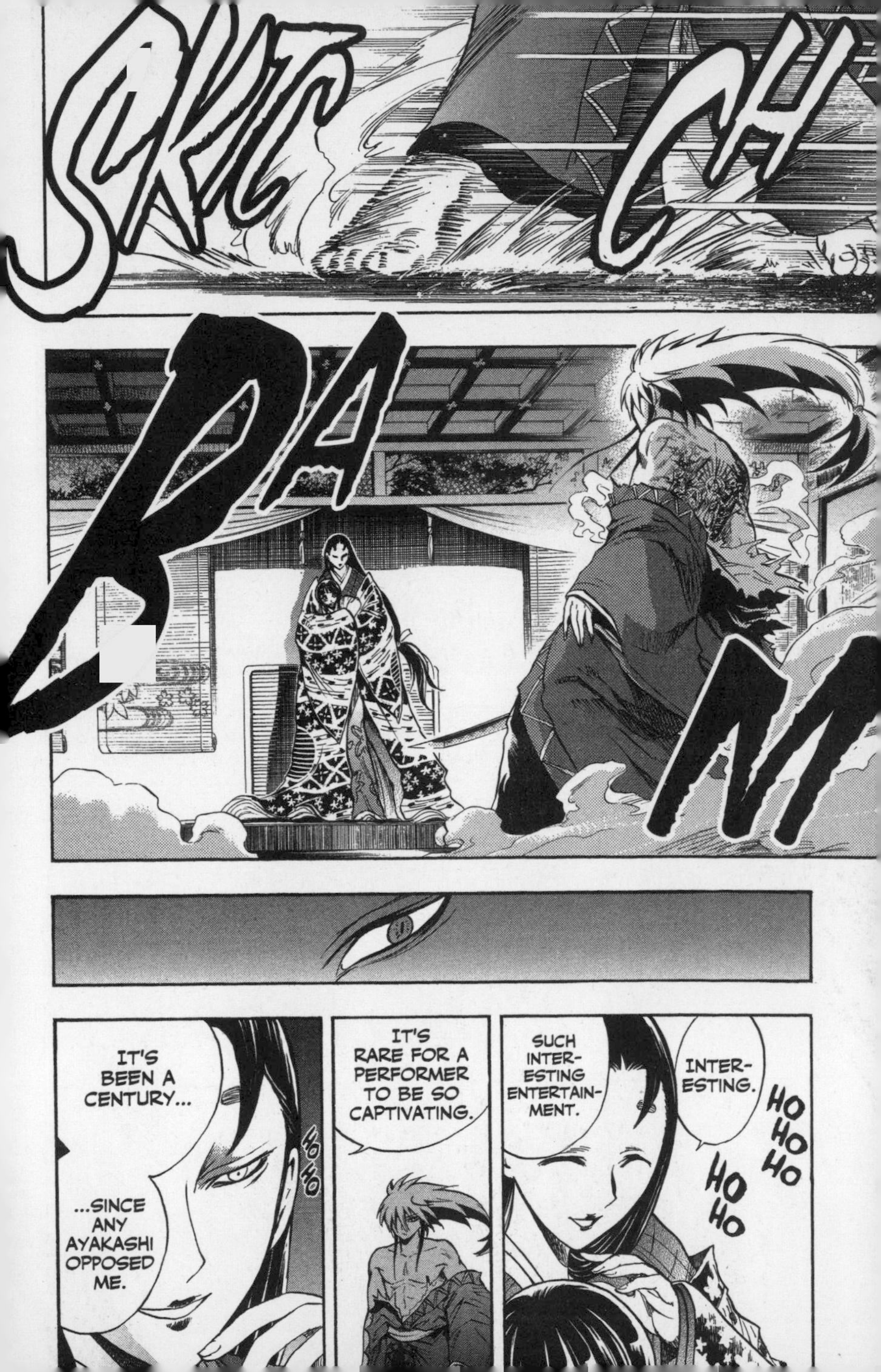
SKT
CH
BA
M
INTER-ESTING.
SUCH INTER-ESTING ENTERTAIN-MENT.
HO HO HO
HO HO HO
IT'S RARE FOR A PERFORMER TO BE SO CAPTIVATING.
IT'S BEEN A CENTURY...
HO HO
...SINCE ANY AYAKASHI OPPOSED ME.

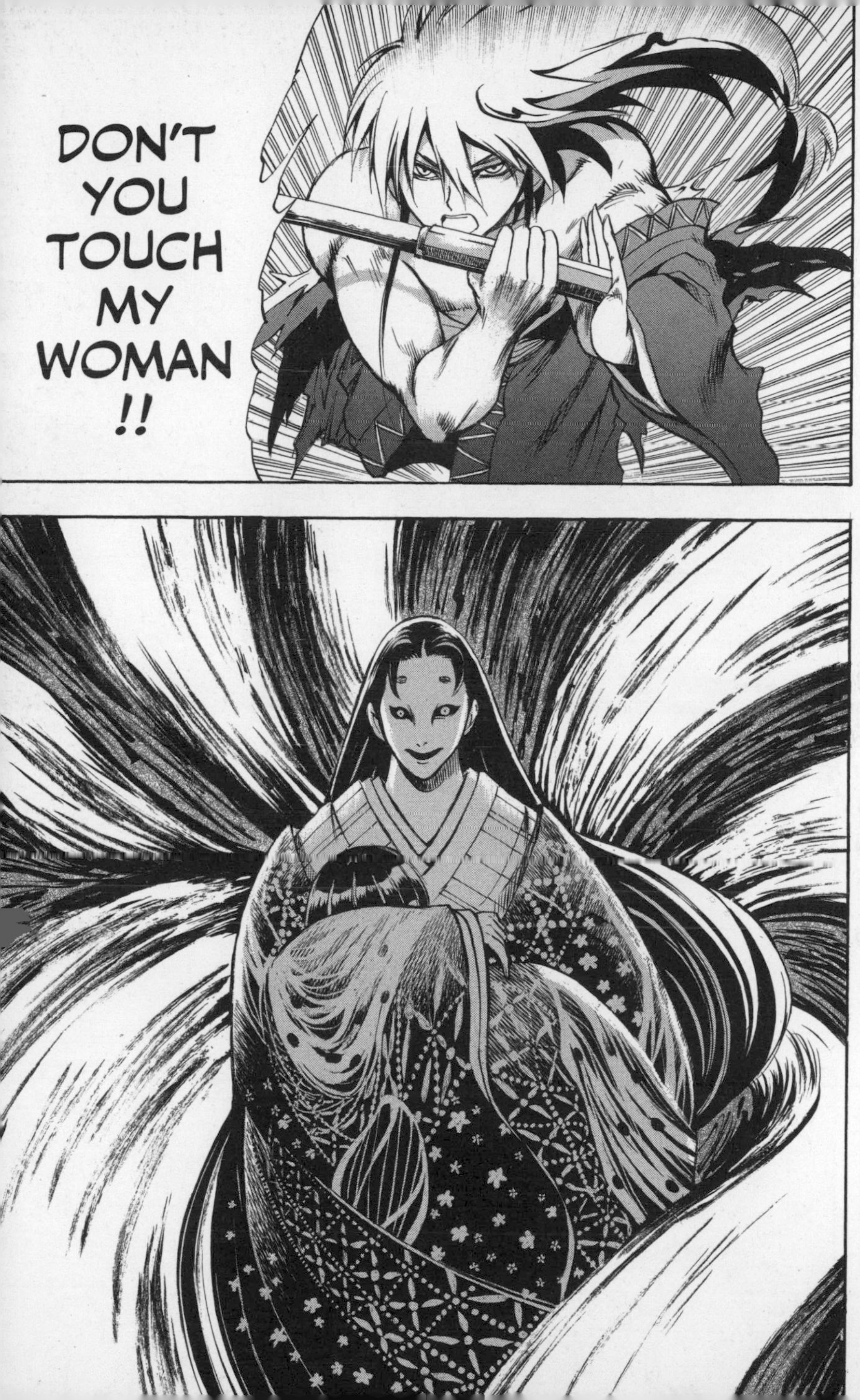
DON'T YOU TOUCH MY WOMAN !!

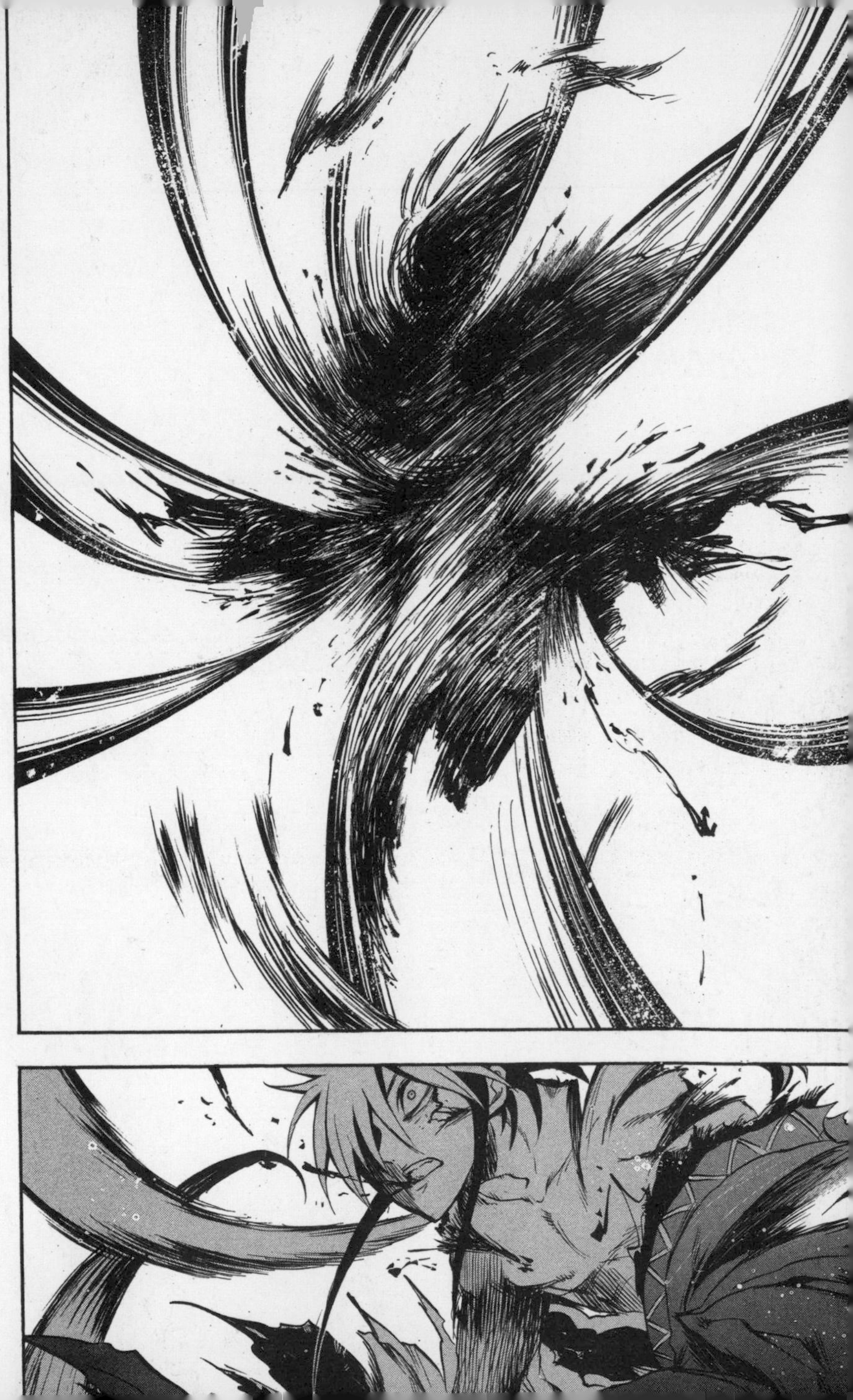

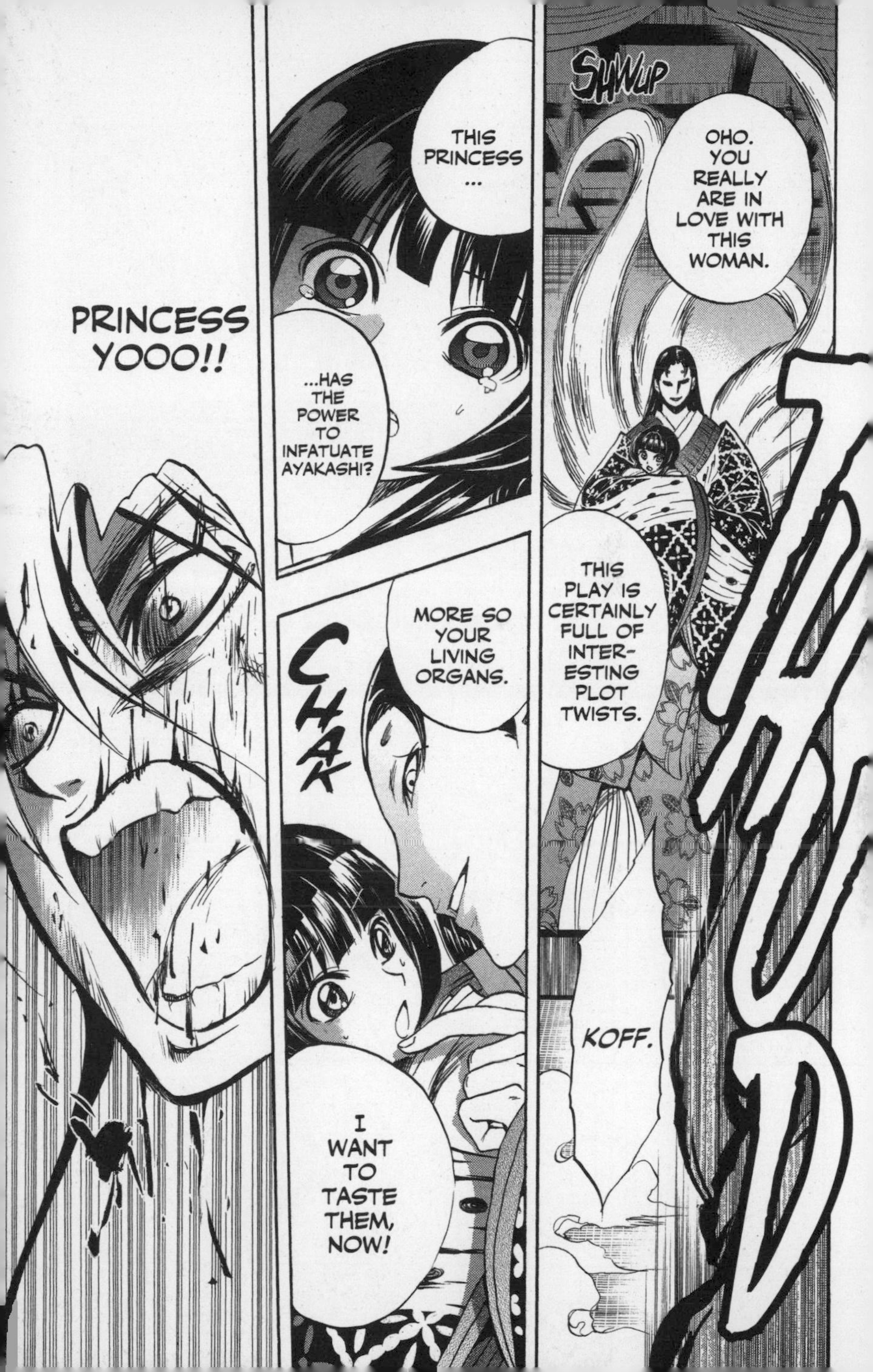
SHWUP
OHO. YOU REALLY ARE IN LOVE WITH THIS WOMAN.
THIS PLAY IS CERTAINLY FULL OF INTER-ESTING PLOT TWISTS.
KOFF.
THIS PRINCESS...
...HAS THE POWER TO INFATUATE AYAKASHI?
MORE SO YOUR LIVING ORGANS.
CHAK
I WANT TO TASTE THEM, NOW!
PRINCESS YOOO!!

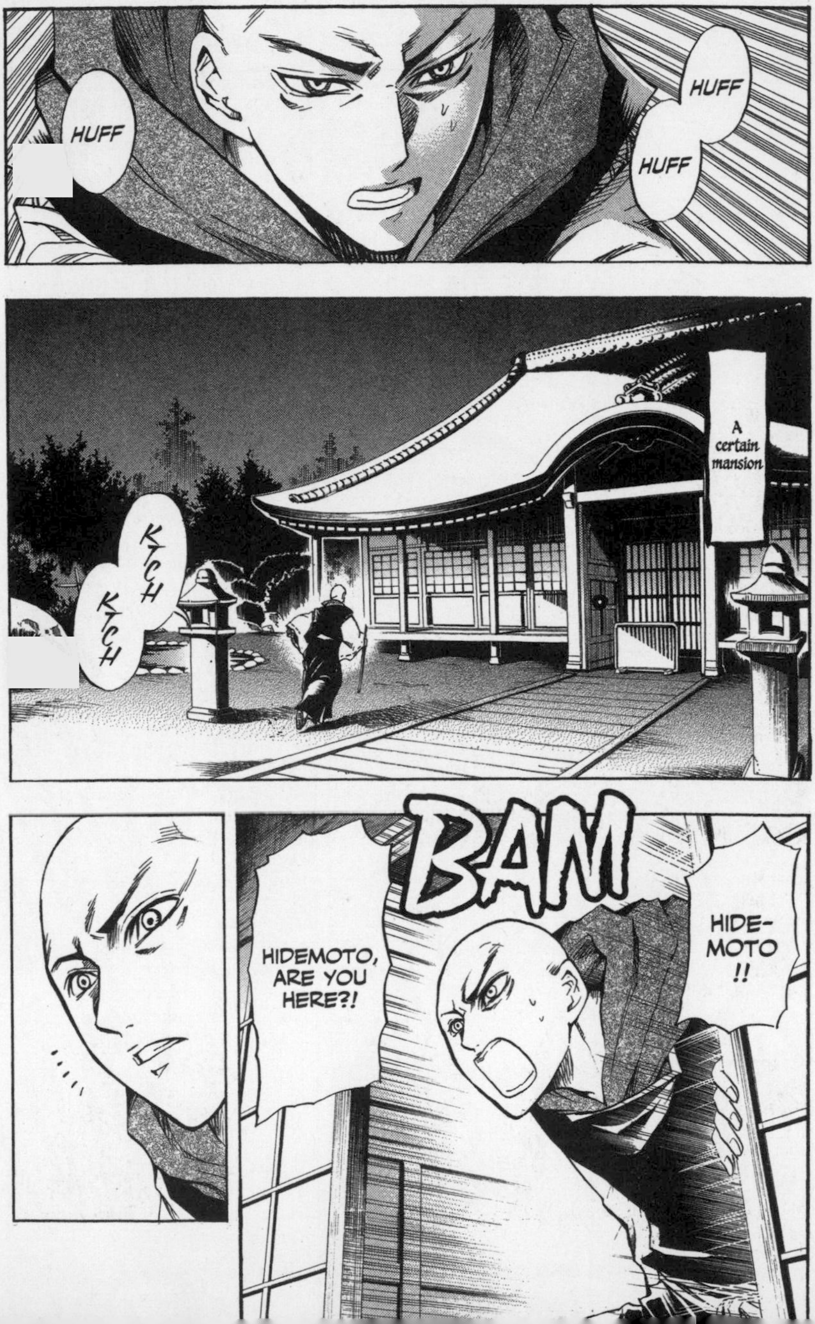
HUFF
HUFF
HUFF
A certain mansion
KTCH
KTCH
BAM
HIDE-MOTO !!
HIDEMOTO, ARE YOU HERE?!
......

READ THIS WAY

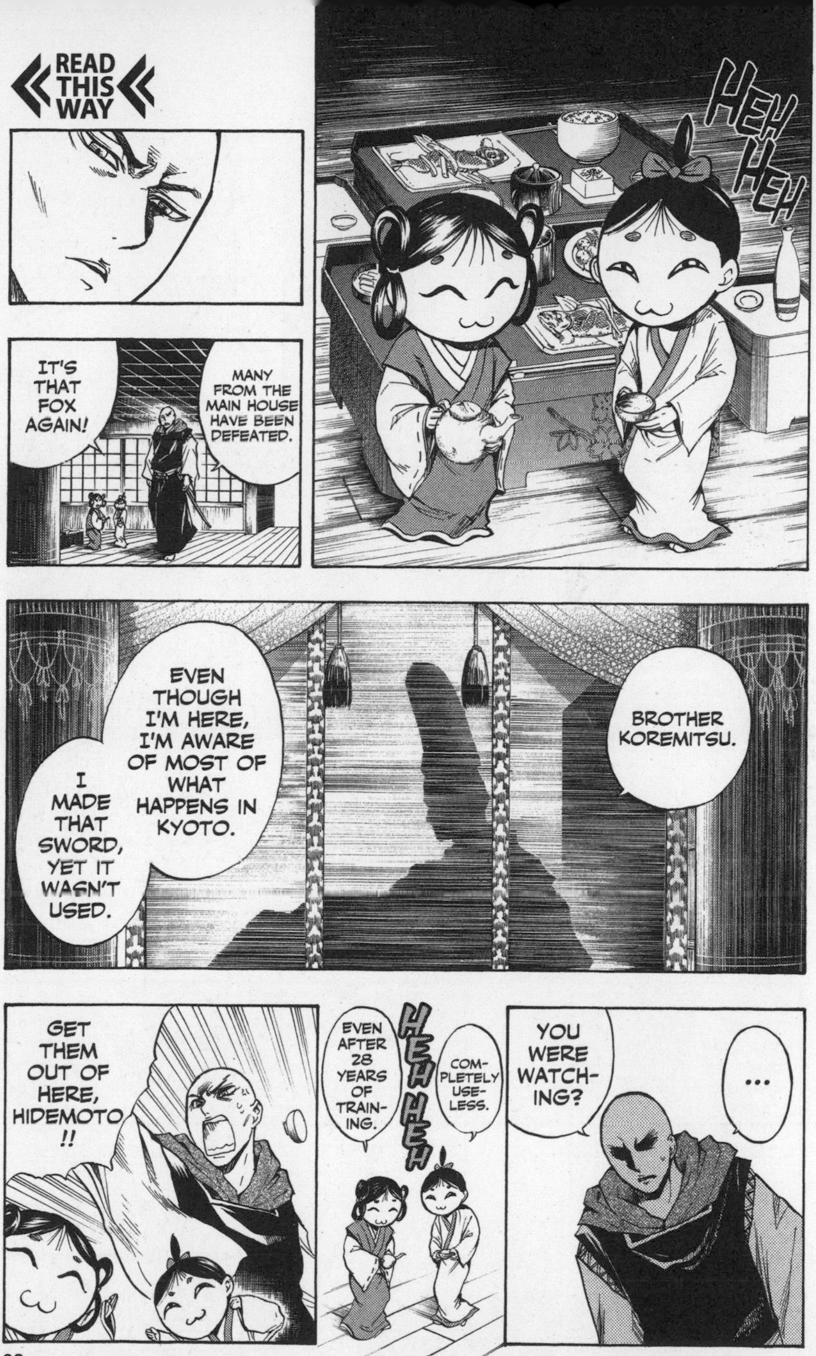
HEH HEH
MANY FROM THE MAIN HOUSE HAVE BEEN DEFEATED.
IT'S THAT FOX AGAIN!
BROTHER KOREMITSU.
EVEN THOUGH I'M HERE, I'M AWARE OF MOST OF WHAT HAPPENS IN KYOTO.
I MADE THAT SWORD, YET IT WASN'T USED.
...
YOU WERE WATCHING?
COMPLETELY USELESS.
HEH HEH
EVEN AFTER 28 YEARS OF TRAINING.
GET THEM OUT OF HERE, HIDEMOTO!!

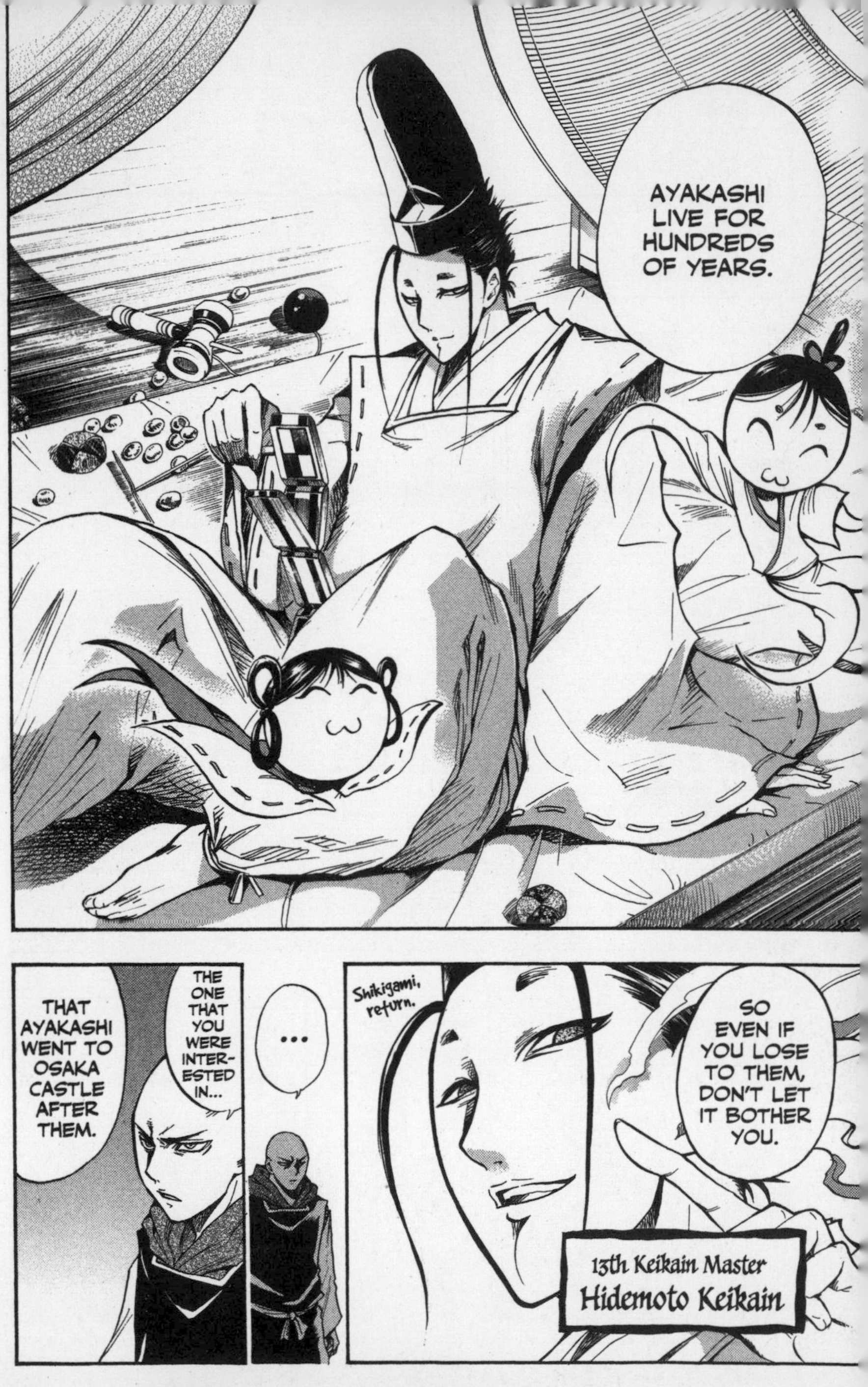
AYAKASHI LIVE FOR HUNDREDS OF YEARS.
SO EVEN IF YOU LOSE TO THEM, DON'T LET IT BOTHER YOU.
Shikigami, return.
13th Keikain Master
Hidemoto Keikain
THE ONE THAT YOU WERE INTER-ESTED IN...
...
THAT AYAKASHI WENT TO OSAKA CASTLE AFTER THEM.

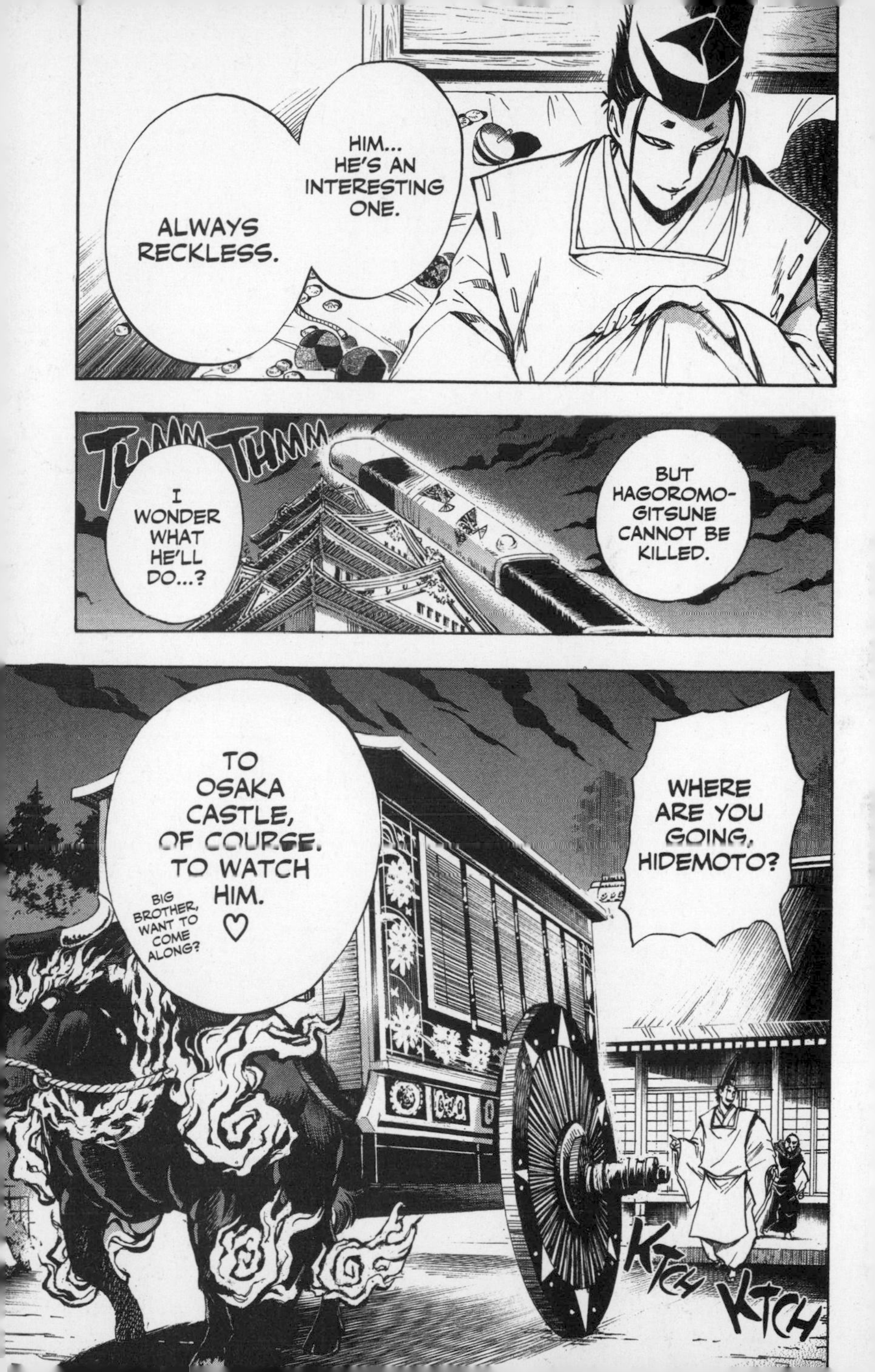
HIM... HE'S AN INTERESTING ONE.
ALWAYS RECKLESS.
THMM THMM
BUT HAGOROMO-GITSUNE CANNOT BE KILLED.
I WONDER WHAT HE'LL DO...?
WHERE ARE YOU GOING, HIDEMOTO?
TO OSAKA CASTLE, OF COURSE. TO WATCH HIM. ♡
BIG BROTHER, WANT TO COME ALONG?
KTCH KTCH

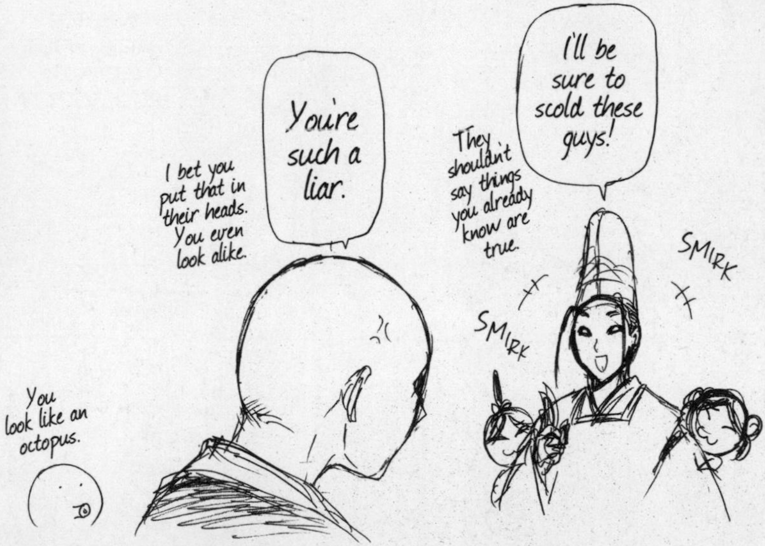
I'll be sure to scold these guys!
They shouldn't say things you already know are true.
SMIRK
SMIRK
You're such a liar.
I bet you put that in their heads. You even look alike.
You look like an octopus.

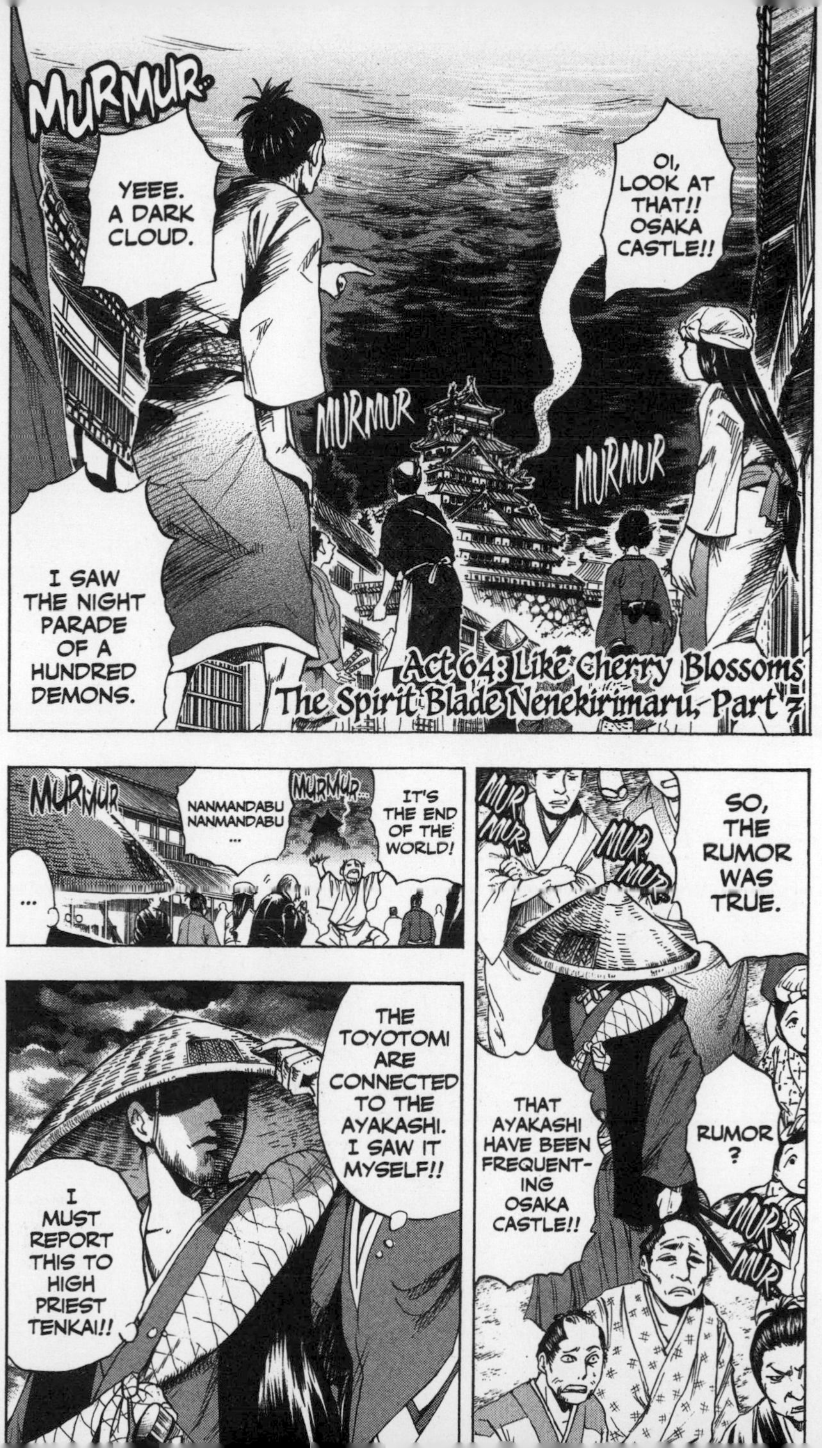
OI, LOOK AT THAT!! OSAKA CASTLE!!
MURMUR..
YEEE. A DARK CLOUD.
MURMUR
MURMUR
I SAW THE NIGHT PARADE OF A HUNDRED DEMONS.
Act 64: Like Cherry Blossoms
The Spirit Blade Nenekirimaru, Part 7
MUR MUR
SO, THE RUMOR WAS TRUE.
MUR MUR
RUMOR?
THAT AYAKASHI HAVE BEEN FREQUENTING OSAKA CASTLE!!
MUR MUR
IT'S THE END OF THE WORLD!
MURMUR...
NANMANDABU NANMANDABU ...
MURMUR
...
THE TOYOTOMI ARE CONNECTED TO THE AYAKASHI. I SAW IT MYSELF!!
I MUST REPORT THIS TO HIGH PRIEST TENKAI!!

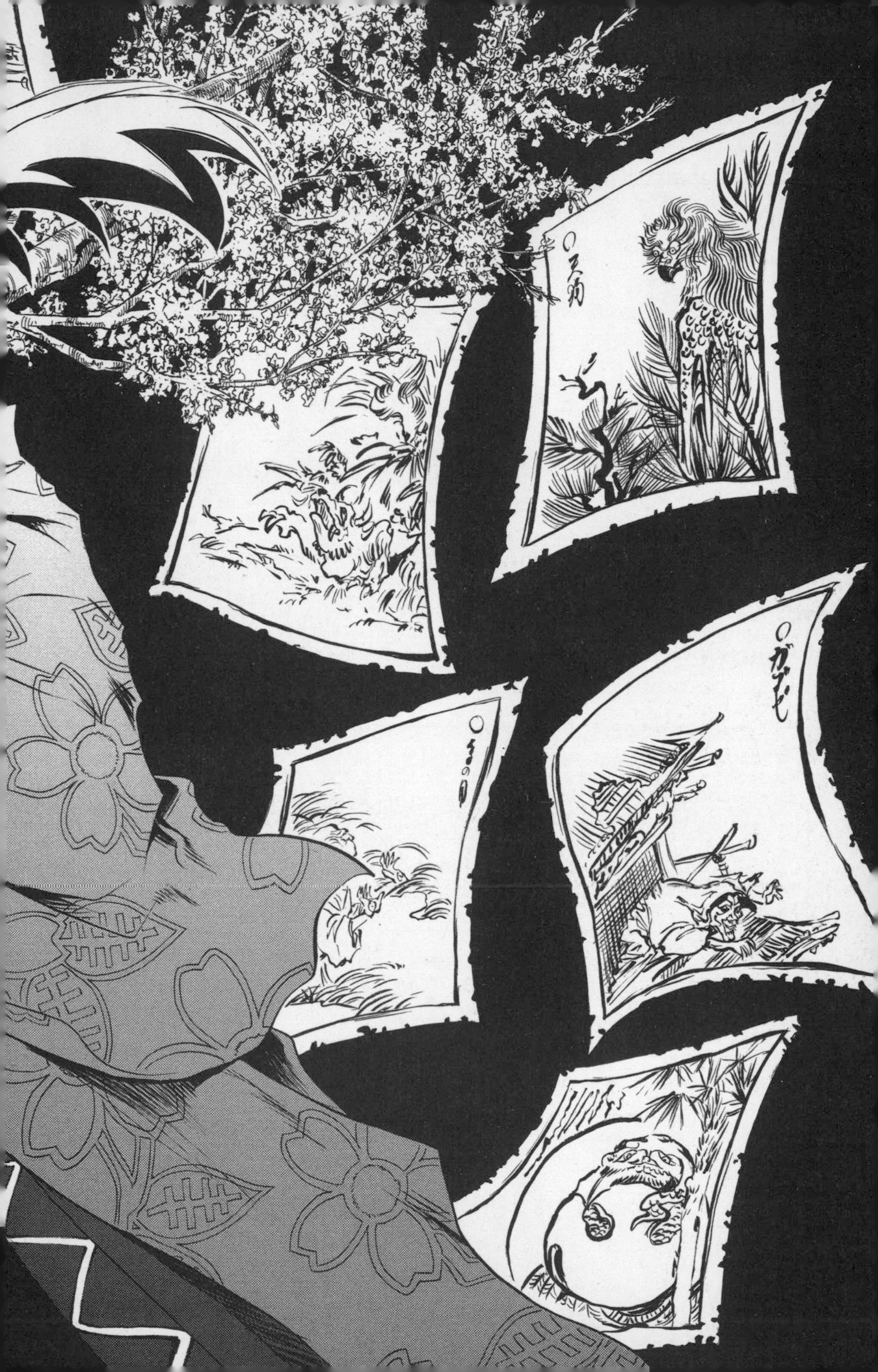
○天狗
○手の目

Act 64:

Like Cherry Blossoms

The Spirit Blade Nenekirimaru, Part 7

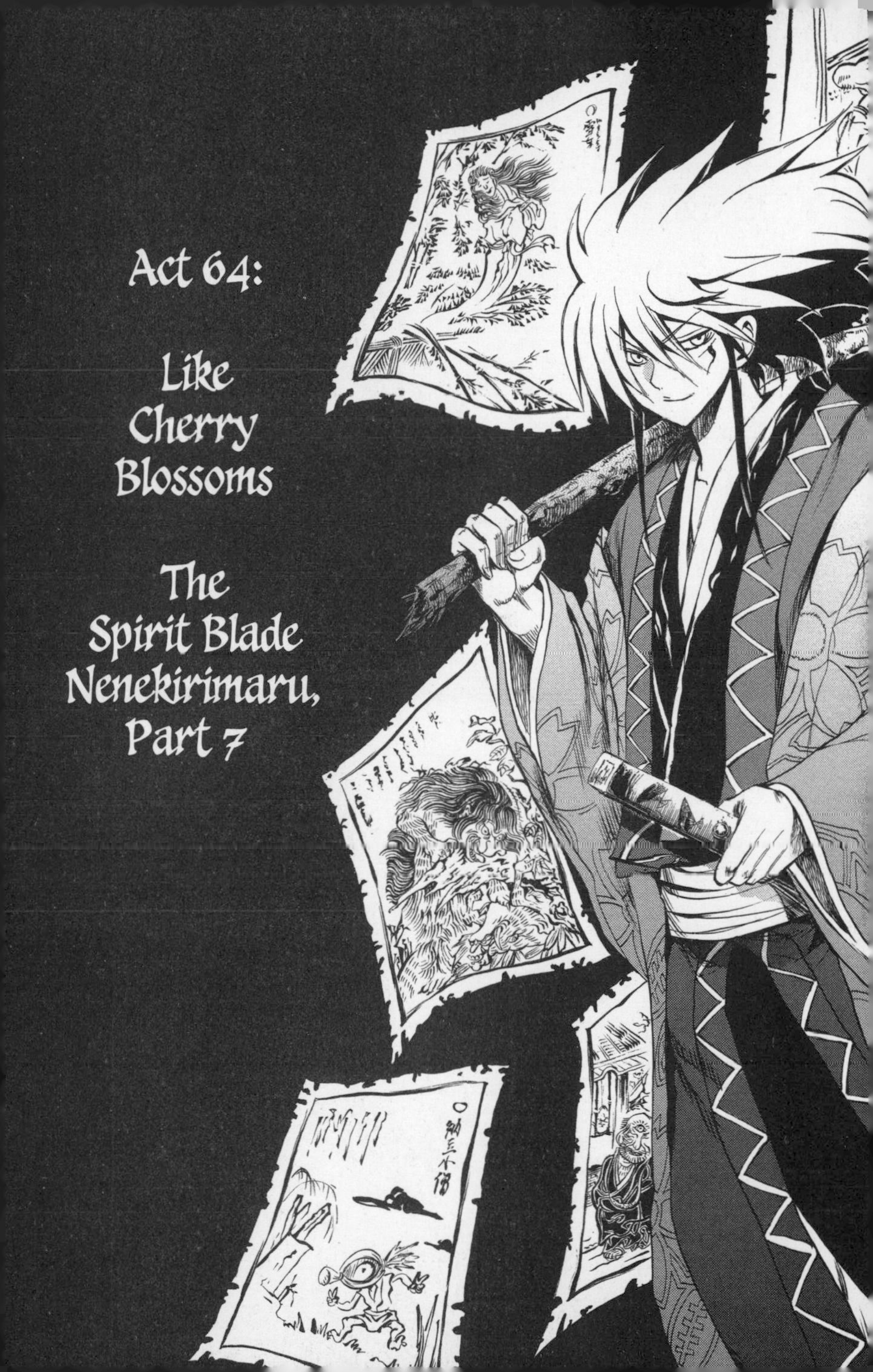

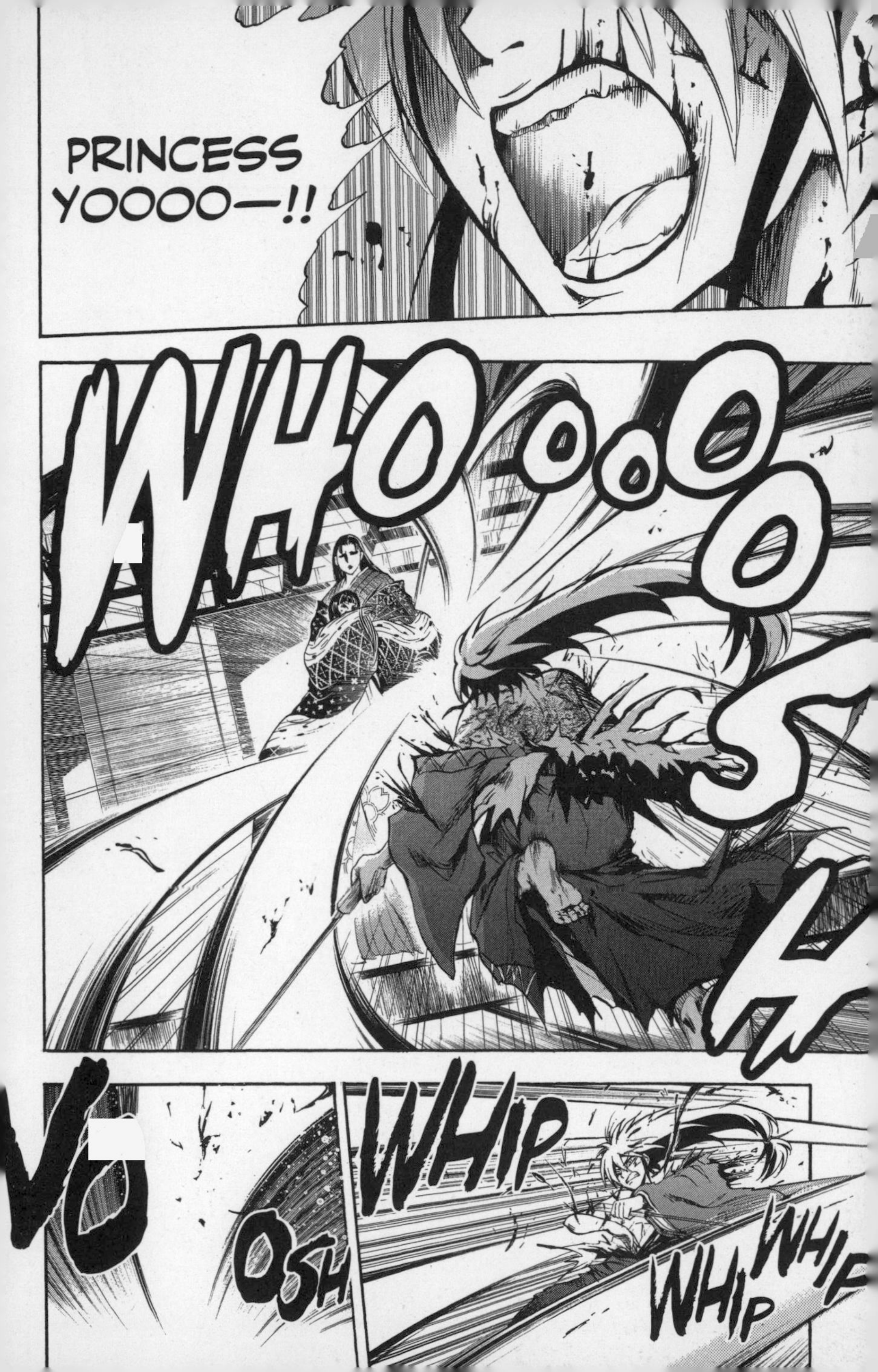
PRINCESS YOOOO—!!
WHOOOOSH
VOOSH
WHIP
WHIP WHIP WHIP

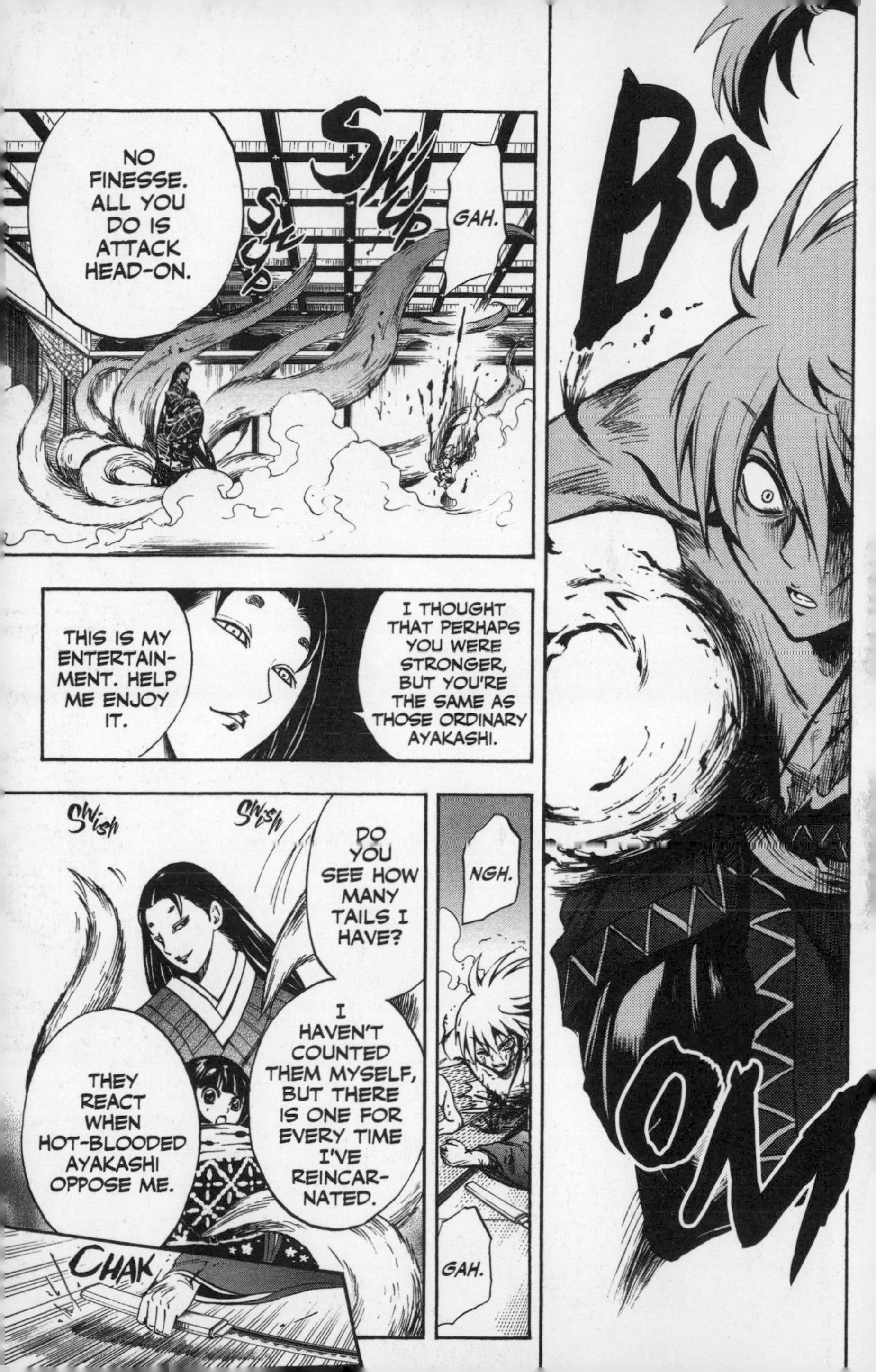
BOOM
SWUP
GAH.
SWUP
NO FINESSE. ALL YOU DO IS ATTACK HEAD-ON.
I THOUGHT THAT PERHAPS YOU WERE STRONGER, BUT YOU'RE THE SAME AS THOSE ORDINARY AYAKASHI.
THIS IS MY ENTERTAIN-MENT. HELP ME ENJOY IT.
NGH.
GAH.
Swish
DO YOU SEE HOW MANY TAILS I HAVE?
Swish
I HAVEN'T COUNTED THEM MYSELF, BUT THERE IS ONE FOR EVERY TIME I'VE REINCAR-NATED.
THEY REACT WHEN HOT-BLOODED AYAKASHI OPPOSE ME.
CHAK

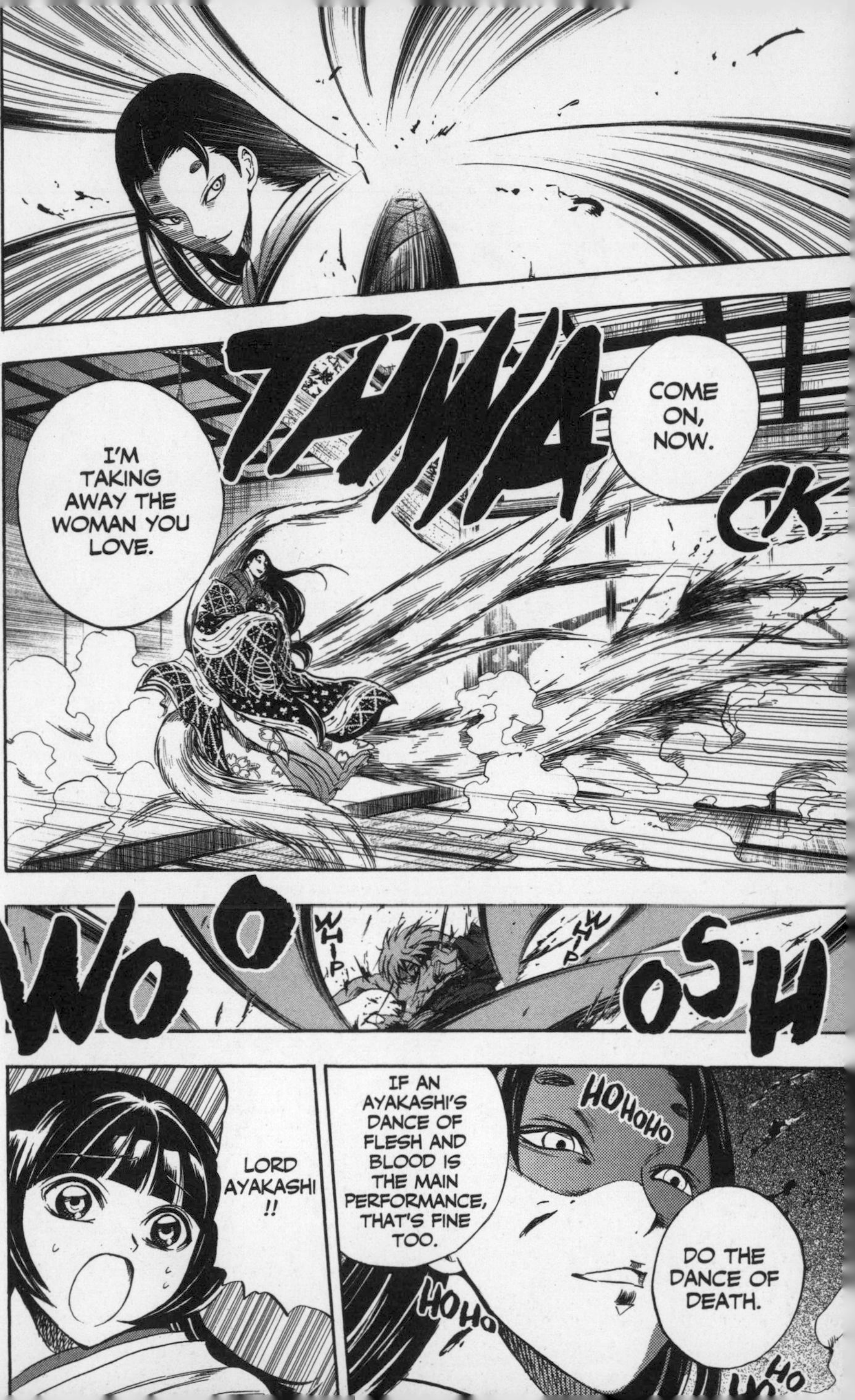
THWACK
COME ON, NOW.
I'M TAKING AWAY THE WOMAN YOU LOVE.
WOOOSH
WHIP
WHIP
HOHOHO
IF AN AYAKASHI'S DANCE OF FLESH AND BLOOD IS THE MAIN PERFORMANCE, THAT'S FINE TOO.
DO THE DANCE OF DEATH.
HOHO
LORD AYAKASHI !!

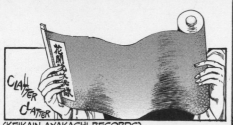

CLATTER
CLATTER

(KEIKAIN AYAKASHI RECORDS)

HAGOROMO-GITSUNE IS NO ORDINARY AYAKASHI.

CLATTER

CLATTER

ACCORDING TO THE KEIKAIN AYAKASHI RECORDS FROM EIGHT GENERATIONS AGO...

...
HAGOROMO-GITSUNE APPEARED DURING TURBULENT TIMES, AND POSSESSED THE BODY OF A YOUNG CHILD IN ORDER TO GROW WITHIN.

WHEN THAT CHILD'S HEART WAS FINALLY CONSUMED WITH DARKNESS, THE BODY WAS TAKEN OVER, AND MATURED.

CLOP
CLOP

CLOP

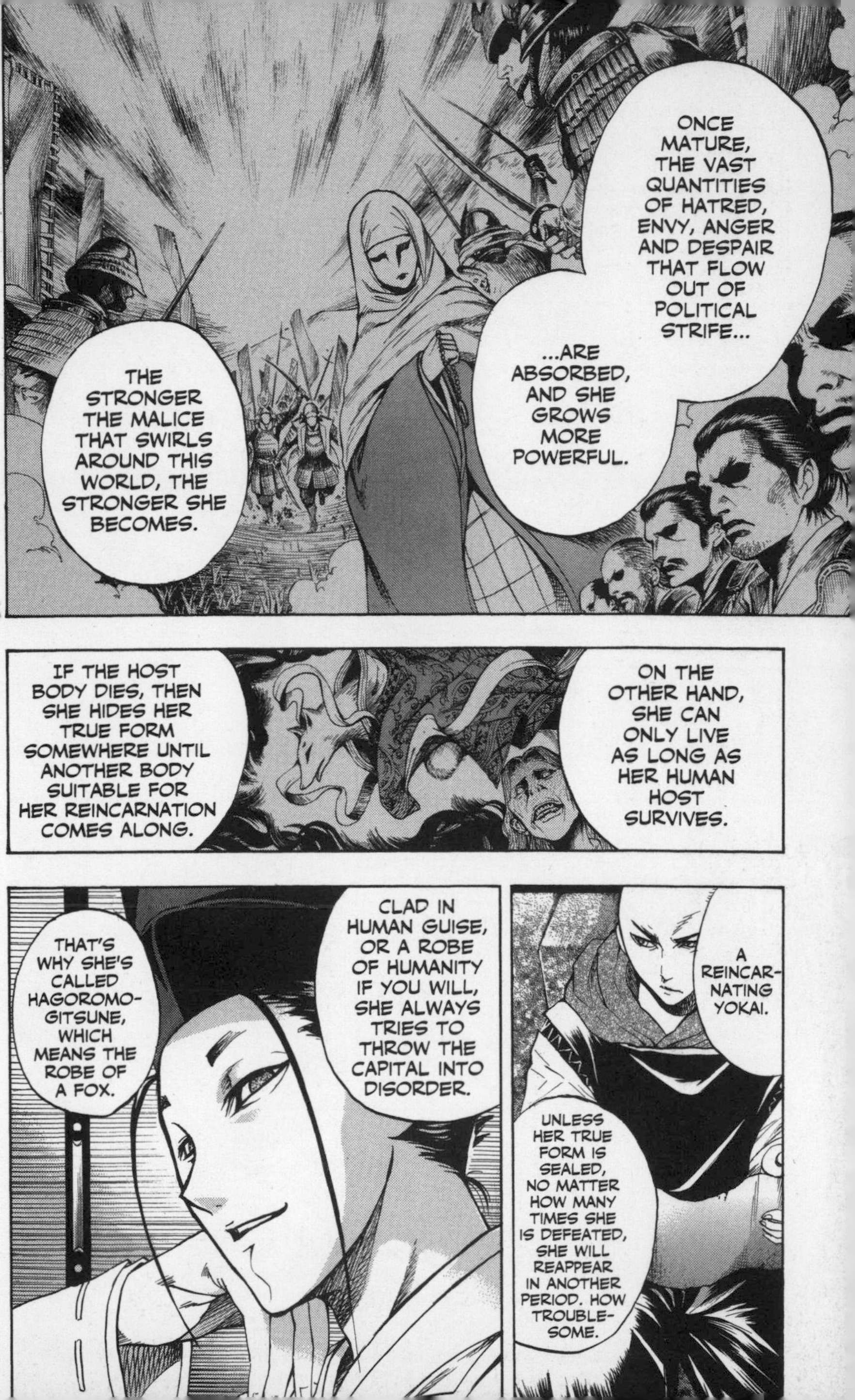
ONCE MATURE, THE VAST QUANTITIES OF HATRED, ENVY, ANGER AND DESPAIR THAT FLOW OUT OF POLITICAL STRIFE...
...ARE ABSORBED, AND SHE GROWS MORE POWERFUL.
THE STRONGER THE MALICE THAT SWIRLS AROUND THIS WORLD, THE STRONGER SHE BECOMES.
ON THE OTHER HAND, SHE CAN ONLY LIVE AS LONG AS HER HUMAN HOST SURVIVES.
IF THE HOST BODY DIES, THEN SHE HIDES HER TRUE FORM SOMEWHERE UNTIL ANOTHER BODY SUITABLE FOR HER REINCARNATION COMES ALONG.
A REINCAR-NATING YOKAI.
UNLESS HER TRUE FORM IS SEALED, NO MATTER HOW MANY TIMES SHE IS DEFEATED, SHE WILL REAPPEAR IN ANOTHER PERIOD. HOW TROUBLE-SOME.
CLAD IN HUMAN GUISE, OR A ROBE OF HUMANITY IF YOU WILL, SHE ALWAYS TRIES TO THROW THE CAPITAL INTO DISORDER.
THAT'S WHY SHE'S CALLED HAGOROMO-GITSUNE, WHICH MEANS THE ROBE OF A FOX.

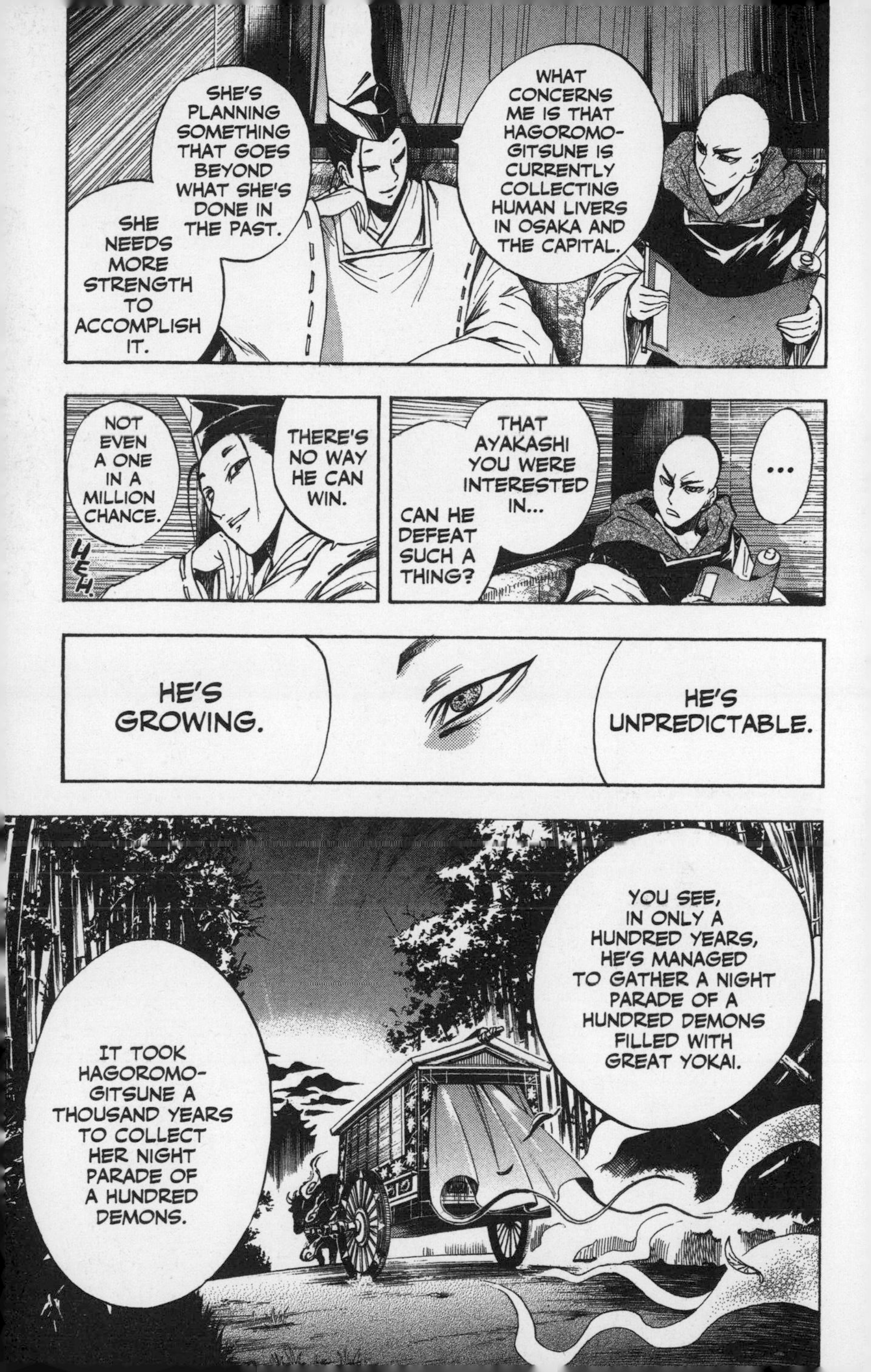
WHAT CONCERNS ME IS THAT HAGOROMO-GITSUNE IS CURRENTLY COLLECTING HUMAN LIVERS IN OSAKA AND THE CAPITAL.
SHE'S PLANNING SOMETHING THAT GOES BEYOND WHAT SHE'S DONE IN THE PAST.
SHE NEEDS MORE STRENGTH TO ACCOMPLISH IT.
...
THAT AYAKASHI YOU WERE INTERESTED IN...
CAN HE DEFEAT SUCH A THING?
THERE'S NO WAY HE CAN WIN.
NOT EVEN A ONE IN A MILLION CHANCE.
HEH.
HE'S UNPREDICTABLE.
HE'S GROWING.
YOU SEE, IN ONLY A HUNDRED YEARS, HE'S MANAGED TO GATHER A NIGHT PARADE OF A HUNDRED DEMONS FILLED WITH GREAT YOKAI.
IT TOOK HAGOROMO-GITSUNE A THOUSAND YEARS TO COLLECT HER NIGHT PARADE OF A HUNDRED DEMONS.

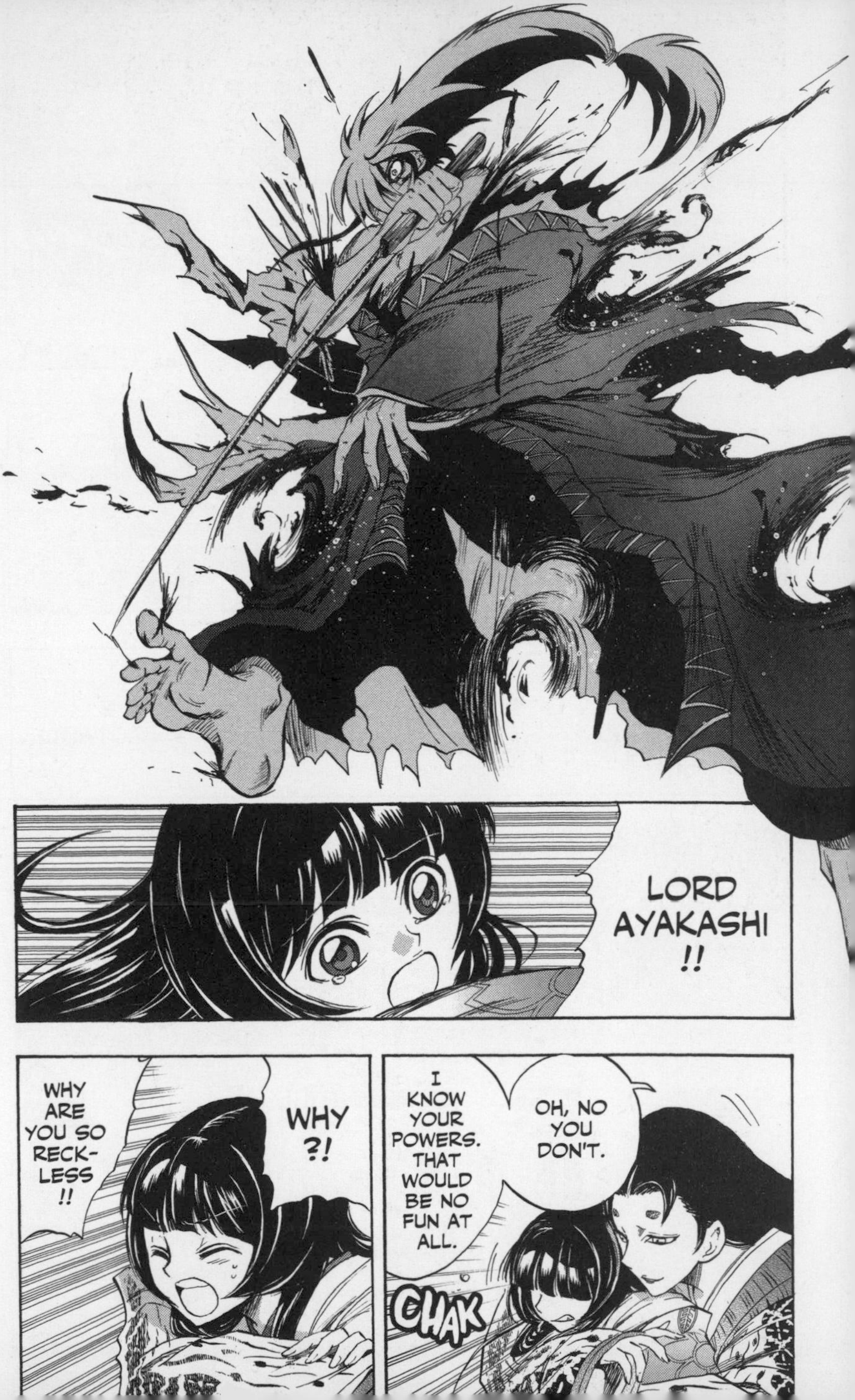
LORD AYAKASHI!!
OH, NO YOU DON'T.
I KNOW YOUR POWERS. THAT WOULD BE NO FUN AT ALL.
CHAK
WHY?!
WHY ARE YOU SO RECK-LESS!!

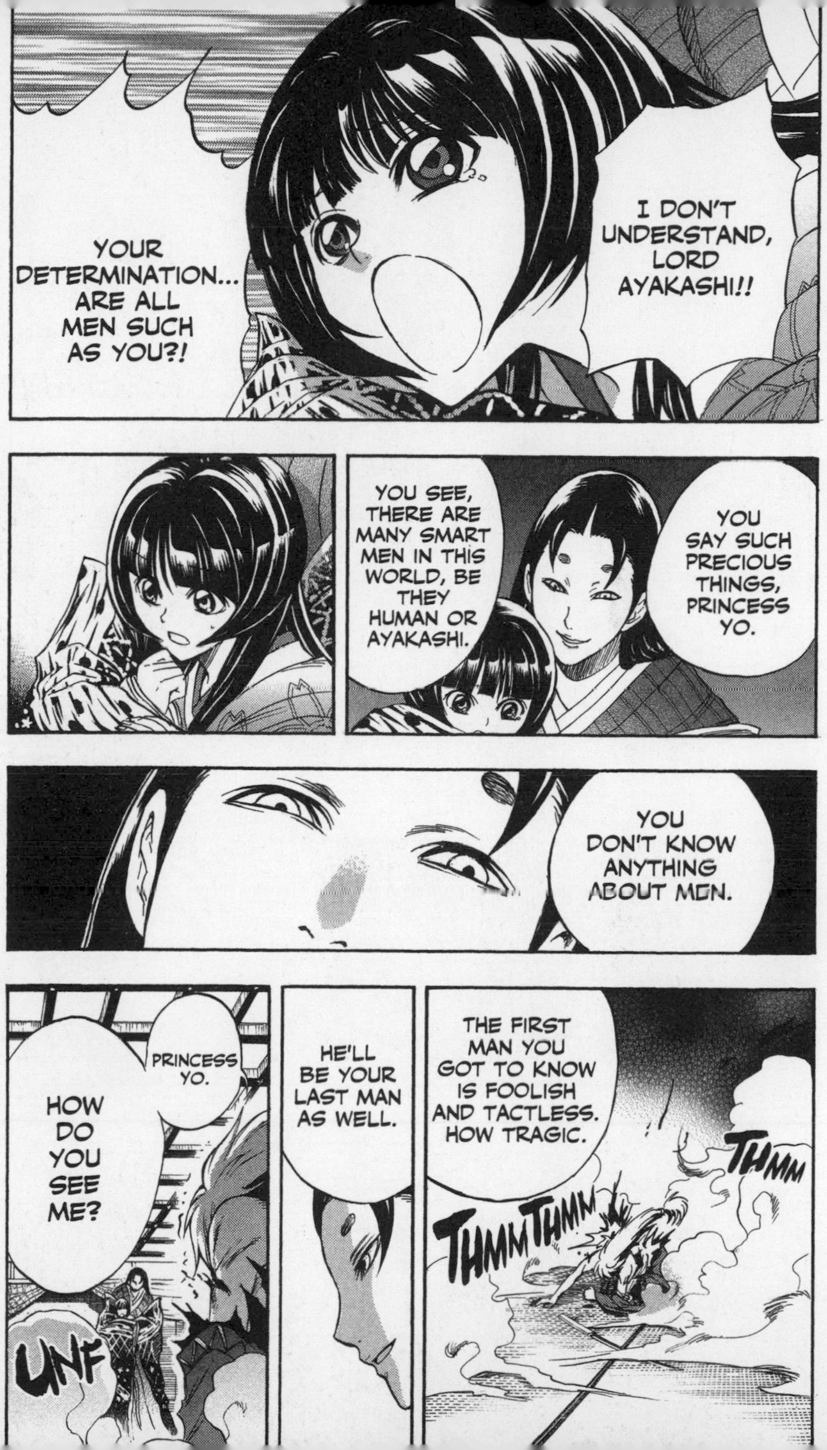
I DON'T UNDERSTAND, LORD AYAKASHI!!
YOUR DETERMINATION... ARE ALL MEN SUCH AS YOU?!
YOU SAY SUCH PRECIOUS THINGS, PRINCESS YO.
YOU SEE, THERE ARE MANY SMART MEN IN THIS WORLD, BE THEY HUMAN OR AYAKASHI.
YOU DON'T KNOW ANYTHING ABOUT MEN.
THE FIRST MAN YOU GOT TO KNOW IS FOOLISH AND TACTLESS. HOW TRAGIC.
THMM
THMMTHMM
HE'LL BE YOUR LAST MAN AS WELL.
PRINCESS YO.
HOW DO YOU SEE ME?
UNF

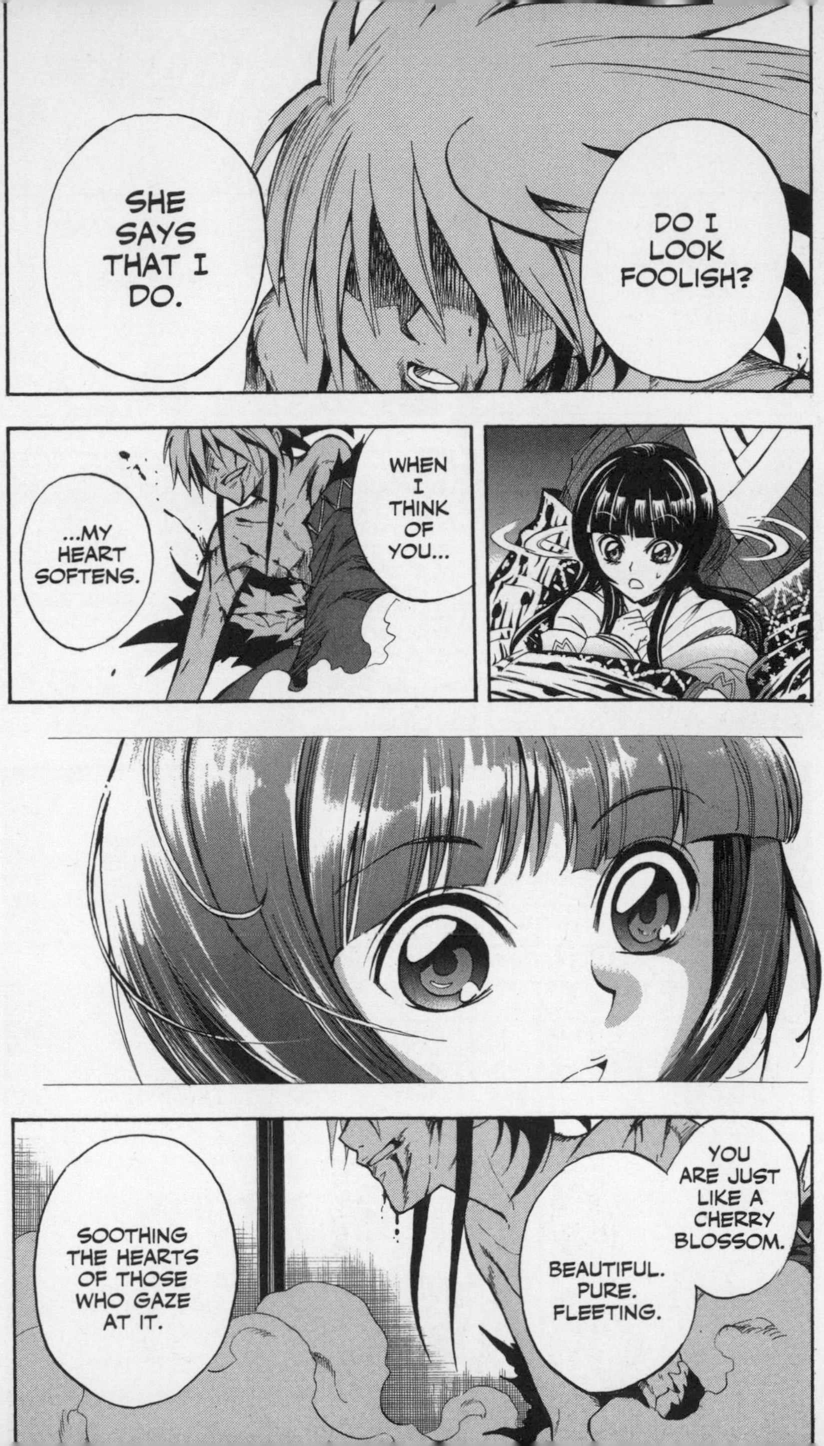
DO I LOOK FOOLISH?
SHE SAYS THAT I DO.
WHEN I THINK OF YOU...
...MY HEART SOFTENS.
YOU ARE JUST LIKE A CHERRY BLOSSOM.
BEAUTIFUL. PURE. FLEETING.
SOOTHING THE HEARTS OF THOSE WHO GAZE AT IT.

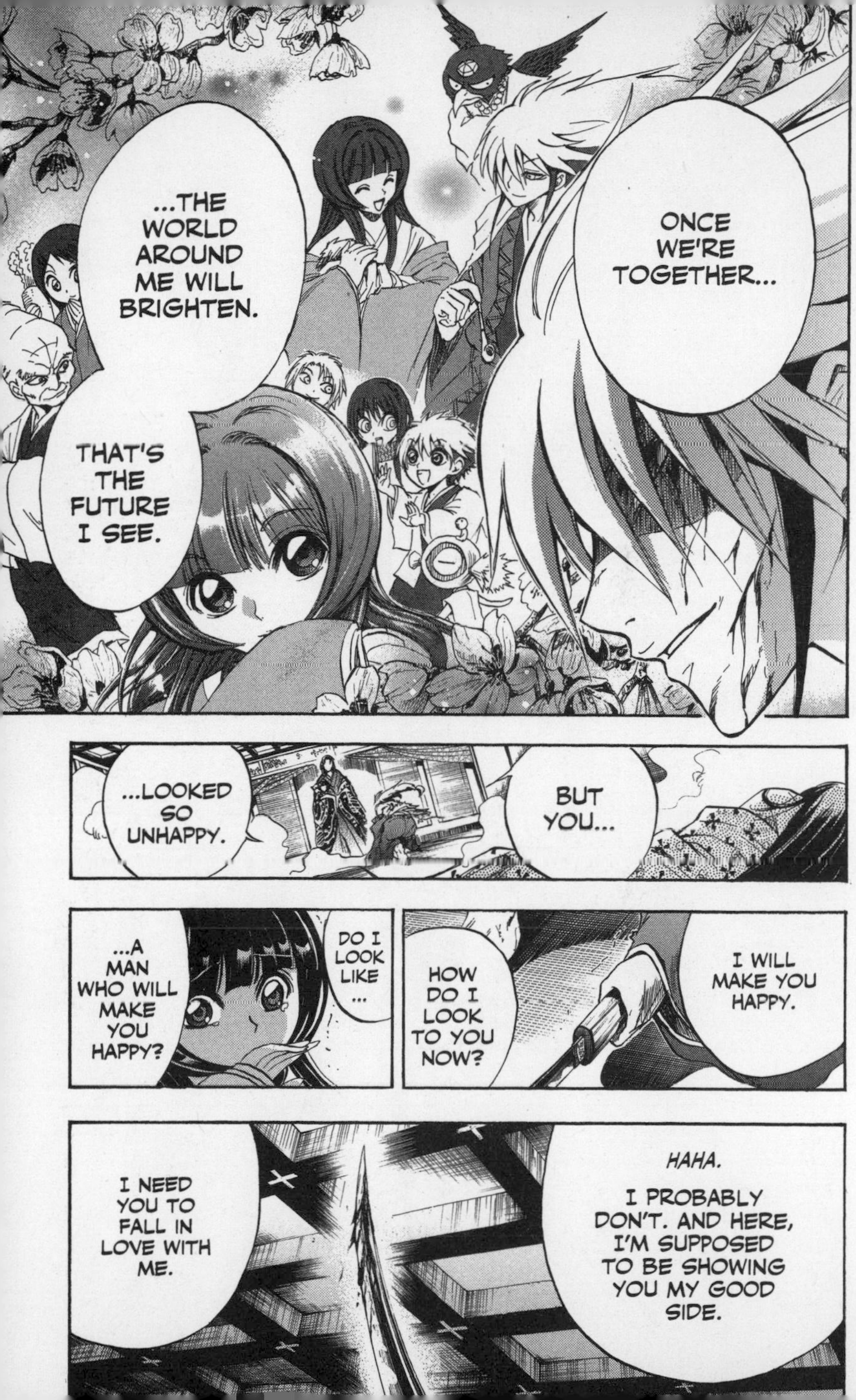
ONCE WE'RE TOGETHER...
...THE WORLD AROUND ME WILL BRIGHTEN.
THAT'S THE FUTURE I SEE.
BUT YOU...
...LOOKED SO UNHAPPY.
I WILL MAKE YOU HAPPY.
HOW DO I LOOK TO YOU NOW?
DO I LOOK LIKE ...
...A MAN WHO WILL MAKE YOU HAPPY?
HAHA.
I PROBABLY DON'T. AND HERE, I'M SUPPOSED TO BE SHOWING YOU MY GOOD SIDE.
I NEED YOU TO FALL IN LOVE WITH ME.

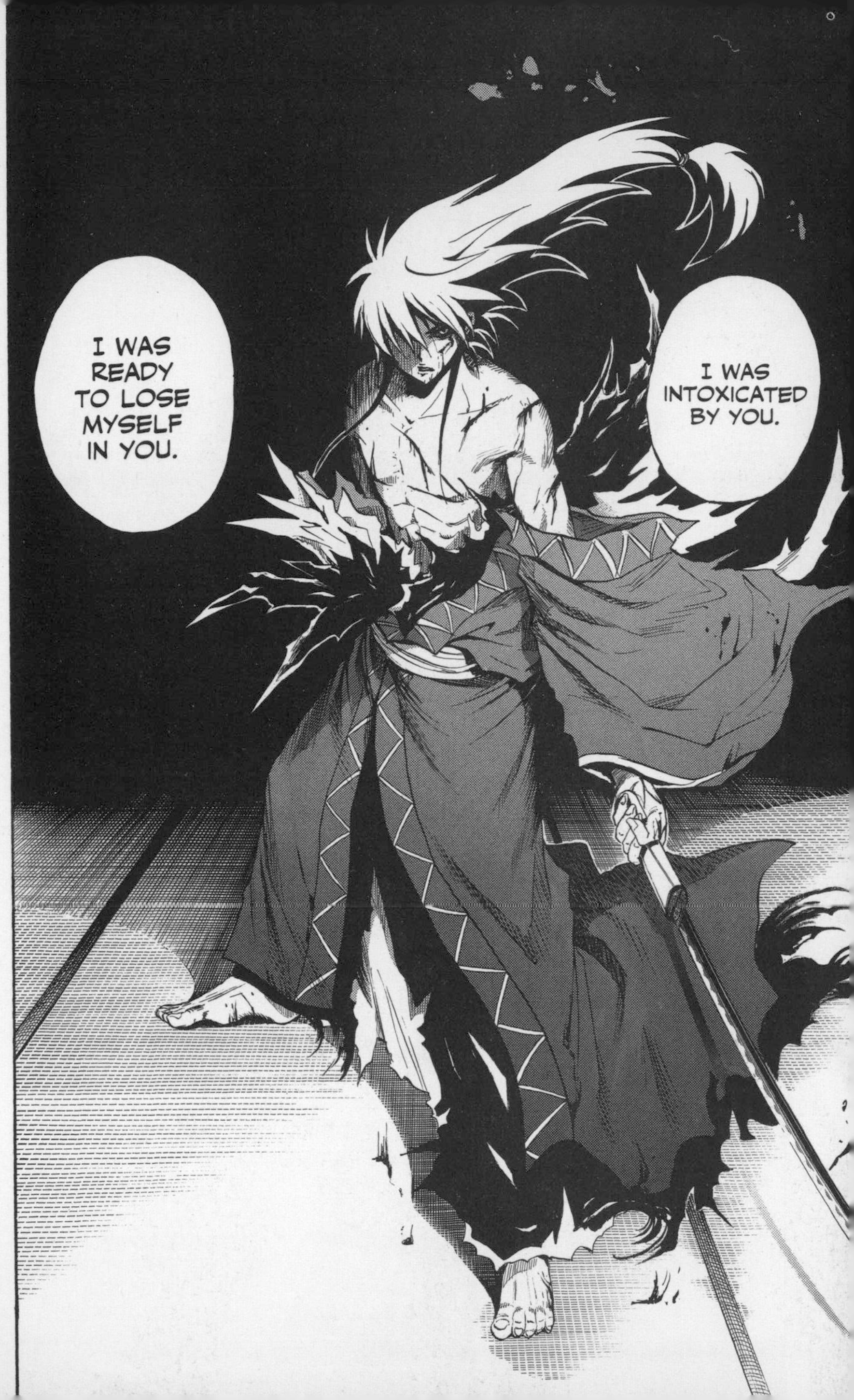
I WAS INTOXICATED BY YOU.
I WAS READY TO LOSE MYSELF IN YOU.

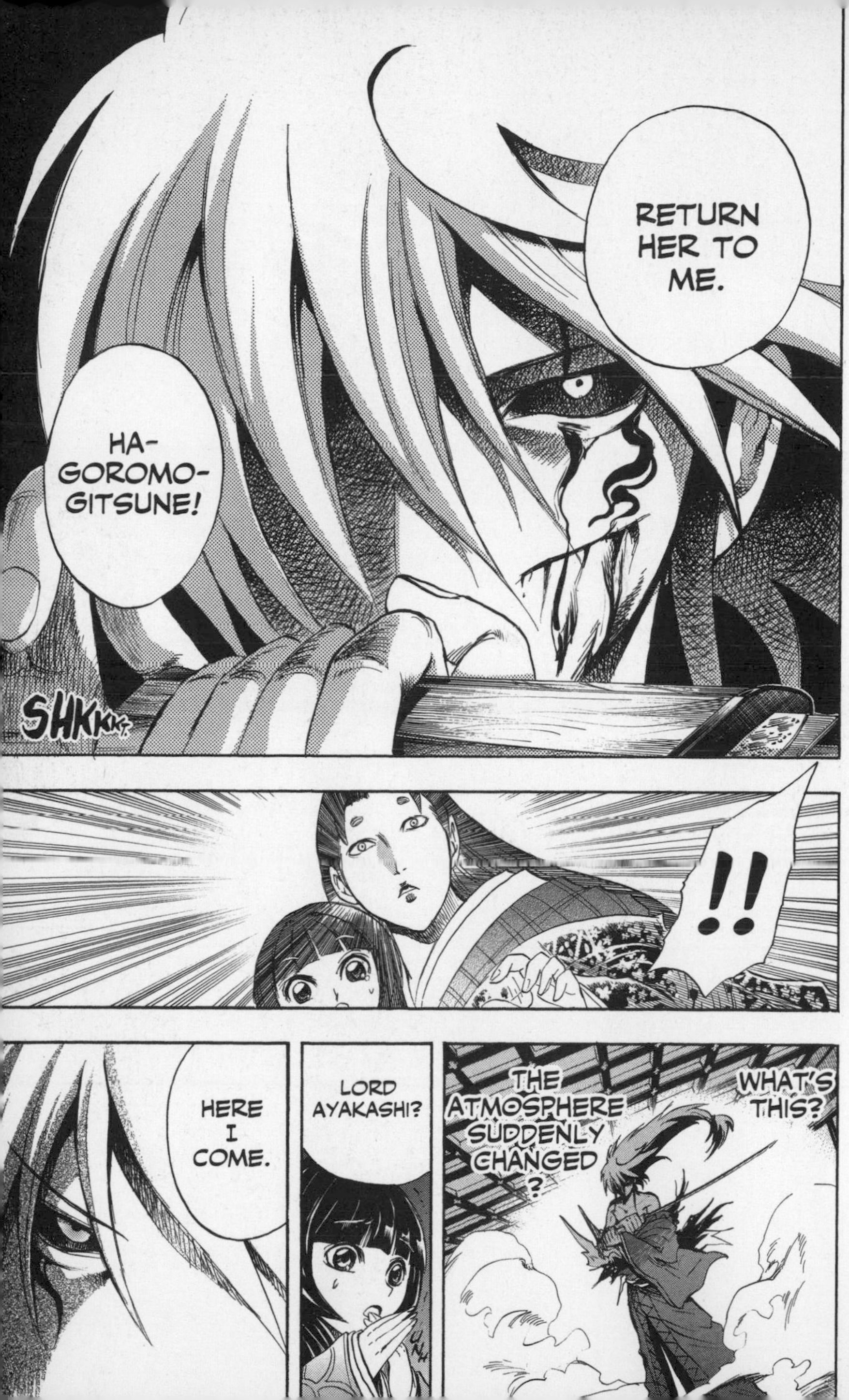
RETURN HER TO ME.
HA-GOROMO-GITSUNE!
SHKKKT
!!
WHAT'S THIS?
THE ATMOSPHERE SUDDENLY CHANGED?
LORD AYAKASHI?
HERE I COME.

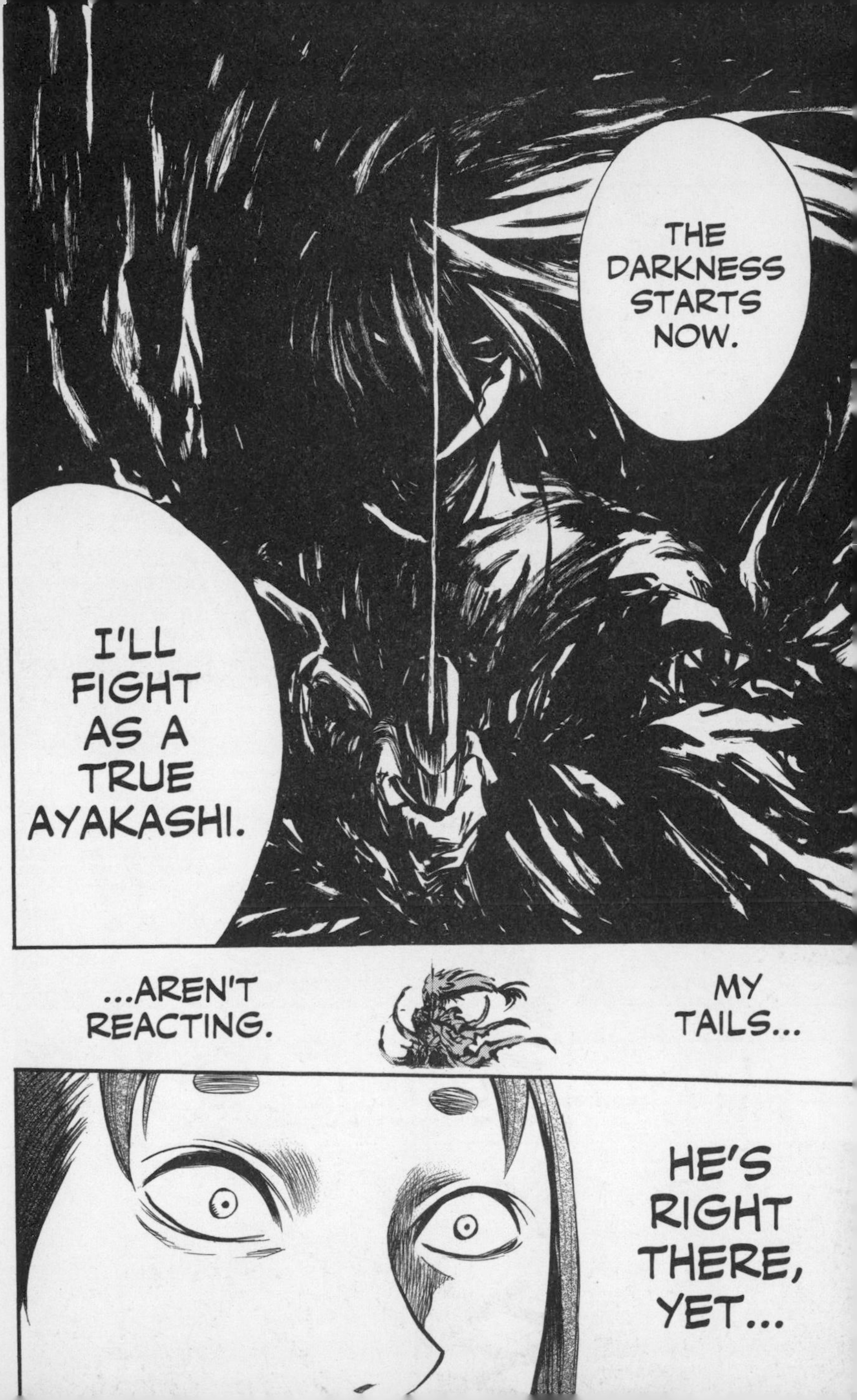
THE DARKNESS STARTS NOW.
I'LL FIGHT AS A TRUE AYAKASHI.
MY TAILS...
...AREN'T REACTING.
HE'S RIGHT THERE, YET...

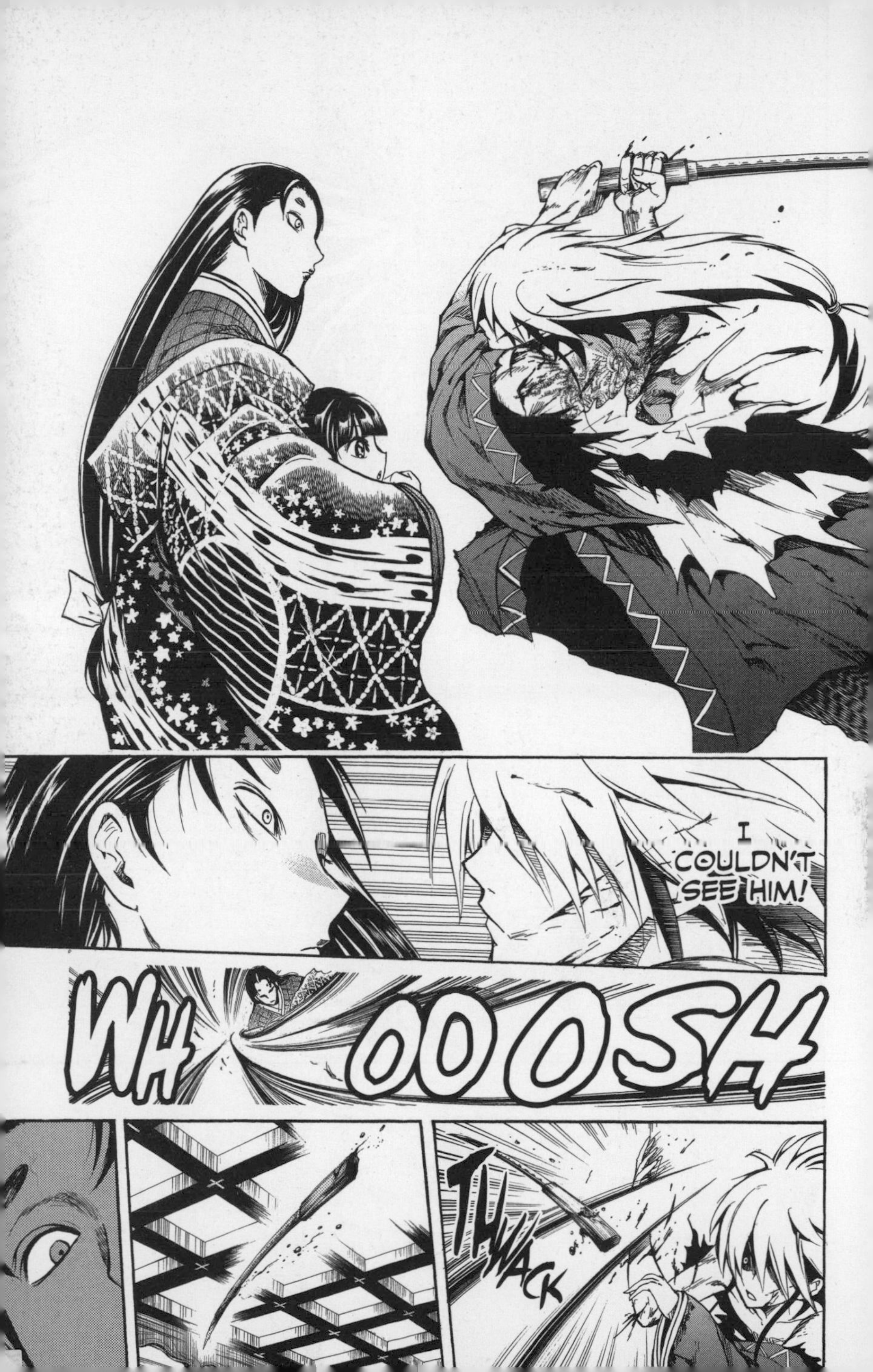
I COULDN'T SEE HIM!
WHOOOSH
THWACK

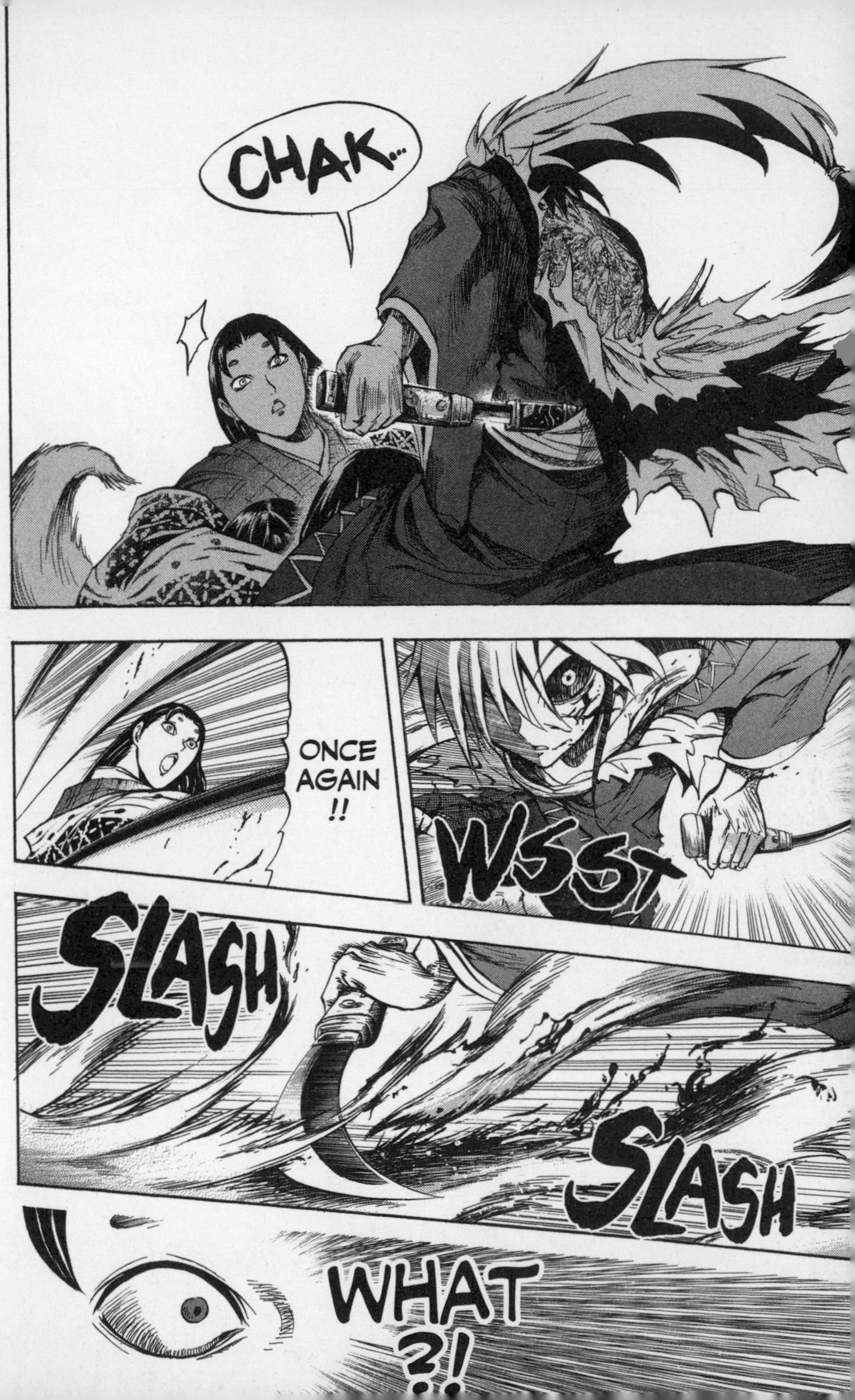
CHAK...
WSST
ONCE AGAIN!!
SLASH
SLASH
WHAT?!

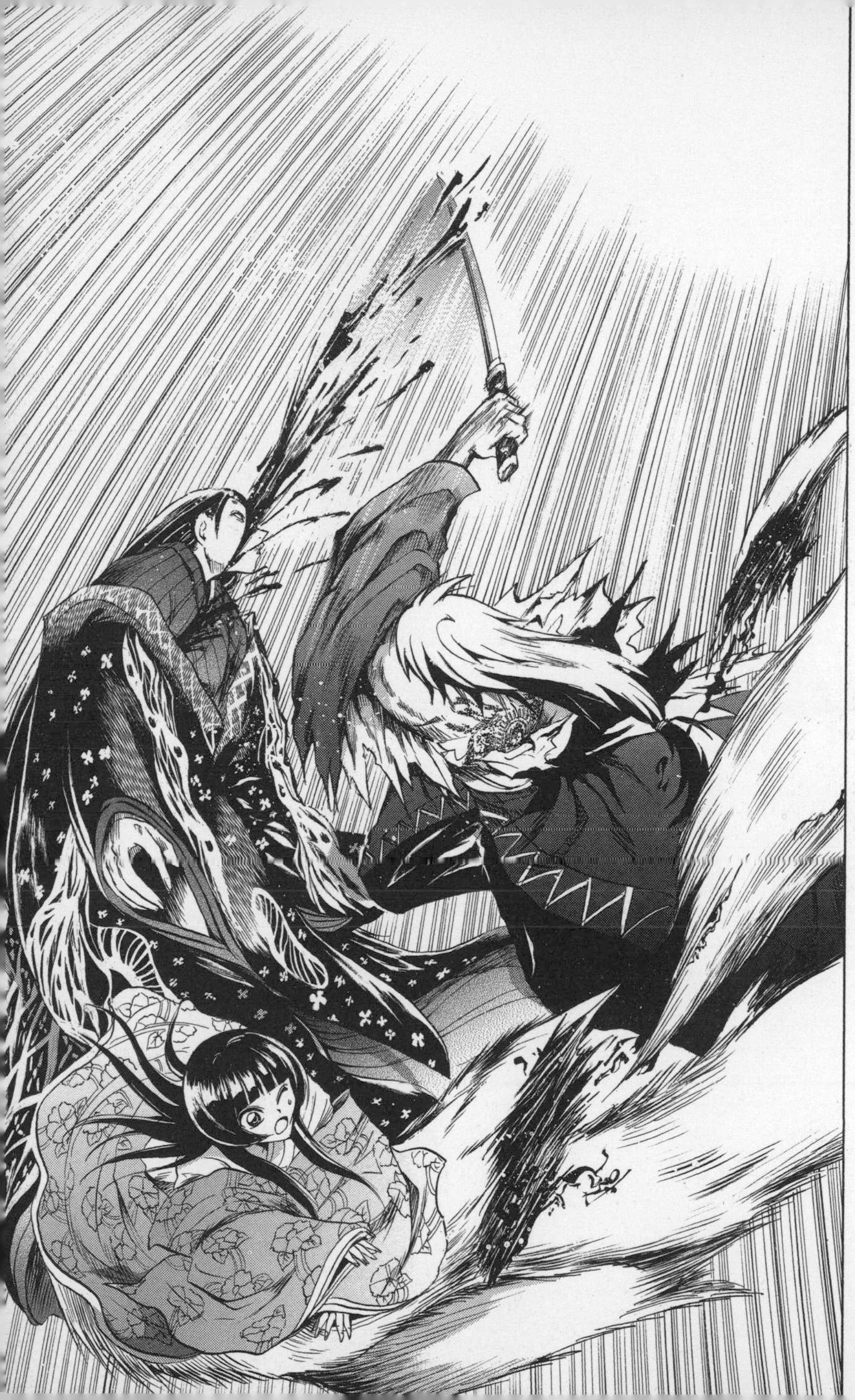

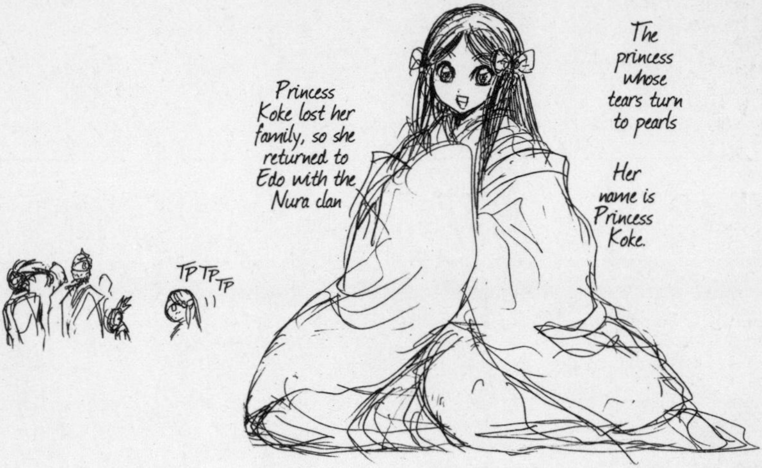
The princess whose tears turn to pearls
Her name is Princess Koke.
Princess Koke lost her family, so she returned to Edo with the Nura clan
TP TP TP

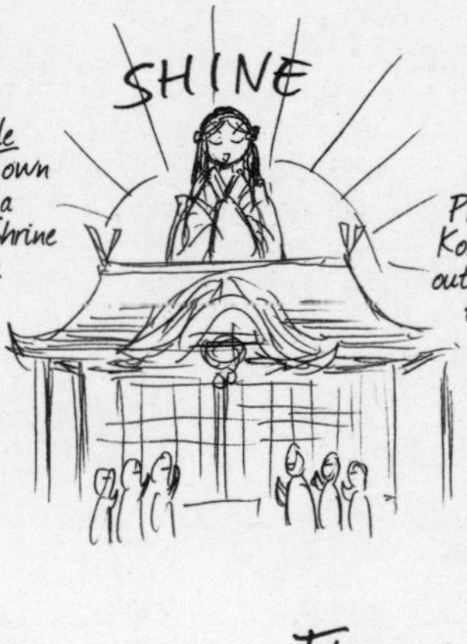
Even in Edo, she was praised.
SHINE
Princess Koke lived out her life there.
And the people of Ukiyoe Town created a Tamakoke Shrine for her.

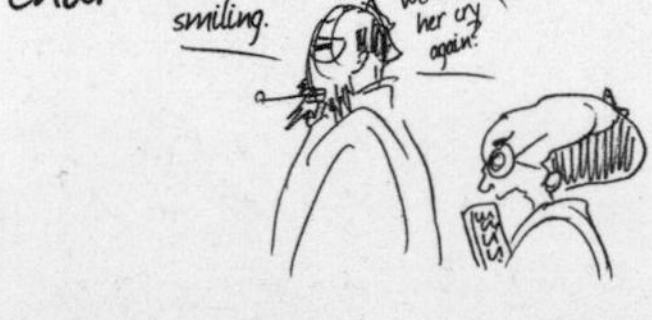
The Nura clan becomes more wealthy when she cries.
You shouldn't say things like that.
Shall we make her cry again?
She looks best when she's smiling.
The end.

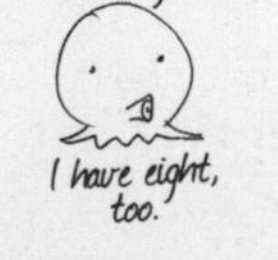
Hagormo-Gitsune has eight
I have eight, too.

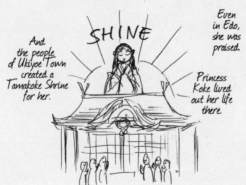

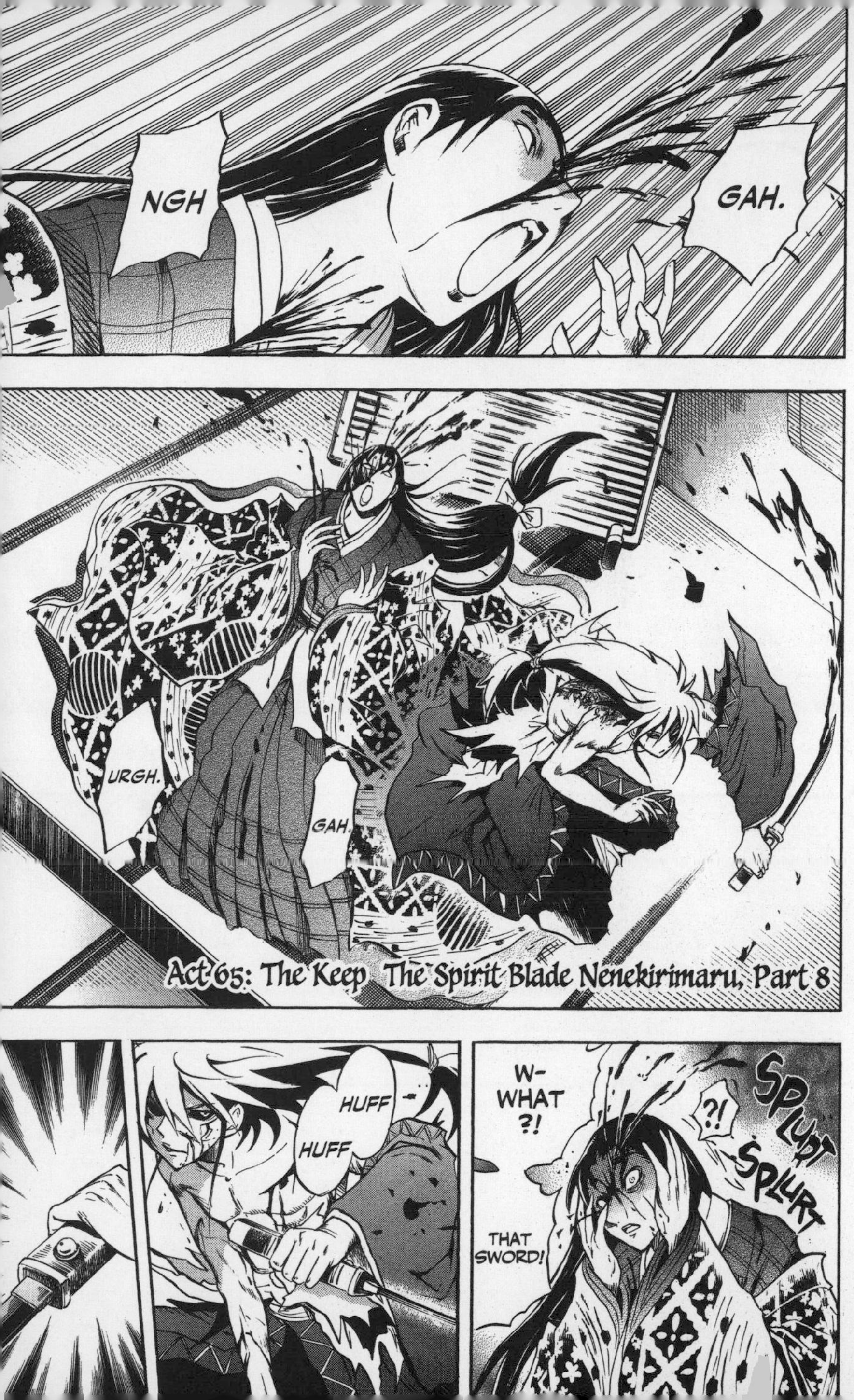
GAH.
NGH
URGH.
GAH.
Act 65: The Keep The Spirit Blade Nenekirimaru, Part 8
SPLURT
SPLURT
?!
W-WHAT ?!
THAT SWORD!
HUFF
HUFF

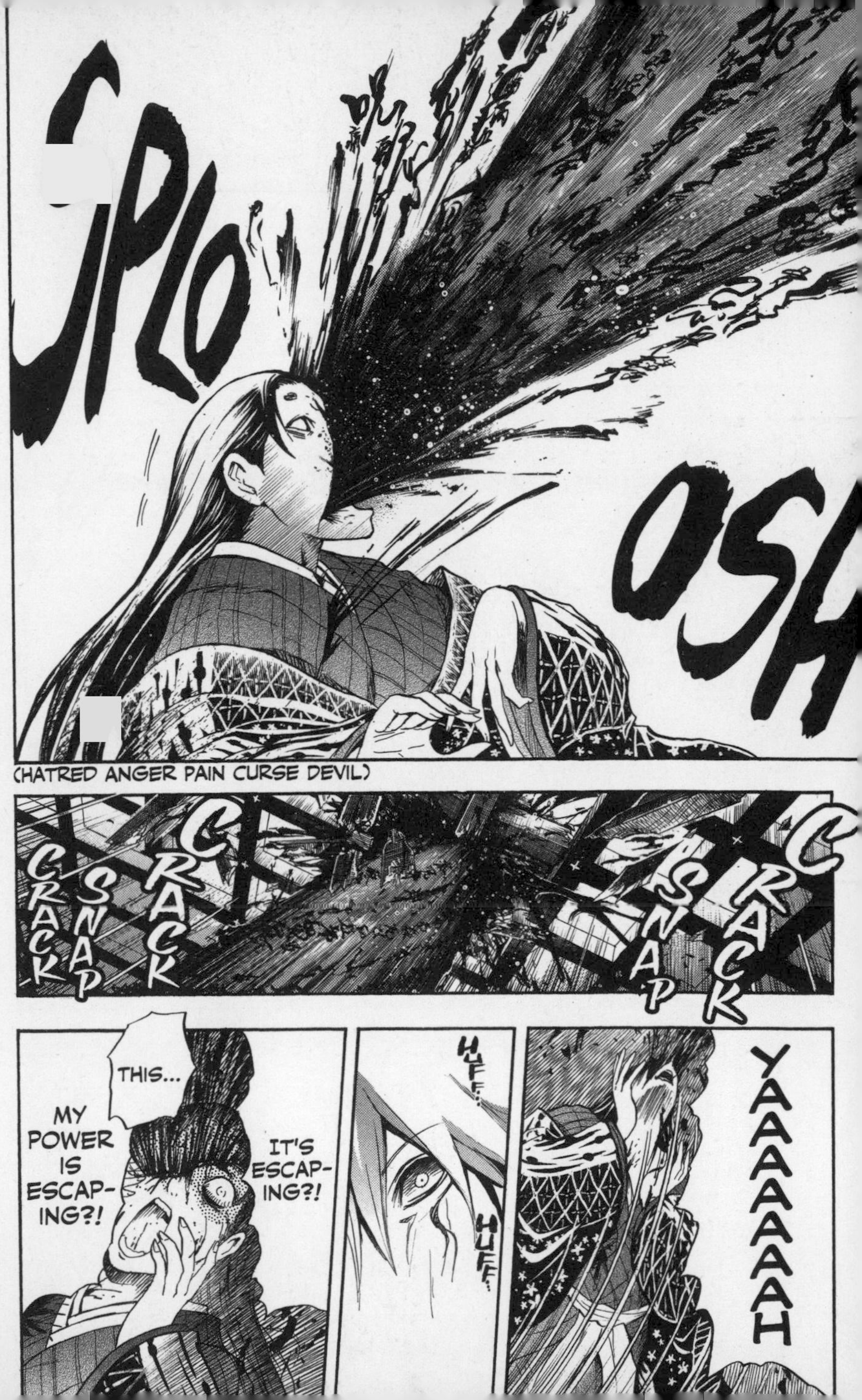
SPLO
OSH
(HATRED ANGER PAIN CURSE DEVIL)
CRACK
SNAP
CRACK
CRACK
SNAP
CRACK
YAAAAAAAH
HUFF...
HUFF...
IT'S ESCAPING?!
THIS...
MY POWER IS ESCAPING?!

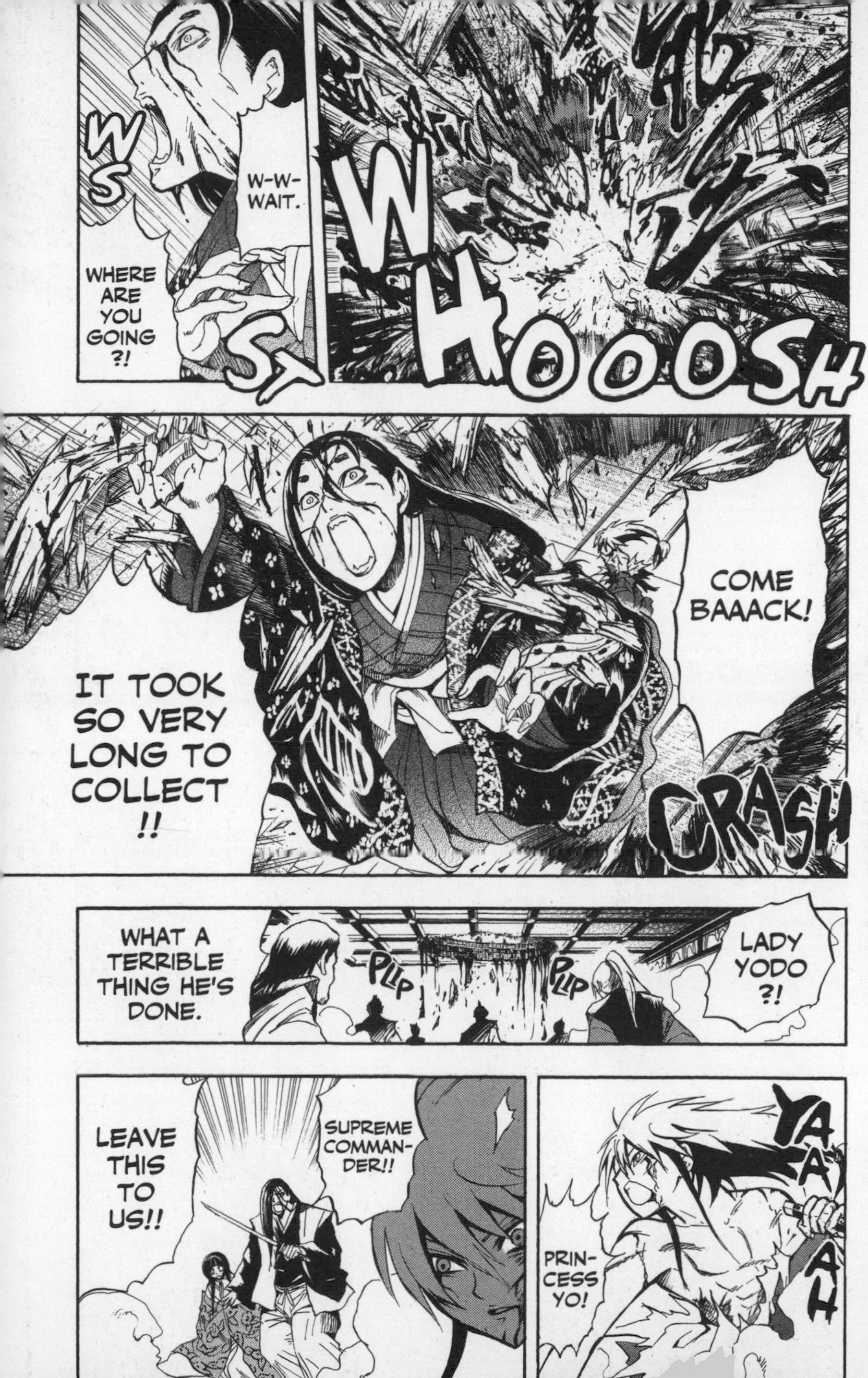
WHOOOSH
W-W-WAIT.
WHERE ARE YOU GOING ?!
WS
ST
COME BAAACK!
CRASH
IT TOOK SO VERY LONG TO COLLECT !!
LADY YODO ?!
PLIP
PLIP
WHAT A TERRIBLE THING HE'S DONE.
YAAAAH
PRINCESS YO!
SUPREME COMMANDER!!
LEAVE THIS TO US!!

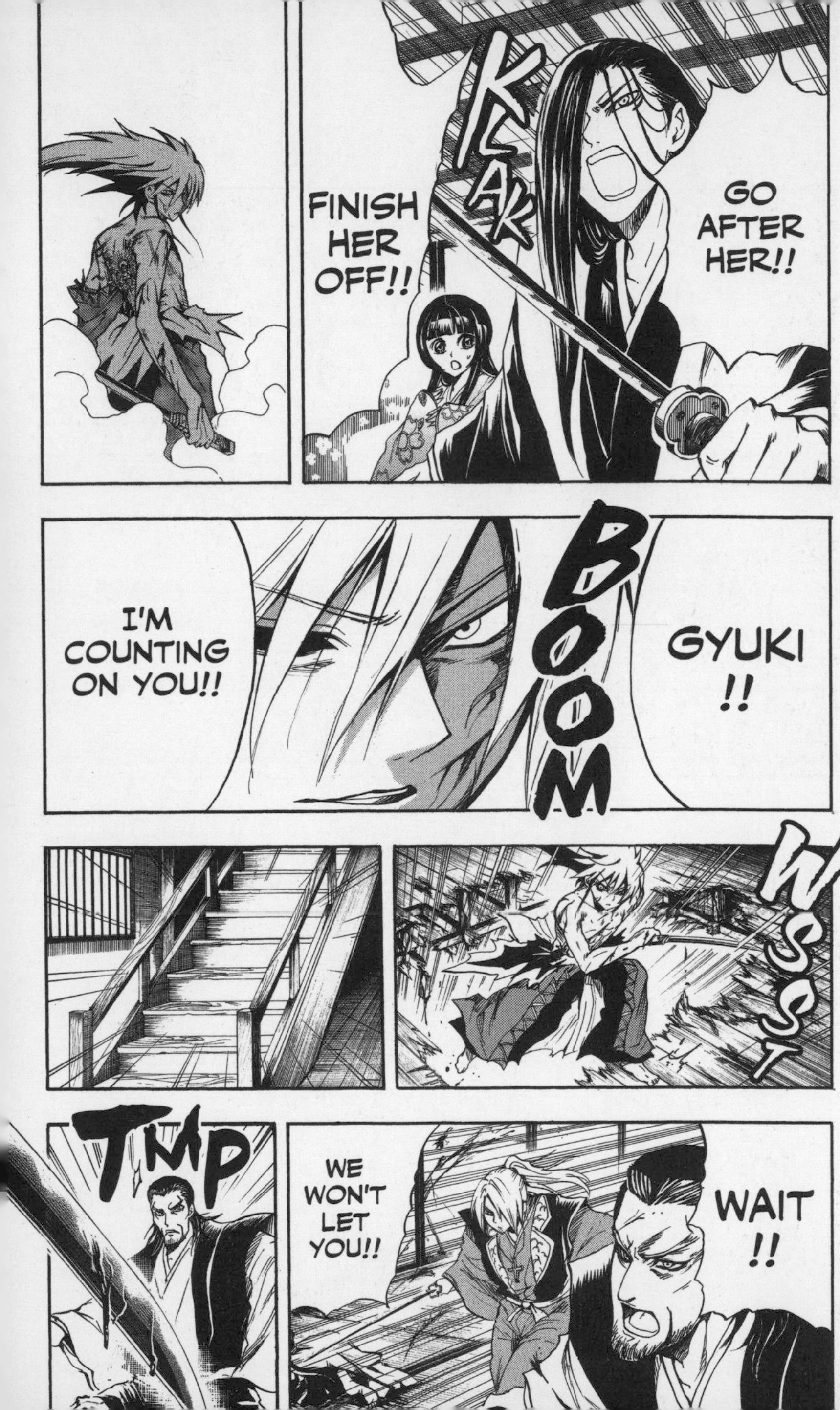
KAK
GO AFTER HER!!
FINISH HER OFF!!
GYUKI !!
BOOM
I'M COUNTING ON YOU!!
WSSST
WAIT !!
WE WON'T LET YOU!!
TMP

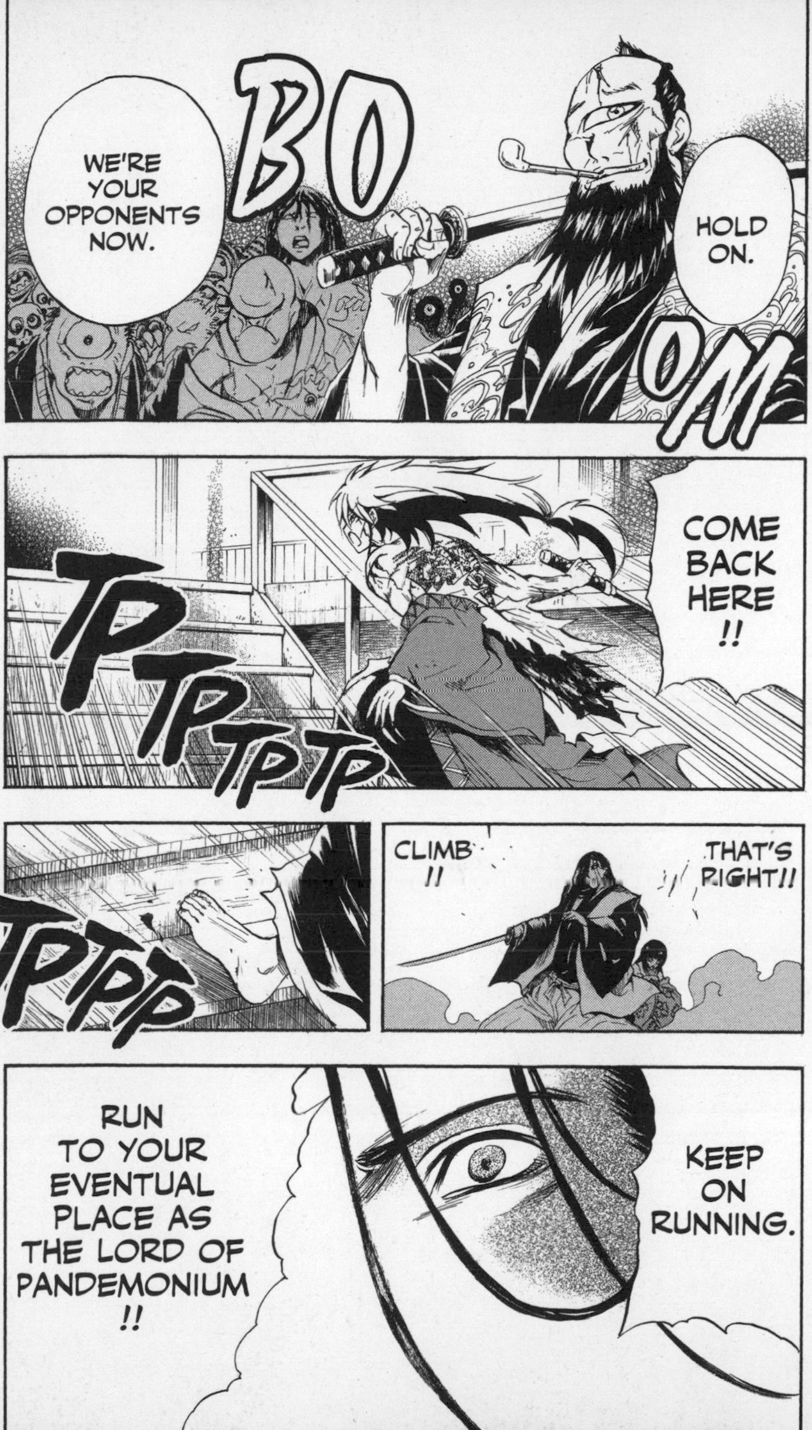
HOLD ON.
BOOM
WE'RE YOUR OPPONENTS NOW.
COME BACK HERE!!
TP TP TPTP
THAT'S RIGHT!!
CLIMB!!
TPTPTP
KEEP ON RUNNING.
RUN TO YOUR EVENTUAL PLACE AS THE LORD OF PANDEMONIUM!!

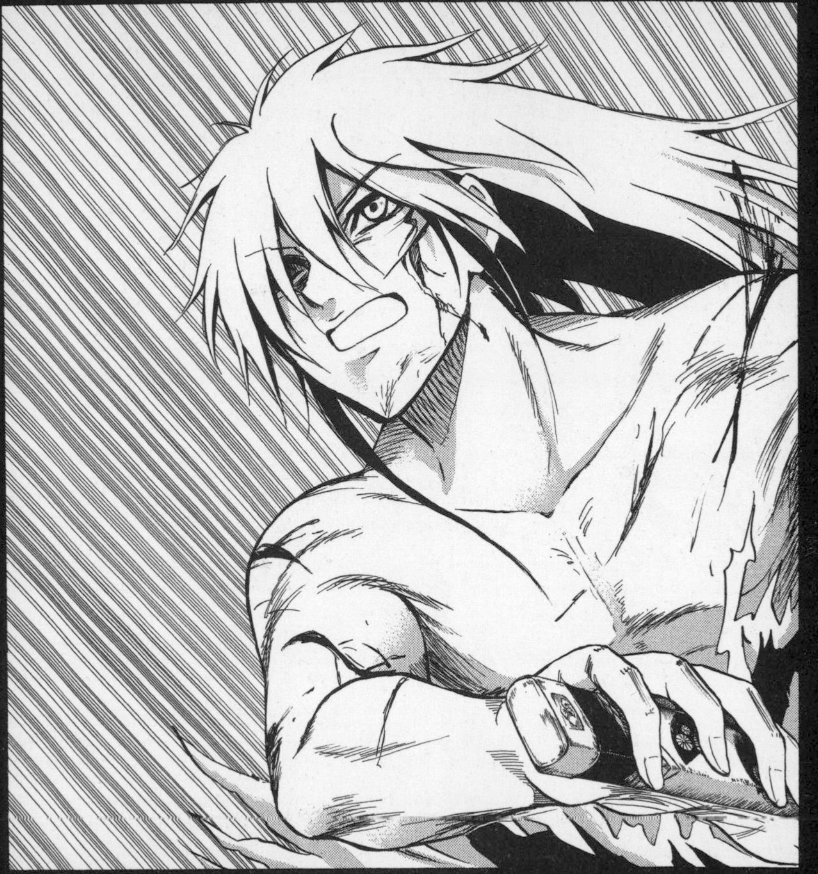

Act 65: The Keep
The Spirit Blade Nenekirimaru
Part 8

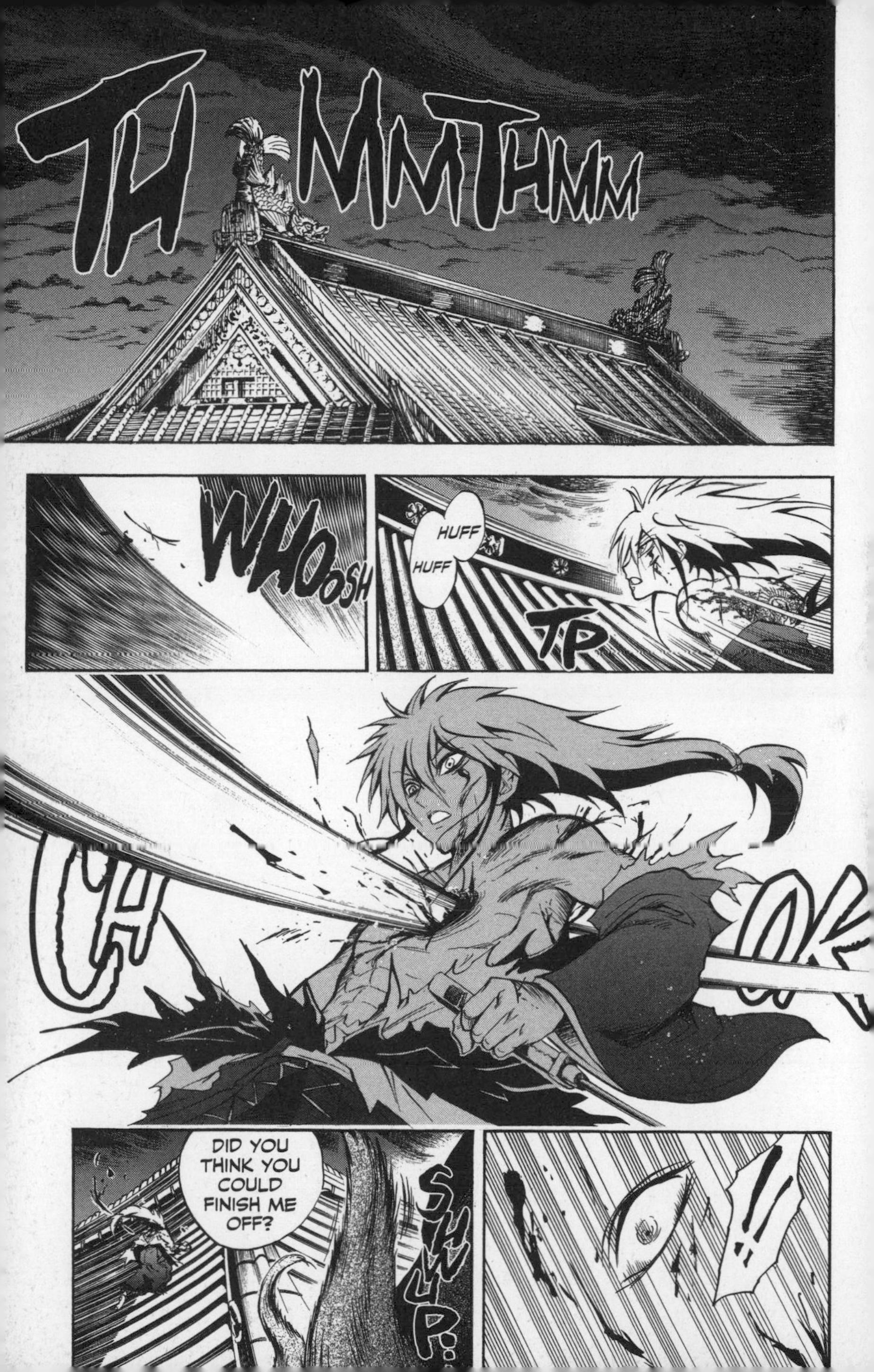

TH
MMTHMM
HUFF
HUFF
TP
WHOOSH
CH
OK
!!
DID YOU THINK YOU COULD FINISH ME OFF?
SHLUP!

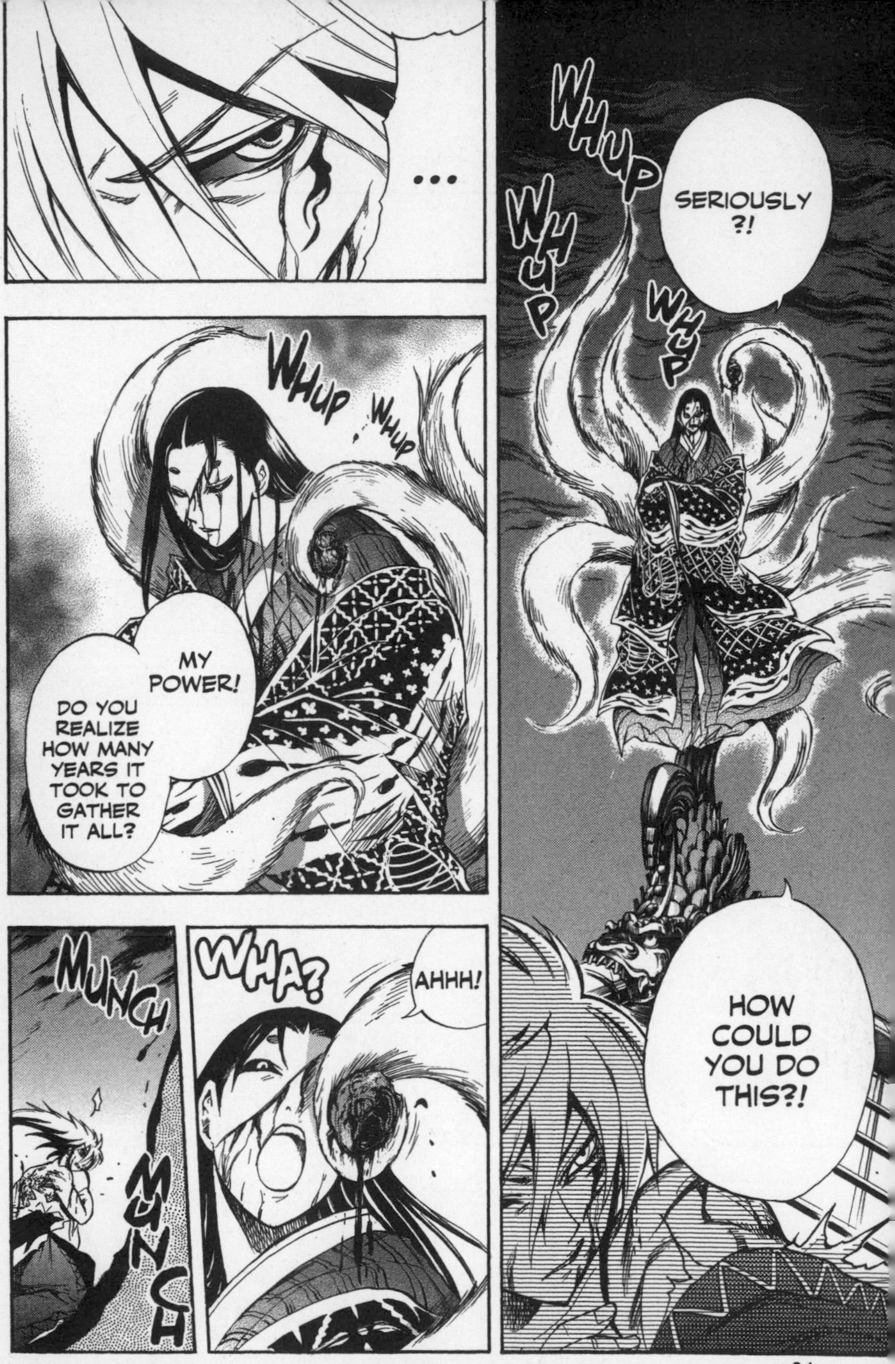
WHUP
SERIOUSLY ?!
WHUP
WHUP
HOW COULD YOU DO THIS?!
...
WHUP
WHUP
MY POWER!
DO YOU REALIZE HOW MANY YEARS IT TOOK TO GATHER IT ALL?
WHA?
AHHH!
MUNCH
MUNCH

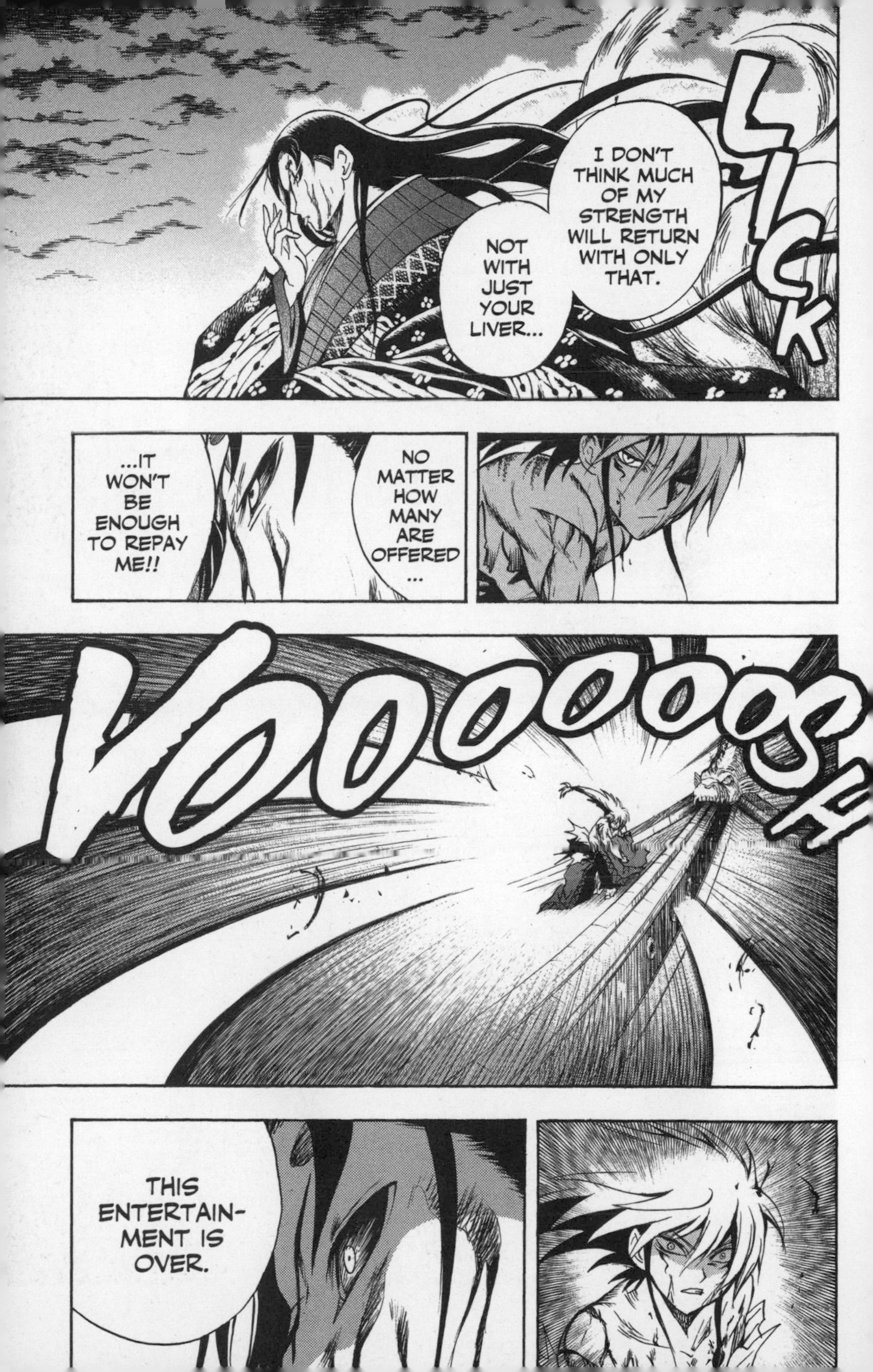
LICK
I DON'T THINK MUCH OF MY STRENGTH WILL RETURN WITH ONLY THAT.
NOT WITH JUST YOUR LIVER...
NO MATTER HOW MANY ARE OFFERED ...
...IT WON'T BE ENOUGH TO REPAY ME!!
VOOOOOSH
THIS ENTERTAINMENT IS OVER.

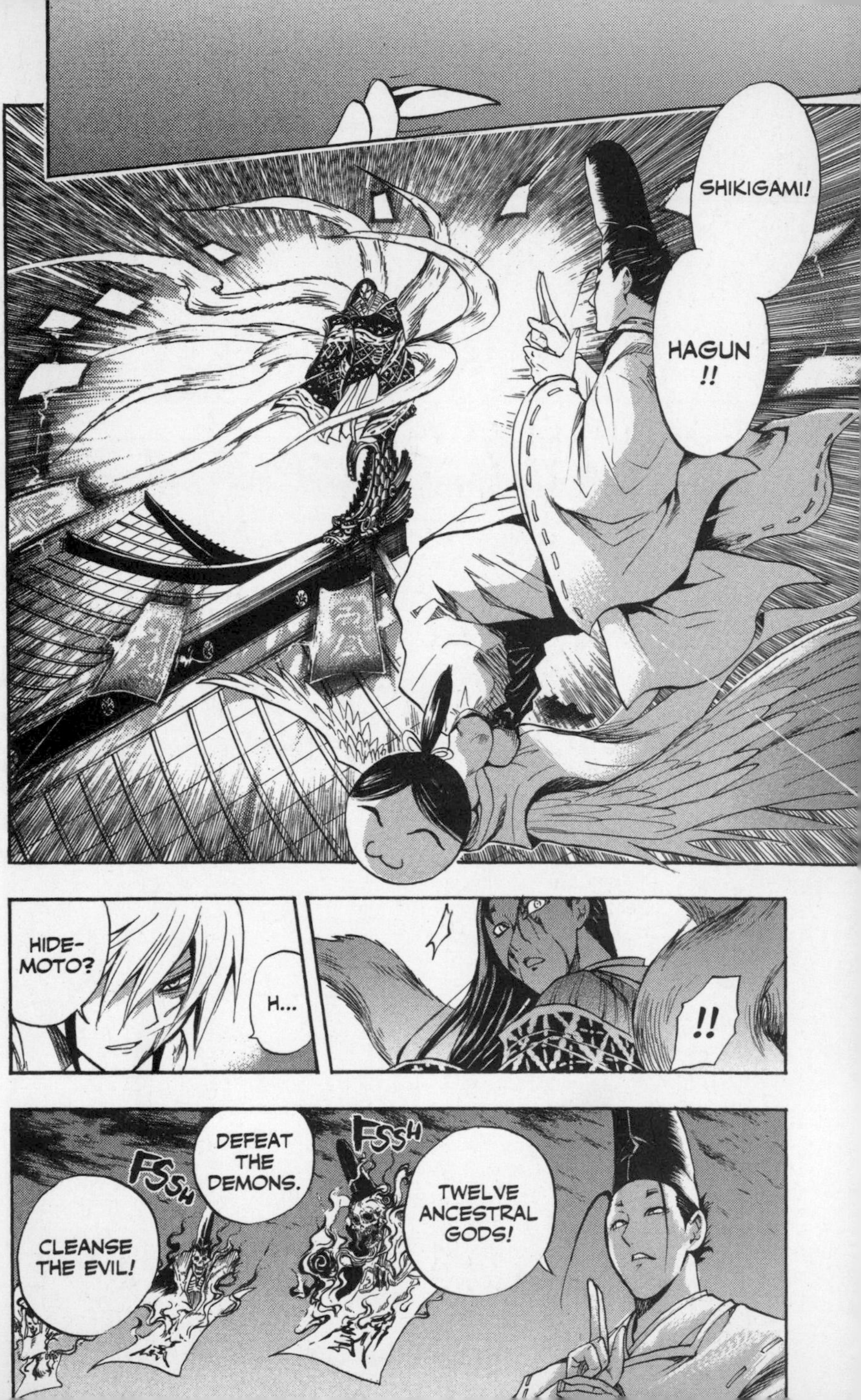
SHIKIGAMI!
HAGUN !!
!!
HIDE-MOTO?
H...
TWELVE ANCESTRAL GODS!
FSSH
DEFEAT THE DEMONS.
FSSH
CLEANSE THE EVIL!

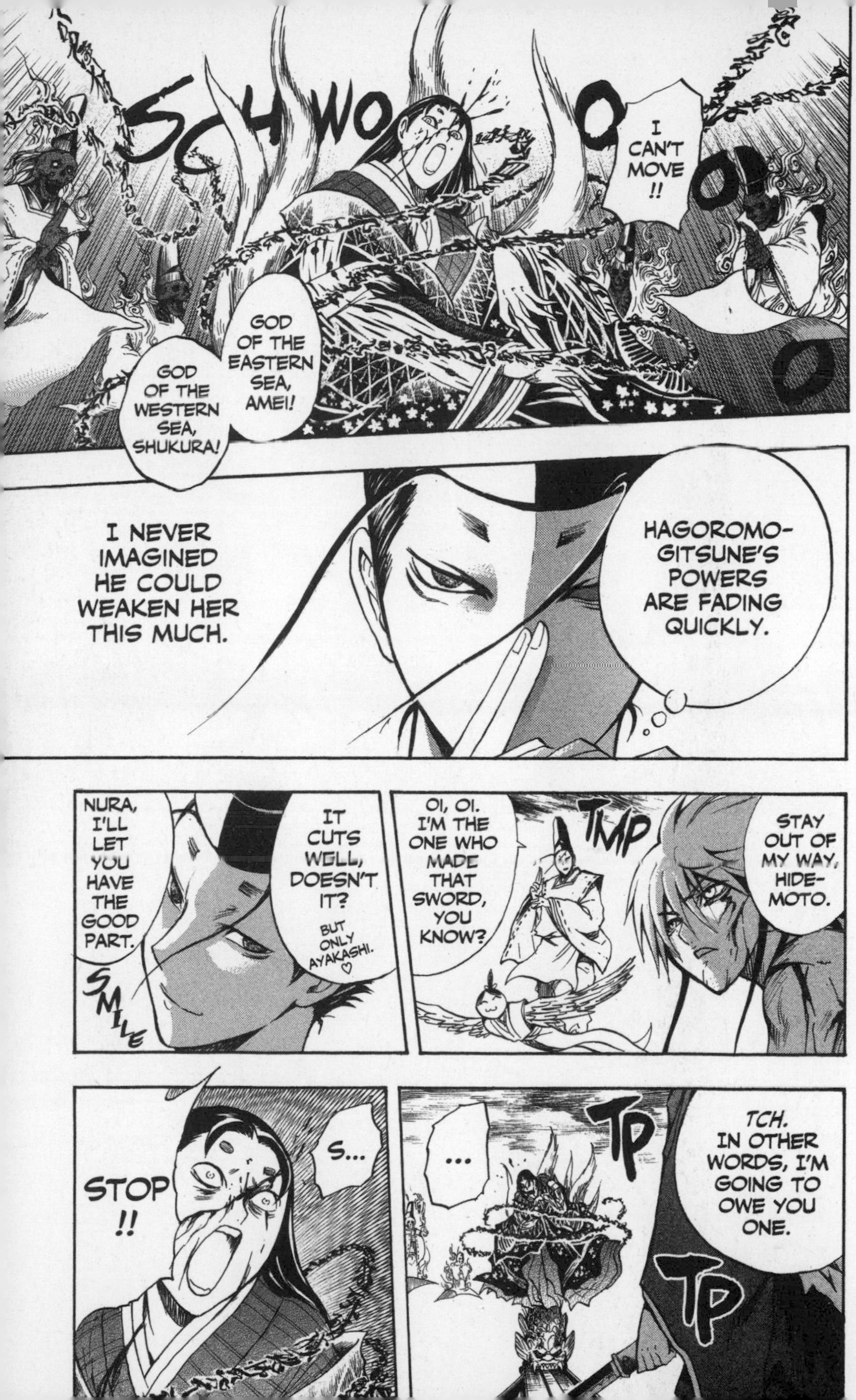
SCHWOOOOO
I CAN'T MOVE !!
GOD OF THE EASTERN SEA, AMEI!
GOD OF THE WESTERN SEA, SHUKURA!
HAGOROMO-GITSUNE'S POWERS ARE FADING QUICKLY.
I NEVER IMAGINED HE COULD WEAKEN HER THIS MUCH.
STAY OUT OF MY WAY, HIDE-MOTO.
TMP
OI, OI. I'M THE ONE WHO MADE THAT SWORD, YOU KNOW?
IT CUTS WELL, DOESN'T IT?
BUT ONLY AYAKASHI. ♡
NURA, I'LL LET YOU HAVE THE GOOD PART.
SMILE
TCH. IN OTHER WORDS, I'M GOING TO OWE YOU ONE.
TP
TP
...
S...
STOP !!

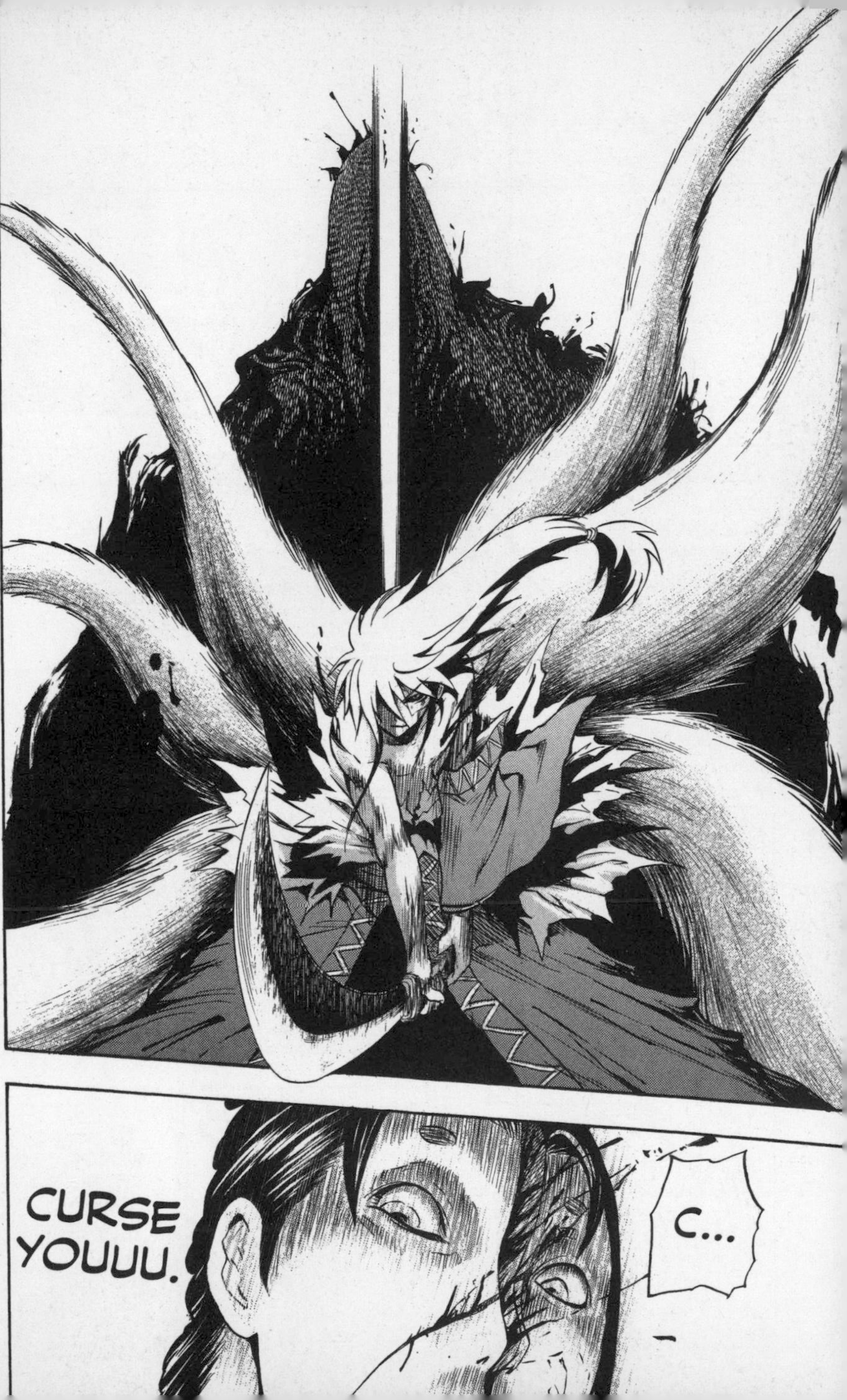
C...
CURSE YOUUU.

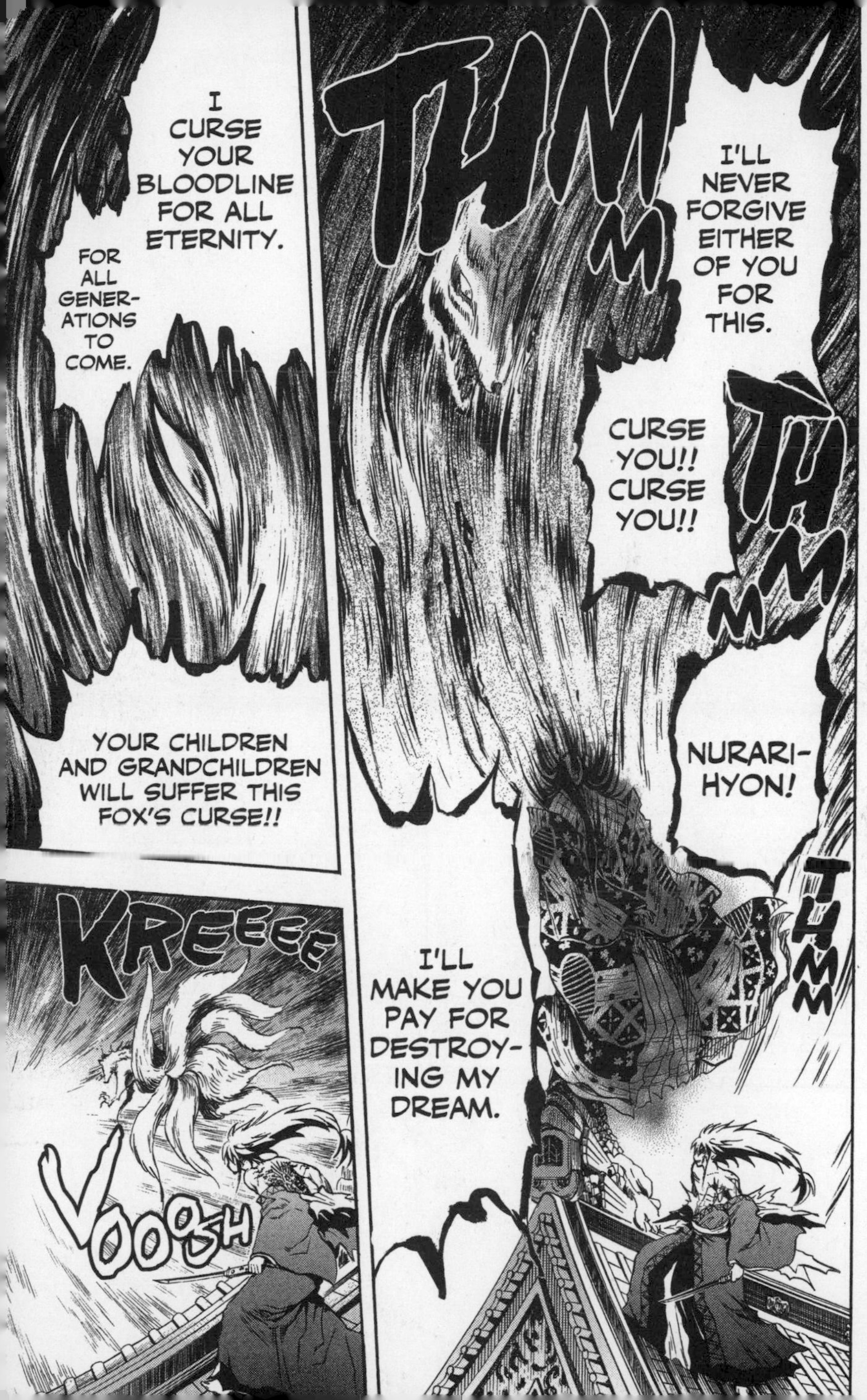
THMM
I'LL NEVER FORGIVE EITHER OF YOU FOR THIS.
CURSE YOU!! CURSE YOU!!
THMMM
NURARI-HYON!
THUMM
I'LL MAKE YOU PAY FOR DESTROY-ING MY DREAM.
I CURSE YOUR BLOODLINE FOR ALL ETERNITY.
FOR ALL GENER-ATIONS TO COME.
YOUR CHILDREN AND GRANDCHILDREN WILL SUFFER THIS FOX'S CURSE!!
KREEEEE
VOOOSH

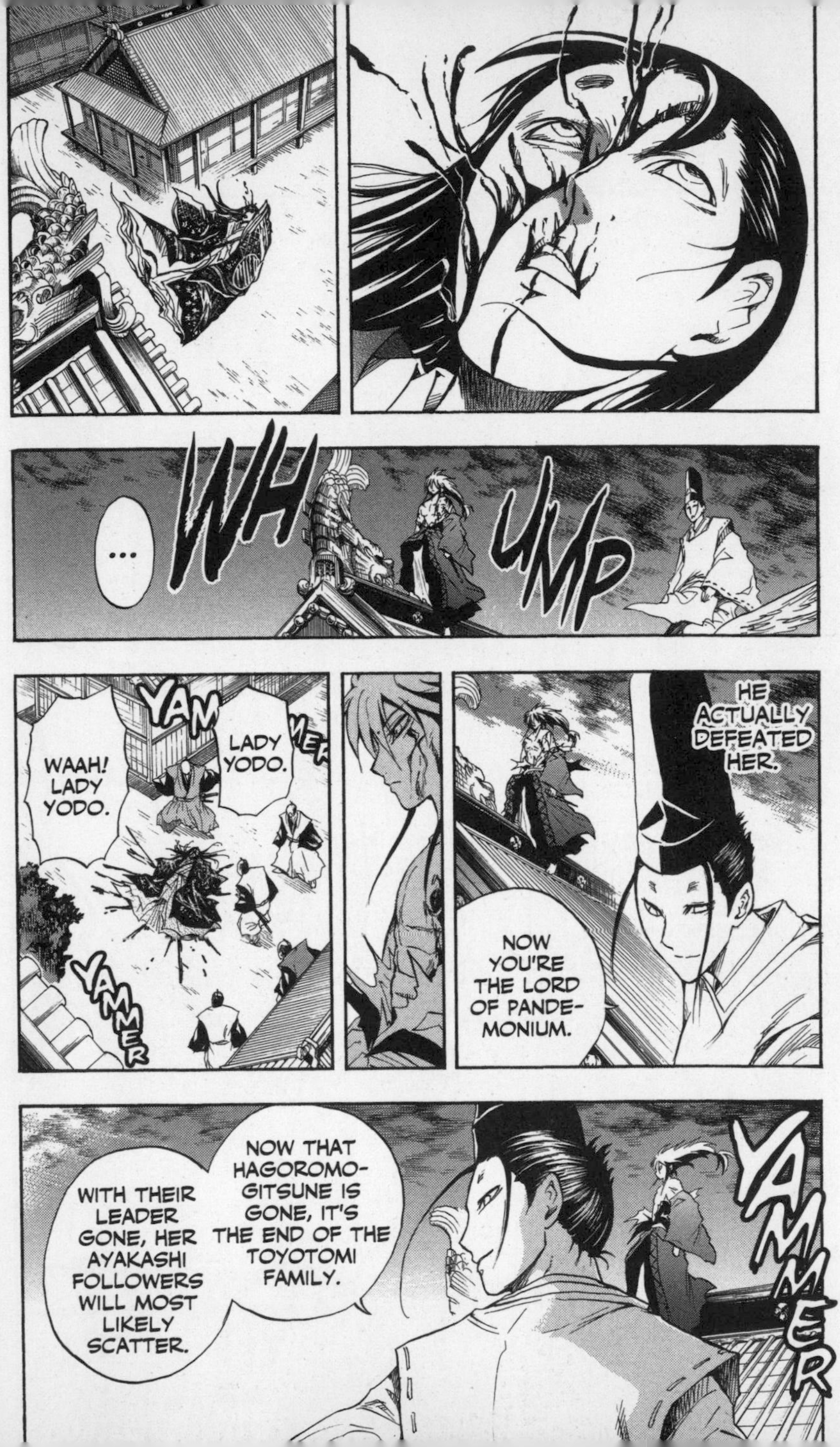
WHUMP
...
HE ACTUALLY DEFEATED HER.
NOW YOU'RE THE LORD OF PANDE-MONIUM.
YAMMER
LADY YODO.
WAAH! LADY YODO.
YAMMER
YAMMER
NOW THAT HAGOROMO-GITSUNE IS GONE, IT'S THE END OF THE TOYOTOMI FAMILY.
WITH THEIR LEADER GONE, HER AYAKASHI FOLLOWERS WILL MOST LIKELY SCATTER.

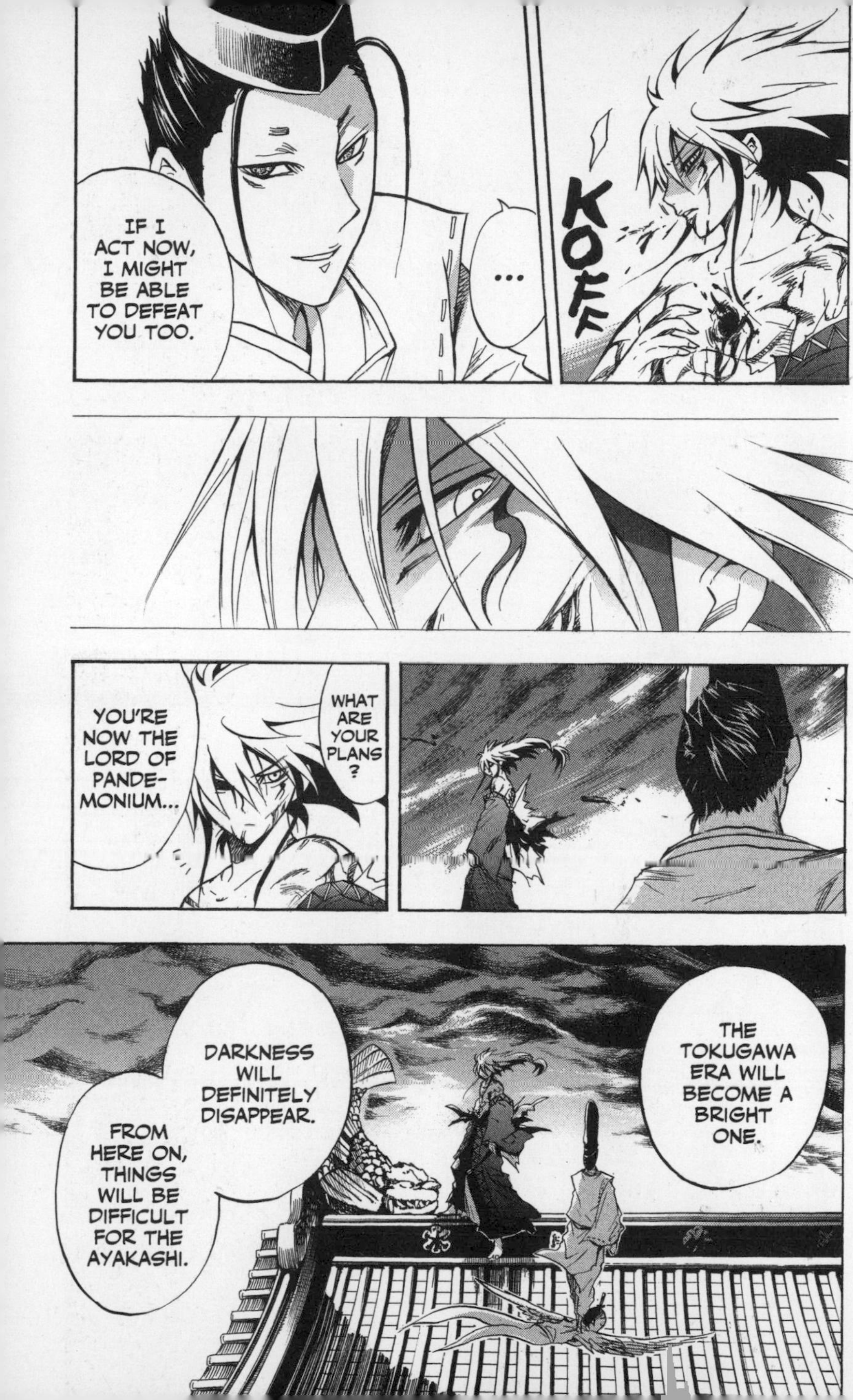
KOFF
...
IF I ACT NOW, I MIGHT BE ABLE TO DEFEAT YOU TOO.
WHAT ARE YOUR PLANS?
YOU'RE NOW THE LORD OF PANDE-MONIUM...
THE TOKUGAWA ERA WILL BECOME A BRIGHT ONE.
DARKNESS WILL DEFINITELY DISAPPEAR.
FROM HERE ON, THINGS WILL BE DIFFICULT FOR THE AYAKASHI.

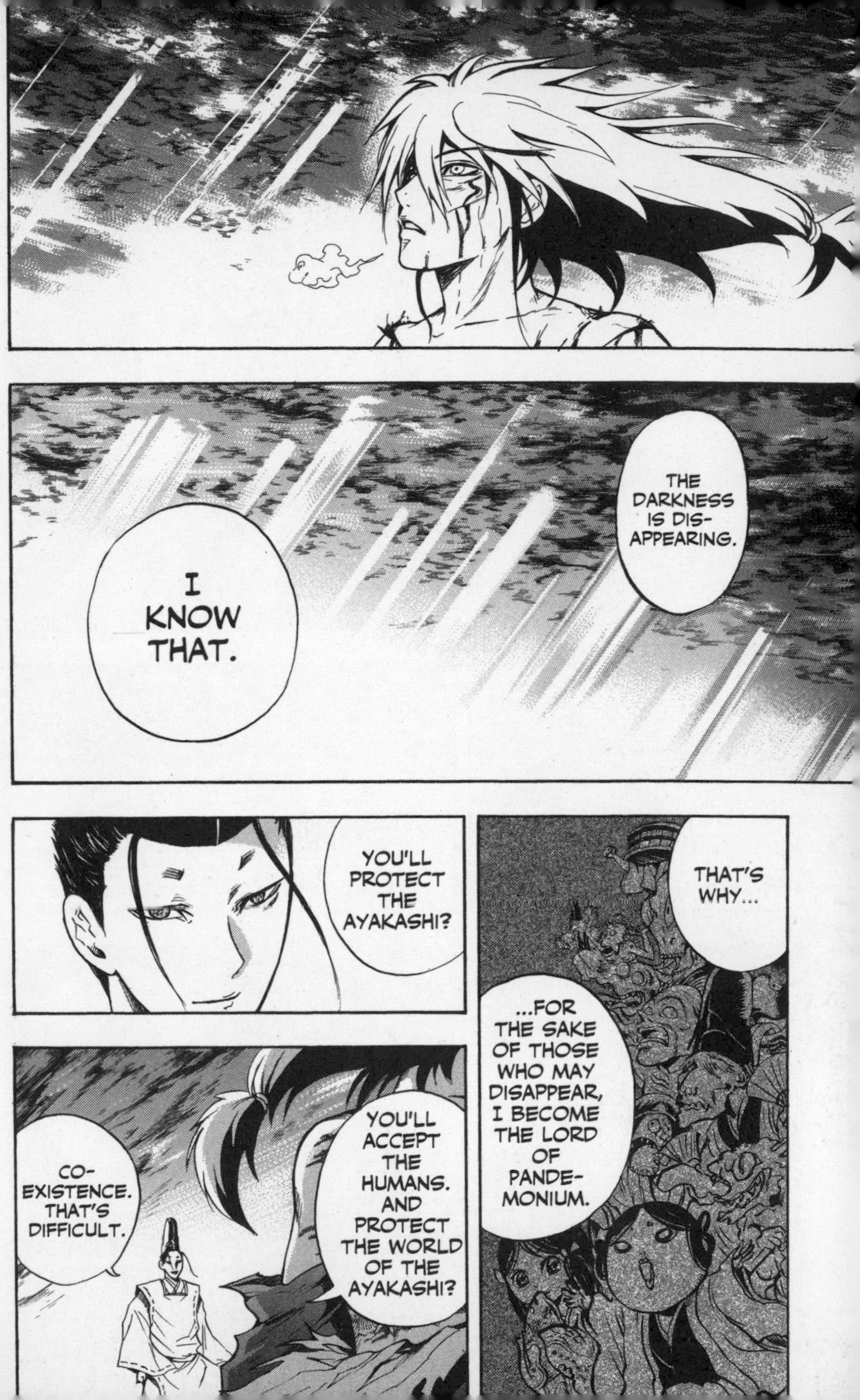
THE DARKNESS IS DIS-APPEARING.
I KNOW THAT.
THAT'S WHY...
...FOR THE SAKE OF THOSE WHO MAY DISAPPEAR, I BECOME THE LORD OF PANDE-MONIUM.
YOU'LL PROTECT THE AYAKASHI?
YOU'LL ACCEPT THE HUMANS. AND PROTECT THE WORLD OF THE AYAKASHI?
CO-EXISTENCE. THAT'S DIFFICULT.

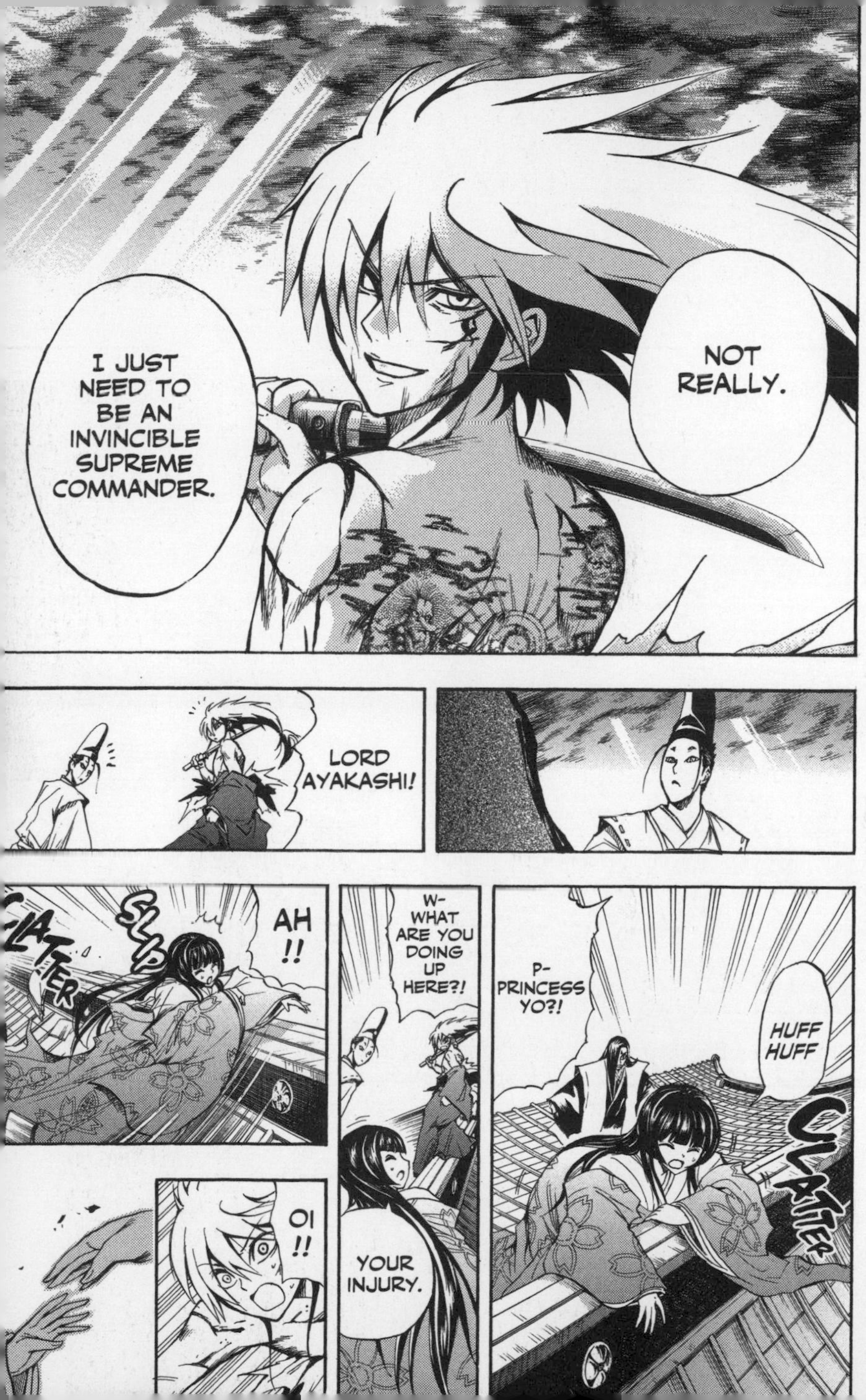
NOT REALLY.
I JUST NEED TO BE AN INVINCIBLE SUPREME COMMANDER.
LORD AYAKASHI!
HUFF HUFF
CLATTER
P- PRINCESS YO?!
W- WHAT ARE YOU DOING UP HERE?!
YOUR INJURY.
AH !!
SLIP
CLATTER
OI !!

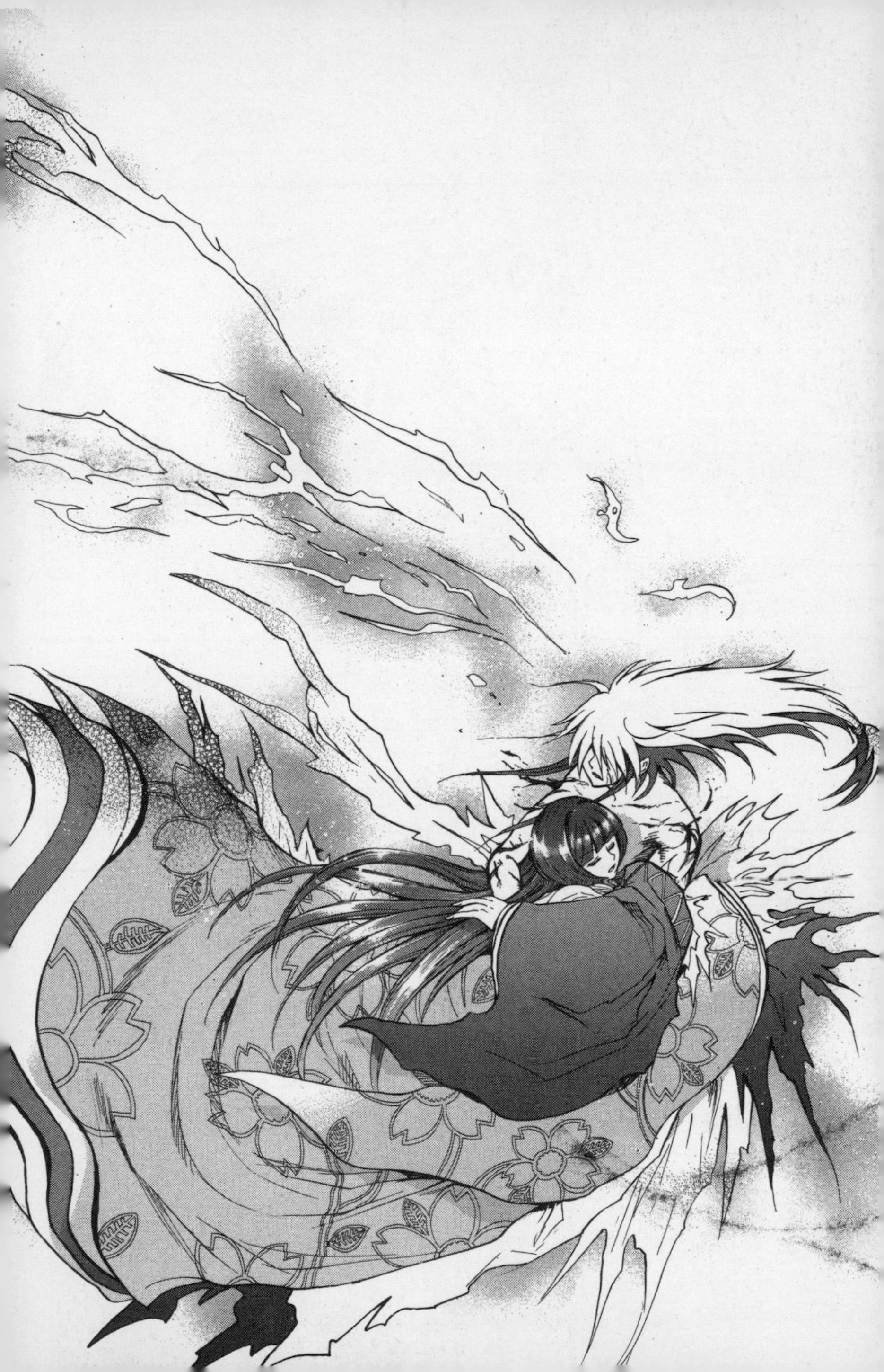

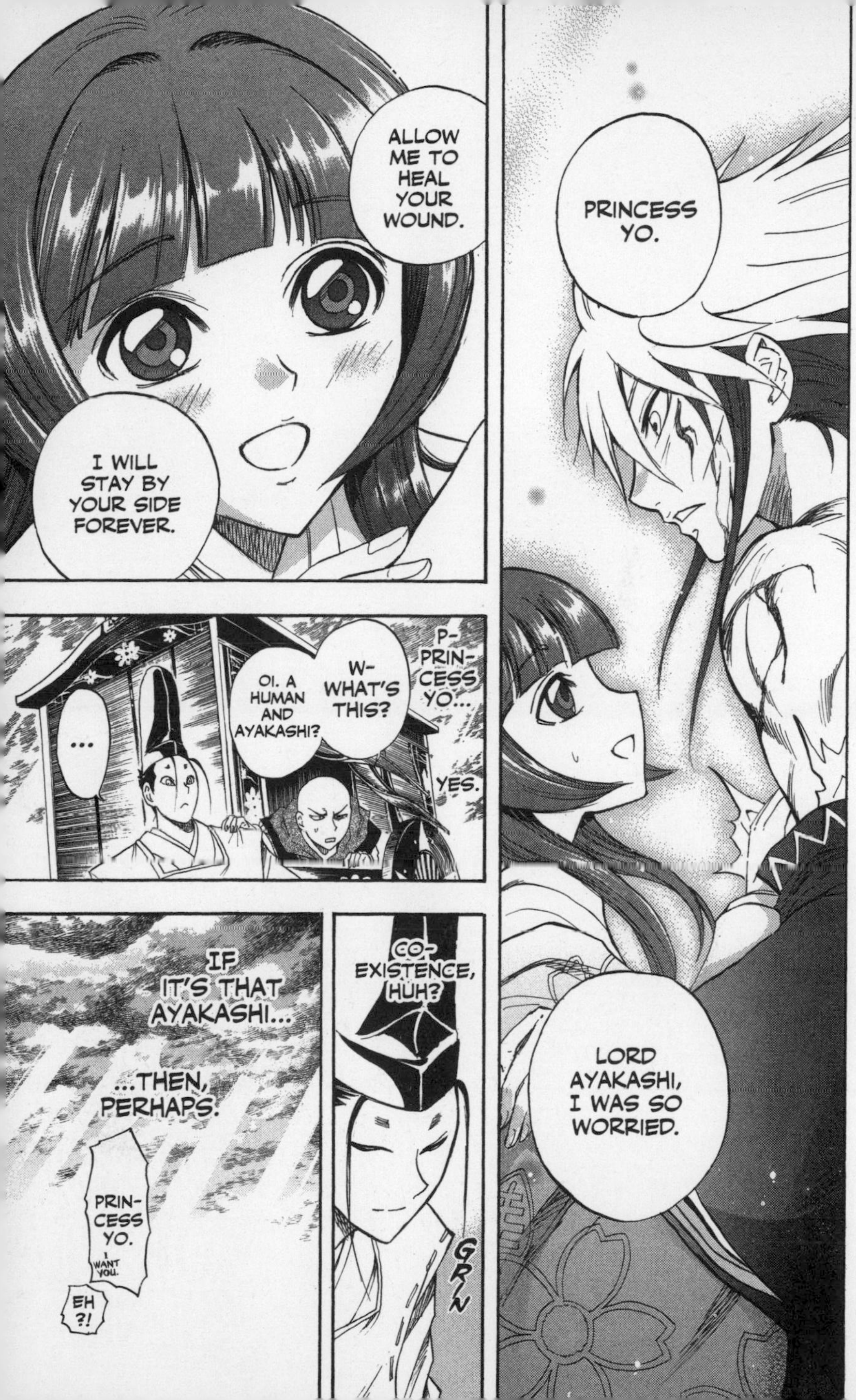
PRINCESS YO.
LORD AYAKASHI, I WAS SO WORRIED.
ALLOW ME TO HEAL YOUR WOUND.
I WILL STAY BY YOUR SIDE FOREVER.
P-PRINCESS YO...
YES.
W-WHAT'S THIS?
OI. A HUMAN AND AYAKASHI?
...
CO-EXISTENCE, HUH?
GRIN
IF IT'S THAT AYAKASHI...
...THEN, PERHAPS.
PRINCESS YO.
I WANT YOU.
EH?!

NURA: RISE OF THE YOKAI CLAN

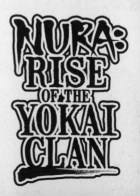

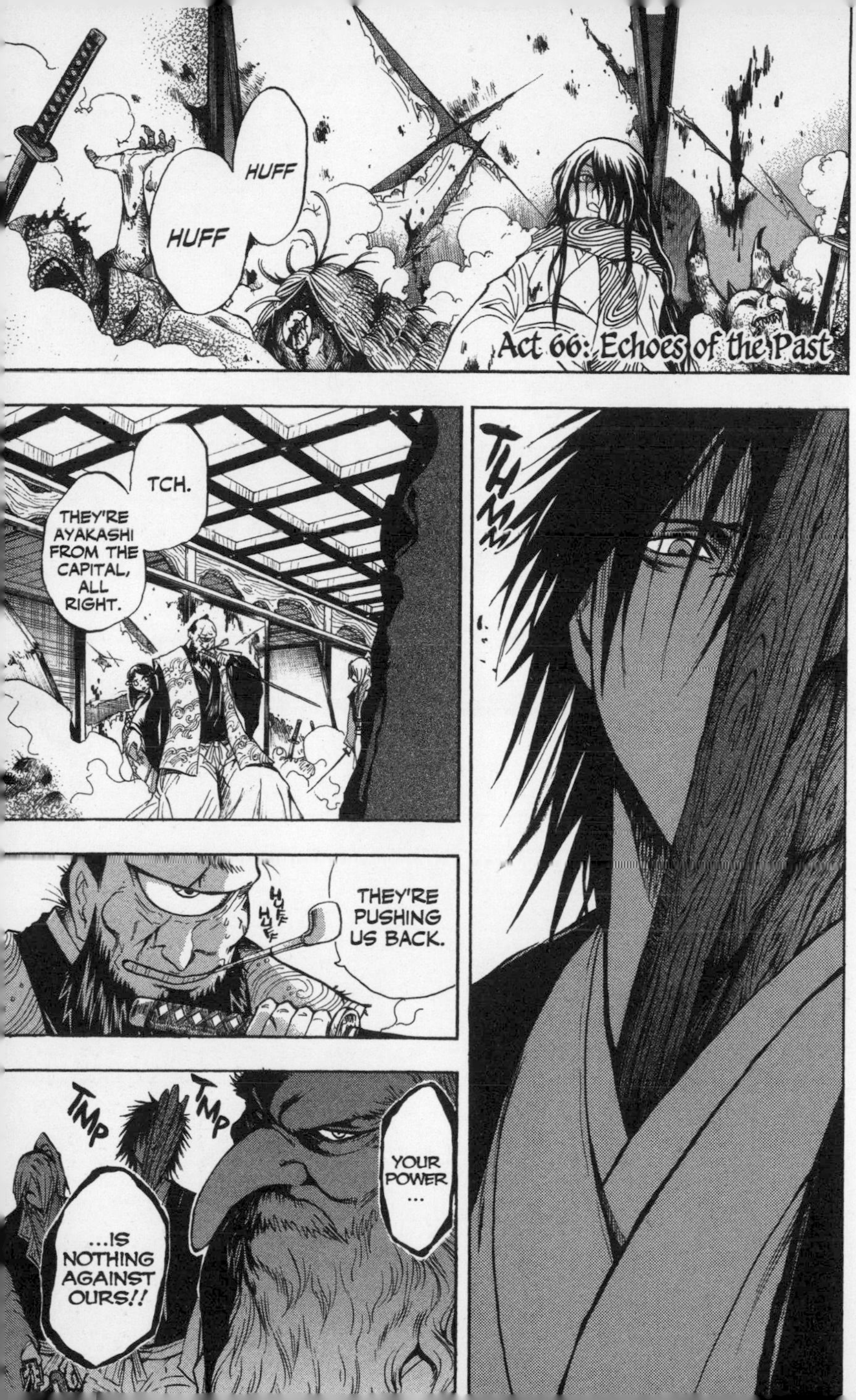
HUFF
HUFF
Act 66: Echoes of the Past
THMM
TCH.
THEY'RE AYAKASHI FROM THE CAPITAL, ALL RIGHT.
HUFF HUFF
THEY'RE PUSHING US BACK.
TMP
TMP
YOUR POWER ...
...IS NOTHING AGAINST OURS!!

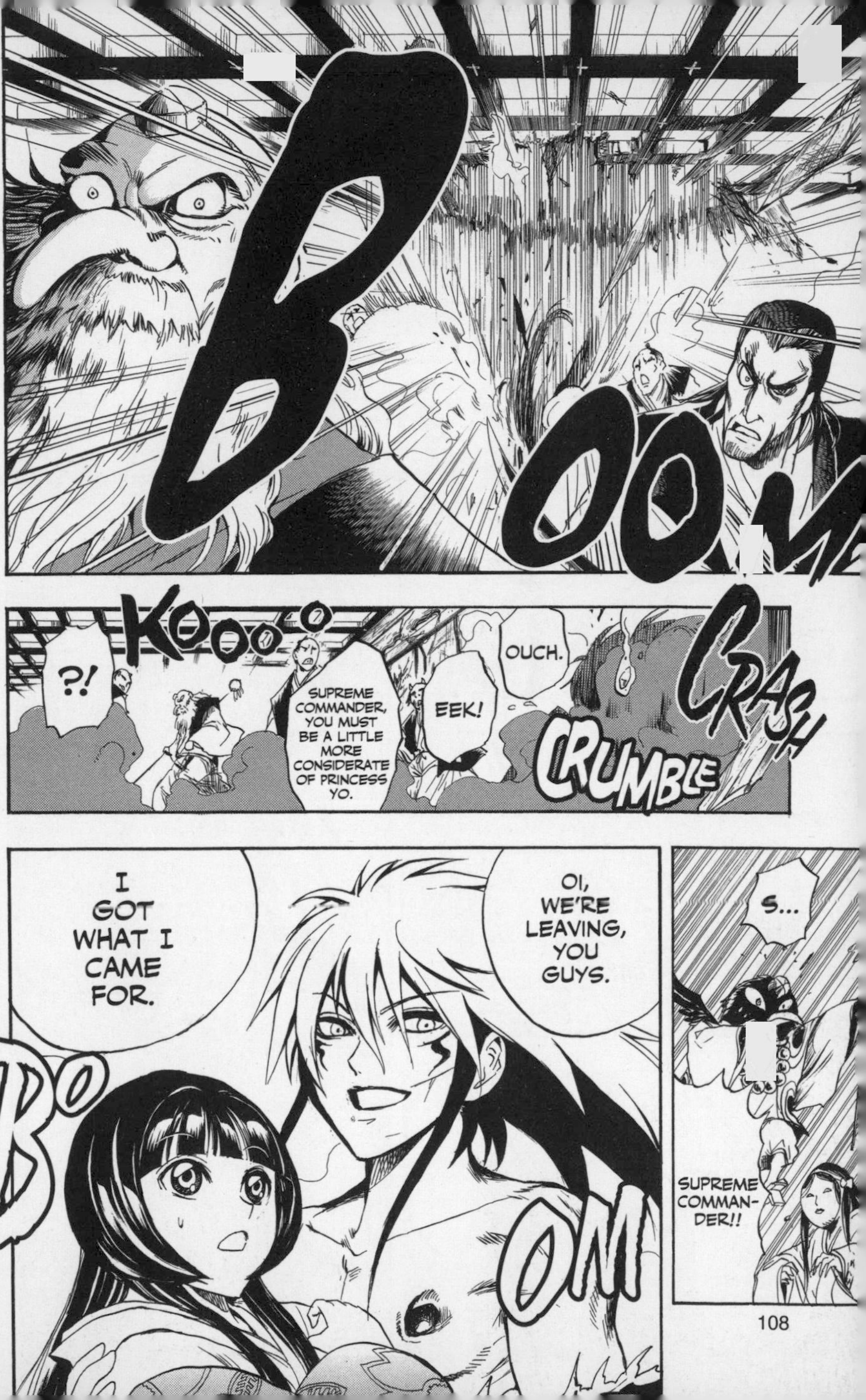
BOOM
CRASH
CRUMBLE
OUCH.
EEK!
SUPREME COMMANDER, YOU MUST BE A LITTLE MORE CONSIDERATE OF PRINCESS YO.
KOOO
?!
S...
SUPREME COMMANDER!!
OI, WE'RE LEAVING, YOU GUYS.
I GOT WHAT I CAME FOR.
BOOM

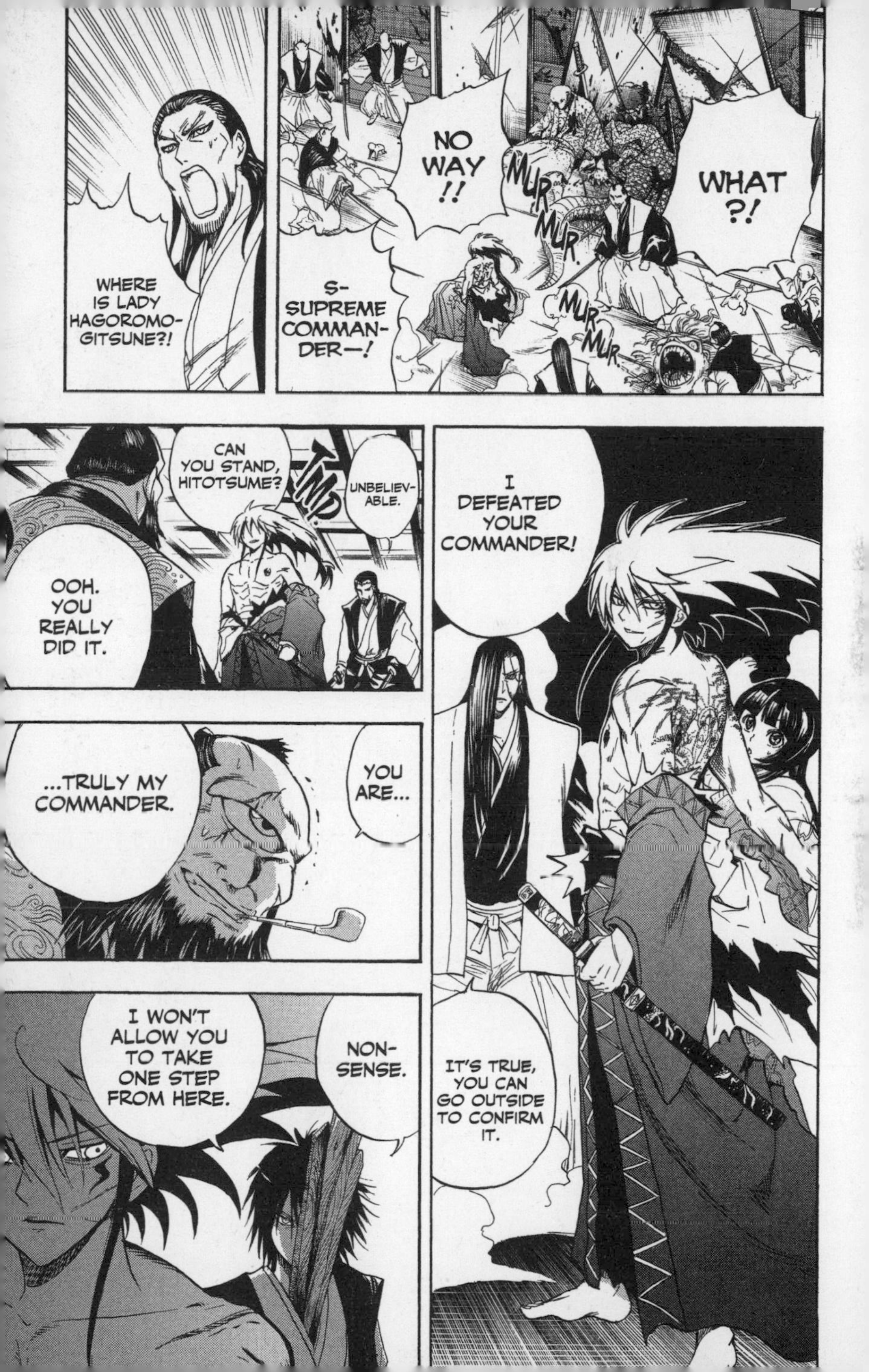
WHAT?!
NO WAY!!
MUR MUR
MUR MUR
S-SUPREME COMMANDER—!
WHERE IS LADY HAGOROMO-GITSUNE?!
I DEFEATED YOUR COMMANDER!
IT'S TRUE, YOU CAN GO OUTSIDE TO CONFIRM IT.
UNBELIEVABLE.
CAN YOU STAND, HITOTSUME?
TMP
OOH. YOU REALLY DID IT.
YOU ARE...
...TRULY MY COMMANDER.
NON-SENSE.
I WON'T ALLOW YOU TO TAKE ONE STEP FROM HERE.

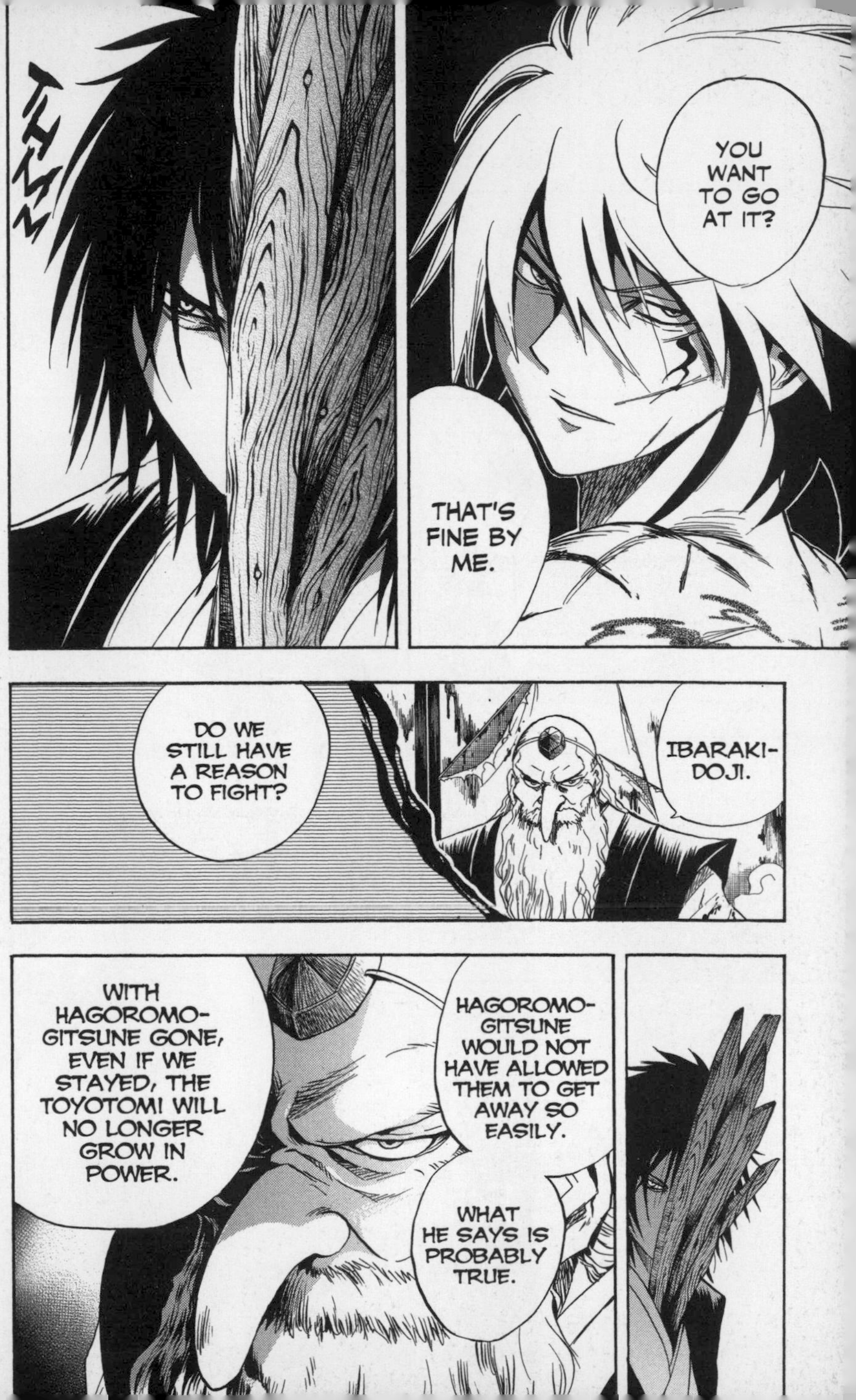

YOU WANT TO GO AT IT?
THAT'S FINE BY ME.
THMM
IBARAKI-DOJI.
DO WE STILL HAVE A REASON TO FIGHT?
HAGOROMO-GITSUNE WOULD NOT HAVE ALLOWED THEM TO GET AWAY SO EASILY.
WITH HAGOROMO-GITSUNE GONE, EVEN IF WE STAYED, THE TOYOTOMI WILL NO LONGER GROW IN POWER.
WHAT HE SAYS IS PROBABLY TRUE.

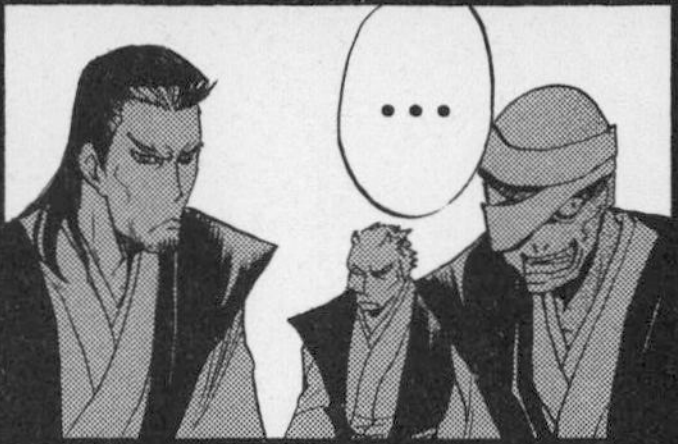
...

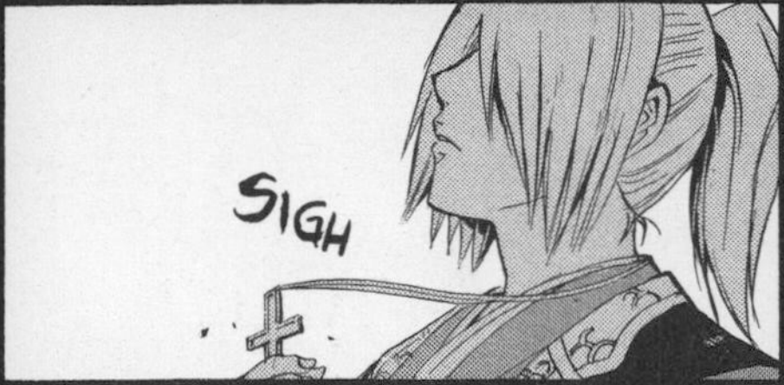
SIGH

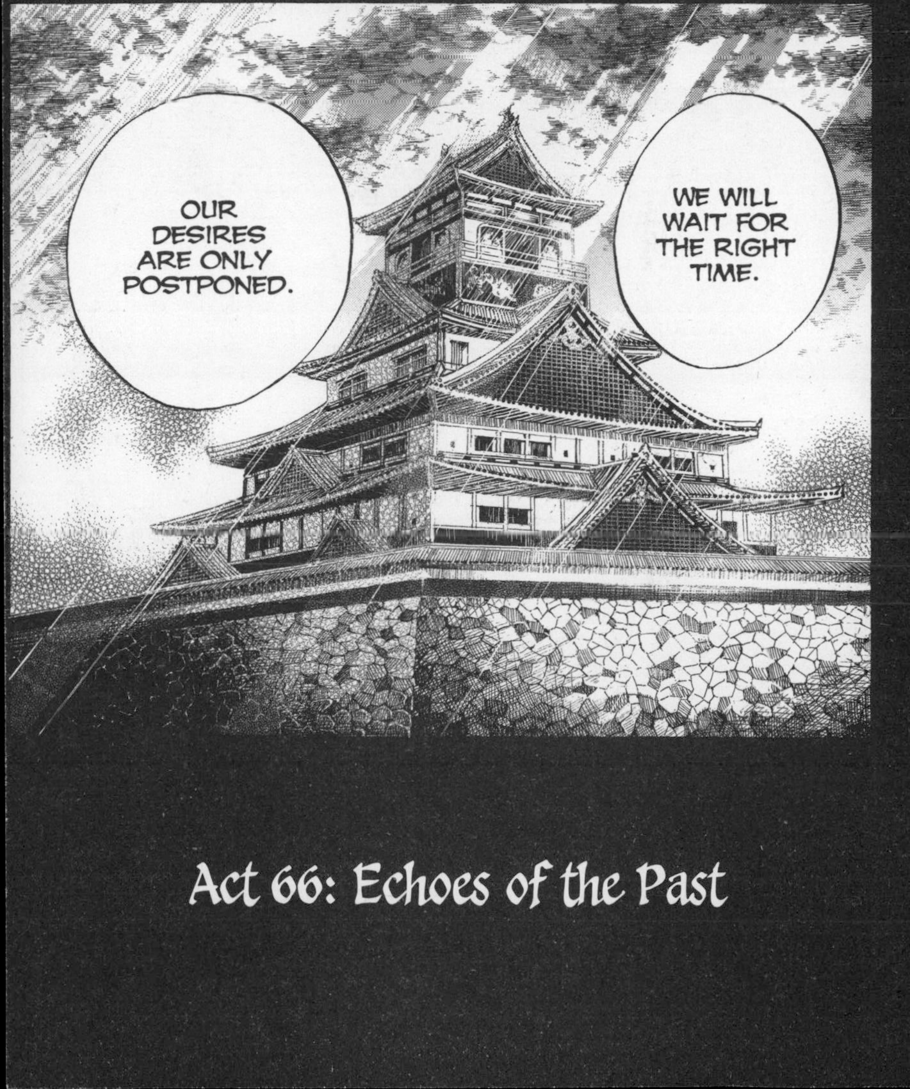
WE WILL WAIT FOR THE RIGHT TIME.
OUR DESIRES ARE ONLY POSTPONED.

Act 66: Echoes of the Past

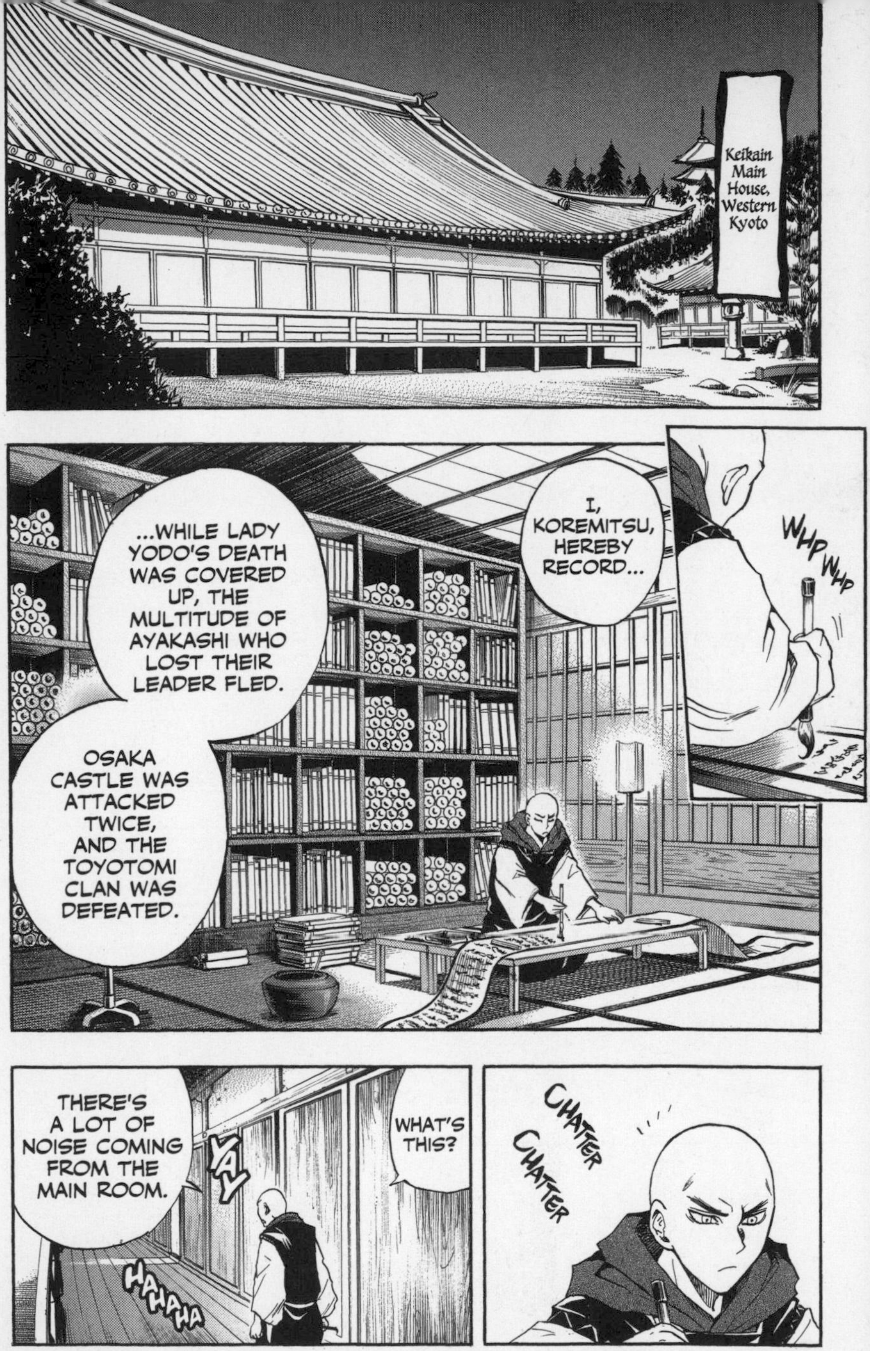
Keikain Main House, Western Kyoto
WHP WHP
I, KOREMITSU, HEREBY RECORD...
...WHILE LADY YODO'S DEATH WAS COVERED UP, THE MULTITUDE OF AYAKASHI WHO LOST THEIR LEADER FLED.
OSAKA CASTLE WAS ATTACKED TWICE, AND THE TOYOTOMI CLAN WAS DEFEATED.
CHATTER CHATTER
WHAT'S THIS?
THERE'S A LOT OF NOISE COMING FROM THE MAIN ROOM.
YAY
HAHAHA

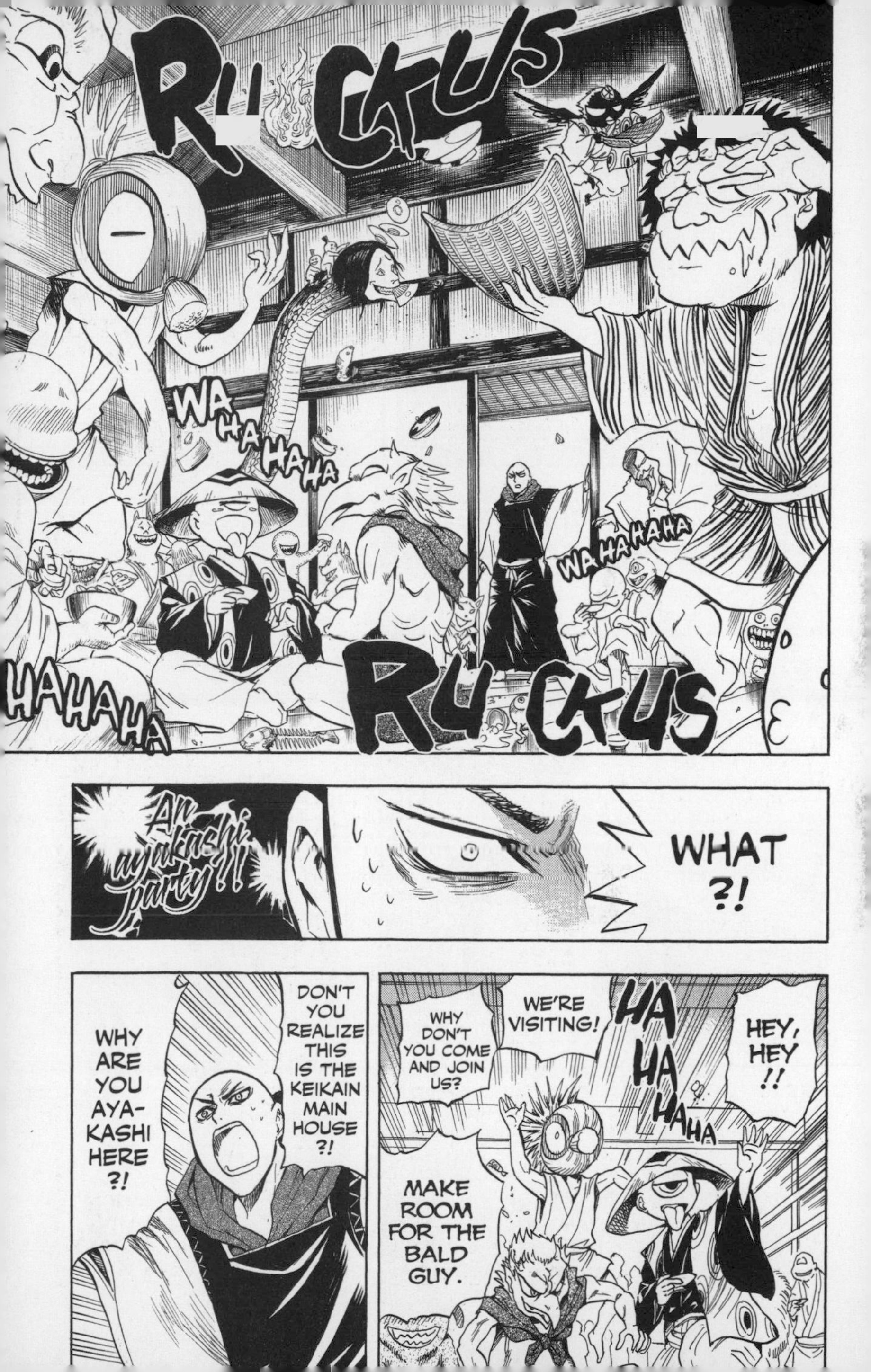
RUCKUS
WAHAHAHAHA
WA HA HAHA
HAHAHAHA
RUCKUS
WHAT ?!
An ayakashi party?!
HEY, HEY!!
HA HA HAHA
WE'RE VISITING!
WHY DON'T YOU COME AND JOIN US?
MAKE ROOM FOR THE BALD GUY.
DON'T YOU REALIZE THIS IS THE KEIKAIN MAIN HOUSE?!
WHY ARE YOU AYAKASHI HERE?!

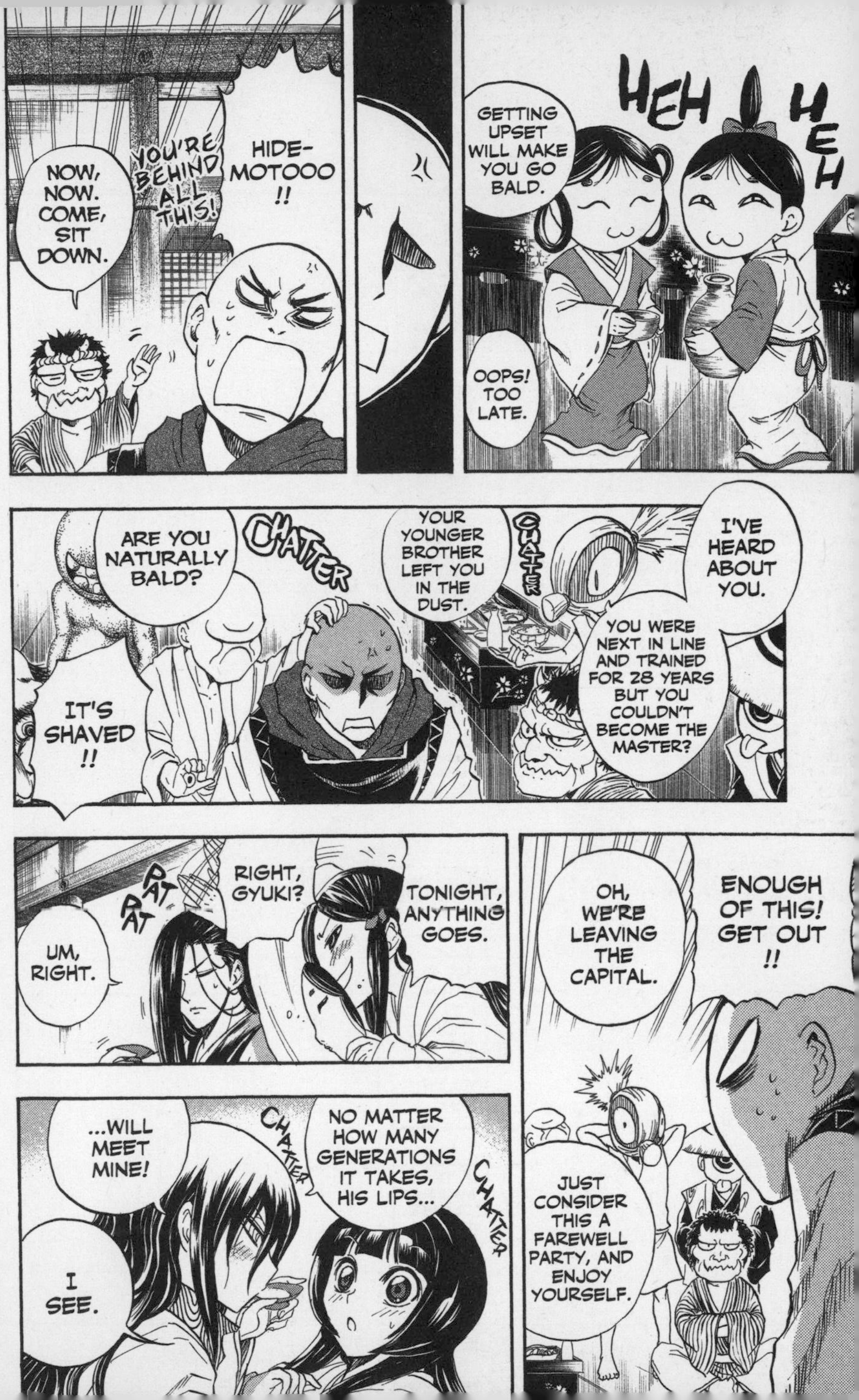
HEH HEH
GETTING UPSET WILL MAKE YOU GO BALD.
OOPS! TOO LATE.
HIDE-MOTOOO!!
YOU'RE BEHIND ALL THIS!
NOW, NOW. COME, SIT DOWN.
I'VE HEARD ABOUT YOU.
YOU WERE NEXT IN LINE AND TRAINED FOR 28 YEARS BUT YOU COULDN'T BECOME THE MASTER?
CHATTER
YOUR YOUNGER BROTHER LEFT YOU IN THE DUST.
CHATTER
ARE YOU NATURALLY BALD?
IT'S SHAVED!!
ENOUGH OF THIS! GET OUT!!
OH, WE'RE LEAVING THE CAPITAL.
JUST CONSIDER THIS A FAREWELL PARTY, AND ENJOY YOURSELF.
TONIGHT, ANYTHING GOES.
RIGHT, GYUKI?
PAT PAT
UM, RIGHT.
CHATTER
NO MATTER HOW MANY GENERATIONS IT TAKES, HIS LIPS...
CHATTER
...WILL MEET MINE!
I SEE.

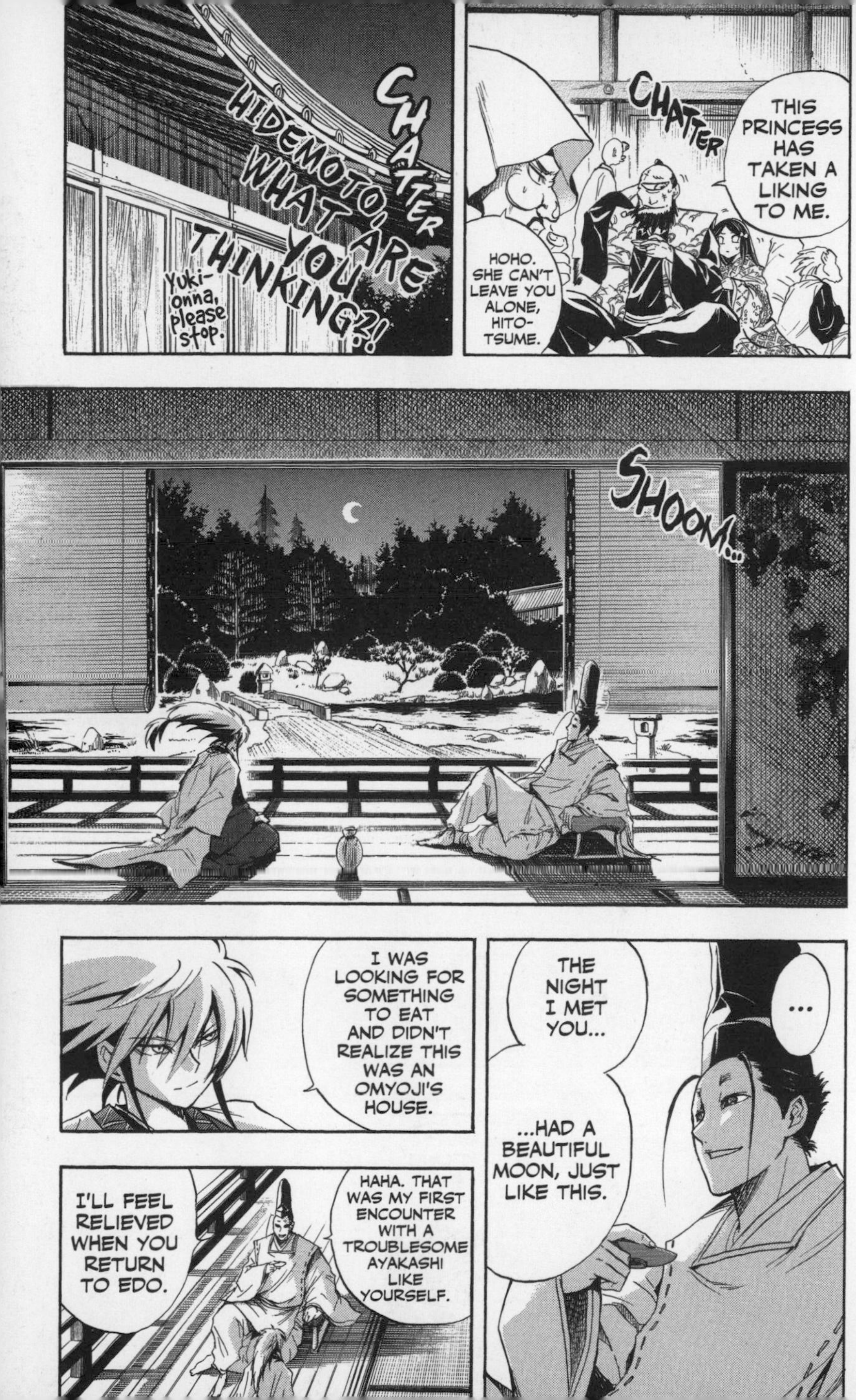
CHATTER
THIS PRINCESS HAS TAKEN A LIKING TO ME.
HOHO. SHE CAN'T LEAVE YOU ALONE, HITO-TSUME.
CHATTER
HIDEMOTO, WHAT ARE YOU THINKING?!
Yuki-onna, please stop.
SHOOM...
...
THE NIGHT I MET YOU...
...HAD A BEAUTIFUL MOON, JUST LIKE THIS.
I WAS LOOKING FOR SOMETHING TO EAT AND DIDN'T REALIZE THIS WAS AN OMYOJI'S HOUSE.
HAHA. THAT WAS MY FIRST ENCOUNTER WITH A TROUBLESOME AYAKASHI LIKE YOURSELF.
I'LL FEEL RELIEVED WHEN YOU RETURN TO EDO.

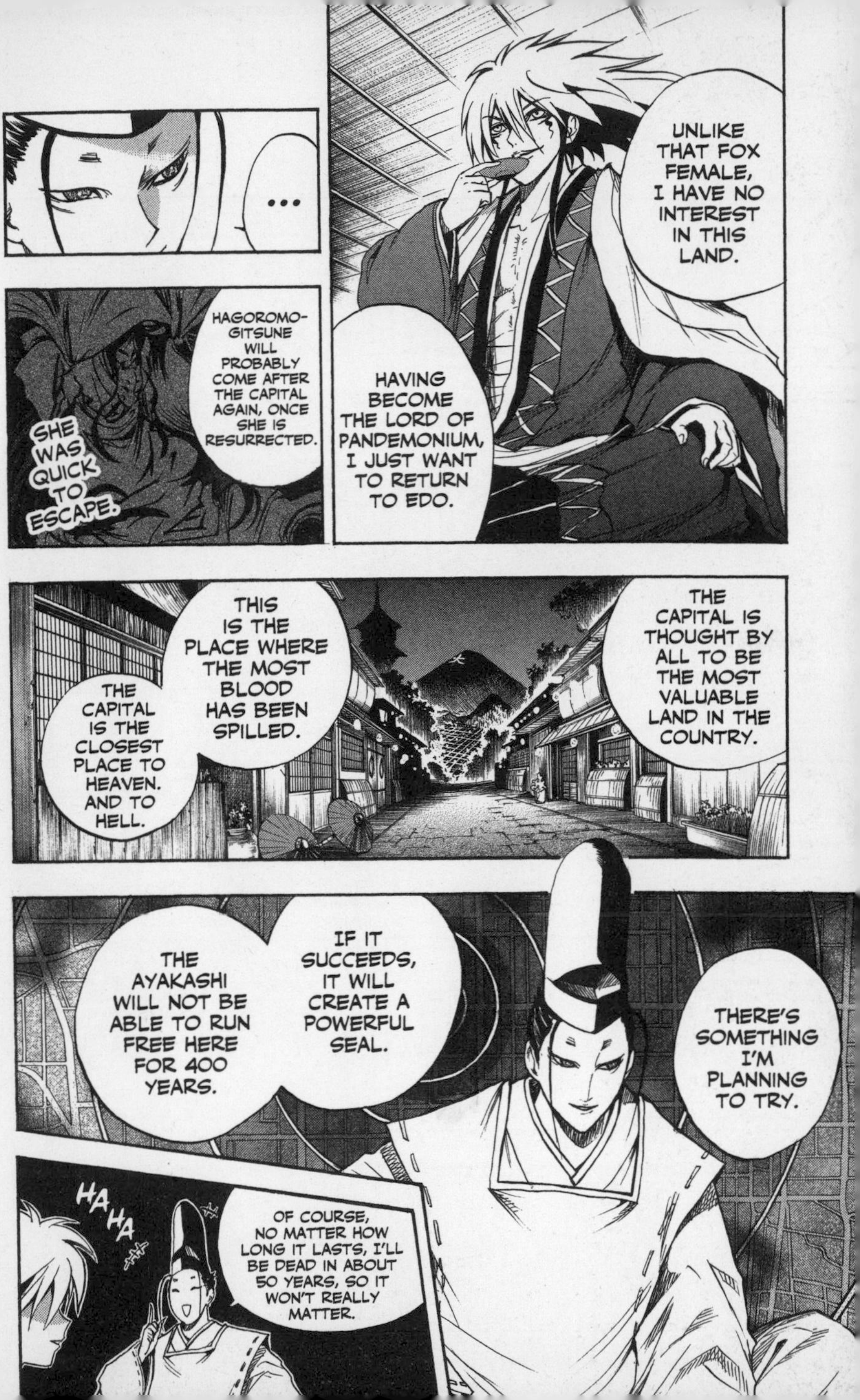
UNLIKE THAT FOX FEMALE, I HAVE NO INTEREST IN THIS LAND.
HAVING BECOME THE LORD OF PANDEMONIUM, I JUST WANT TO RETURN TO EDO.
...
HAGOROMO-GITSUNE WILL PROBABLY COME AFTER THE CAPITAL AGAIN, ONCE SHE IS RESURRECTED.
SHE WAS QUICK TO ESCAPE.
THE CAPITAL IS THOUGHT BY ALL TO BE THE MOST VALUABLE LAND IN THE COUNTRY.
THIS IS THE PLACE WHERE THE MOST BLOOD HAS BEEN SPILLED.
THE CAPITAL IS THE CLOSEST PLACE TO HEAVEN. AND TO HELL.
THERE'S SOMETHING I'M PLANNING TO TRY.
IF IT SUCCEEDS, IT WILL CREATE A POWERFUL SEAL.
THE AYAKASHI WILL NOT BE ABLE TO RUN FREE HERE FOR 400 YEARS.
OF COURSE, NO MATTER HOW LONG IT LASTS, I'LL BE DEAD IN ABOUT 50 YEARS, SO IT WON'T REALLY MATTER.
HA HA

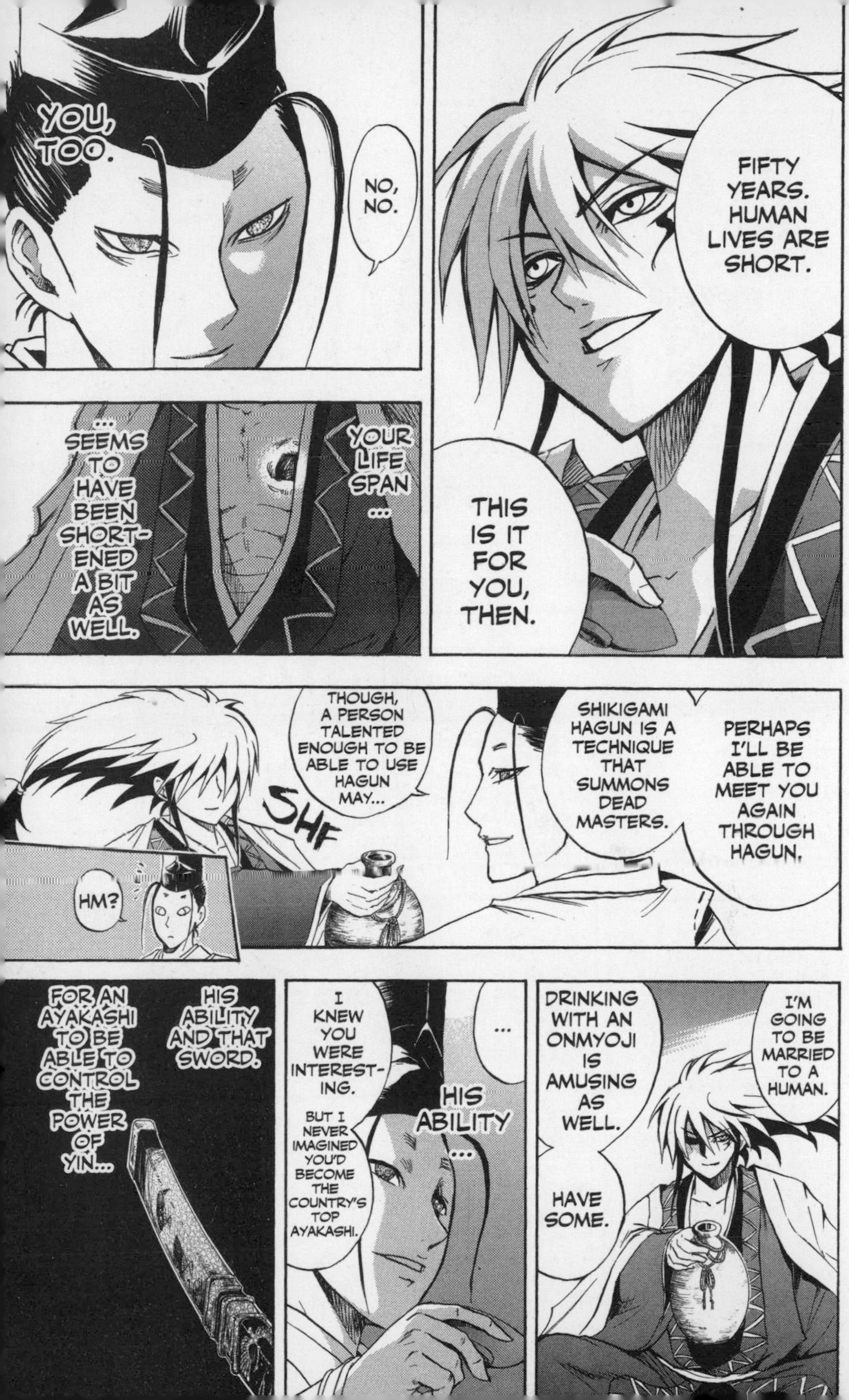
FIFTY YEARS. HUMAN LIVES ARE SHORT.
THIS IS IT FOR YOU, THEN.
NO, NO.
YOU, TOO.
YOUR LIFE SPAN ...
... SEEMS TO HAVE BEEN SHORTENED A BIT AS WELL.
PERHAPS I'LL BE ABLE TO MEET YOU AGAIN THROUGH HAGUN.
SHIKIGAMI HAGUN IS A TECHNIQUE THAT SUMMONS DEAD MASTERS.
THOUGH, A PERSON TALENTED ENOUGH TO BE ABLE TO USE HAGUN MAY...
SHF
HM?
I'M GOING TO BE MARRIED TO A HUMAN.
DRINKING WITH AN ONMYOJI IS AMUSING AS WELL.
HAVE SOME.
...
I KNEW YOU WERE INTEREST-ING.
HIS ABILITY ...
BUT I NEVER IMAGINED YOU'D BECOME THE COUNTRY'S TOP AYAKASHI.
HIS ABILITY AND THAT SWORD.
FOR AN AYAKASHI TO BE ABLE TO CONTROL THE POWER OF YIN...

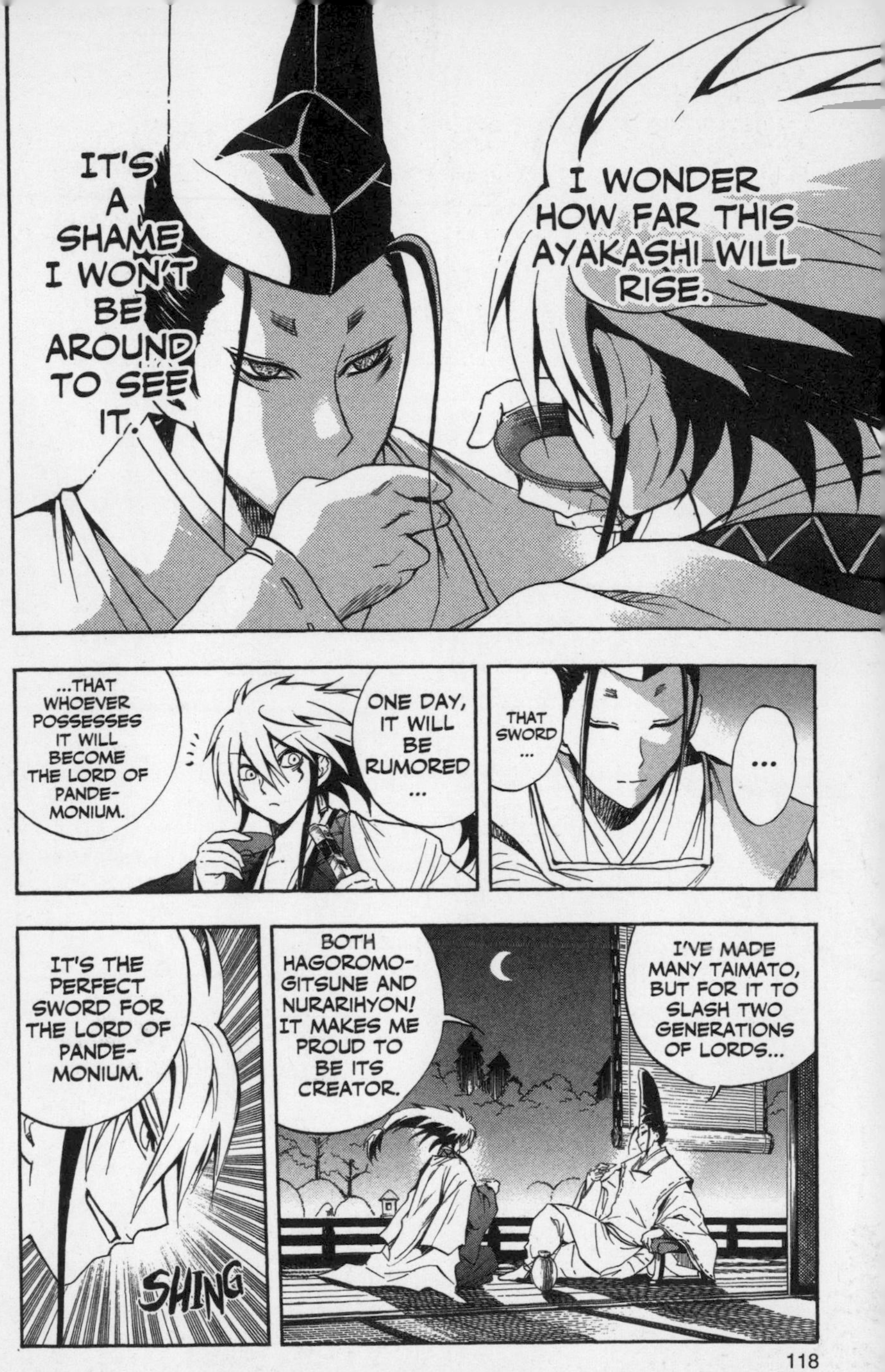
I WONDER HOW FAR THIS AYAKASHI WILL RISE.
IT'S A SHAME I WON'T BE AROUND TO SEE IT...
...
THAT SWORD ...
ONE DAY, IT WILL BE RUMORED ...
...THAT WHOEVER POSSESSES IT WILL BECOME THE LORD OF PANDEMONIUM.
I'VE MADE MANY TAIMATO, BUT FOR IT TO SLASH TWO GENERATIONS OF LORDS...
BOTH HAGOROMO-GITSUNE AND NURARIHYON! IT MAKES ME PROUD TO BE ITS CREATOR.
IT'S THE PERFECT SWORD FOR THE LORD OF PANDEMONIUM.
SHING

READ THIS WAY

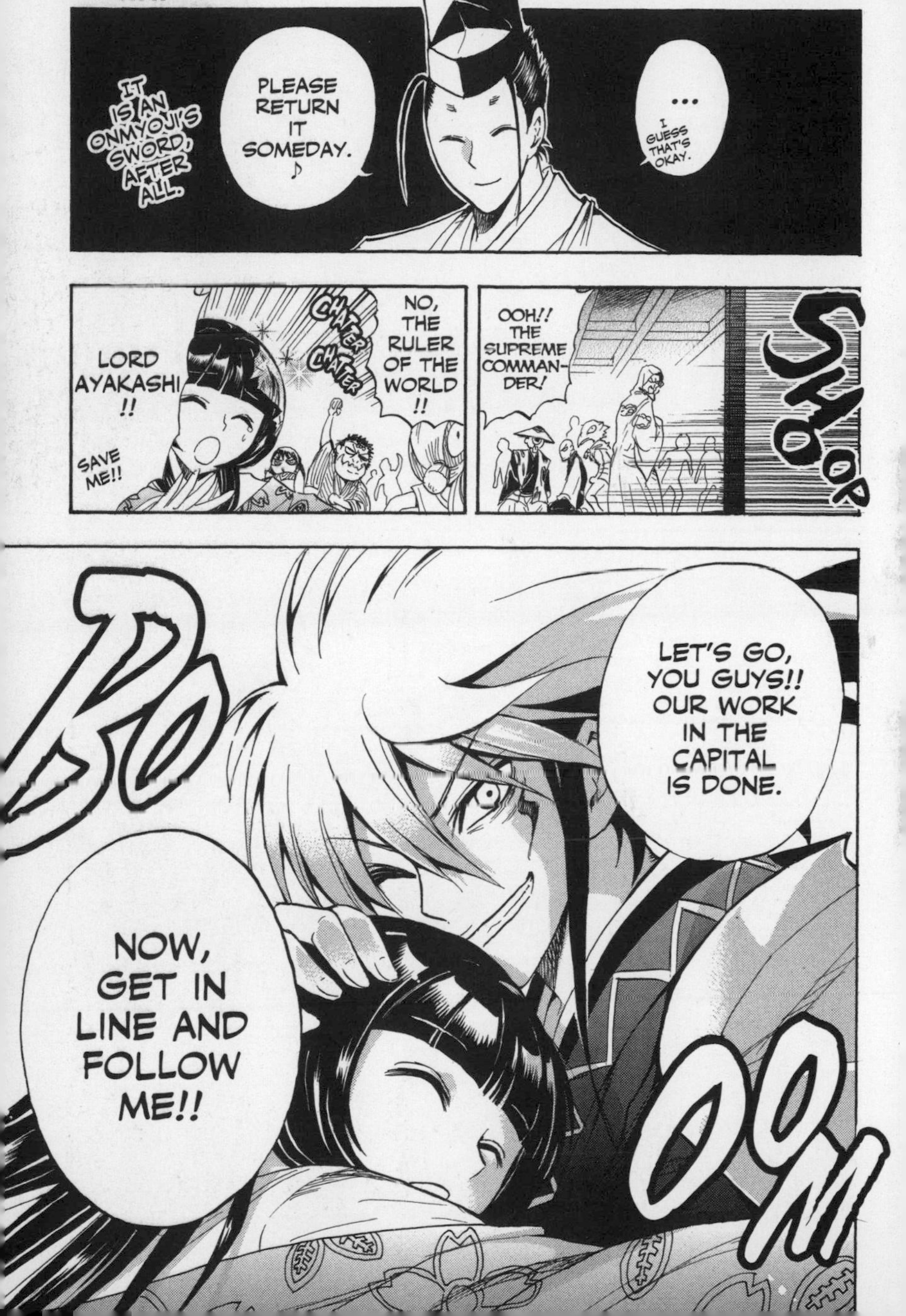
...
I GUESS THAT'S OKAY.
PLEASE RETURN IT SOMEDAY. ♪
IT IS AN ONMYOJI'S SWORD, AFTER ALL.
SHOOP
OOH!! THE SUPREME COMMANDER!
NO, THE RULER OF THE WORLD!!
CHATER CHATER
LORD AYAKASHI!!
SAVE ME!!
LET'S GO, YOU GUYS!! OUR WORK IN THE CAPITAL IS DONE.
NOW, GET IN LINE AND FOLLOW ME!!
BOOOM

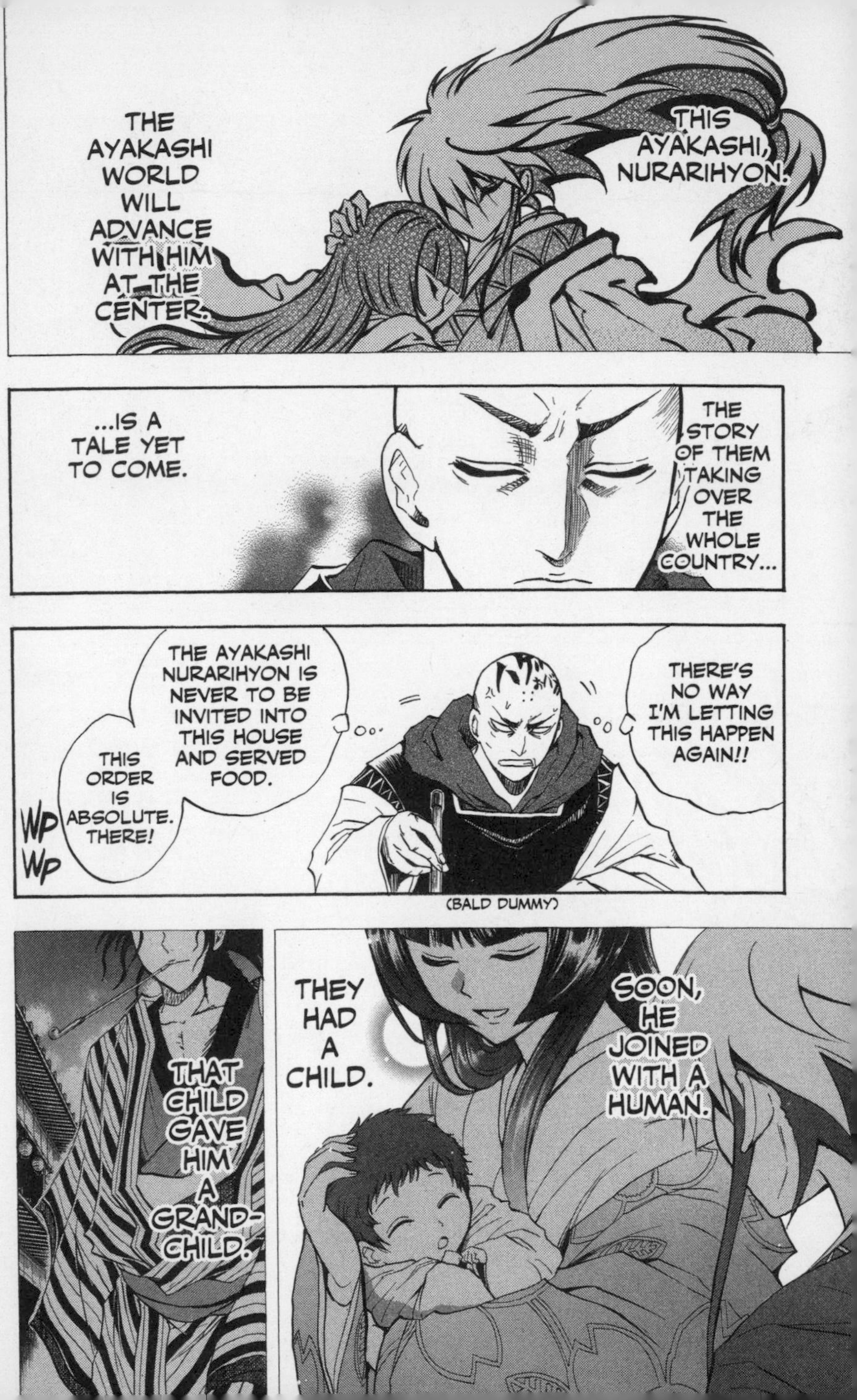
THIS AYAKASHI, NURARIHYON.
THE AYAKASHI WORLD WILL ADVANCE WITH HIM AT THE CENTER.
THE STORY OF THEM TAKING OVER THE WHOLE COUNTRY...
...IS A TALE YET TO COME.
THERE'S NO WAY I'M LETTING THIS HAPPEN AGAIN!!
THE AYAKASHI NURARIHYON IS NEVER TO BE INVITED INTO THIS HOUSE AND SERVED FOOD.
THIS ORDER IS ABSOLUTE. THERE!
WP WP
(BALD DUMMY)
SOON, HE JOINED WITH A HUMAN.
THEY HAD A CHILD.
THAT CHILD GAVE HIM A GRAND-CHILD.

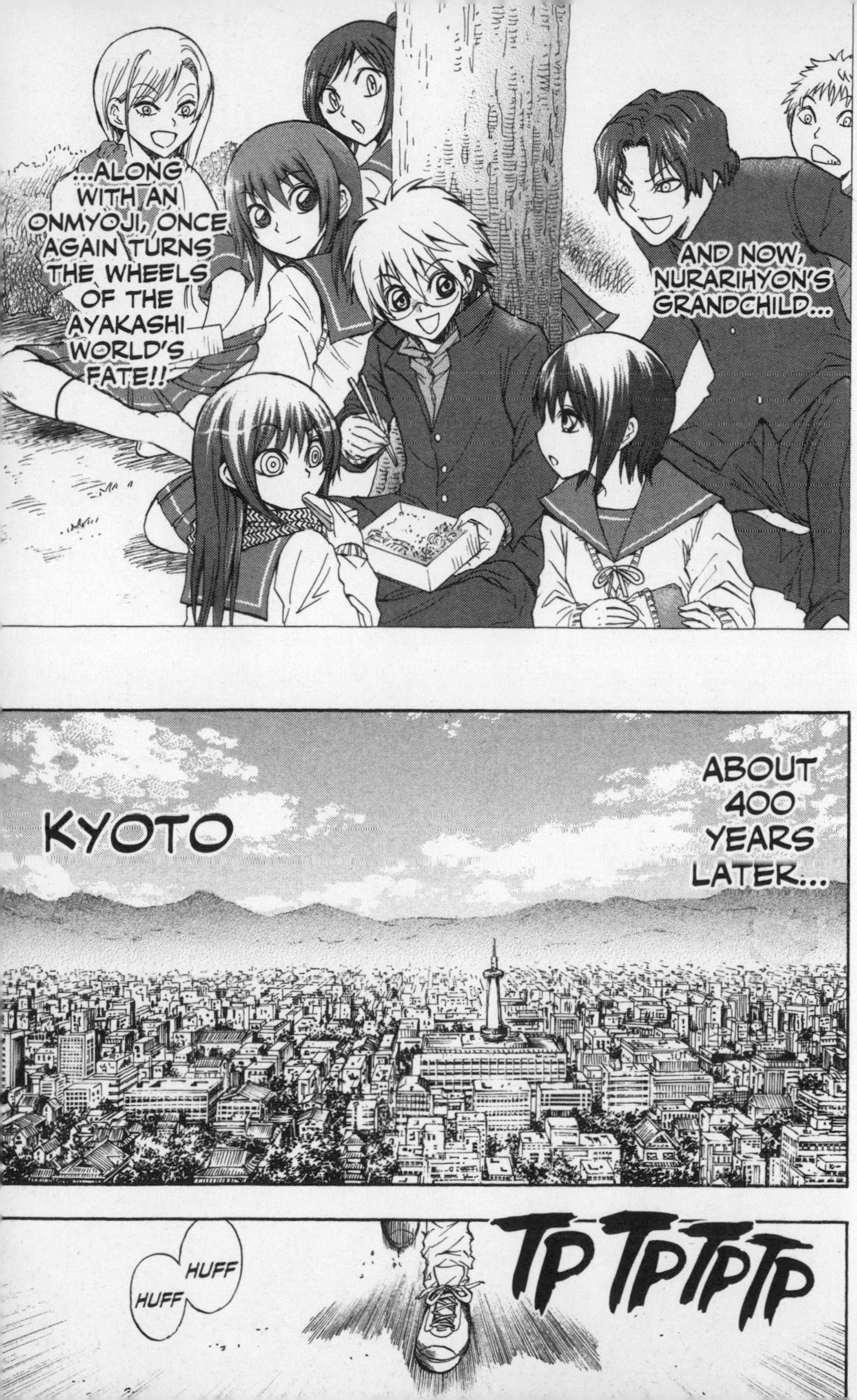
AND NOW, NURARIHYON'S GRANDCHILD...
...ALONG WITH AN ONMYOJI, ONCE AGAIN TURNS THE WHEELS OF THE AYAKASHI WORLD'S FATE!!
ABOUT 400 YEARS LATER...
KYOTO
TP TPTPTP
HUFF HUFF

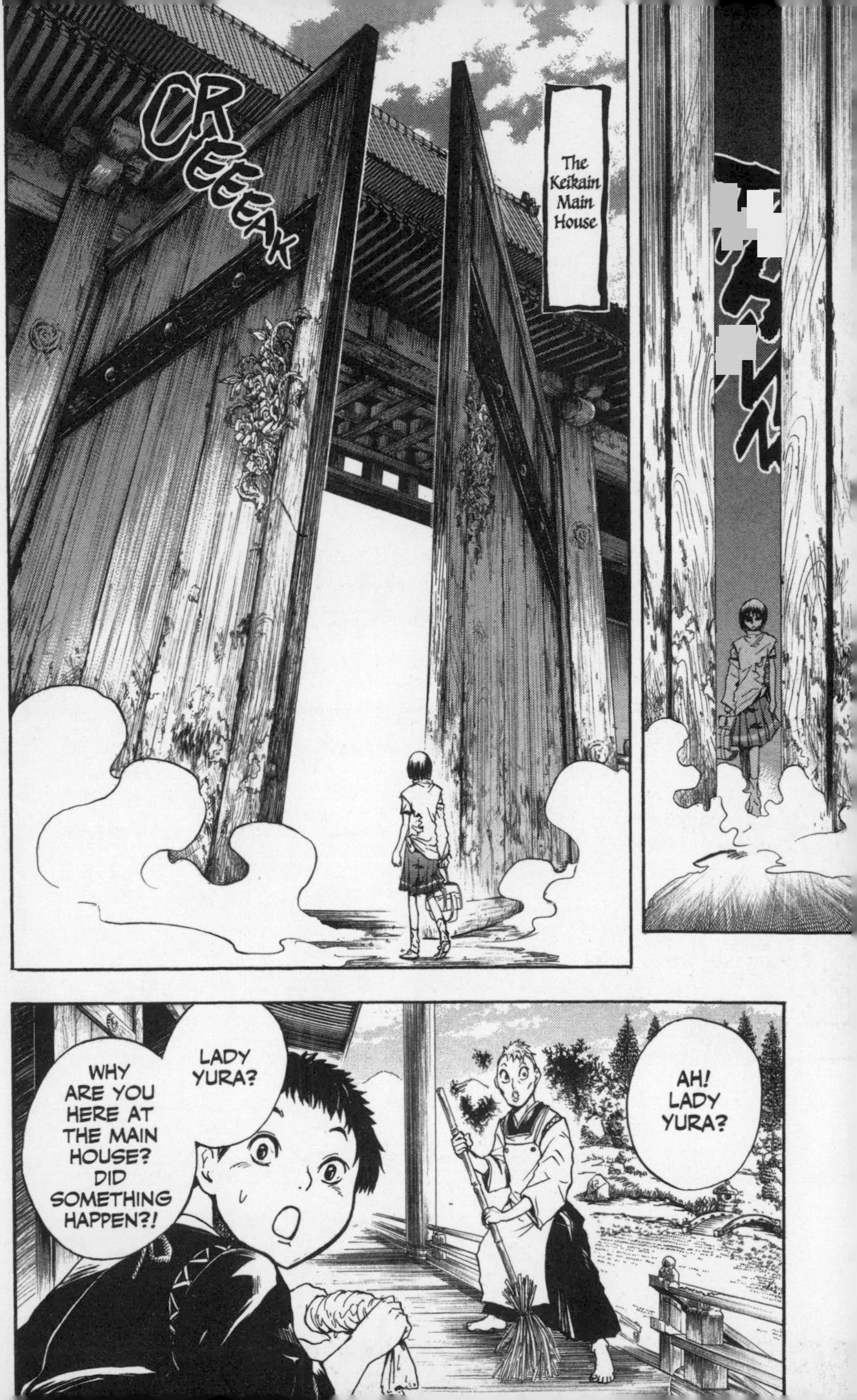
CREEEAK
The Keikain Main House
AH! LADY YURA?
LADY YURA?
WHY ARE YOU HERE AT THE MAIN HOUSE? DID SOMETHING HAPPEN?!

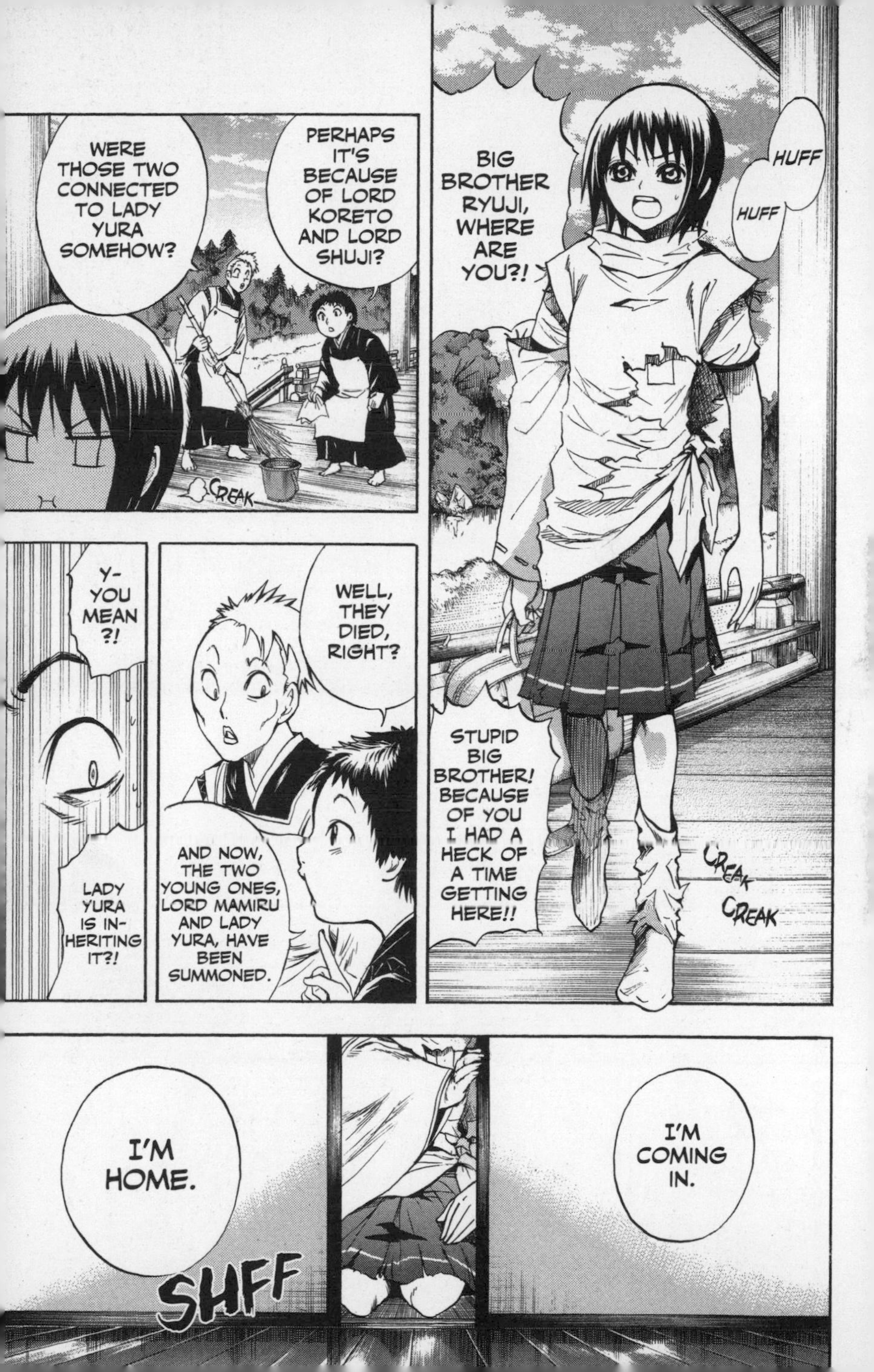
HUFF
HUFF
BIG BROTHER RYUJI, WHERE ARE YOU?!
STUPID BIG BROTHER! BECAUSE OF YOU I HAD A HECK OF A TIME GETTING HERE!!
CREAK
CREAK
PERHAPS IT'S BECAUSE OF LORD KORETO AND LORD SHUJI?
WERE THOSE TWO CONNECTED TO LADY YURA SOMEHOW?
CREAK
WELL, THEY DIED, RIGHT?
AND NOW, THE TWO YOUNG ONES, LORD MAMIRU AND LADY YURA, HAVE BEEN SUMMONED.
Y-YOU MEAN ?!
LADY YURA IS IN-HERITING IT?!
I'M COMING IN.
I'M HOME.
SHFF

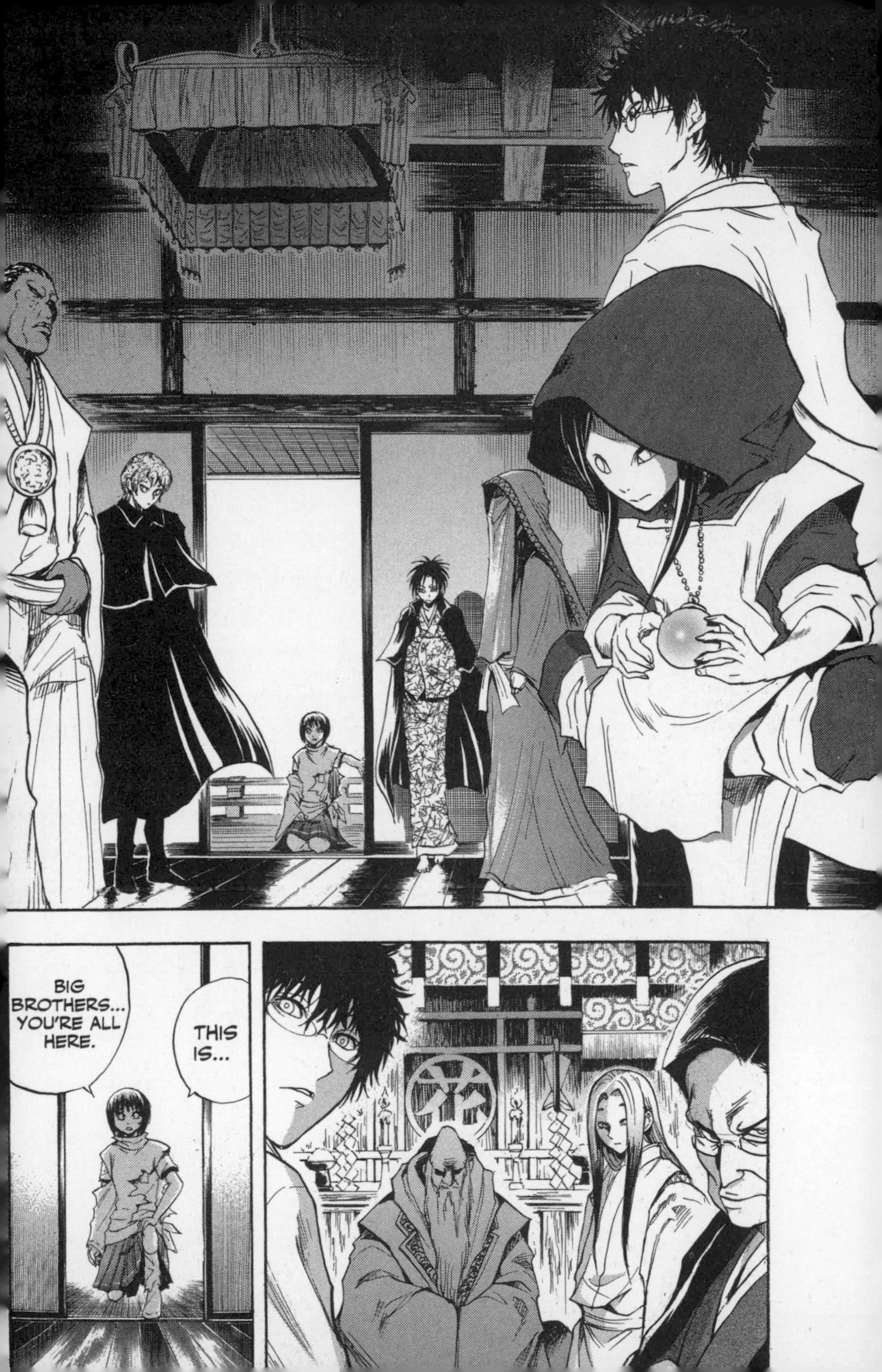
BIG BROTHERS... YOU'RE ALL HERE.
THIS IS...

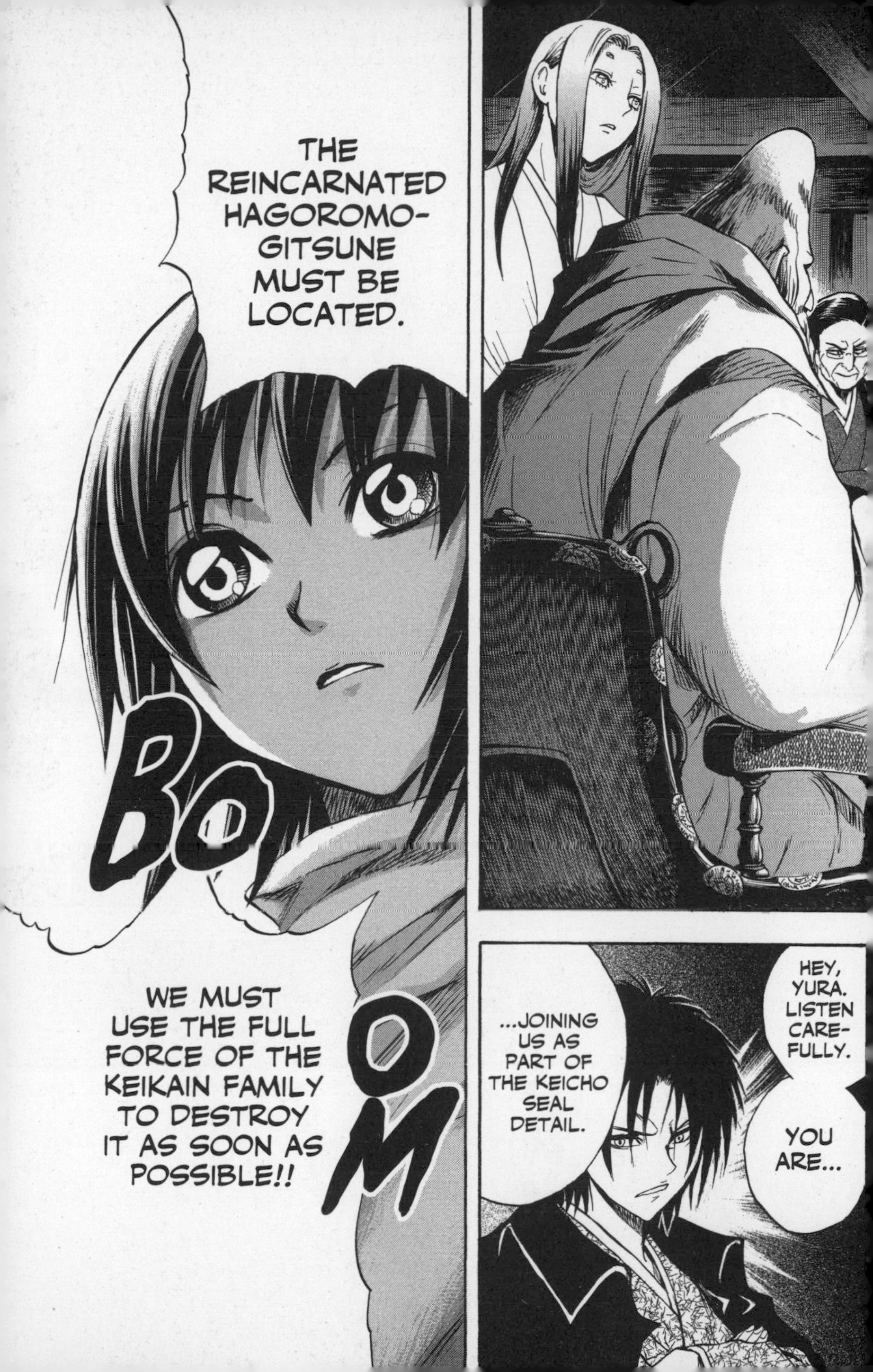
HEY, YURA. LISTEN CARE-FULLY.
YOU ARE...
...JOINING US AS PART OF THE KEICHO SEAL DETAIL.
THE REINCARNATED HAGOROMO-GITSUNE MUST BE LOCATED.
BOOM
WE MUST USE THE FULL FORCE OF THE KEIKAIN FAMILY TO DESTROY IT AS SOON AS POSSIBLE!!

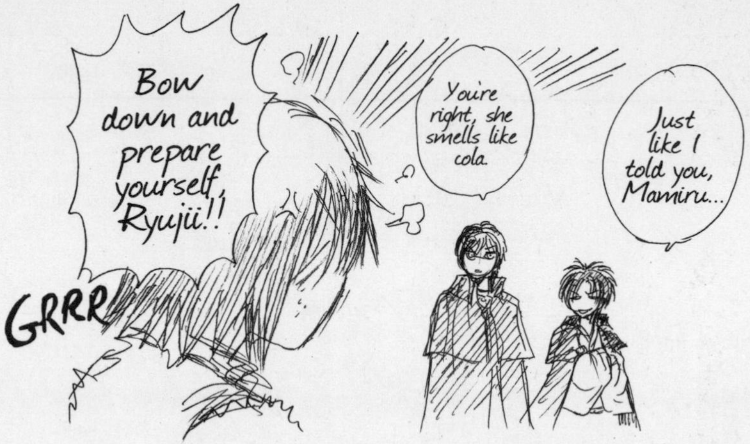
Just like I told you, Mamiru...
You're right, she smells like cola.
Bow down and prepare yourself, Ryujii!!
GRRR

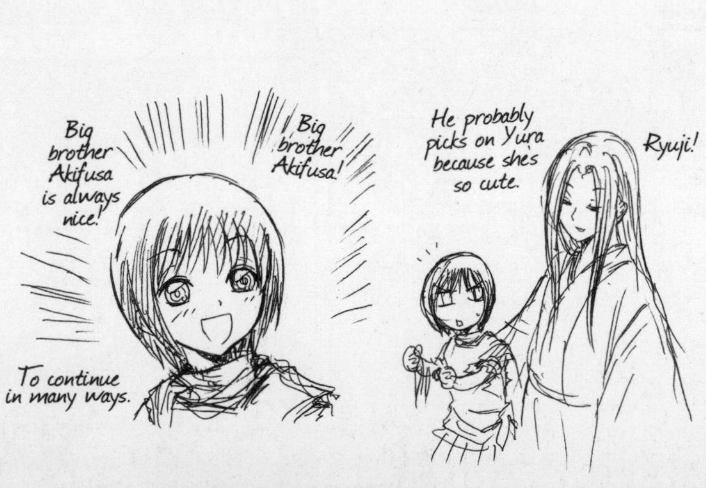
Ryuji!
He probably picks on Yura because she's so cute.
Big brother Akifusa!
Big brother Akifusa is always nice!
To continue in many ways.

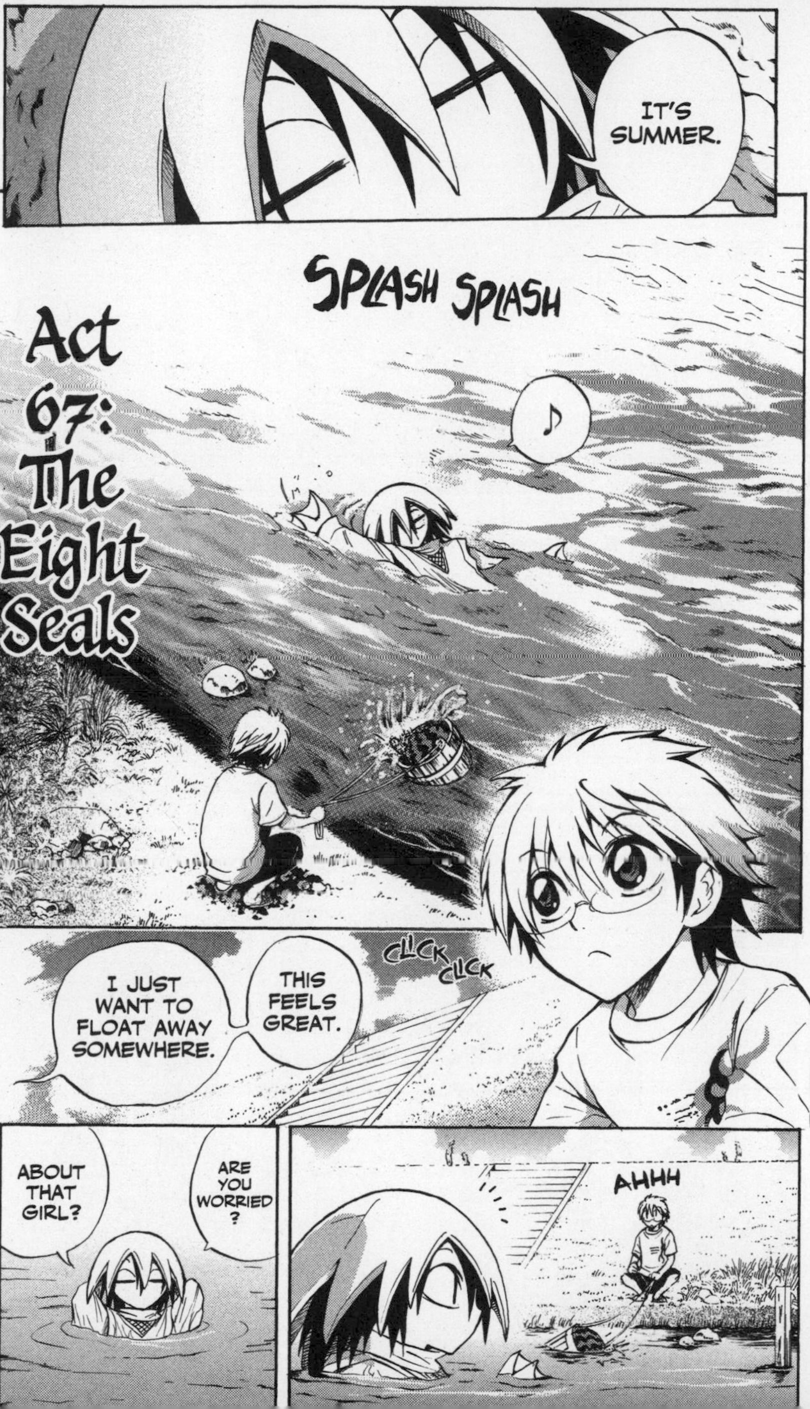
IT'S SUMMER.
SPLASH SPLASH
Act 67: The Eight Seals
♪
CLICK CLICK
THIS FEELS GREAT.
I JUST WANT TO FLOAT AWAY SOMEWHERE.
AHHH
ARE YOU WORRIED?
ABOUT THAT GIRL?

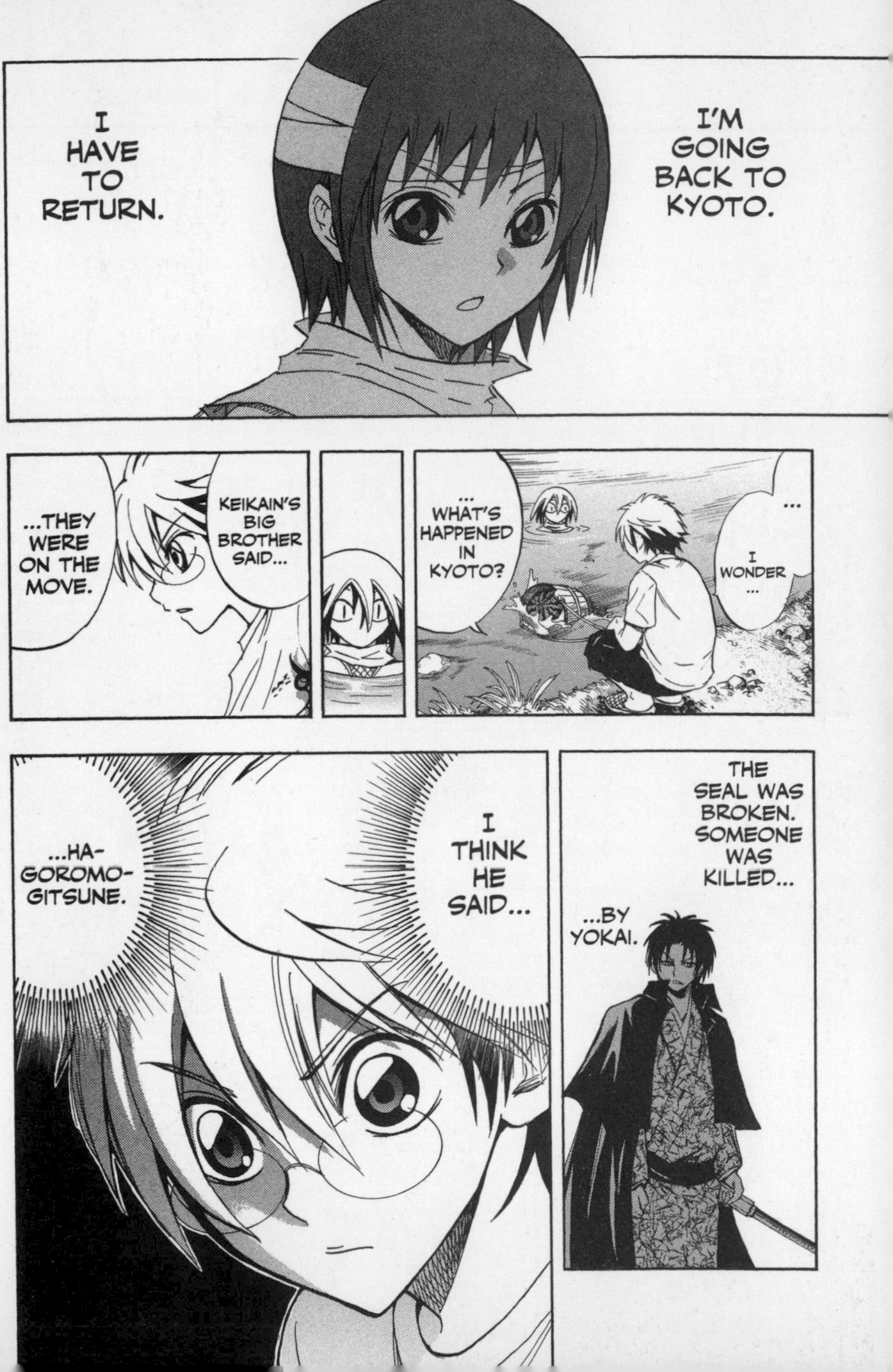
I'M GOING BACK TO KYOTO.
I HAVE TO RETURN.
...
I WONDER ...
... WHAT'S HAPPENED IN KYOTO?
KEIKAIN'S BIG BROTHER SAID...
...THEY WERE ON THE MOVE.
THE SEAL WAS BROKEN. SOMEONE WAS KILLED...
...BY YOKAI.
I THINK HE SAID...
...HA-GOROMO-GITSUNE.

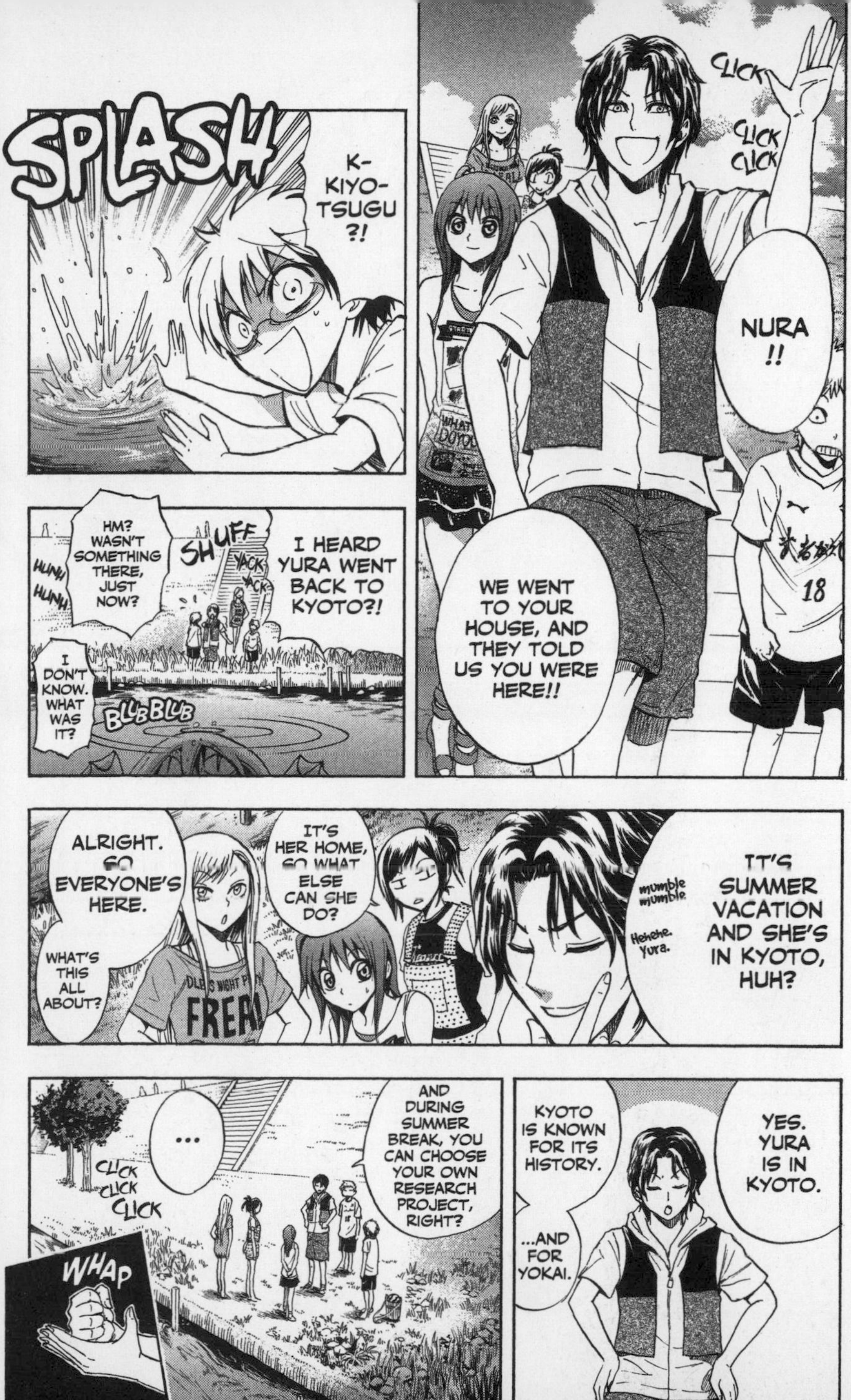
CLICK
CLICK CLICK
NURA!!
WE WENT TO YOUR HOUSE, AND THEY TOLD US YOU WERE HERE!!
SPLASH
K-KIYOTSUGU?!
I HEARD YURA WENT BACK TO KYOTO?!
SHUFF
YACK YACK
HUNH HUNH
HM? WASN'T SOMETHING THERE, JUST NOW?
I DON'T KNOW. WHAT WAS IT?
BLUB BLUB
IT'S SUMMER VACATION AND SHE'S IN KYOTO, HUH?
mumble mumble
Hehehe. Yura.
IT'S HER HOME, SO WHAT ELSE CAN SHE DO?
ALRIGHT. SO EVERYONE'S HERE.
WHAT'S THIS ALL ABOUT?
YES. YURA IS IN KYOTO.
KYOTO IS KNOWN FOR ITS HISTORY.
...AND FOR YOKAI.
AND DURING SUMMER BREAK, YOU CAN CHOOSE YOUR OWN RESEARCH PROJECT, RIGHT?
...
CLICK CLICK CLICK
WHAP

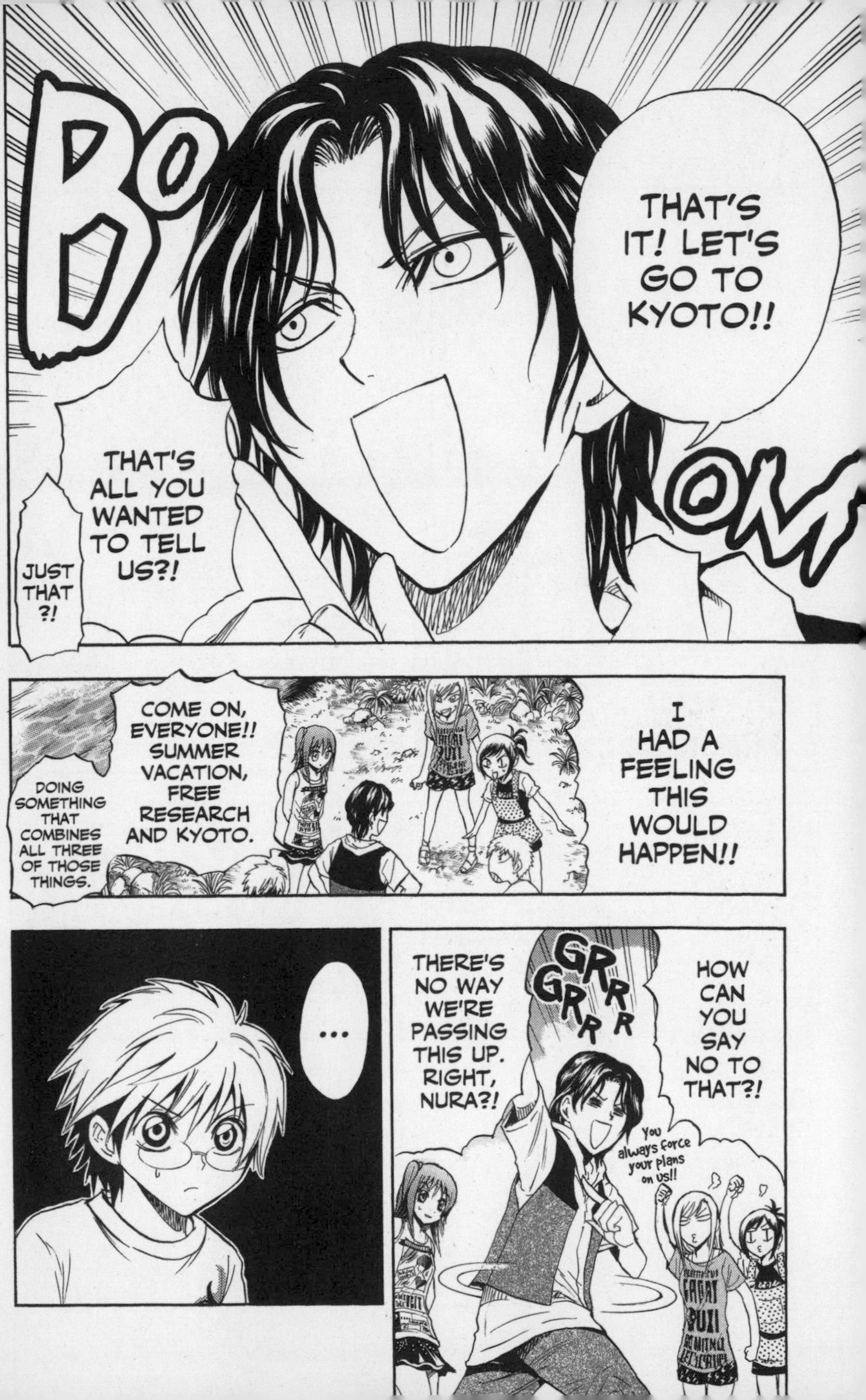
THAT'S IT! LET'S GO TO KYOTO!!
BOOM
THAT'S ALL YOU WANTED TO TELL US?!
JUST THAT?!
I HAD A FEELING THIS WOULD HAPPEN!!
COME ON, EVERYONE!! SUMMER VACATION, FREE RESEARCH AND KYOTO.
DOING SOMETHING THAT COMBINES ALL THREE OF THOSE THINGS.
HOW CAN YOU SAY NO TO THAT?!
GRRR GRRR
THERE'S NO WAY WE'RE PASSING THIS UP. RIGHT, NURA?!
You always force your plans on us!!
...

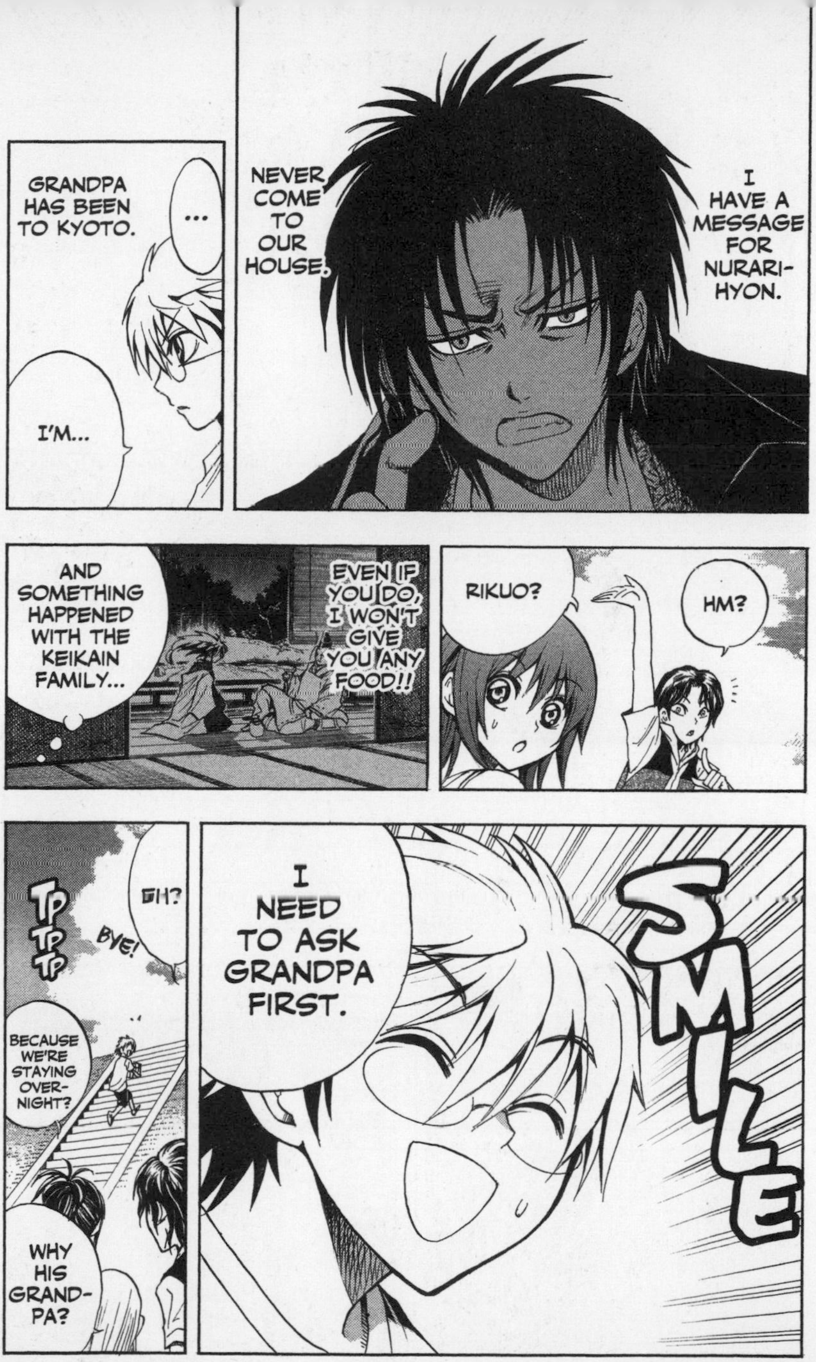
I HAVE A MESSAGE FOR NURARI-HYON.
NEVER COME TO OUR HOUSE.
...
GRANDPA HAS BEEN TO KYOTO.
I'M...
HM?
RIKUO?
EVEN IF YOU DO, I WON'T GIVE YOU ANY FOOD!!
AND SOMETHING HAPPENED WITH THE KEIKAIN FAMILY...
SMILE
I NEED TO ASK GRANDPA FIRST.
EH?
BYE!
TP TP TP
BECAUSE WE'RE STAYING OVER-NIGHT?
WHY HIS GRANDPA?

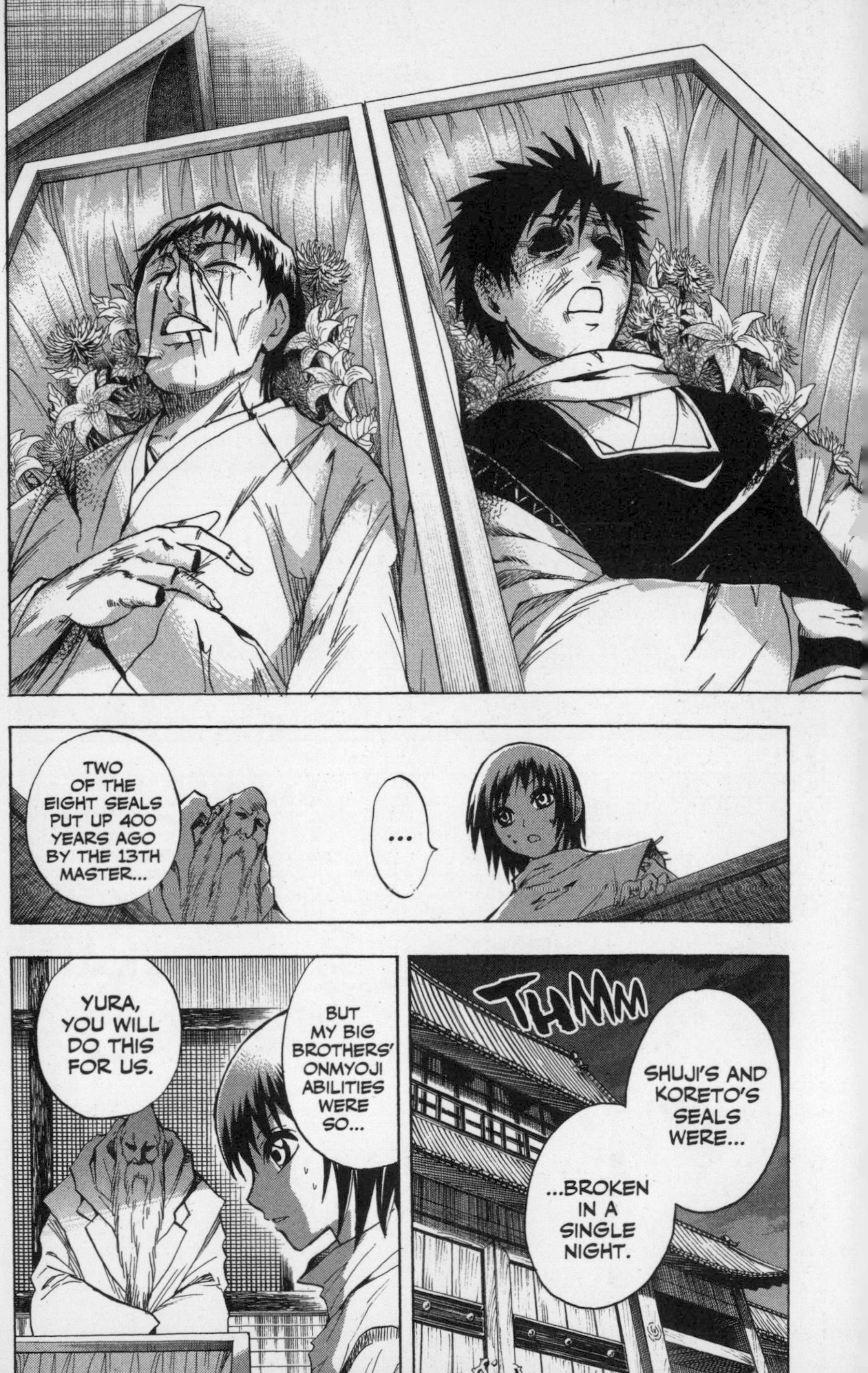
...
TWO OF THE EIGHT SEALS PUT UP 400 YEARS AGO BY THE 13TH MASTER...
THMM
SHUJI'S AND KORETO'S SEALS WERE...
...BROKEN IN A SINGLE NIGHT.
BUT MY BIG BROTHERS' ONMYOJI ABILITIES WERE SO...
YURA, YOU WILL DO THIS FOR US.

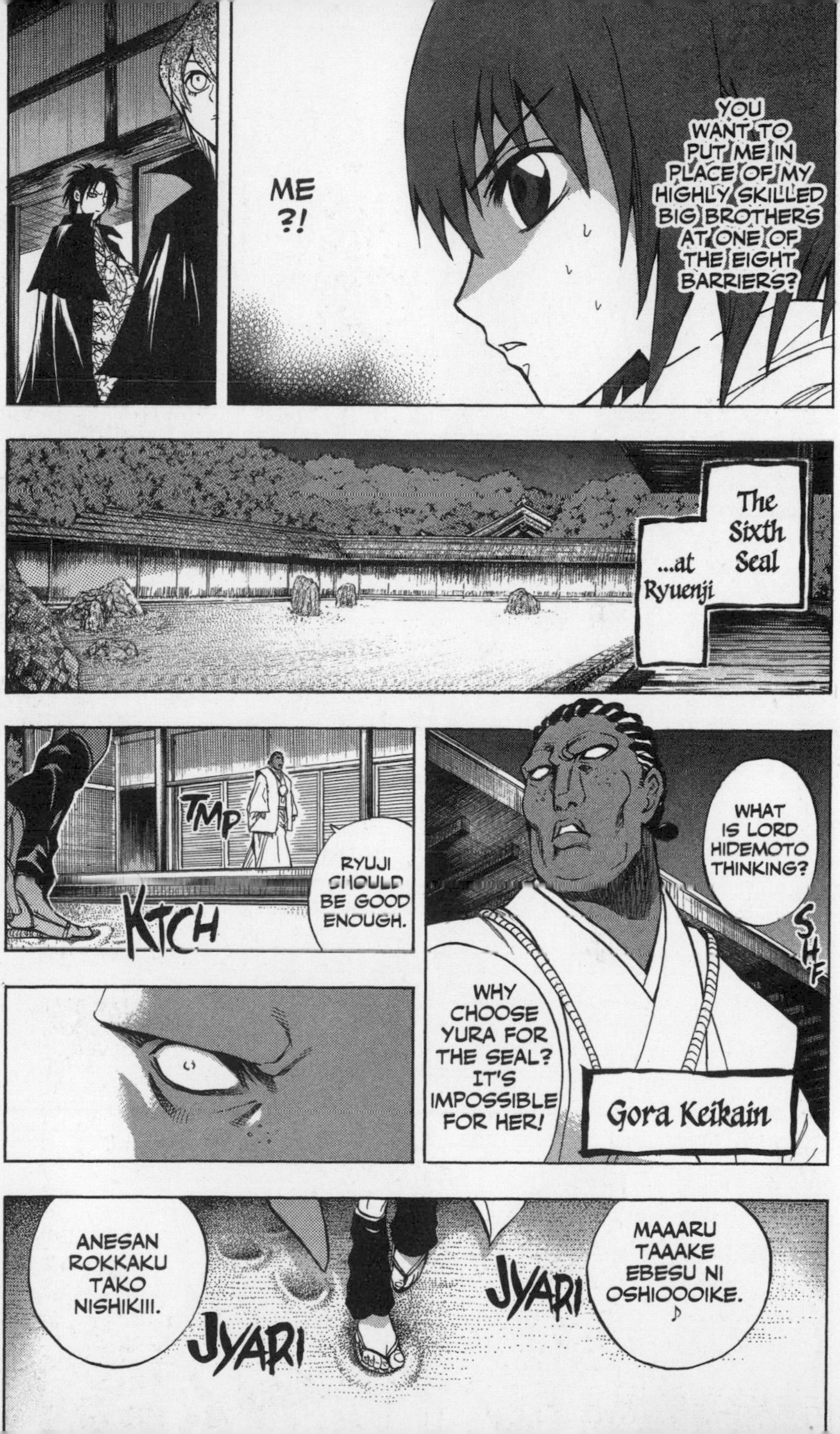
YOU WANT TO PUT ME IN PLACE OF MY HIGHLY SKILLED BIG BROTHERS AT ONE OF THE EIGHT BARRIERS?
ME ?!
The Sixth Seal
...at Ryuenji
WHAT IS LORD HIDEMOTO THINKING?
SHF
WHY CHOOSE YURA FOR THE SEAL? IT'S IMPOSSIBLE FOR HER!
Gora Keikain
TMP
RYUJI SHOULD BE GOOD ENOUGH.
KTCH
MAAARU TAAAKE EBESU NI OSHIOOOIKE. ♪
JYARI
ANESAN ROKKAKU TAKO NISHIKIII.
JYARI

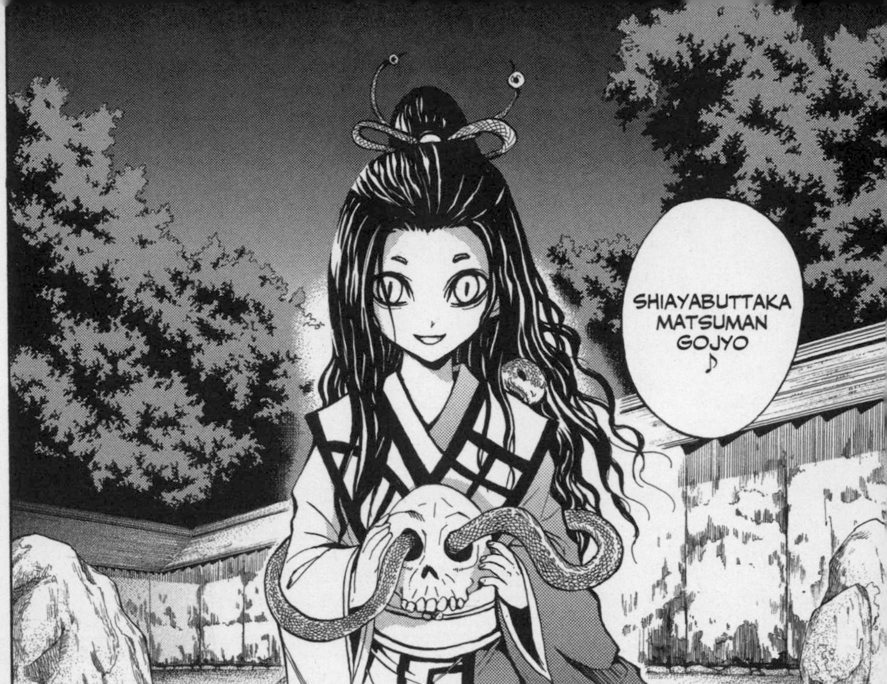
SHIAYABUTTAKA MATSUMAN GOJYO ♪

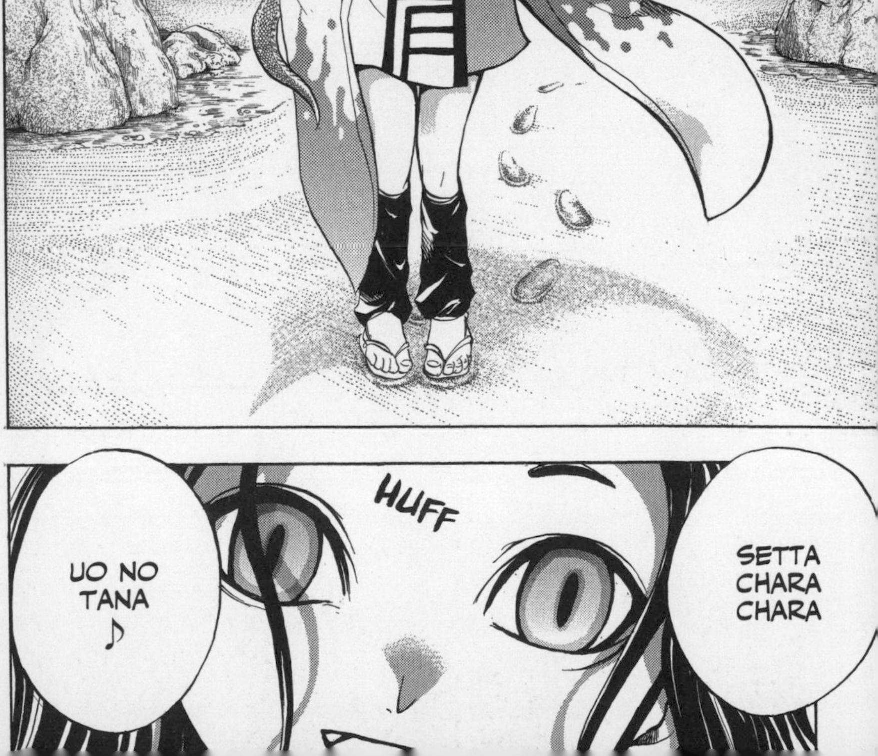
SETTA CHARA CHARA
HUFF
UO NO TANA ♪

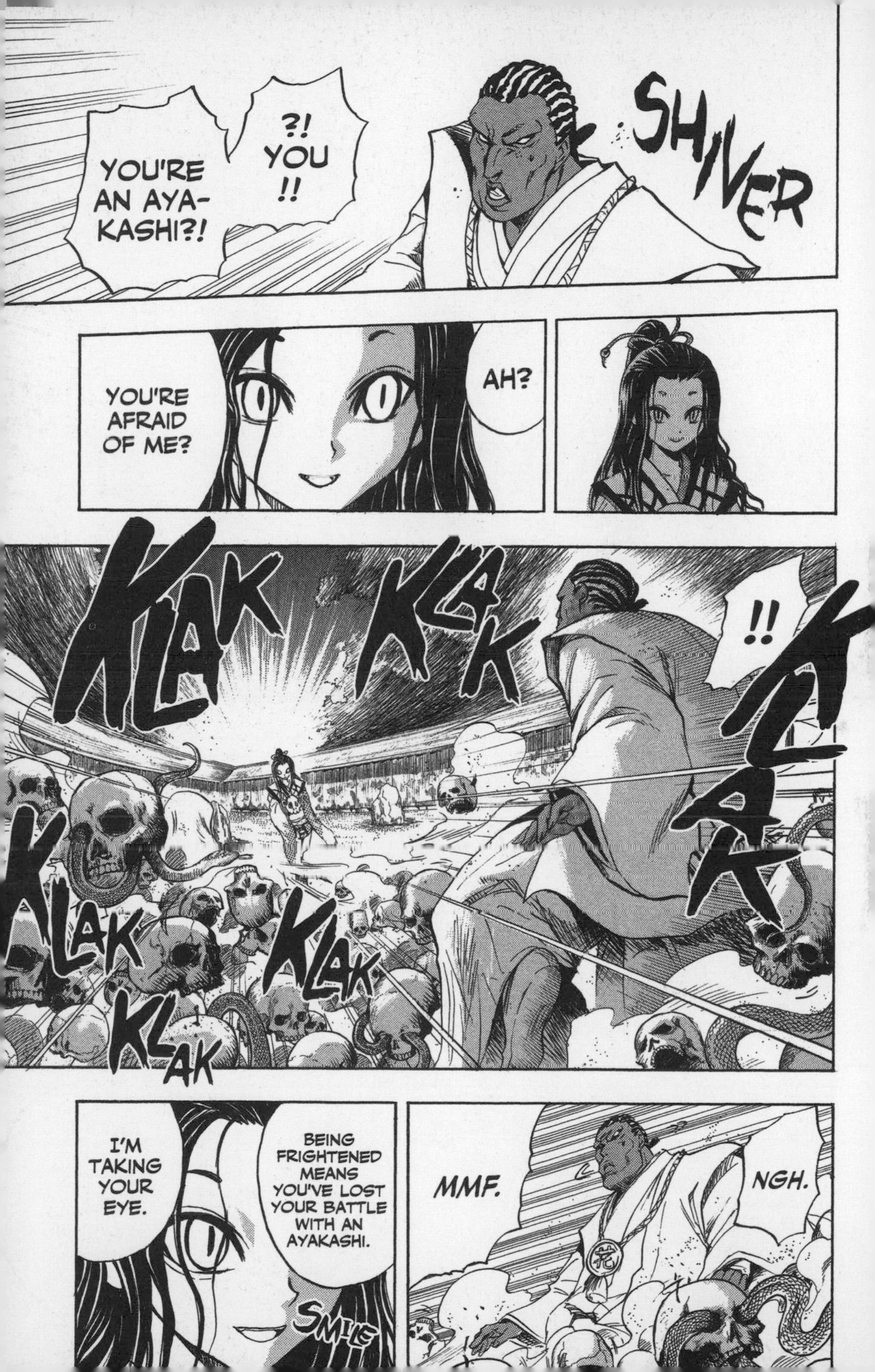
SHIVER
?! YOU !!
YOU'RE AN AYA-KASHI?!
AH?
YOU'RE AFRAID OF ME?
KLAK
!!
KLAK KLAK
KLAK
KLAK
KLAK
KLAK
NGH.
MMF.
BEING FRIGHTENED MEANS YOU'VE LOST YOUR BATTLE WITH AN AYAKASHI.
I'M TAKING YOUR EYE.
SMILE

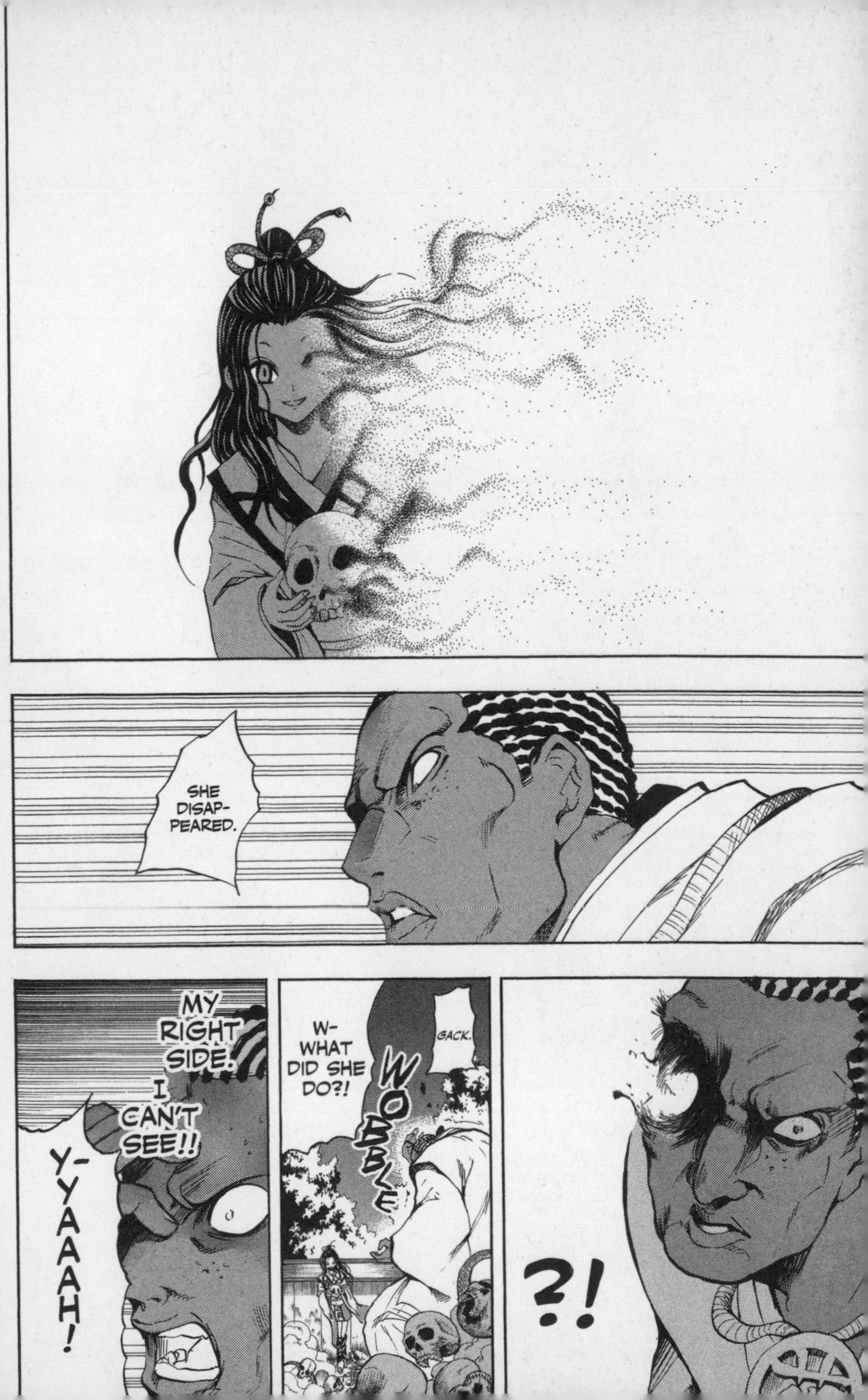
SHE DISAP-PEARED.
?!
GACK.
W- WHAT DID SHE DO?!
WOBBLE
MY RIGHT SIDE. I CAN'T SEE!!
Y-YAAAH!

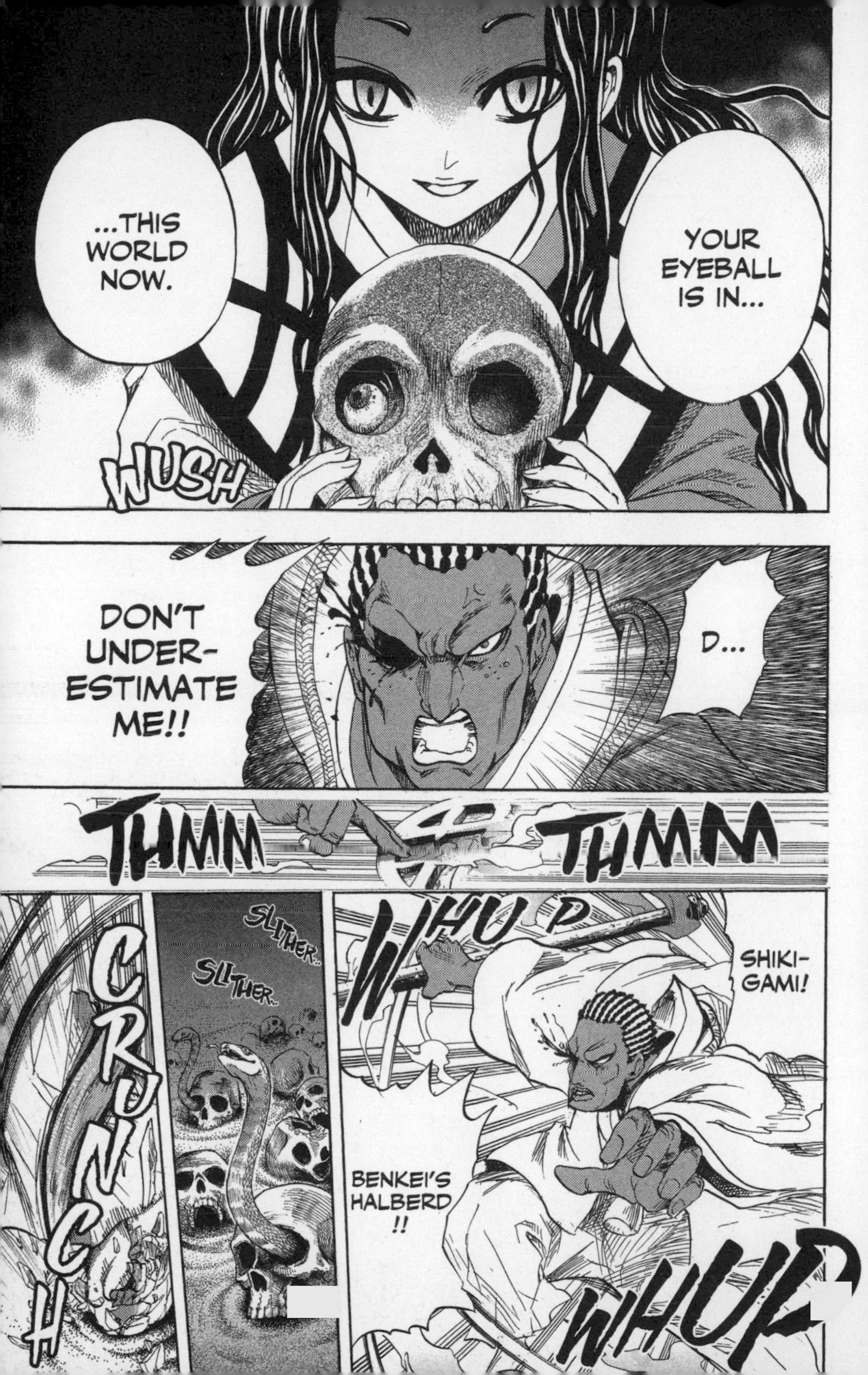
YOUR EYEBALL IS IN...
...THIS WORLD NOW.
WUSH
D...
DON'T UNDER-ESTIMATE ME!!
THMM
THMM
WHUP
SHIKI-GAMI!
BENKEI'S HALBERD !!
WHUP
SLITHER..
SLITHER..
CRUNCH

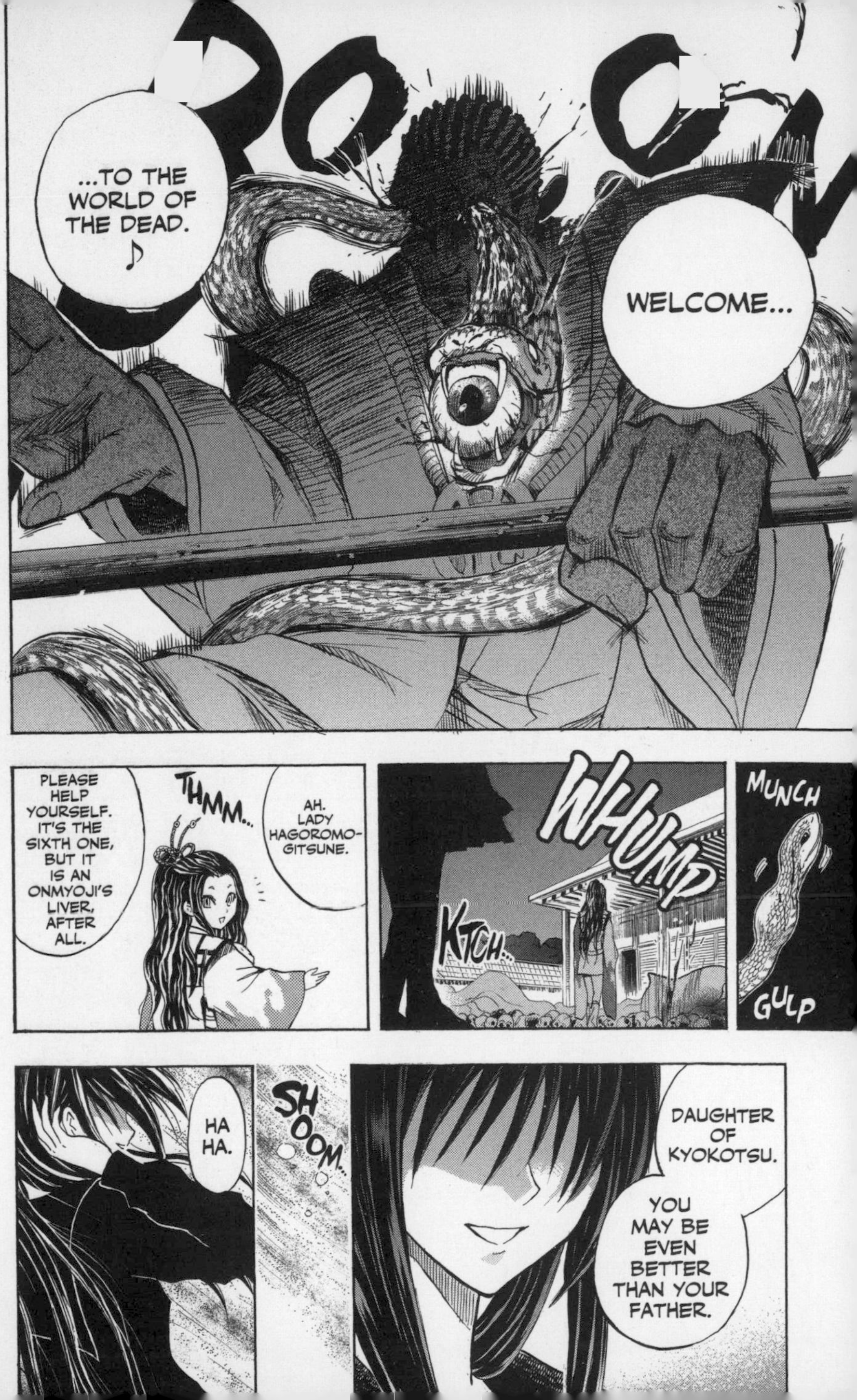
WELCOME...
...TO THE WORLD OF THE DEAD. ♪
MUNCH
GULP
WHUMP
KTCH...
AH. LADY HAGOROMO-GITSUNE.
THMM...
PLEASE HELP YOURSELF. IT'S THE SIXTH ONE, BUT IT IS AN ONMYOJI'S LIVER, AFTER ALL.
DAUGHTER OF KYOKOTSU.
YOU MAY BE EVEN BETTER THAN YOUR FATHER.
SHOOM...
HA HA.

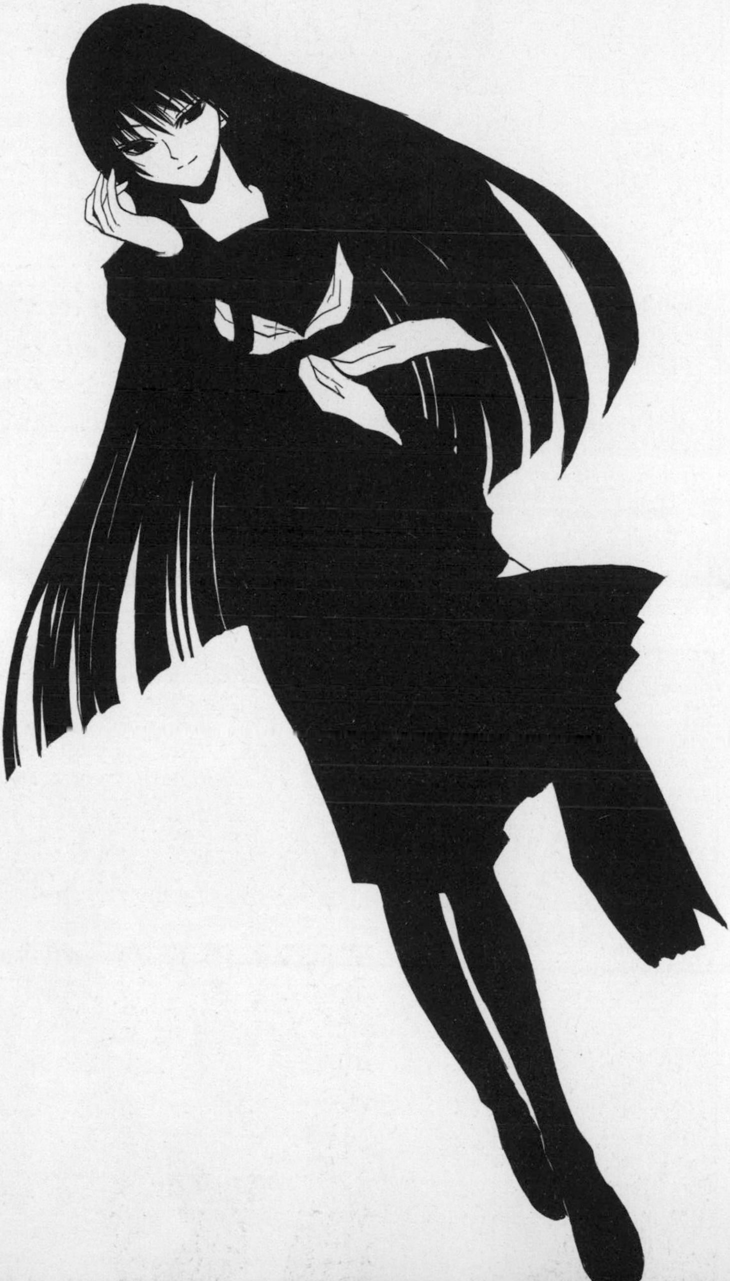

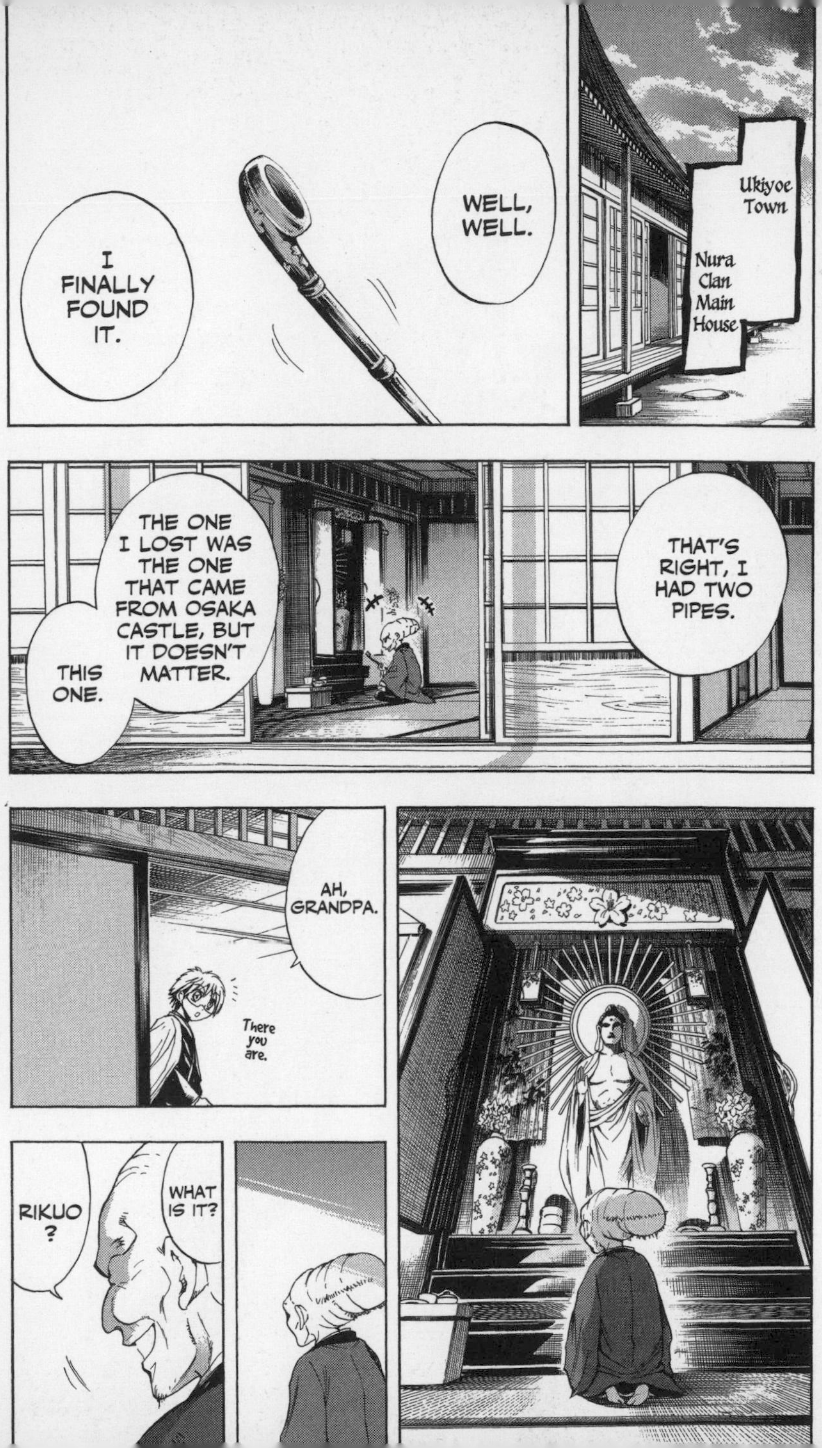
Ukiyoe Town
Nura Clan Main House
WELL, WELL.
I FINALLY FOUND IT.
THAT'S RIGHT, I HAD TWO PIPES.
THE ONE I LOST WAS THE ONE THAT CAME FROM OSAKA CASTLE, BUT IT DOESN'T MATTER.
THIS ONE.
AH, GRANDPA.
There you are.
WHAT IS IT?
RIKUO?

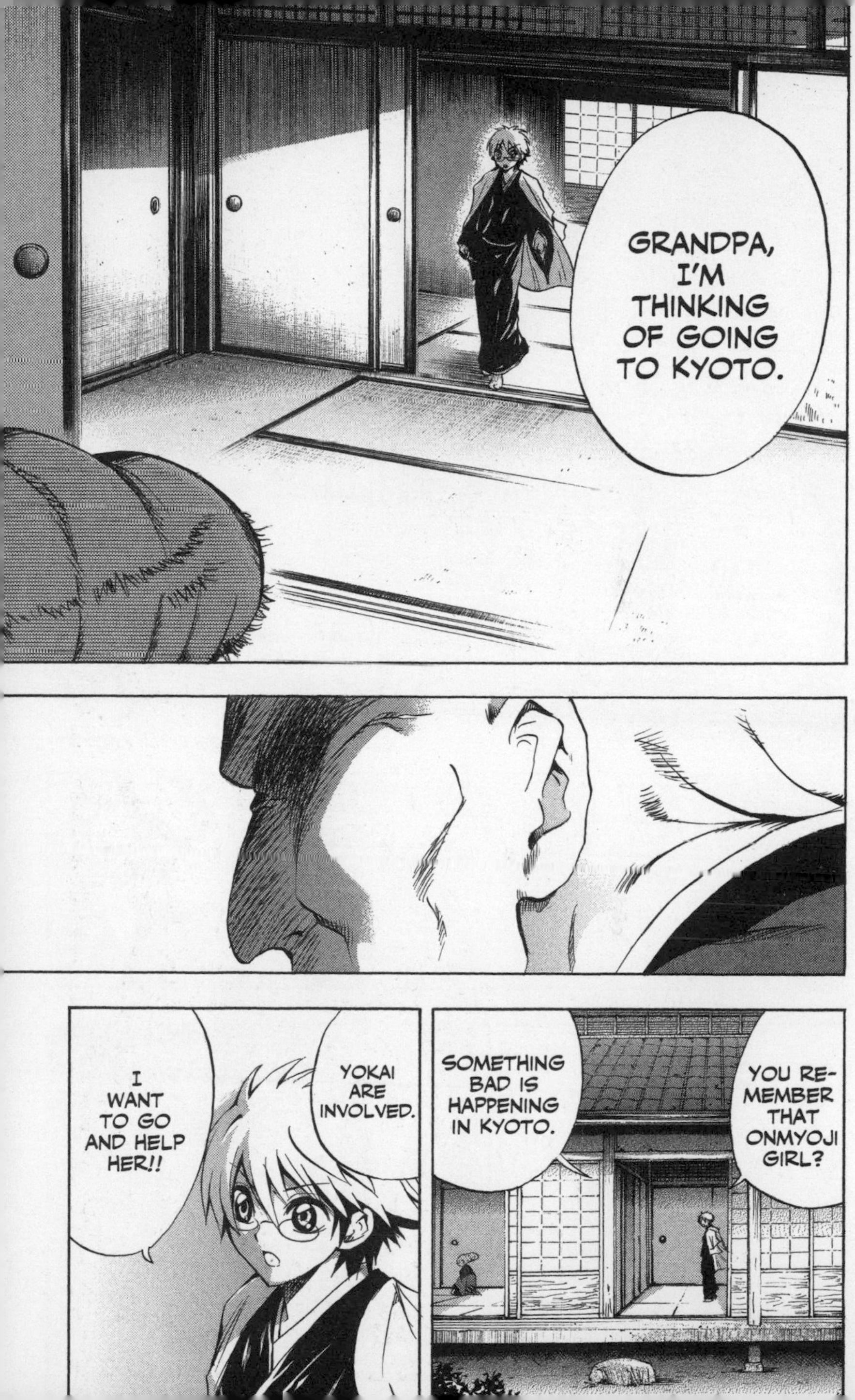
GRANDPA, I'M THINKING OF GOING TO KYOTO.
YOU RE-MEMBER THAT ONMYOJI GIRL?
SOMETHING BAD IS HAPPENING IN KYOTO.
YOKAI ARE INVOLVED.
I WANT TO GO AND HELP HER!!

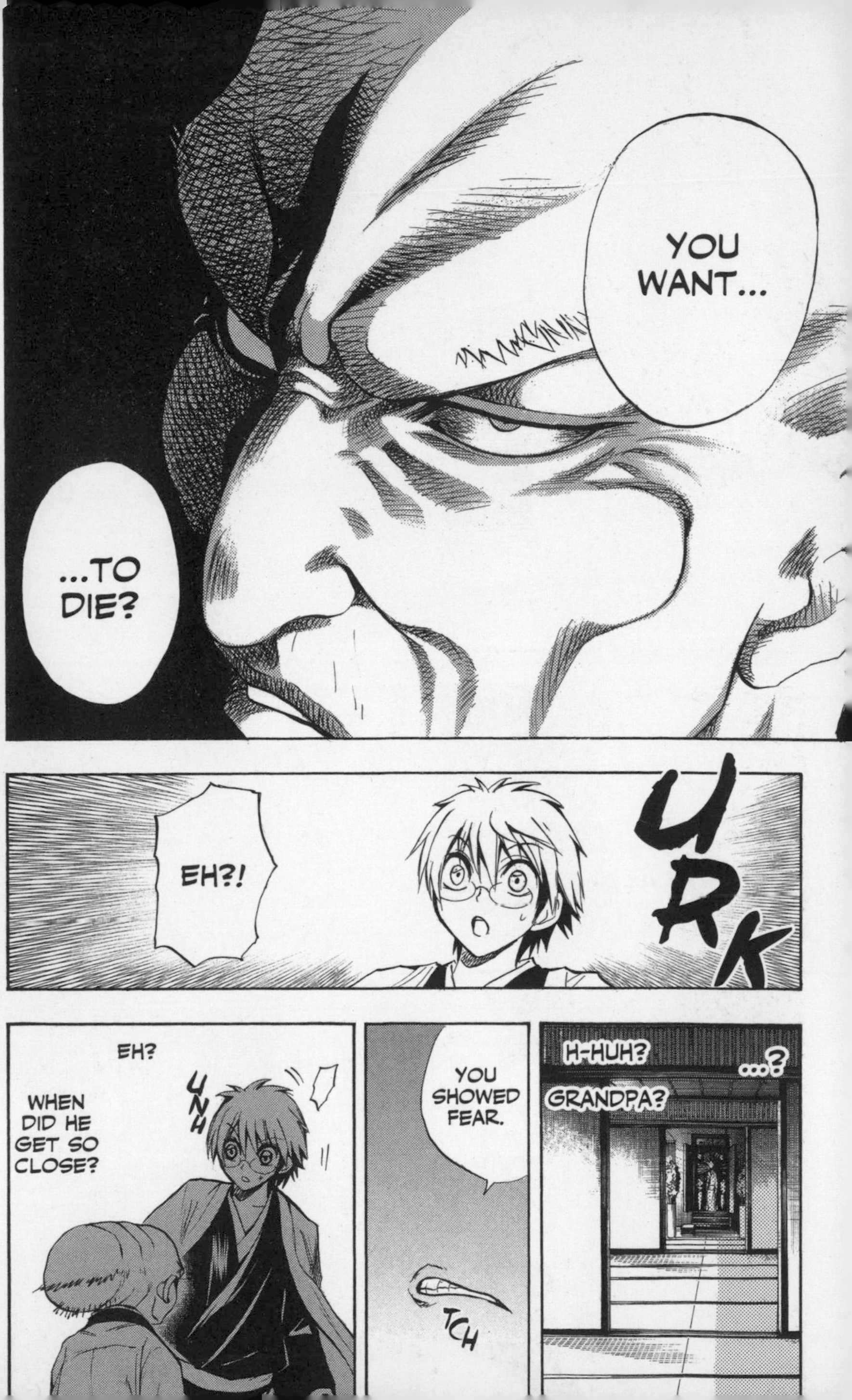
YOU WANT...
...TO DIE?
URK
EH?!
H-HUH?
...?
GRANDPA?
YOU SHOWED FEAR.
TCH
UNH
!
EH?
WHEN DID HE GET SO CLOSE?

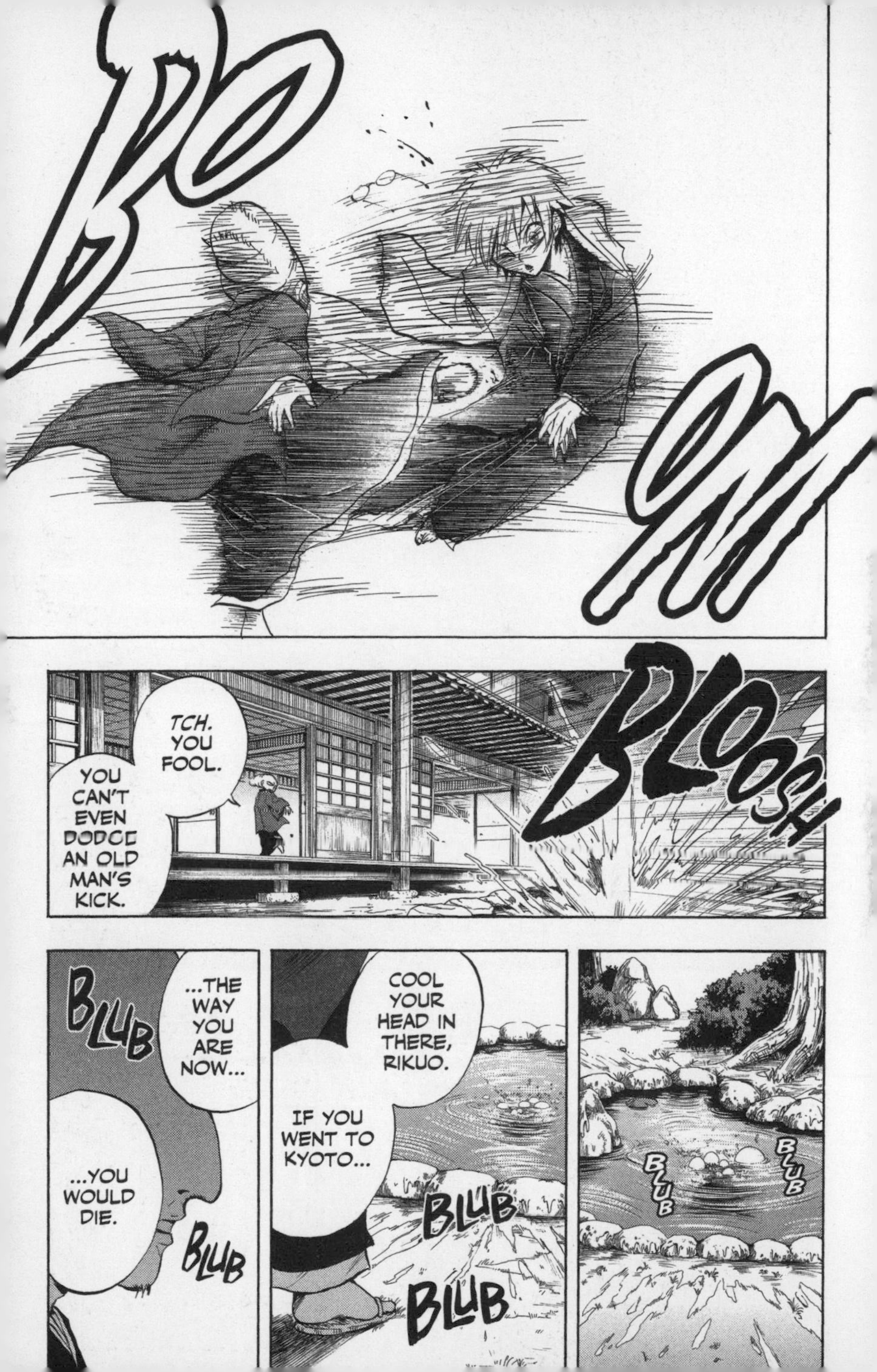

BLOOSH
TCH. YOU FOOL.
YOU CAN'T EVEN DODGE AN OLD MAN'S KICK.
BLUB
BLUB
COOL YOUR HEAD IN THERE, RIKUO.
IF YOU WENT TO KYOTO...
BLUB
BLUB
...THE WAY YOU ARE NOW...
...YOU WOULD DIE.
BLUB
BLUB

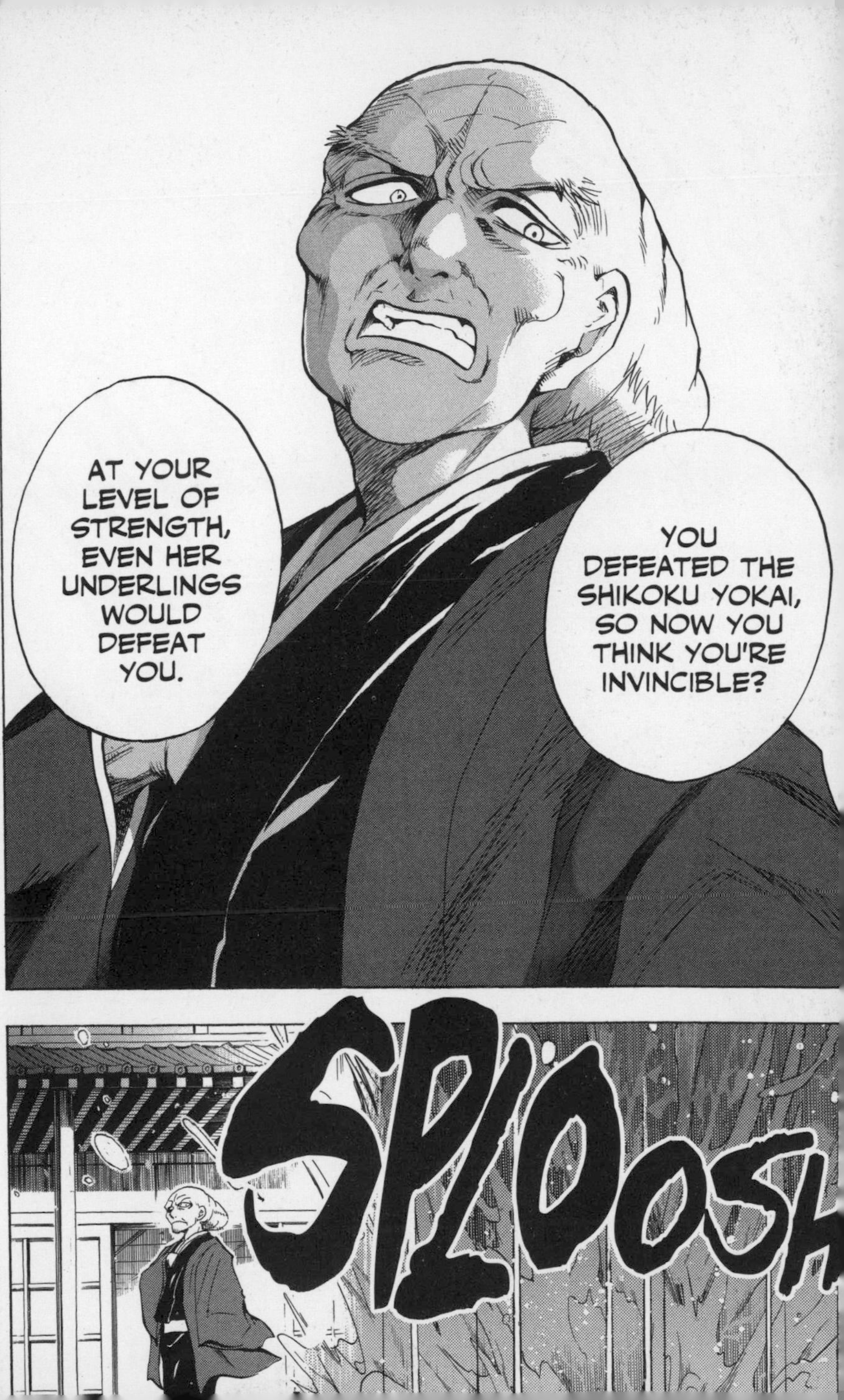
YOU DEFEATED THE SHIKOKU YOKAI, SO NOW YOU THINK YOU'RE INVINCIBLE?
AT YOUR LEVEL OF STRENGTH, EVEN HER UNDERLINGS WOULD DEFEAT YOU.
SPLOOSH

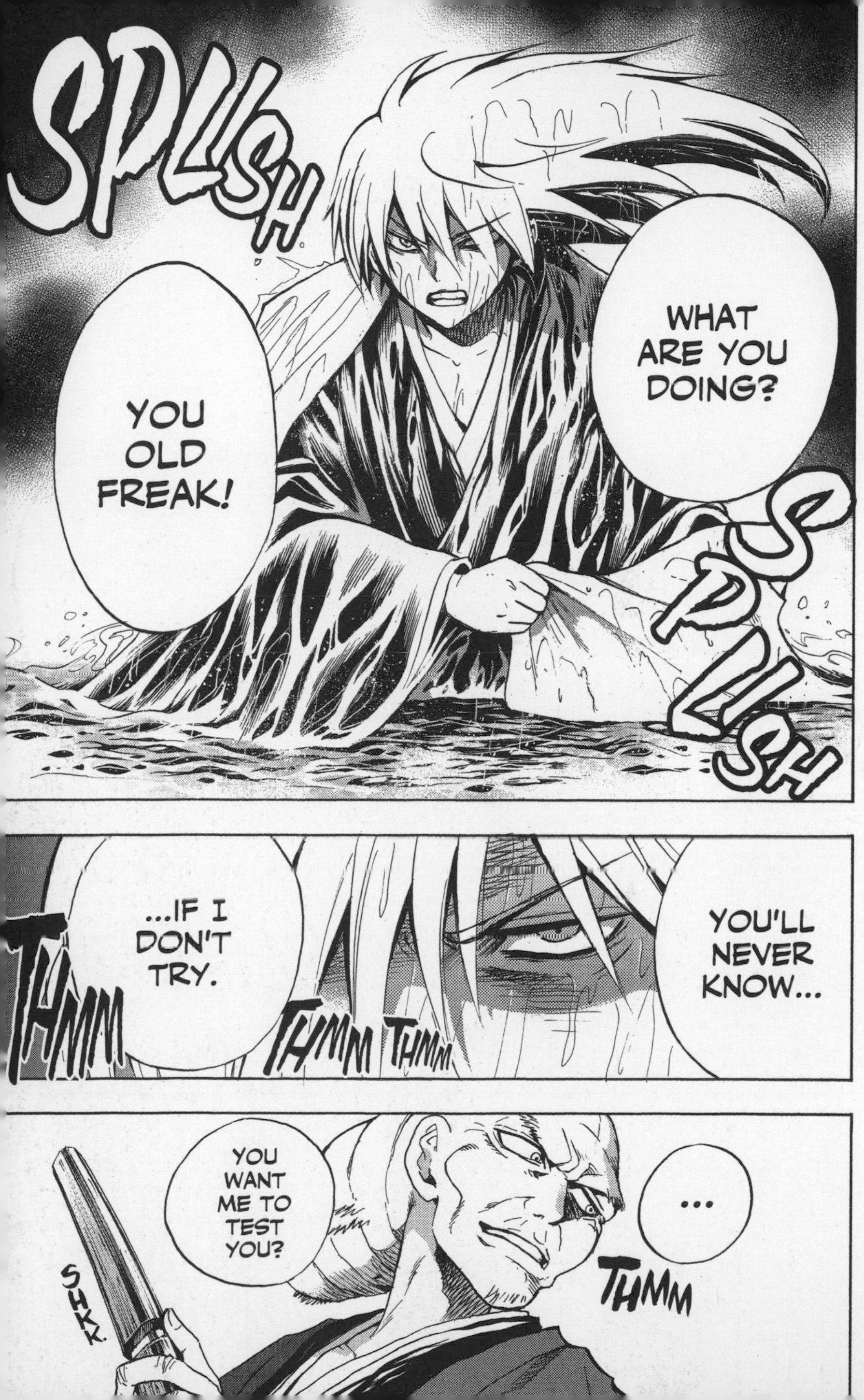
SPLUSH
WHAT ARE YOU DOING?
YOU OLD FREAK!
SPLUSH
YOU'LL NEVER KNOW...
...IF I DON'T TRY.
THMM THMM
THMM
...
YOU WANT ME TO TEST YOU?
THMM
SHKK.

NURA: RISE OF THE YOKAI CLAN

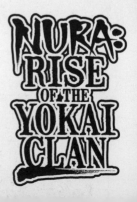

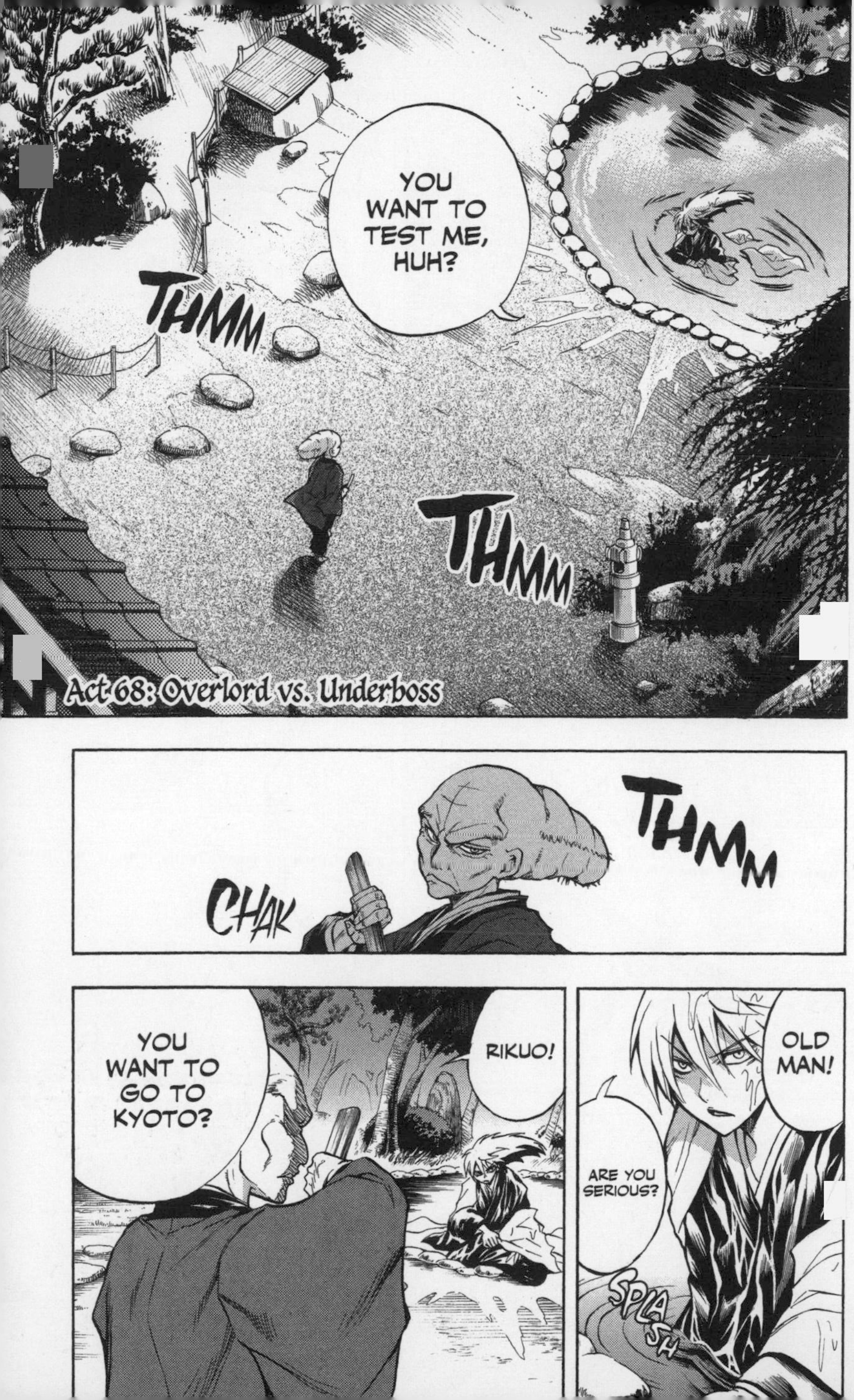
YOU WANT TO TEST ME, HUH?
THMM
THMM
Act 68: Overlord vs. Underboss
THMM
CHAK
OLD MAN!
ARE YOU SERIOUS?
SPLASH
RIKUO!
YOU WANT TO GO TO KYOTO?

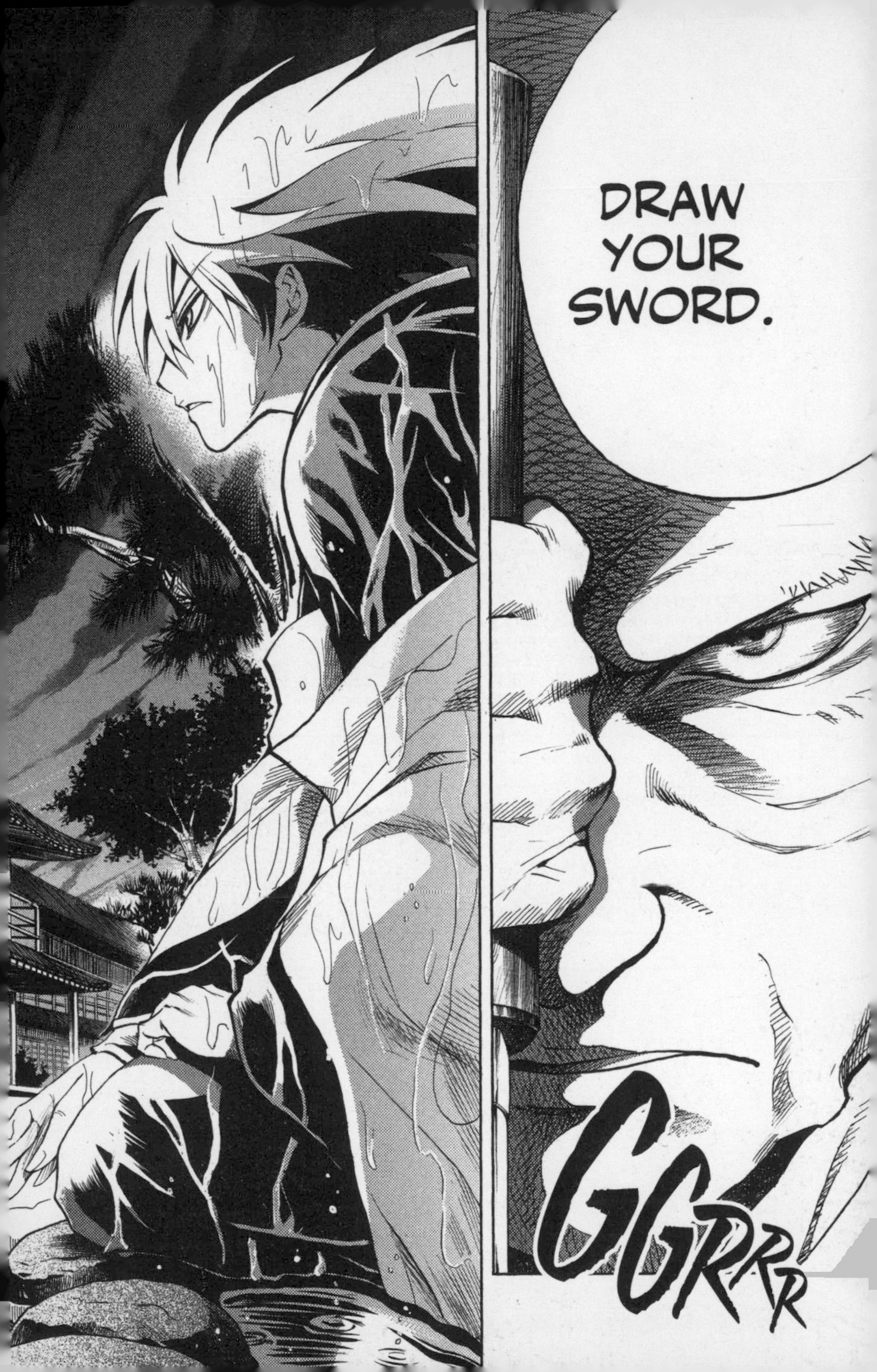
DRAW YOUR SWORD.
GGRRRR

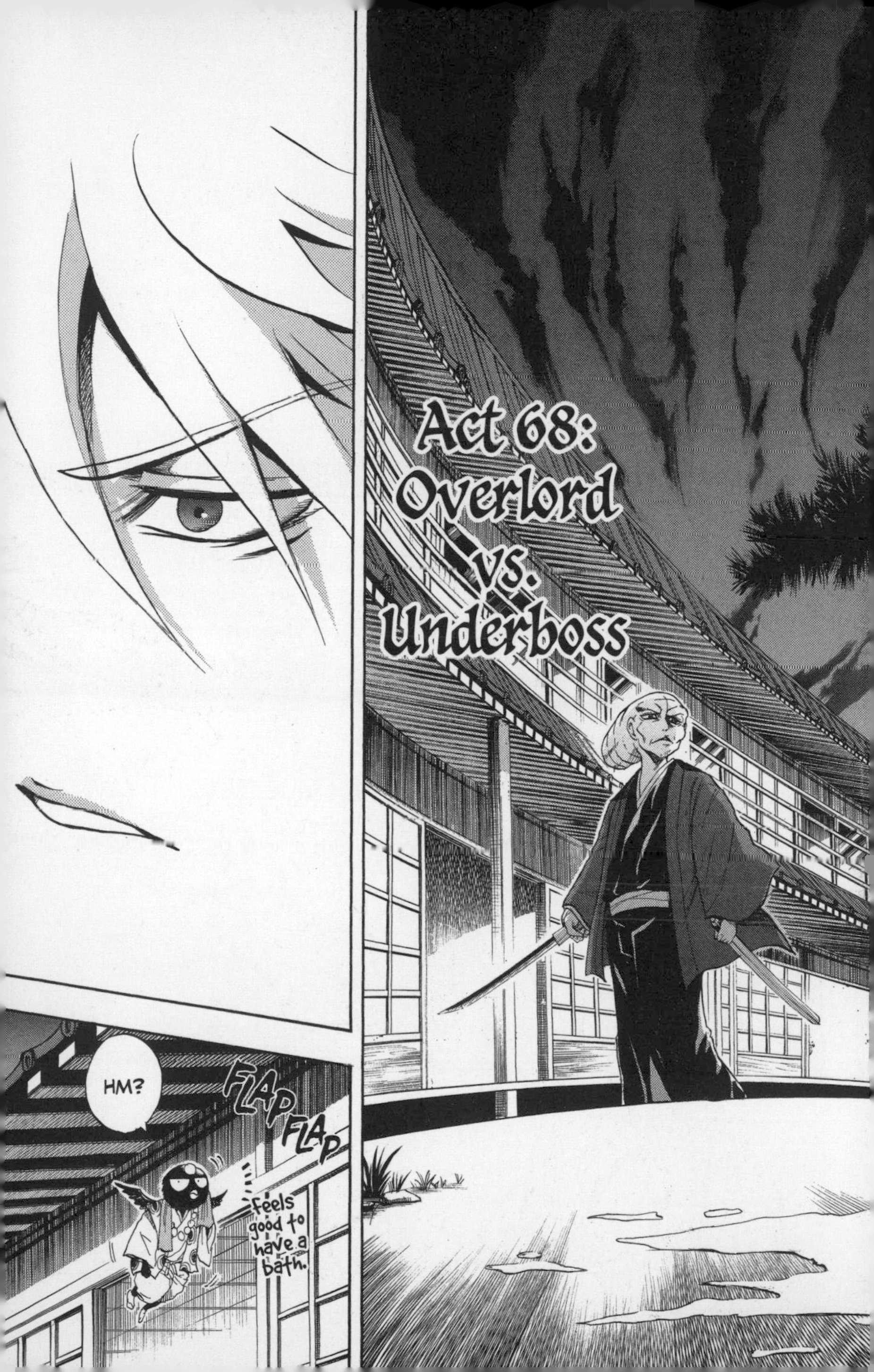
Act 68:
Overlord
vs.
Underboss
FLAP FLAP
HM?
feels good to have a bath.

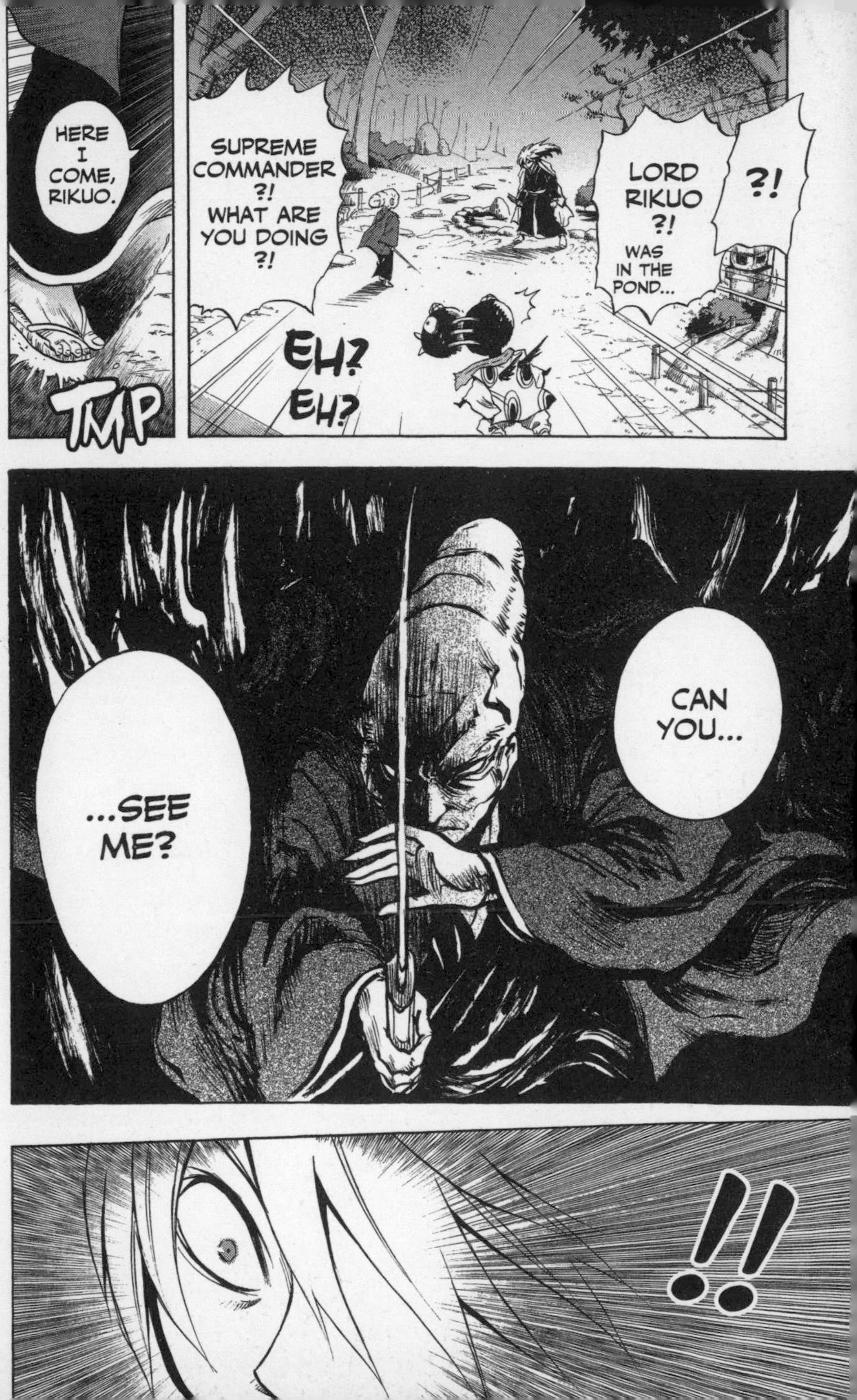
?!
LORD RIKUO ?! WAS IN THE POND...
SUPREME COMMANDER ?! WHAT ARE YOU DOING ?!
EH? EH?
HERE I COME, RIKUO.
TMP
CAN YOU...
...SEE ME?
!!

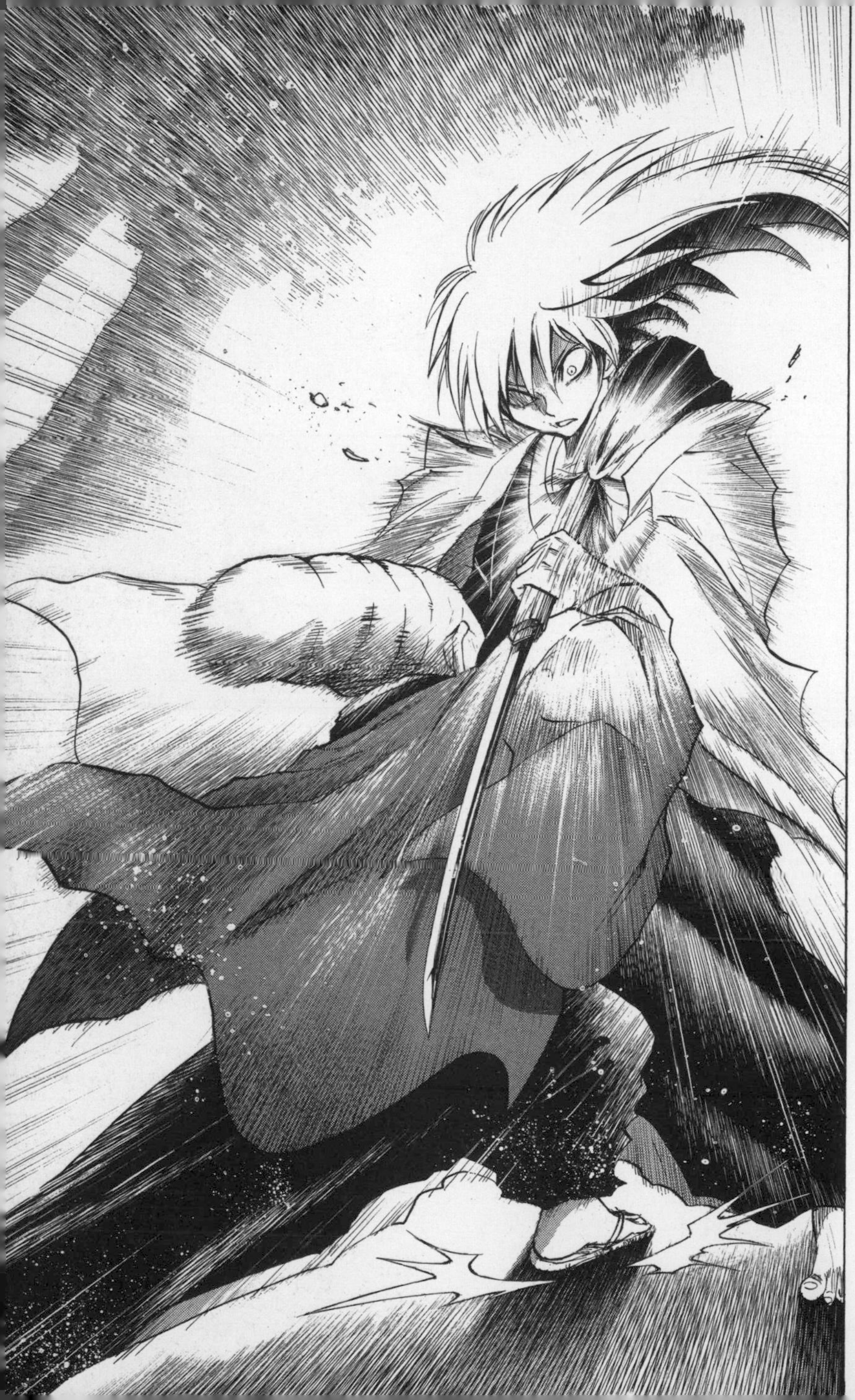

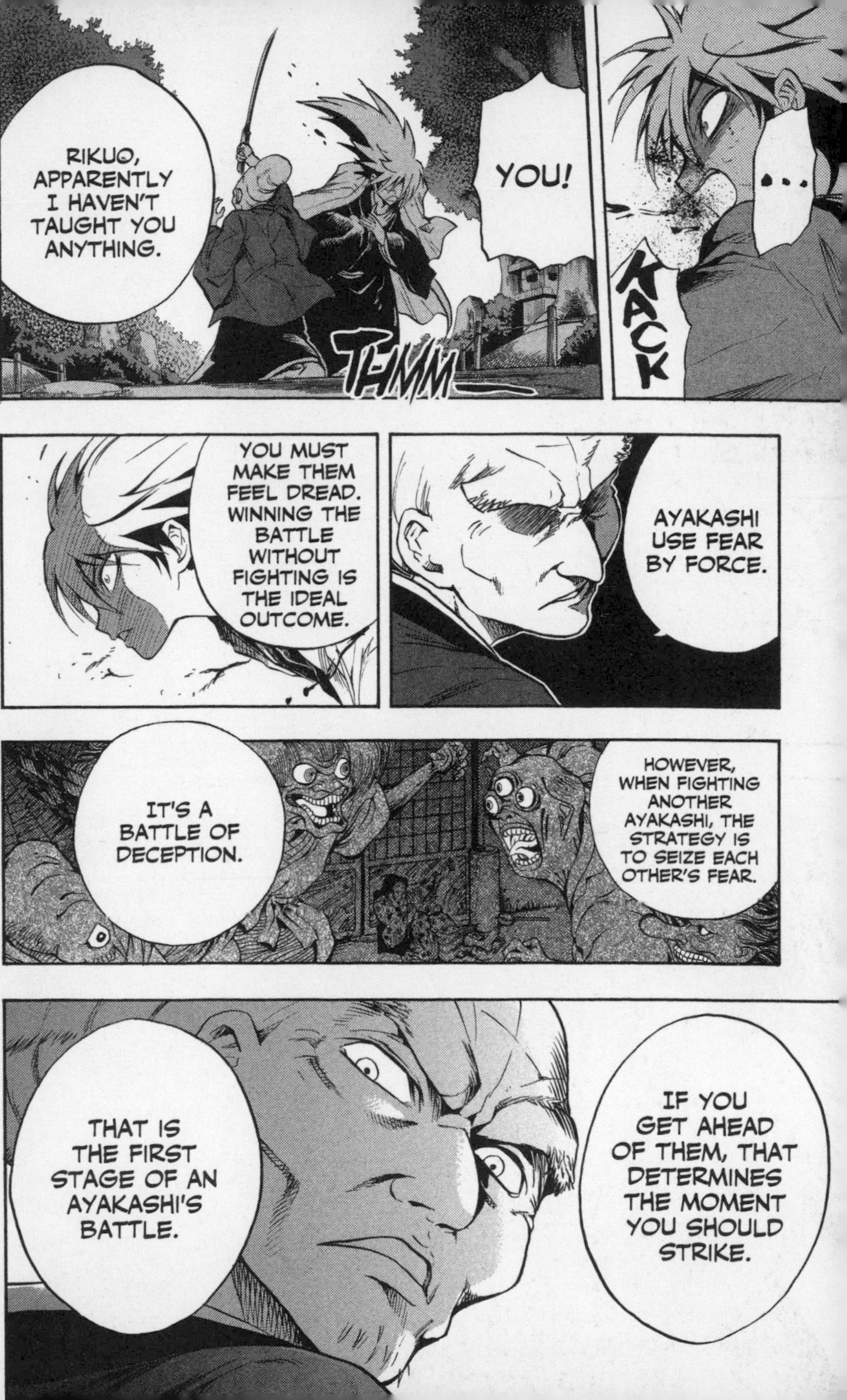
...
KACK
YOU!
RIKUO, APPARENTLY I HAVEN'T TAUGHT YOU ANYTHING.
THMM
AYAKASHI USE FEAR BY FORCE.
YOU MUST MAKE THEM FEEL DREAD. WINNING THE BATTLE WITHOUT FIGHTING IS THE IDEAL OUTCOME.
HOWEVER, WHEN FIGHTING ANOTHER AYAKASHI, THE STRATEGY IS TO SEIZE EACH OTHER'S FEAR.
IT'S A BATTLE OF DECEPTION.
IF YOU GET AHEAD OF THEM, THAT DETERMINES THE MOMENT YOU SHOULD STRIKE.
THAT IS THE FIRST STAGE OF AN AYAKASHI'S BATTLE.

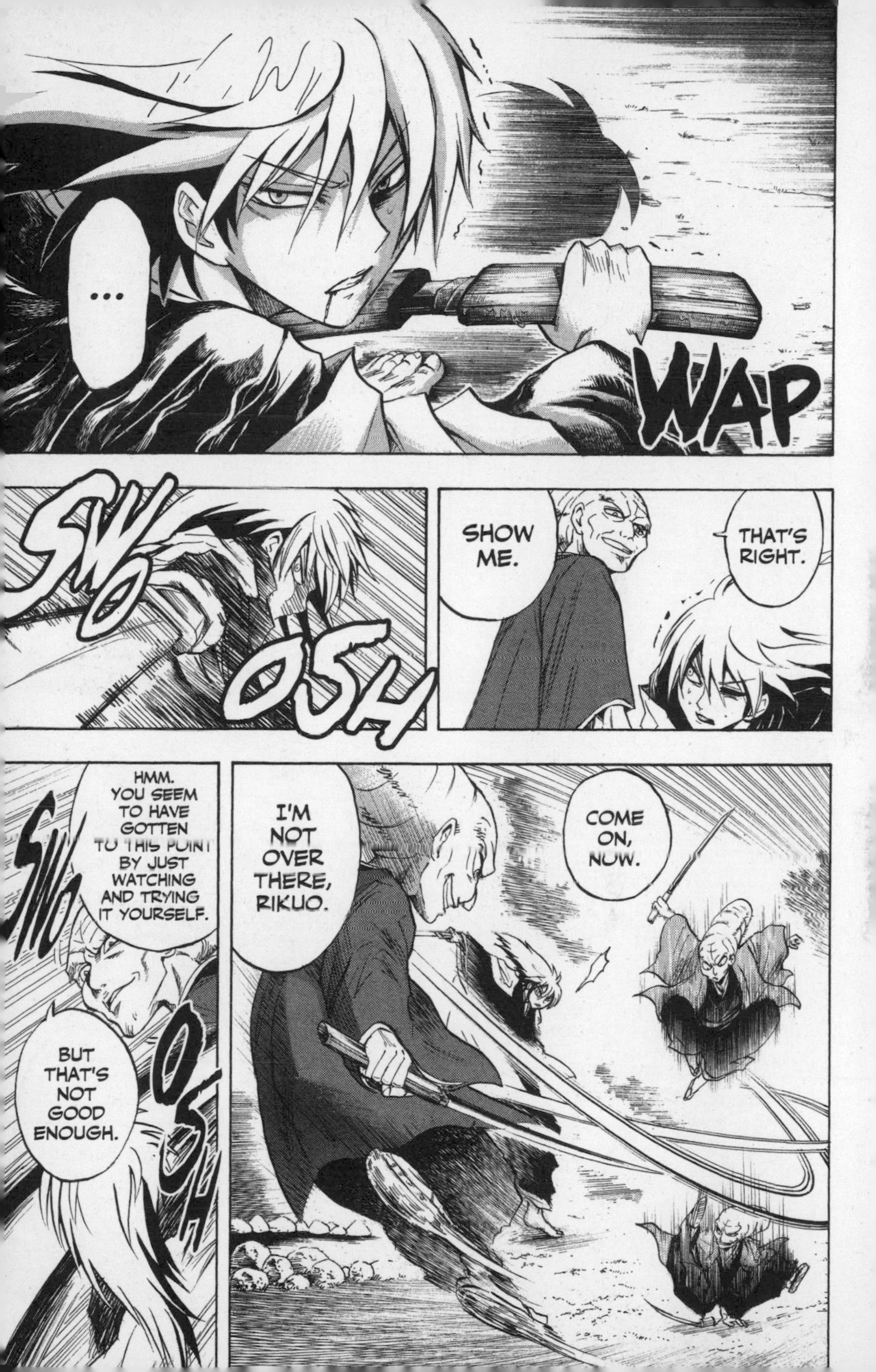
...
WAP
THAT'S RIGHT.
SHOW ME.
SWOOSH
COME ON, NOW.
I'M NOT OVER THERE, RIKUO.
HMM. YOU SEEM TO HAVE GOTTEN TO THIS POINT BY JUST WATCHING AND TRYING IT YOURSELF.
BUT THAT'S NOT GOOD ENOUGH.
SWOOSH

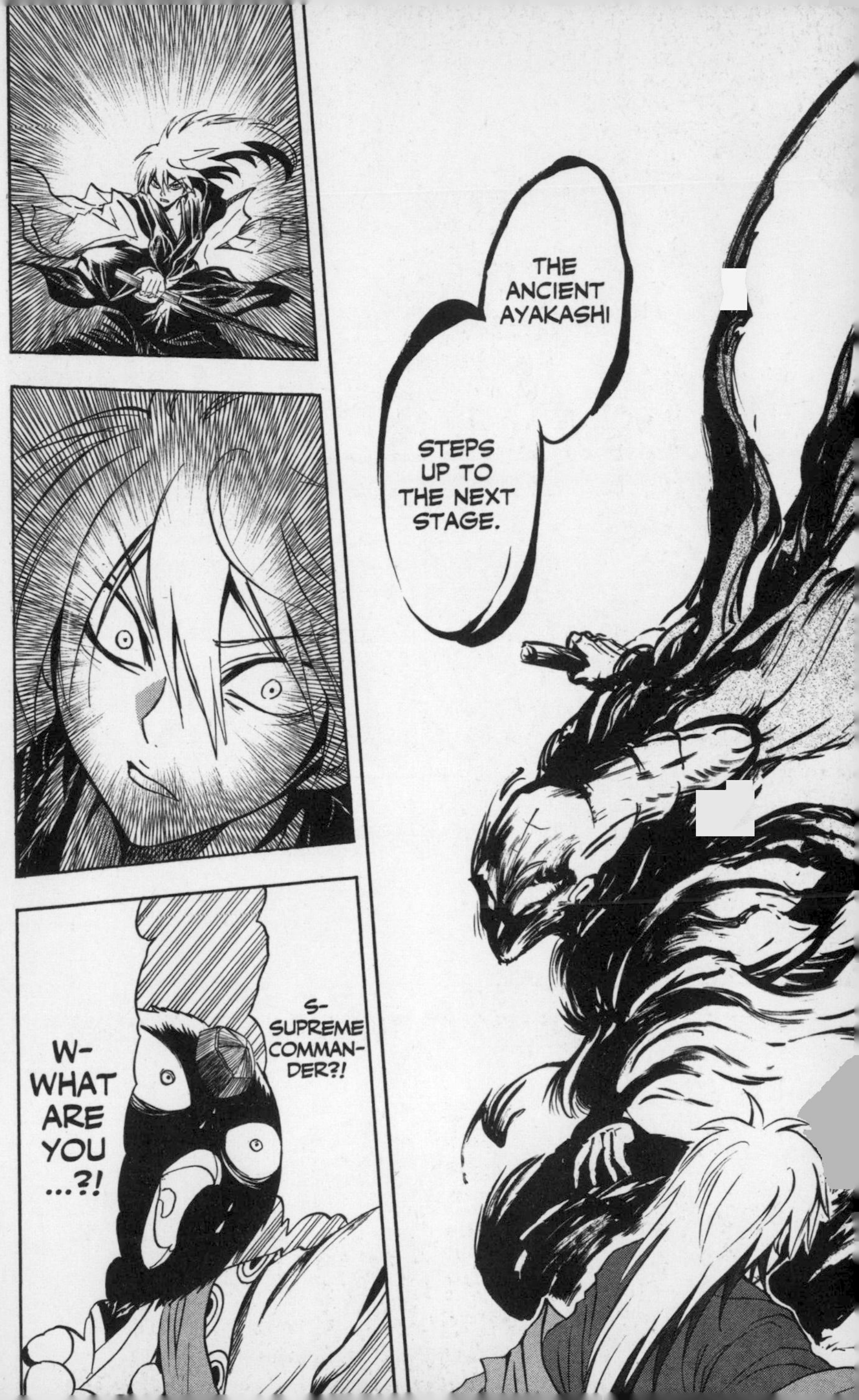
THE ANCIENT AYAKASHI
STEPS UP TO THE NEXT STAGE.
S-SUPREME COMMANDER?!
W-WHAT ARE YOU ...?!

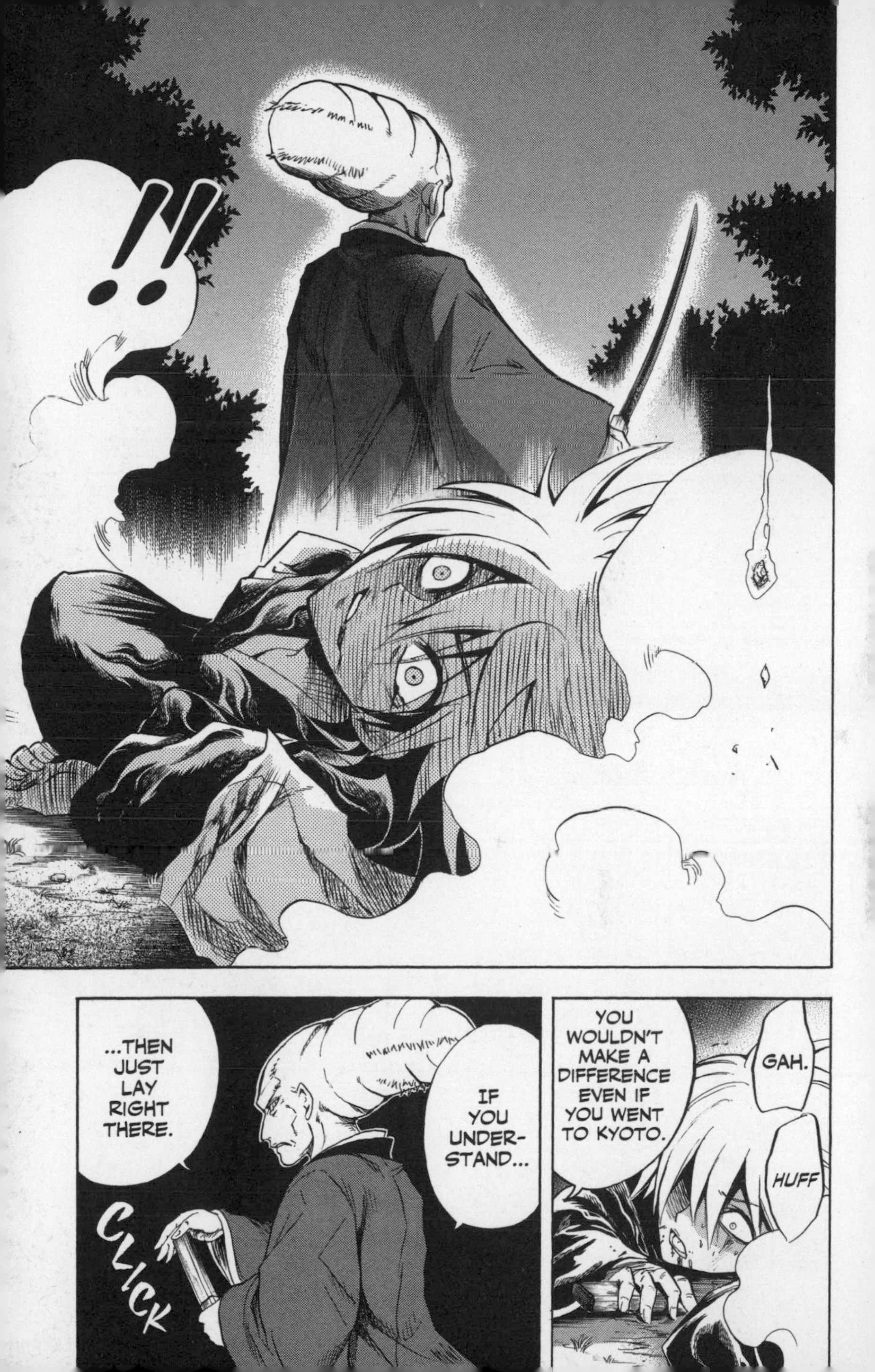
!!
GAH.
YOU WOULDN'T MAKE A DIFFERENCE EVEN IF YOU WENT TO KYOTO.
HUFF
IF YOU UNDER-STAND...
...THEN JUST LAY RIGHT THERE.
CLICK

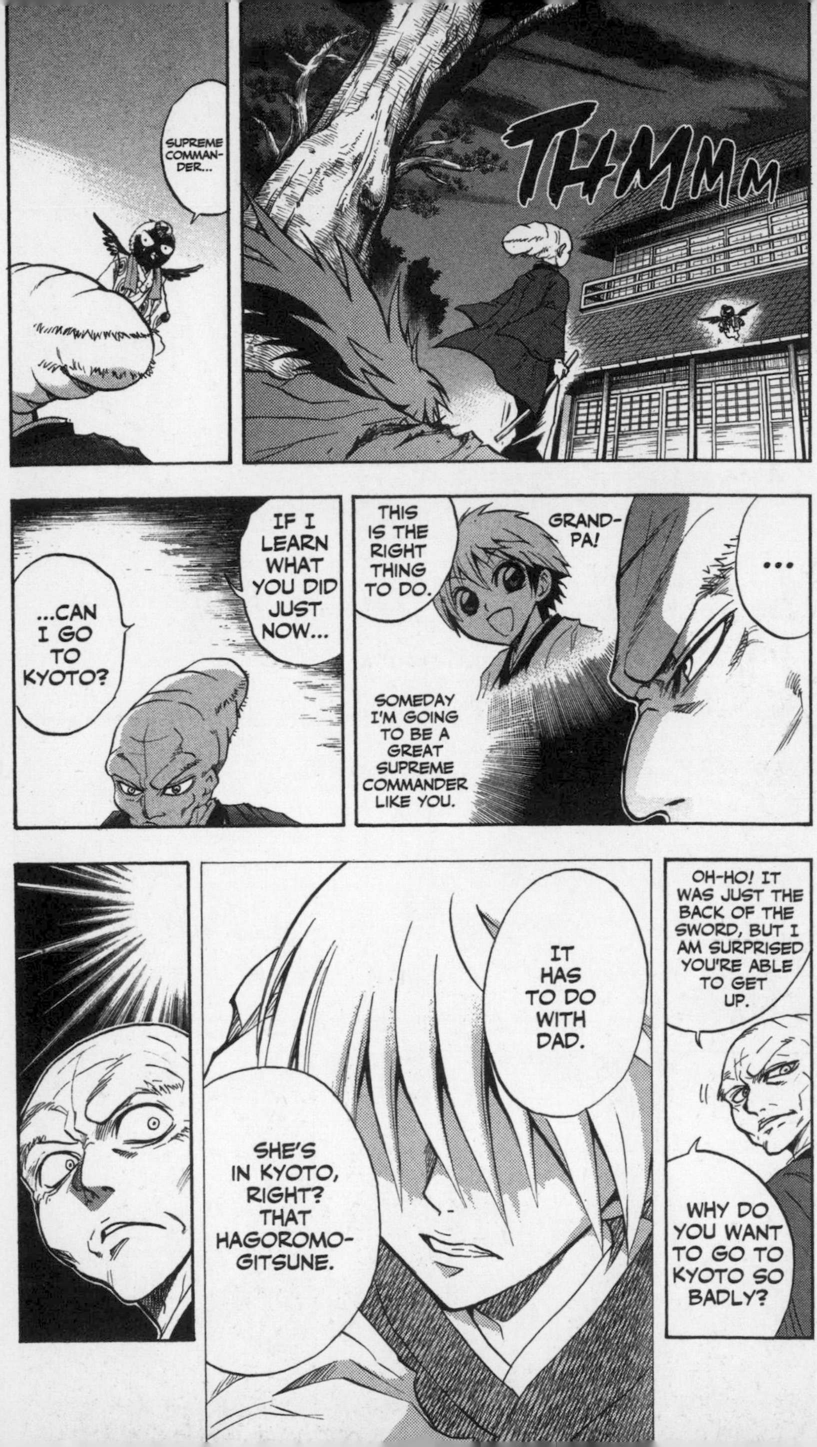
THMMM
SUPREME COMMANDER...
...
GRANDPA!
THIS IS THE RIGHT THING TO DO.
SOMEDAY I'M GOING TO BE A GREAT SUPREME COMMANDER LIKE YOU.
IF I LEARN WHAT YOU DID JUST NOW...
...CAN I GO TO KYOTO?
OH-HO! IT WAS JUST THE BACK OF THE SWORD, BUT I AM SURPRISED YOU'RE ABLE TO GET UP.
WHY DO YOU WANT TO GO TO KYOTO SO BADLY?
IT HAS TO DO WITH DAD.
SHE'S IN KYOTO, RIGHT? THAT HAGOROMO-GITSUNE.

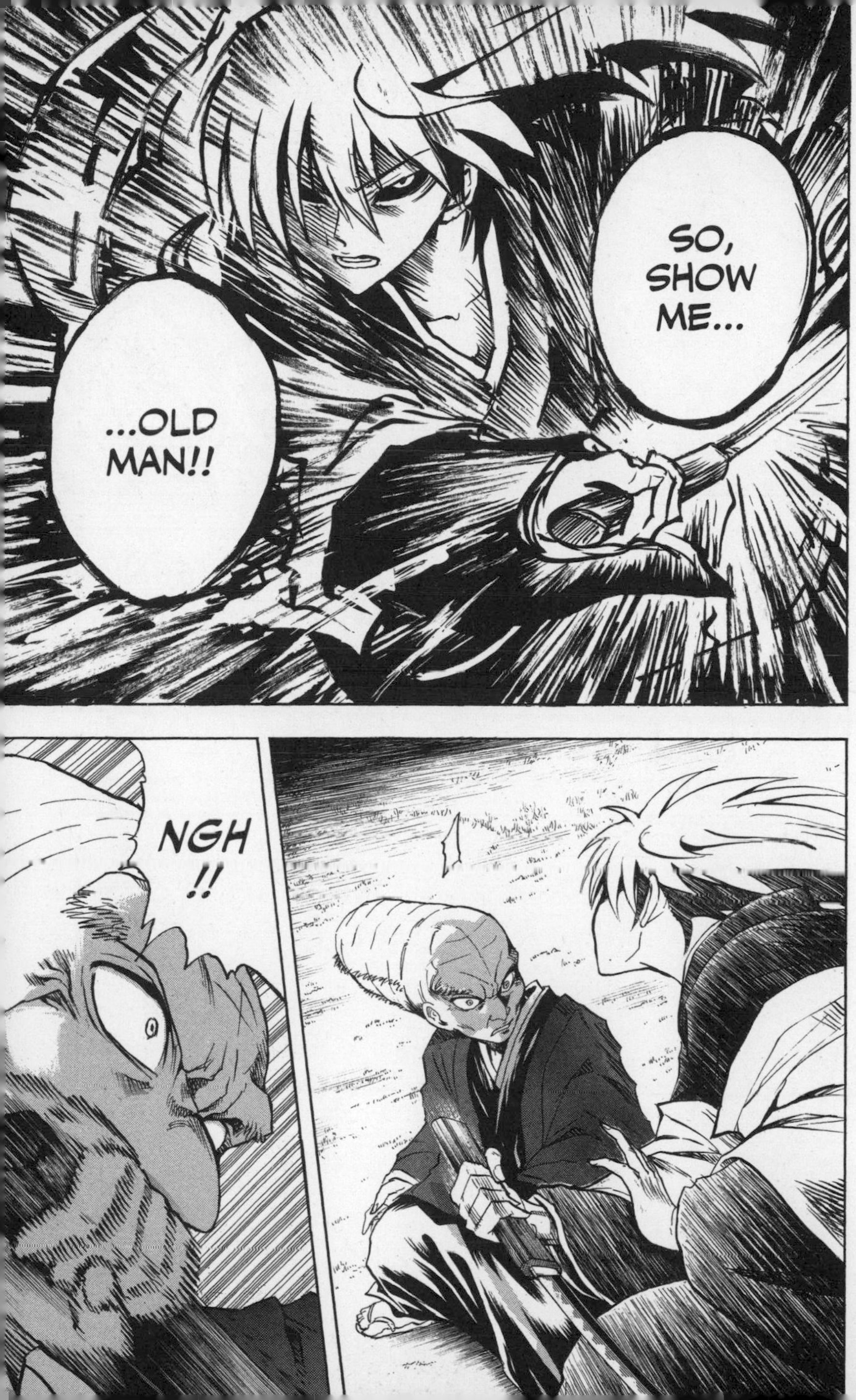
SO, SHOW ME...
...OLD MAN!!
NGH !!

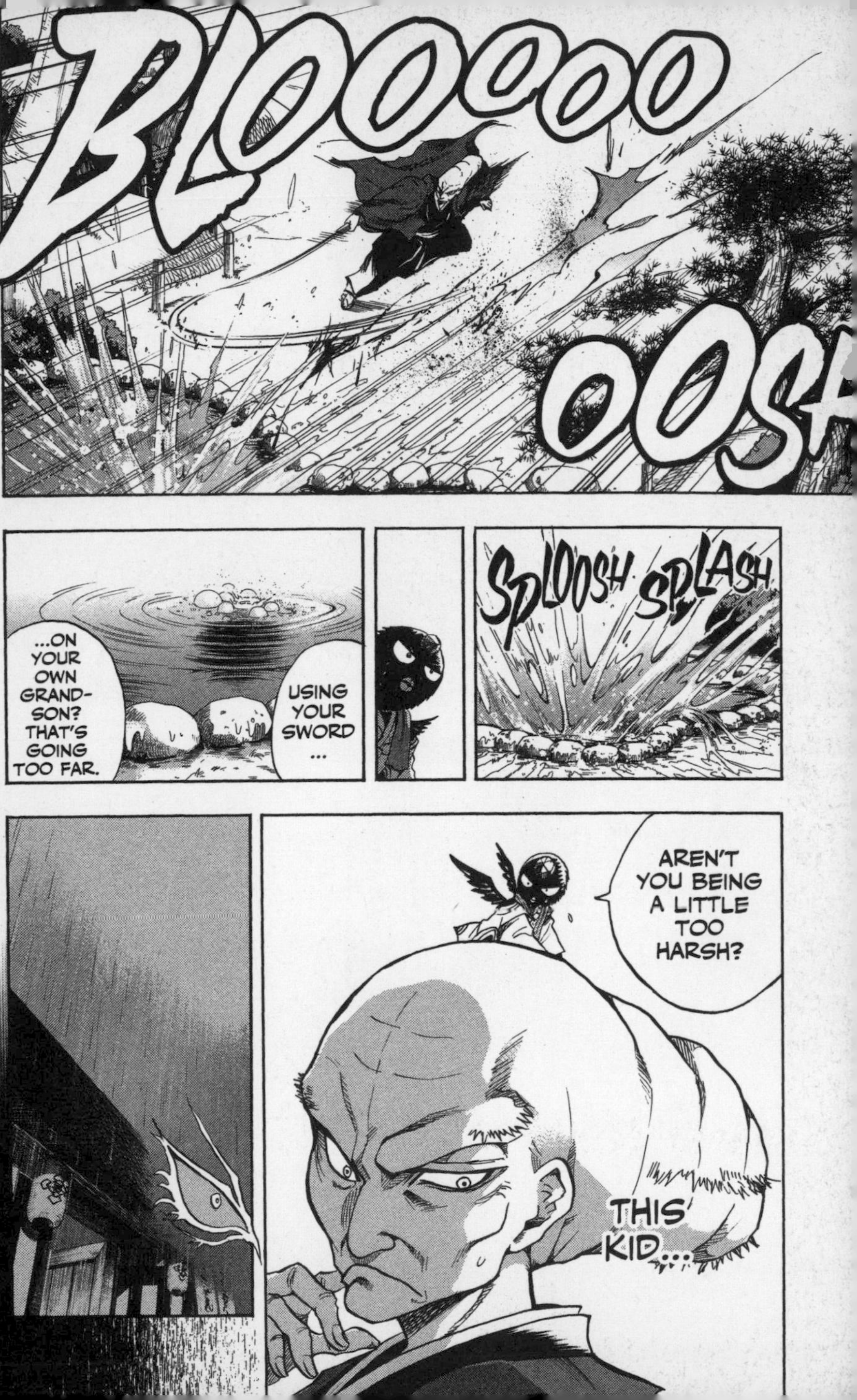
BLOOOOO
OOSH
SPLOOSH SPLASH
USING YOUR SWORD...
...ON YOUR OWN GRANDSON? THAT'S GOING TOO FAR.
AREN'T YOU BEING A LITTLE TOO HARSH?
THIS KID...

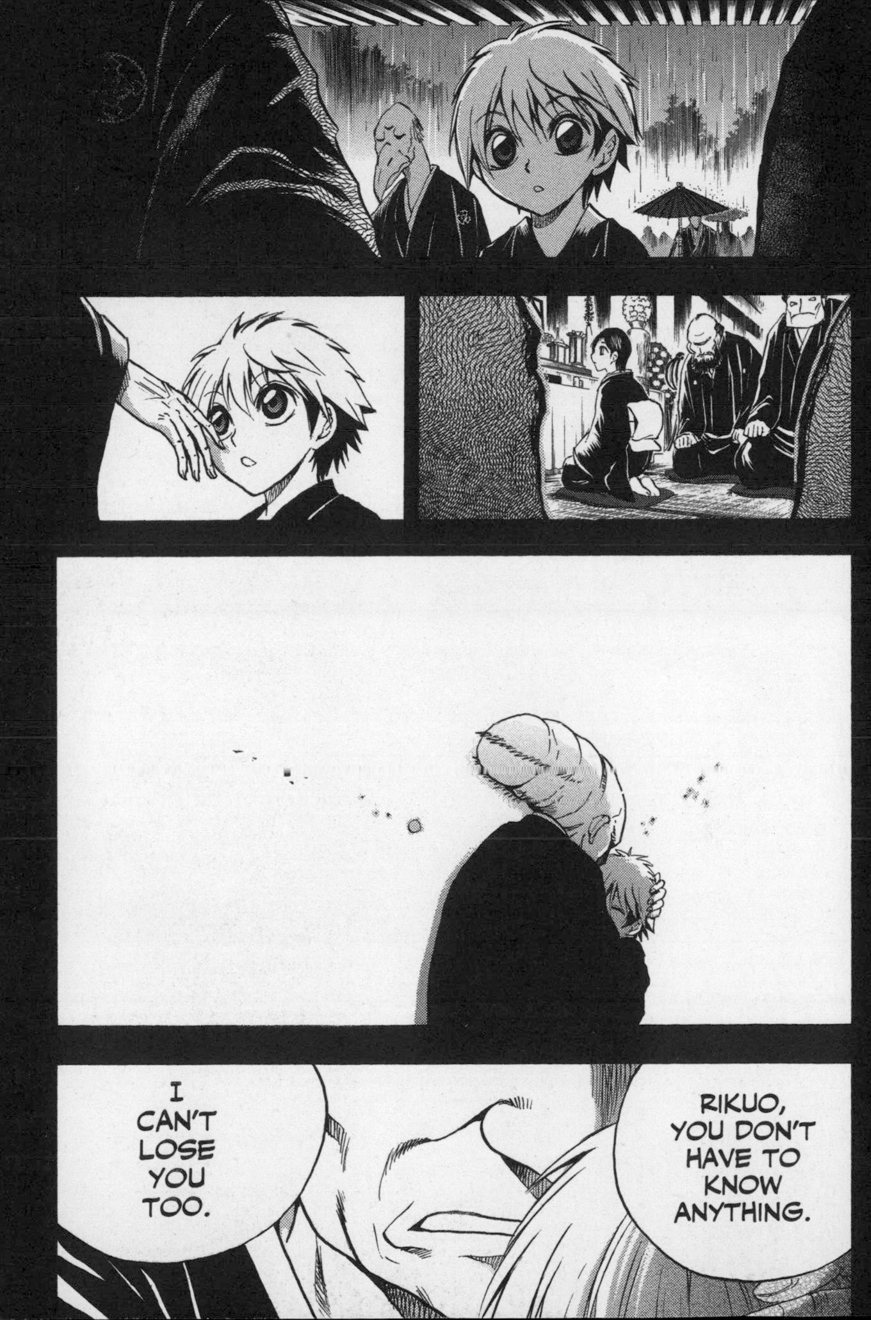
RIKUO, YOU DON'T HAVE TO KNOW ANYTHING.
I CAN'T LOSE YOU TOO.

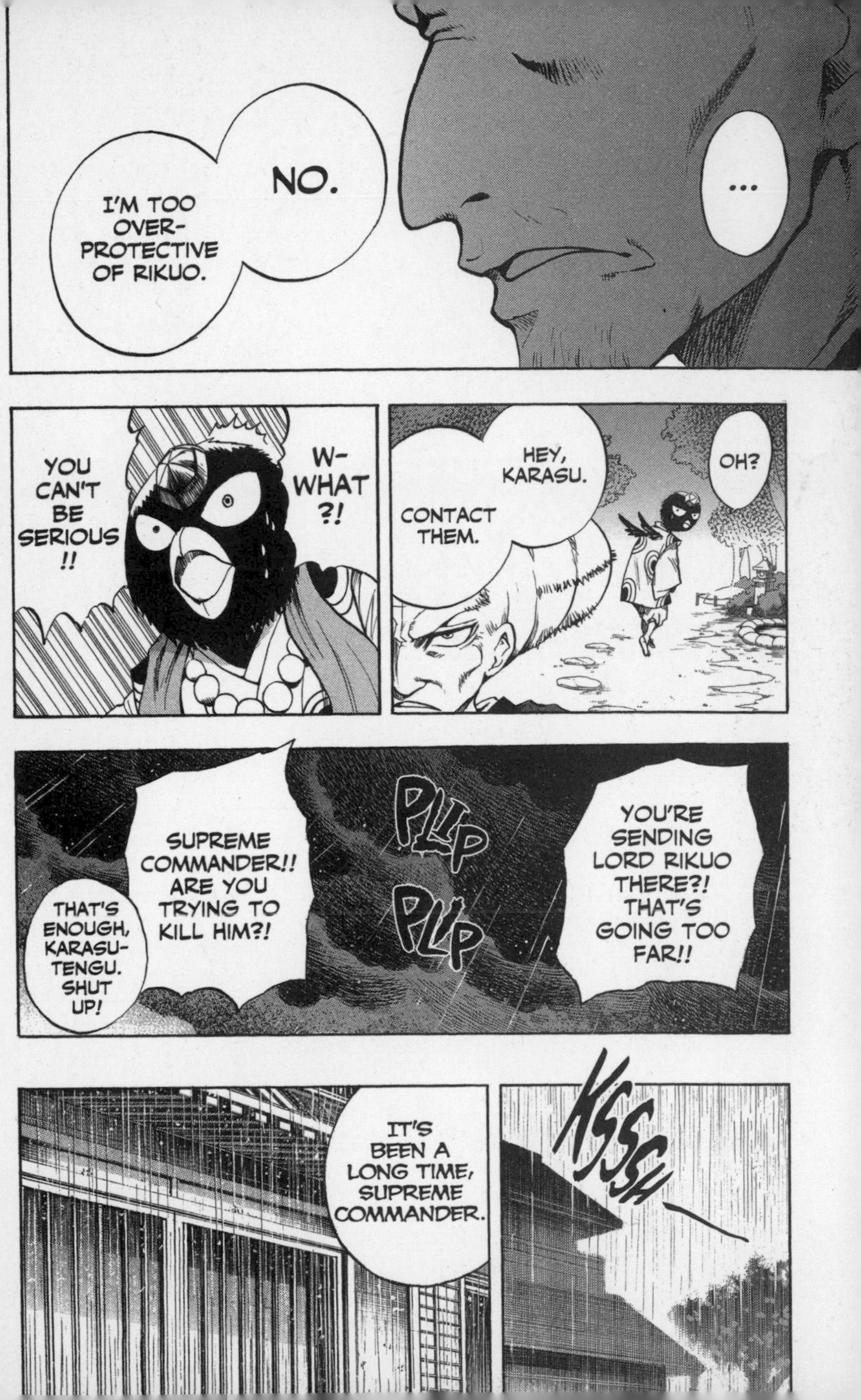
...
NO.
I'M TOO OVER-PROTECTIVE OF RIKUO.
OH?
HEY, KARASU.
CONTACT THEM.
W-WHAT?!
YOU CAN'T BE SERIOUS!!
YOU'RE SENDING LORD RIKUO THERE?! THAT'S GOING TOO FAR!!
PLIP
PLIP
SUPREME COMMANDER!! ARE YOU TRYING TO KILL HIM?!
THAT'S ENOUGH, KARASU-TENGU. SHUT UP!
KSSSH
IT'S BEEN A LONG TIME, SUPREME COMMANDER.

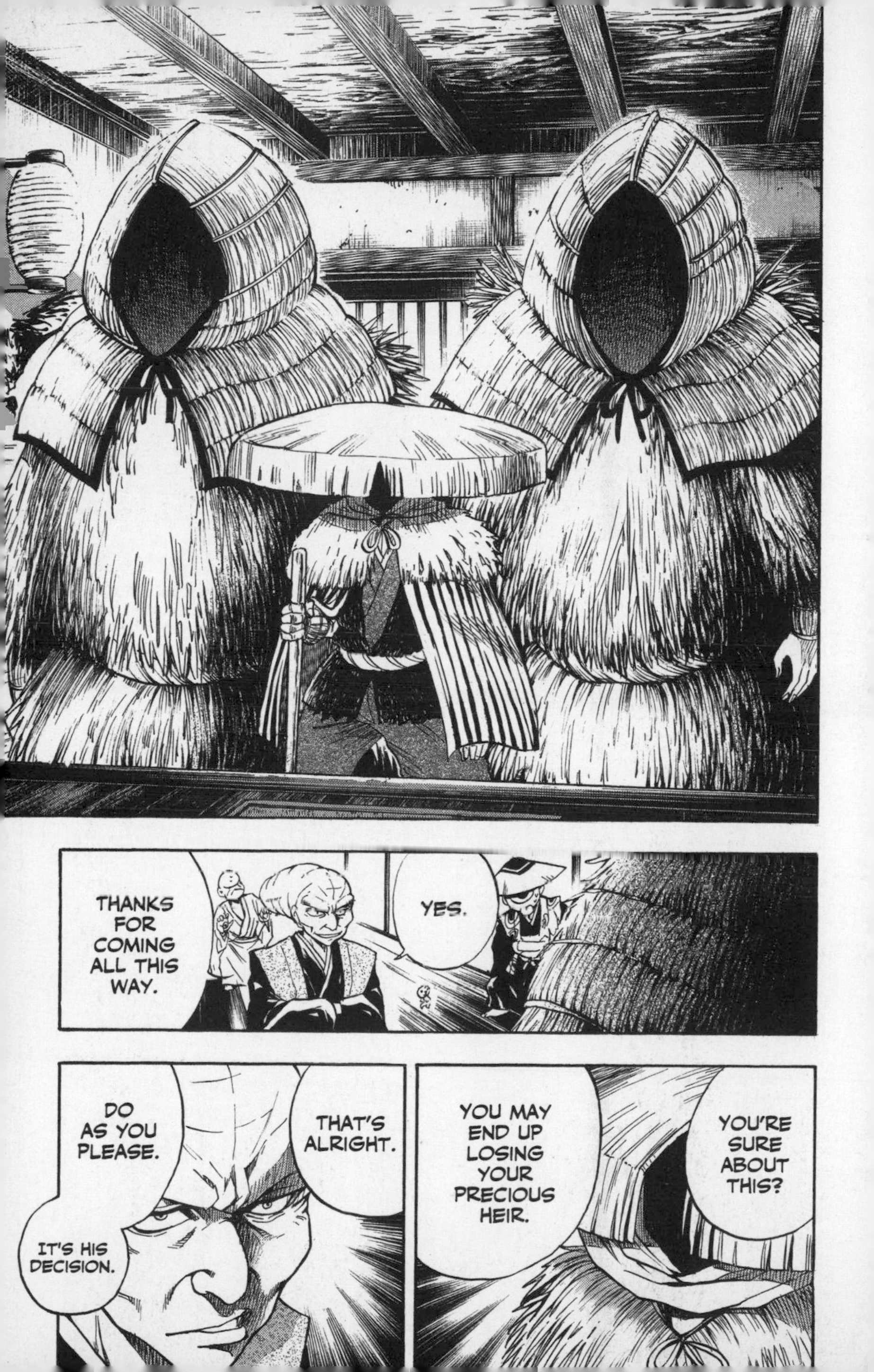
YES.
THANKS FOR COMING ALL THIS WAY.
YOU'RE SURE ABOUT THIS?
YOU MAY END UP LOSING YOUR PRECIOUS HEIR.
THAT'S ALRIGHT.
DO AS YOU PLEASE.
IT'S HIS DECISION.

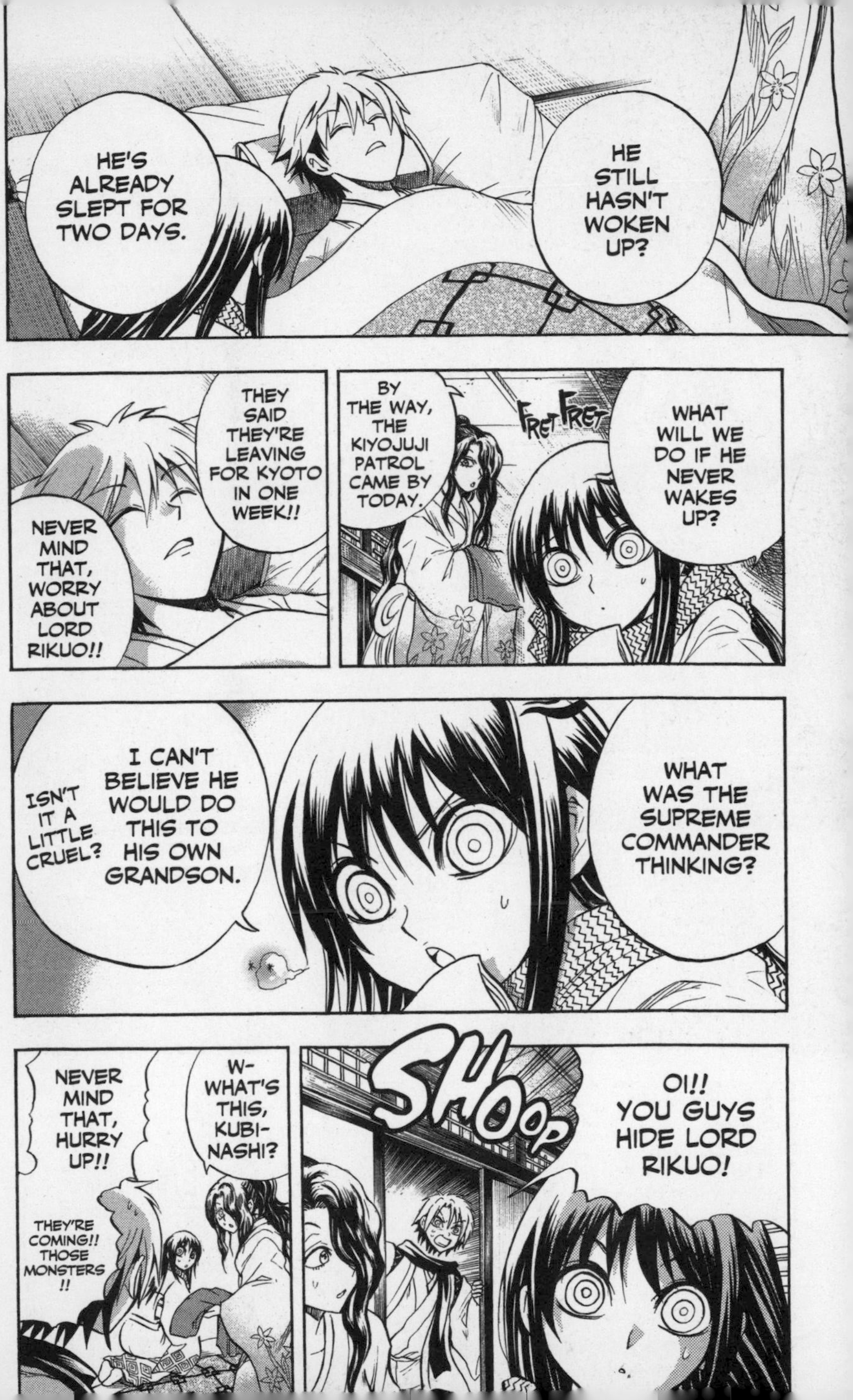
HE STILL HASN'T WOKEN UP?
HE'S ALREADY SLEPT FOR TWO DAYS.
WHAT WILL WE DO IF HE NEVER WAKES UP?
FRET FRET
BY THE WAY, THE KIYOJUJI PATROL CAME BY TODAY.
THEY SAID THEY'RE LEAVING FOR KYOTO IN ONE WEEK!!
NEVER MIND THAT, WORRY ABOUT LORD RIKUO!!
WHAT WAS THE SUPREME COMMANDER THINKING?
I CAN'T BELIEVE HE WOULD DO THIS TO HIS OWN GRANDSON.
ISN'T IT A LITTLE CRUEL?
SHOOP
OI!! YOU GUYS HIDE LORD RIKUO!
W-WHAT'S THIS, KUBI-NASHI?
NEVER MIND THAT, HURRY UP!!
THEY'RE COMING!! THOSE MONSTERS!!

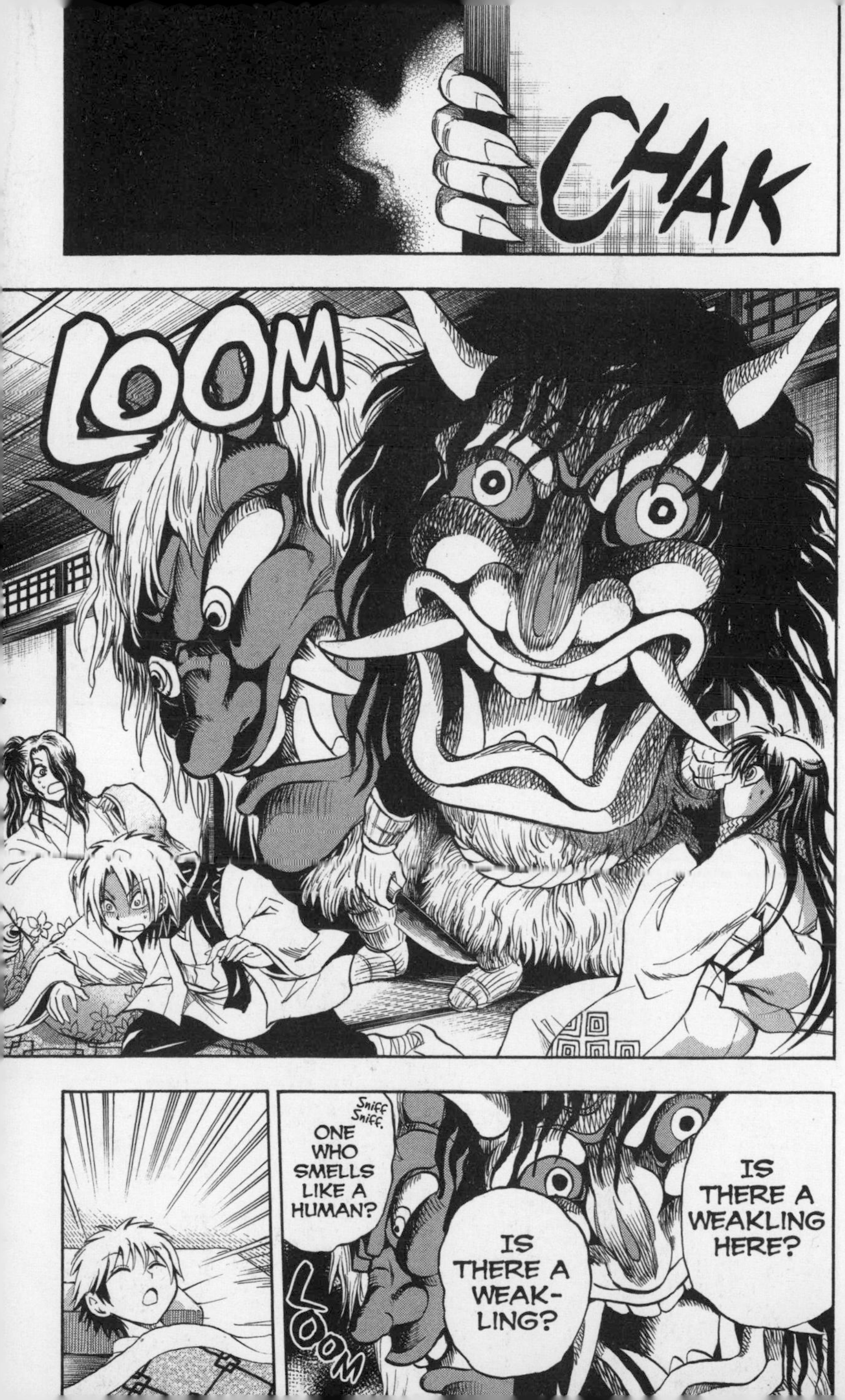
CHAK
LOOM
IS THERE A WEAKLING HERE?
IS THERE A WEAK-LING?
Sniff Sniff.
ONE WHO SMELLS LIKE A HUMAN?
LOOM

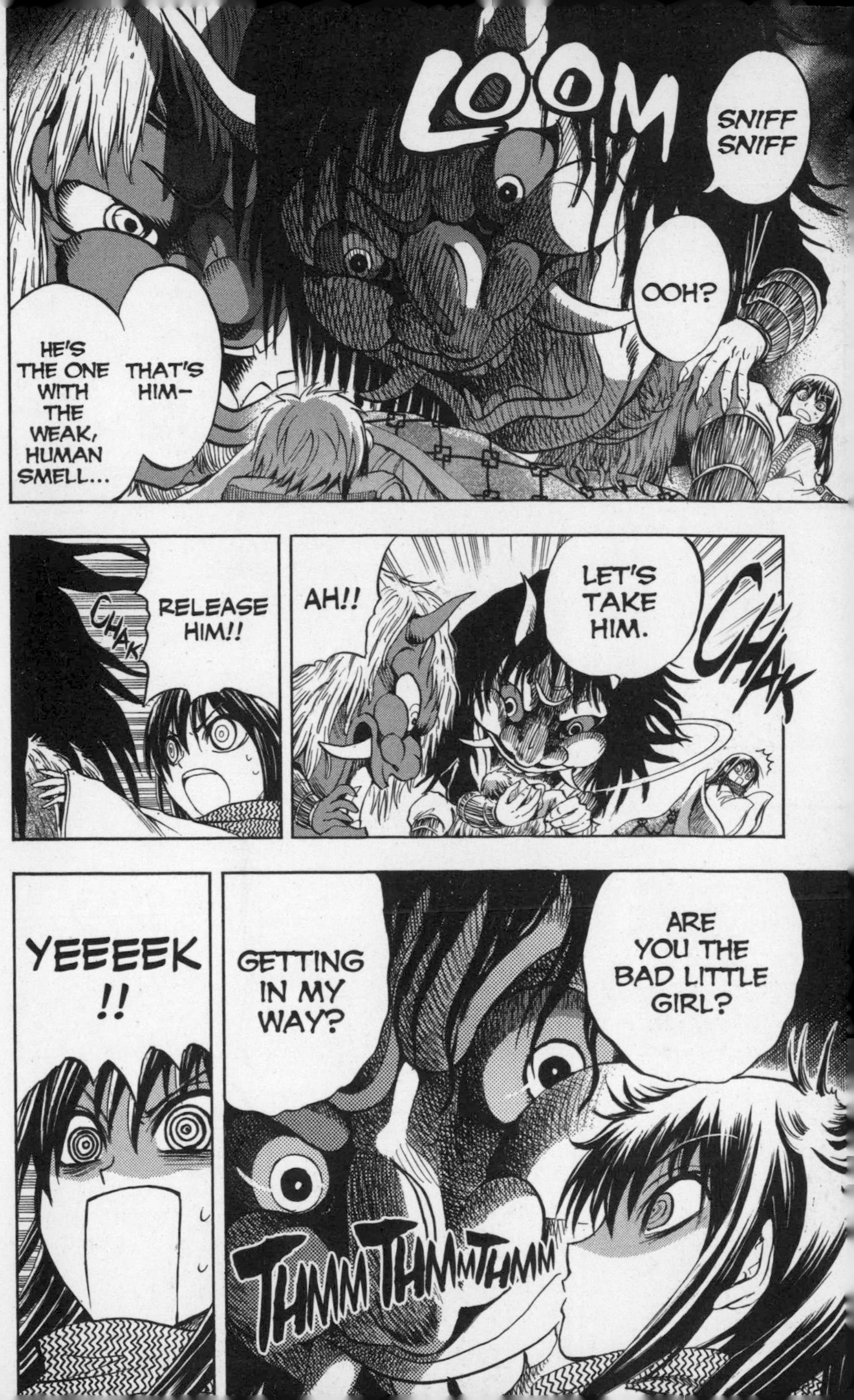
SNIFF SNIFF
LOOM
OOH?
THAT'S HIM— HE'S THE ONE WITH THE WEAK, HUMAN SMELL...
LET'S TAKE HIM.
CHAK
AH!!
RELEASE HIM!!
CHAK
ARE YOU THE BAD LITTLE GIRL?
GETTING IN MY WAY?
THMM THMM THMM
YEEEEK!!

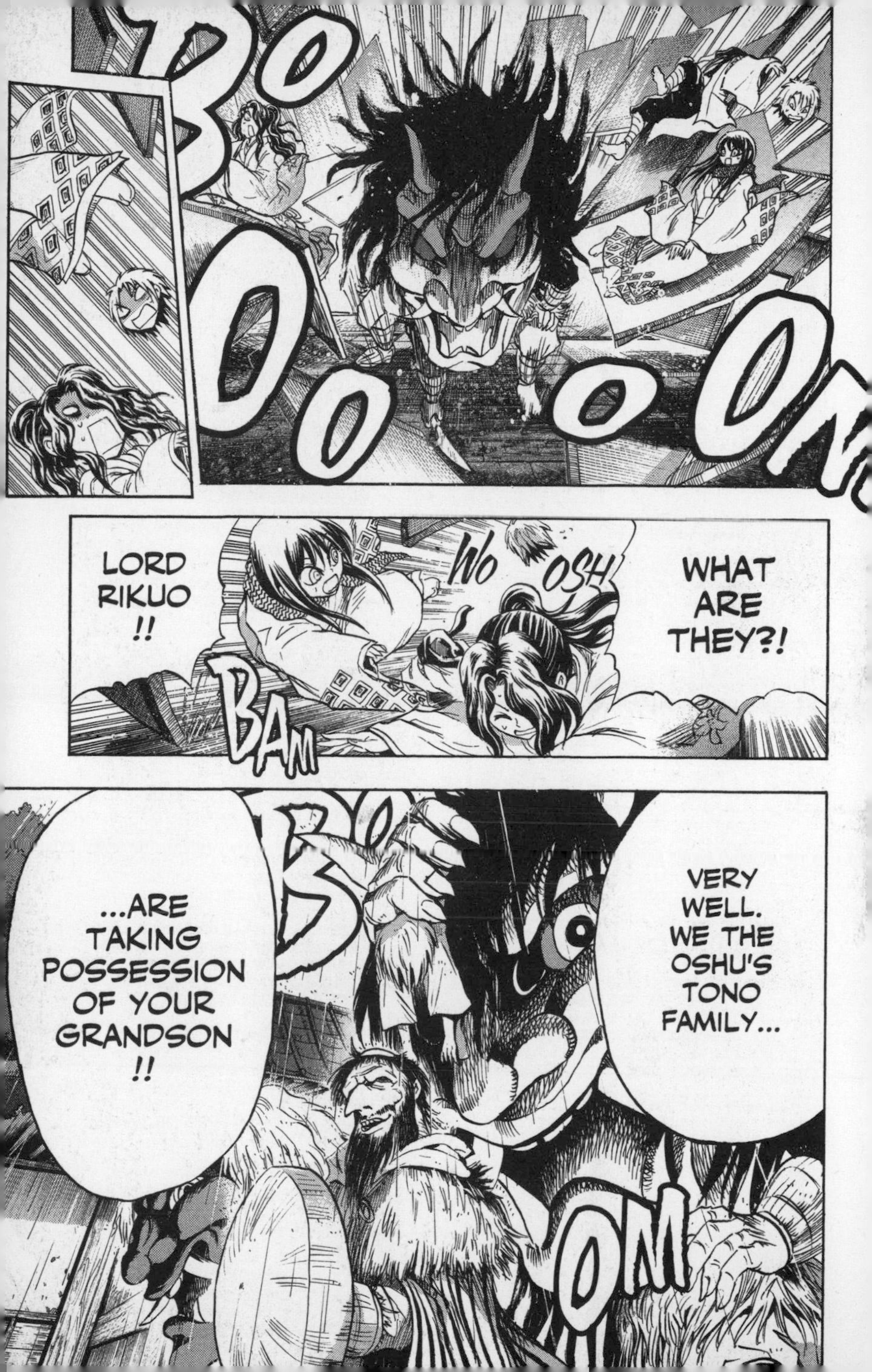
WHAT ARE THEY?!
WOOSH
LORD RIKUO !!
BAM
VERY WELL. WE THE OSHU'S TONO FAMILY...
...ARE TAKING POSSESSION OF YOUR GRANDSON !!

KIYOTSUGU'S YOKAI BRAIN

#8 FIELD TRIP EDITION

Q: RYUJI, YOUR WATER BOTTLE HAS YOUR NAME ON IT, BUT DO YOU HAVE A HABIT OF WRITING YOUR NAME ON ALL YOUR BELONGINGS? *-KUROGOMAPU RIN, SAITAMA PREFECTURE*

RYUJI: ARE YOU KIDDING ME? I'VE BEEN USING THIS SINCE I WAS A KID, AND IT'S SPECIFICALLY FOR SHIKIGAMI SO I CAN'T REPLACE IT THAT EASILY. BY THE WAY, IT'S NOT WRITTEN, IT'S CARVED.

Q: MAKI, DO YOU COLOR YOUR HAIR? *-I'M A FIRST YEAR MIDDLE SCHOOL STUDENT, GUNMA PREFECTURE*

MAKI: SOMEONE ASKED ME A QUESTION!! YES, YES. I'D BE LYING IF I TOLD YOU IT WAS NATURAL, BUT IF I GO INTO MORE DETAIL THEN I MIGHT GET ACCUSED OF BREAKING SCHOOL REGULATIONS!! COME TO THINK OF IT, IS RIKUO'S HAIR NATURAL? THE UPSIDE DOWN COLORS REMIND ME OF FLAN.

RIKUO: EH? MY HAIR'S NOT DYED.

KIYOTSUGU: THAT'S SUSPICIOUS, NURA!! THAT STRANGE HAIR COLORING OF YOURS IS VERY SUSPICIOUS. I WONDER IF YOU'RE HALF-POSSESSED BY YOKAI?

RIKUO: EHHHH?! W-WHAT WOULD MAKE YOU THINK THAT? A-ANYWAY, PLEASE KEEP SENDING YOUR QUESTIONS, EVERYONE!!

KIYO: **YAHOO!** HOW IS EVERYONE?! I'M VERY HAPPY THAT WE'VE GOTTEN SO MANY QUESTIONS LATELY, BUT I CAN'T ANSWER THEM ALL MYSELF!! SO, I'M GOING TO HAVE VARIOUS PEOPLE FROM ALL OVER THE NATION TO HELP ME!! LET'S GET STARTED, NURA-BABY!!

RIKUO: EH? WHY DID YOU PICK ME?! WHOA! WHY ARE YOU TOUCHING ME LIKE THAT?!

Q: YURA, WHICH SHIKIGAMI DO YOU LIKE THE BEST? MINE IS TANRO! I LIKE DOGS! *-KATSUMARU, KAGAWA PREFECTURE*

YURA: HO-HO! TANRO MUST BE HAPPY, BUT HE'S NOT A DOG. HE'S ACTUALLY A SHIKIGAMI OF THE NOW-EXTINCT JAPANESE WOLF. ROKUSON IS AN EZO DEER. UM.I CAN'T CHOOSE ONE THAT I LIKE MORE THAN THE OTHERS. THEY'RE ALL GREAT! AND I DON'T HAVE TO FEED THEM! BY THE WAY, BUKYOKU IS A FALLEN WARRIOR SHIKIGAMI!!

Q: INCLUDING THE LEADER, HOW MANY MEMBERS ARE THERE IN THE TEAM NIGHT PARADE OF A HUNDRED DEMONS MOTORCYCLE GANG? *-RIPPO, SHIZUOKA PREFECTURE*

AOTABO: BEFORE I JOINED, THERE WERE SUPPOSEDLY 108, BUT I SENT A FEW TO THE HOSPITAL, SO NOW THERE ARE EXACTLY 100. I DON'T HAVE MY OWN CLAN, BUT HAVING A TEAM LIKE THIS MAKES ME THINK IT MAY NOT BE SO BAD.

Q: QUESTION FOR KANA! HOW MANY PEOPLE HAVE TOLD YOU THAT THEY LIKE YOU? *-TOMO, SAITAMA PREFECTURE.*

KANA: EHH?! A QUESTION LIKE THAT IS A LITTLE UNCOMFORTABLE TO ANSWER. I'M SO EMBARASSED. BUT, I THINK MAYBE MORE HAVE SINCE I STARTED MIDDLE SCHOOL? I REALLY DON'T KNOW!

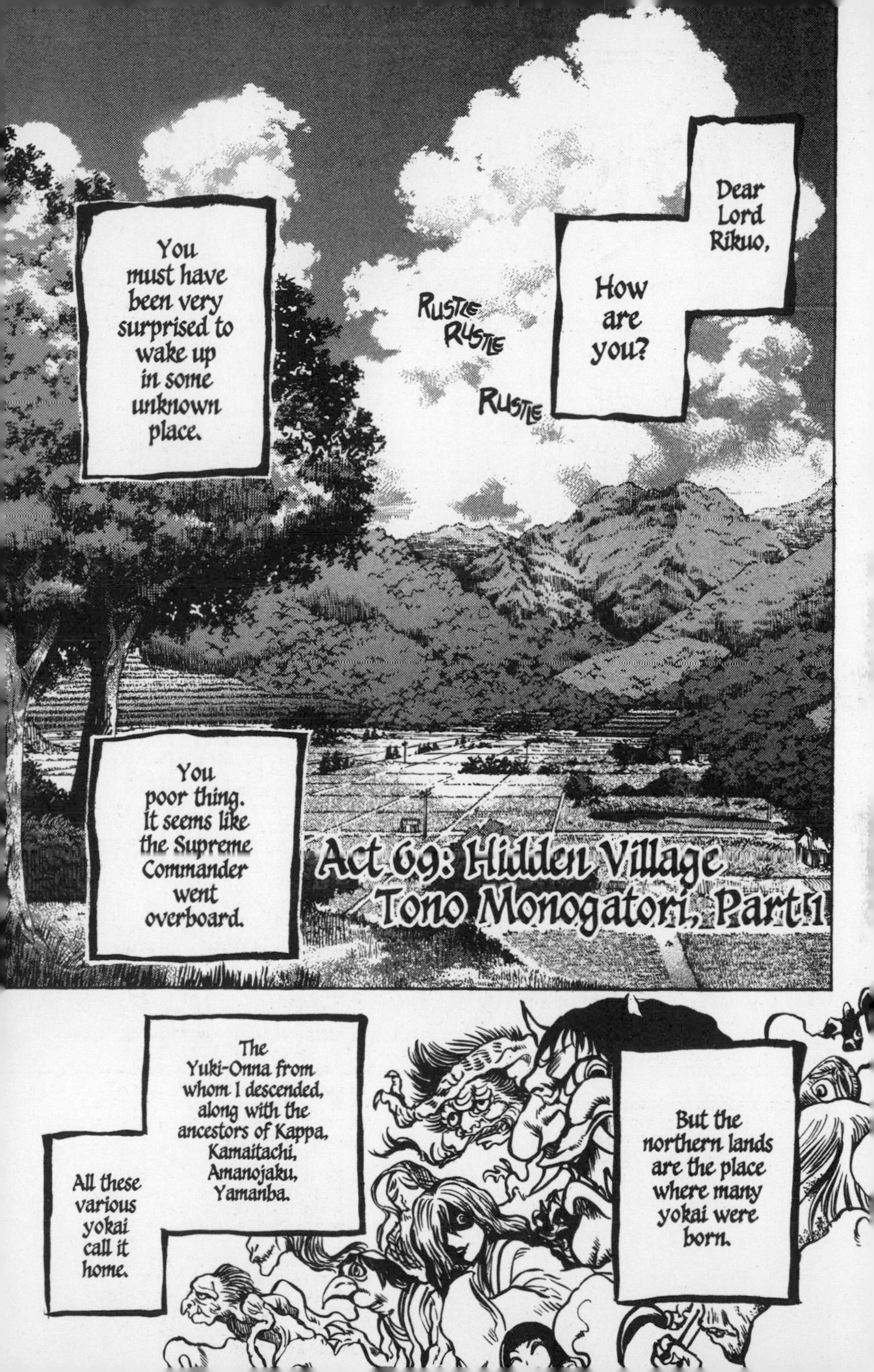
Dear Lord Rikuo,
How are you?
RUSTLE RUSTLE
RUSTLE
You must have been very surprised to wake up in some unknown place.
You poor thing. It seems like the Supreme Commander went overboard.
Act 69: Hidden Village Tono Monogatori, Part 1
But the northern lands are the place where many yokai were born.
The Yuki-Onna from whom I descended, along with the ancestors of Kappa, Kamaitachi, Amanojaku, Yamanba.
All these various yokai call it home.

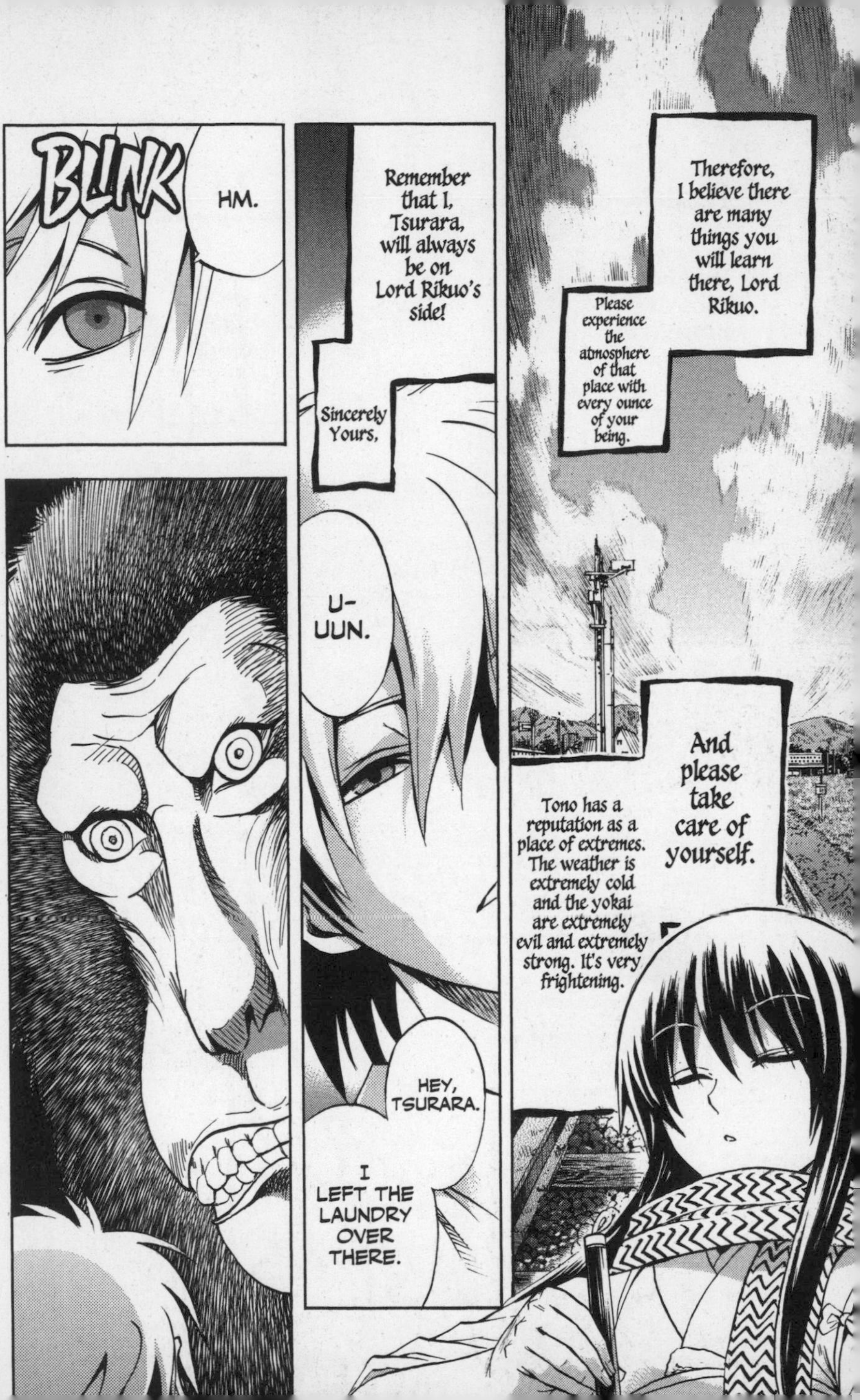
Therefore, I believe there are many things you will learn there, Lord Rikuo.
Please experience the atmosphere of that place with every ounce of your being.
And please take care of yourself.
Tono has a reputation as a place of extremes. The weather is extremely cold and the yokai are extremely evil and extremely strong. It's very frightening.
Remember that I, Tsurara, will always be on Lord Rikuo's side!
Sincerely Yours,
U-UUN.
HEY, TSURARA.
I LEFT THE LAUNDRY OVER THERE.
BLINK
HM.

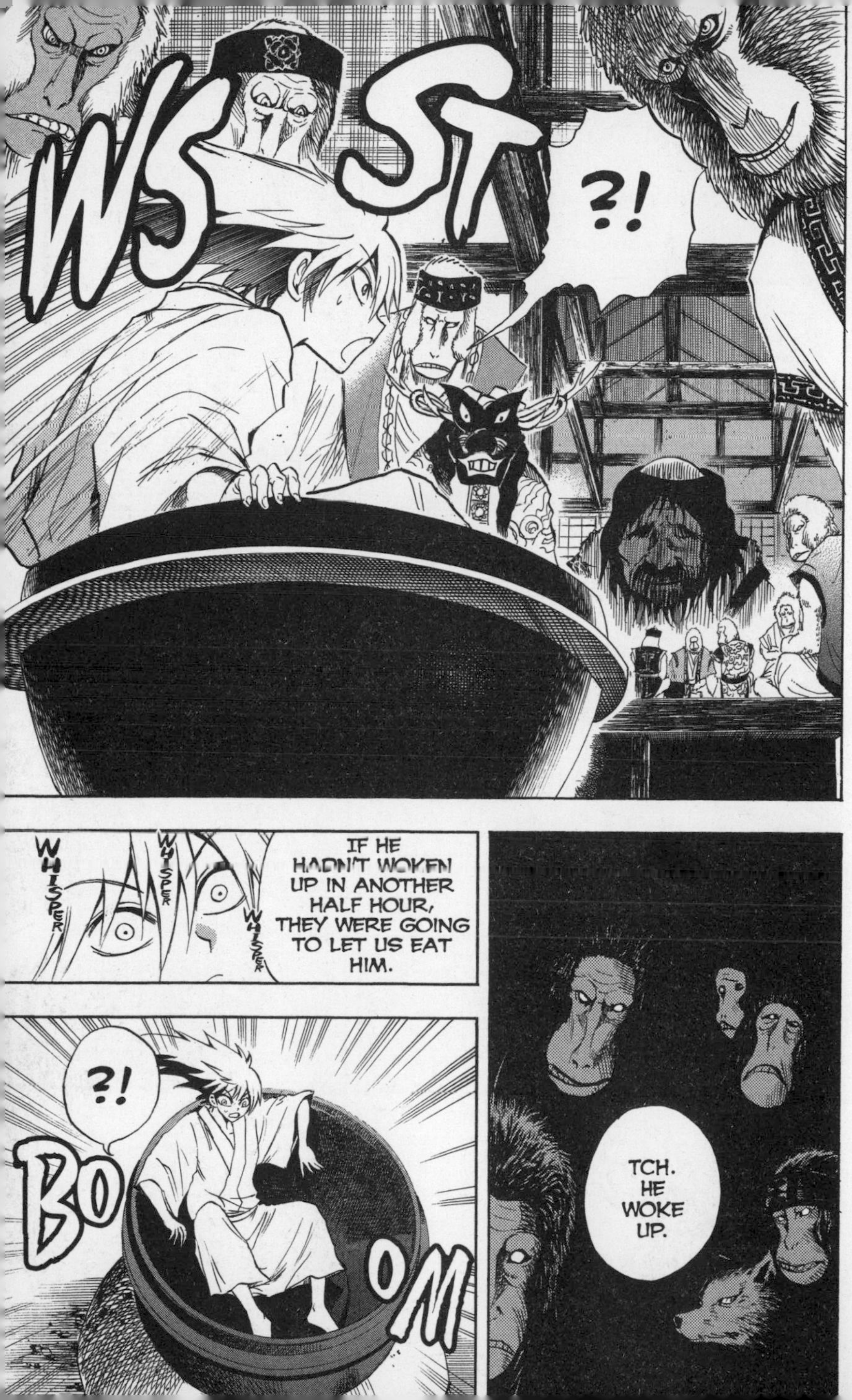
WS ST
?!
TCH. HE WOKE UP.
WHISPER
WHISPER
WHISPER
IF HE HADN'T WOKEN UP IN ANOTHER HALF HOUR, THEY WERE GOING TO LET US EAT HIM.
?!
BO OM

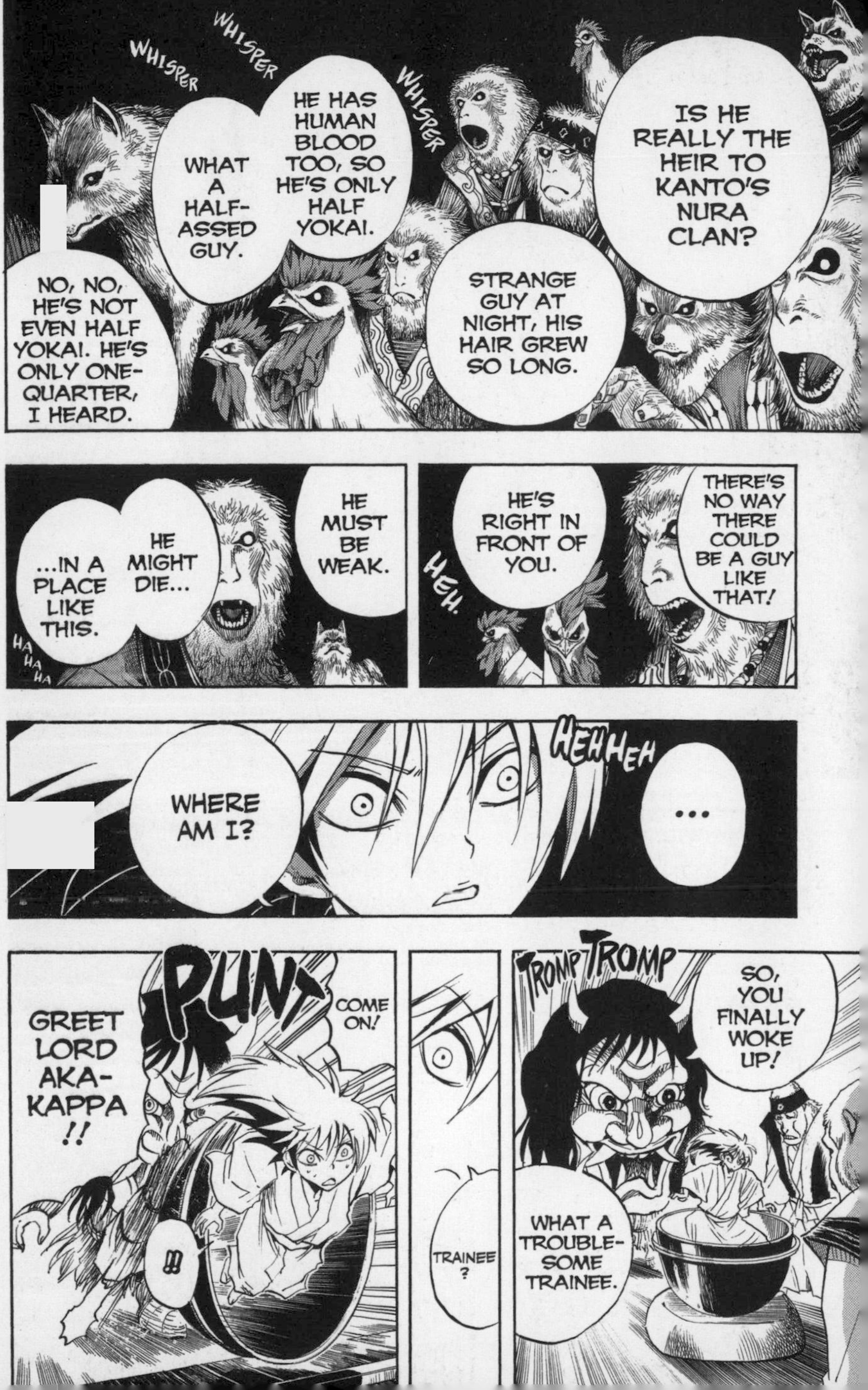
IS HE REALLY THE HEIR TO KANTO'S NURA CLAN?
WHISPER
HE HAS HUMAN BLOOD TOO, SO HE'S ONLY HALF YOKAI.
WHISPER
STRANGE GUY AT NIGHT, HIS HAIR GREW SO LONG.
WHAT A HALF-ASSED GUY.
WHISPER
NO, NO, HE'S NOT EVEN HALF YOKAI. HE'S ONLY ONE-QUARTER, I HEARD.
THERE'S NO WAY THERE COULD BE A GUY LIKE THAT!
HE'S RIGHT IN FRONT OF YOU.
HEH.
HE MUST BE WEAK.
HE MIGHT DIE...
...IN A PLACE LIKE THIS.
HA HA HA
...
HEHHEH
WHERE AM I?
TROMP TROMP
SO, YOU FINALLY WOKE UP!
WHAT A TROUBLE-SOME TRAINEE.
TRAINEE?
COME ON!
PUNT
GREET LORD AKA-KAPPA!!
!!

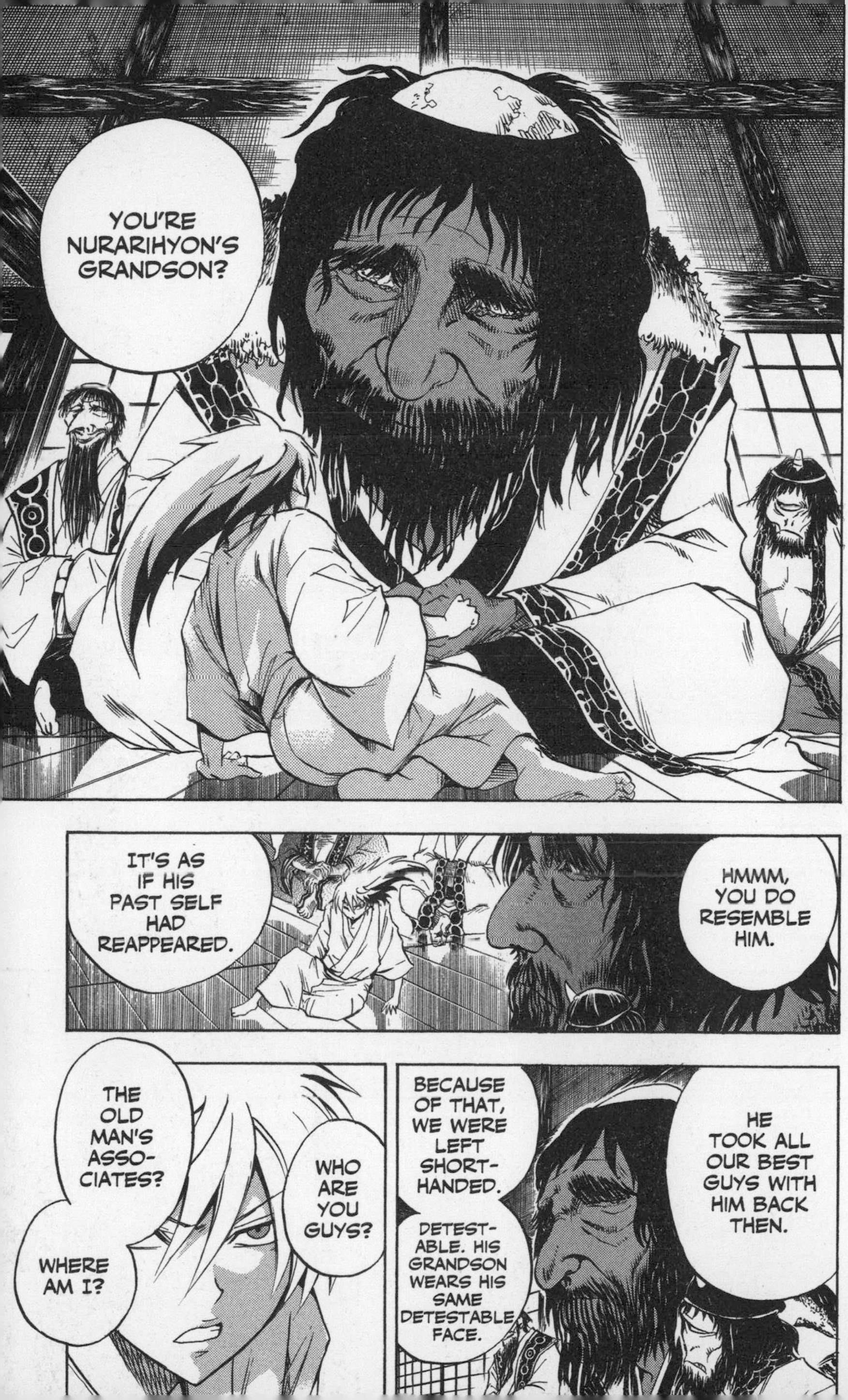
YOU'RE NURARIHYON'S GRANDSON?
HMMM, YOU DO RESEMBLE HIM.
IT'S AS IF HIS PAST SELF HAD REAPPEARED.
HE TOOK ALL OUR BEST GUYS WITH HIM BACK THEN.
BECAUSE OF THAT, WE WERE LEFT SHORT-HANDED.
DETEST-ABLE. HIS GRANDSON WEARS HIS SAME DETESTABLE FACE.
WHO ARE YOU GUYS?
THE OLD MAN'S ASSO-CIATES?
WHERE AM I?

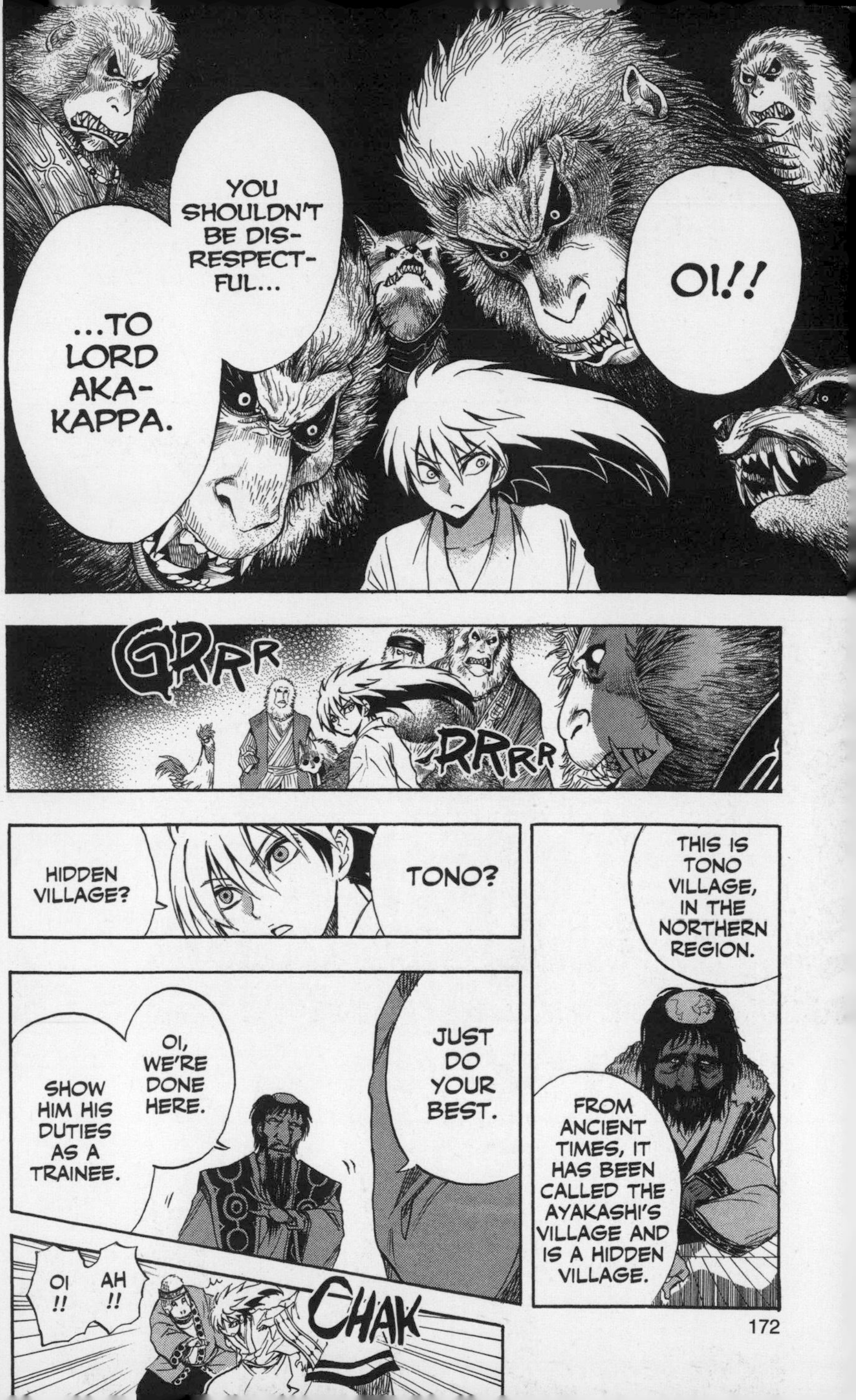
OI!!
YOU SHOULDN'T BE DIS-RESPECT-FUL...
...TO LORD AKA-KAPPA.
GRRR
RRRR
THIS IS TONO VILLAGE, IN THE NORTHERN REGION.
FROM ANCIENT TIMES, IT HAS BEEN CALLED THE AYAKASHI'S VILLAGE AND IS A HIDDEN VILLAGE.
TONO?
HIDDEN VILLAGE?
JUST DO YOUR BEST.
OI, WE'RE DONE HERE.
SHOW HIM HIS DUTIES AS A TRAINEE.
CHAK
AH !!
OI !!

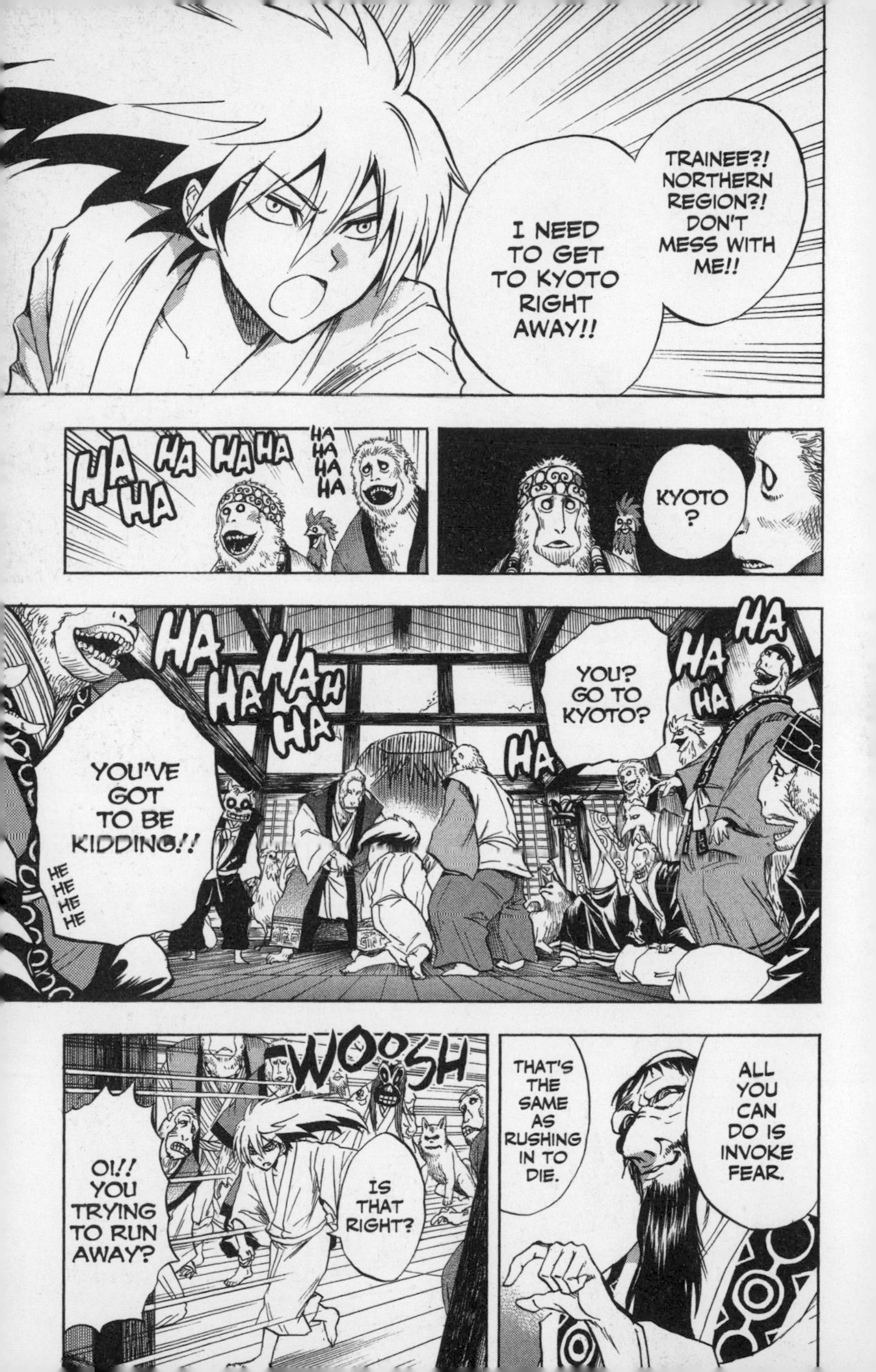
TRAINEE?! NORTHERN REGION?! DON'T MESS WITH ME!!
I NEED TO GET TO KYOTO RIGHT AWAY!!
KYOTO?
HA HA HA HA
HA HA HA HA HA HA
HA HA
HA HA HA
YOU? GO TO KYOTO?
HA
HA HA HAH HA
YOU'VE GOT TO BE KIDDING!!
HE HE HE HE
ALL YOU CAN DO IS INVOKE FEAR.
THAT'S THE SAME AS RUSHING IN TO DIE.
WOOSH
IS THAT RIGHT?
OI!! YOU TRYING TO RUN AWAY?

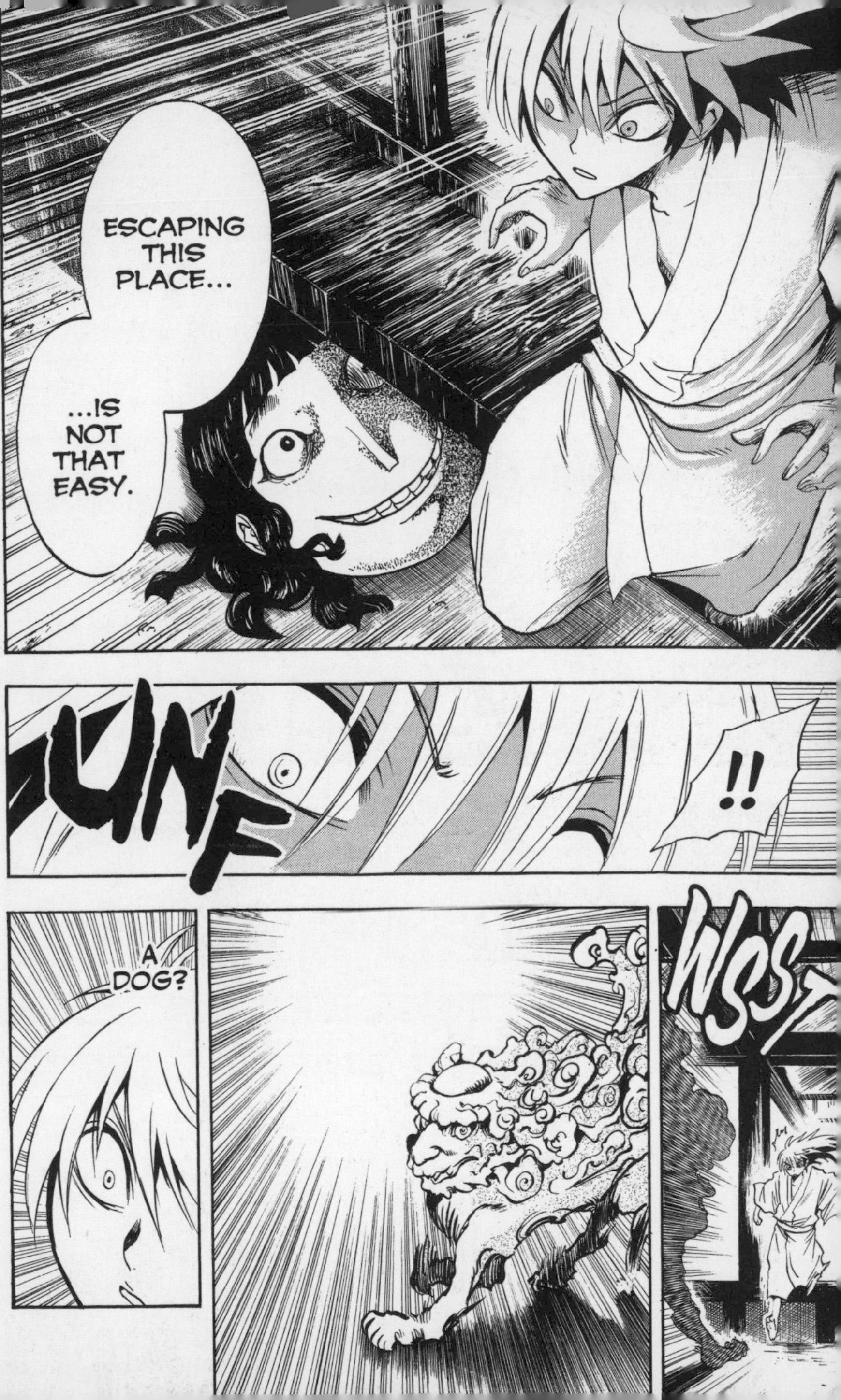
ESCAPING THIS PLACE...
...IS NOT THAT EASY.
!!
UNF
WSS
A DOG?

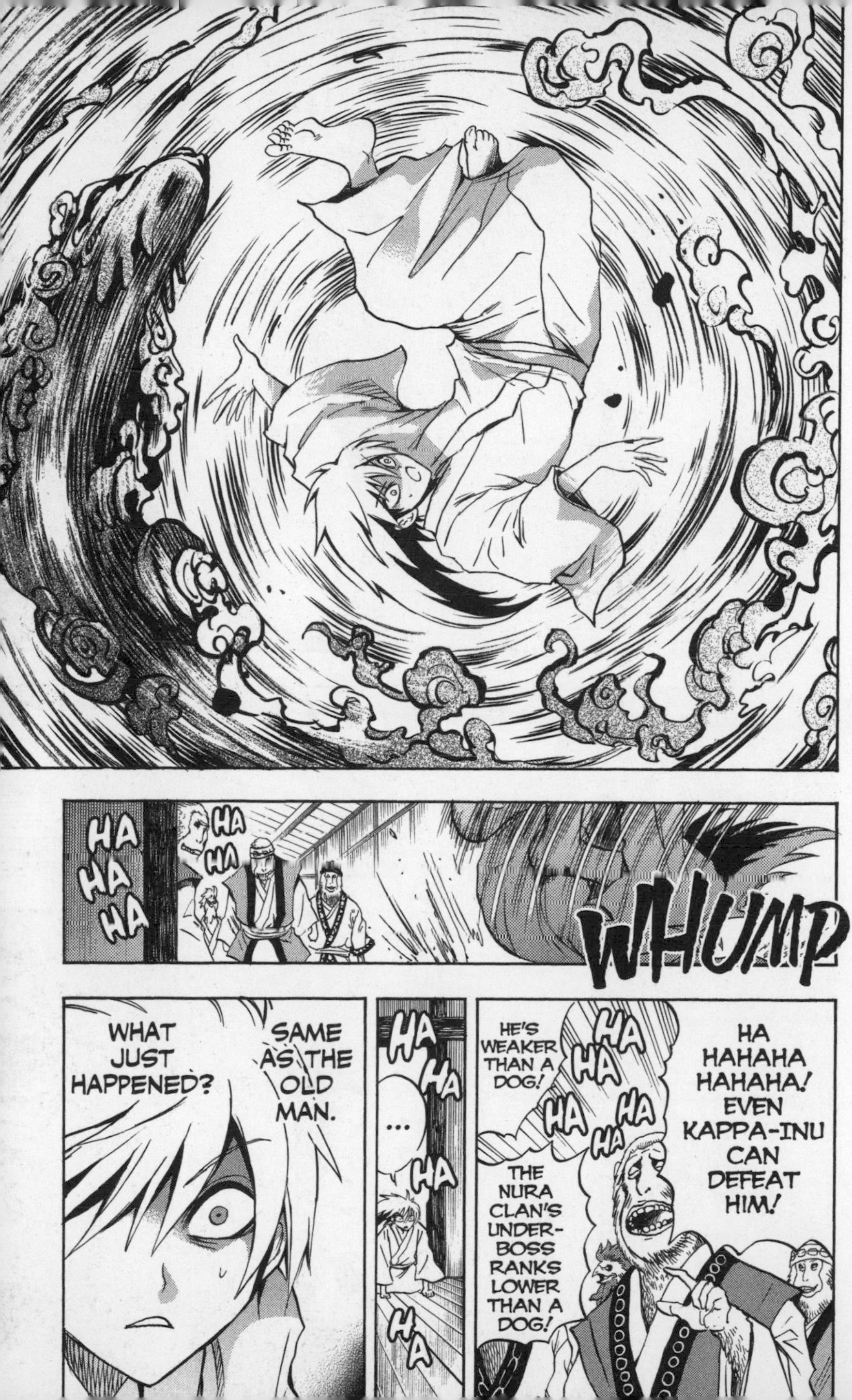
WHUMP
HA HA
HA HA HA
HA HAHAHA HAHAHA! EVEN KAPPA-INU CAN DEFEAT HIM!
HA HA
HE'S WEAKER THAN A DOG!
HA HA HA HA
THE NURA CLAN'S UNDER-BOSS RANKS LOWER THAN A DOG!
HA HA
...
HA
HA
SAME AS THE OLD MAN.
WHAT JUST HAPPENED?

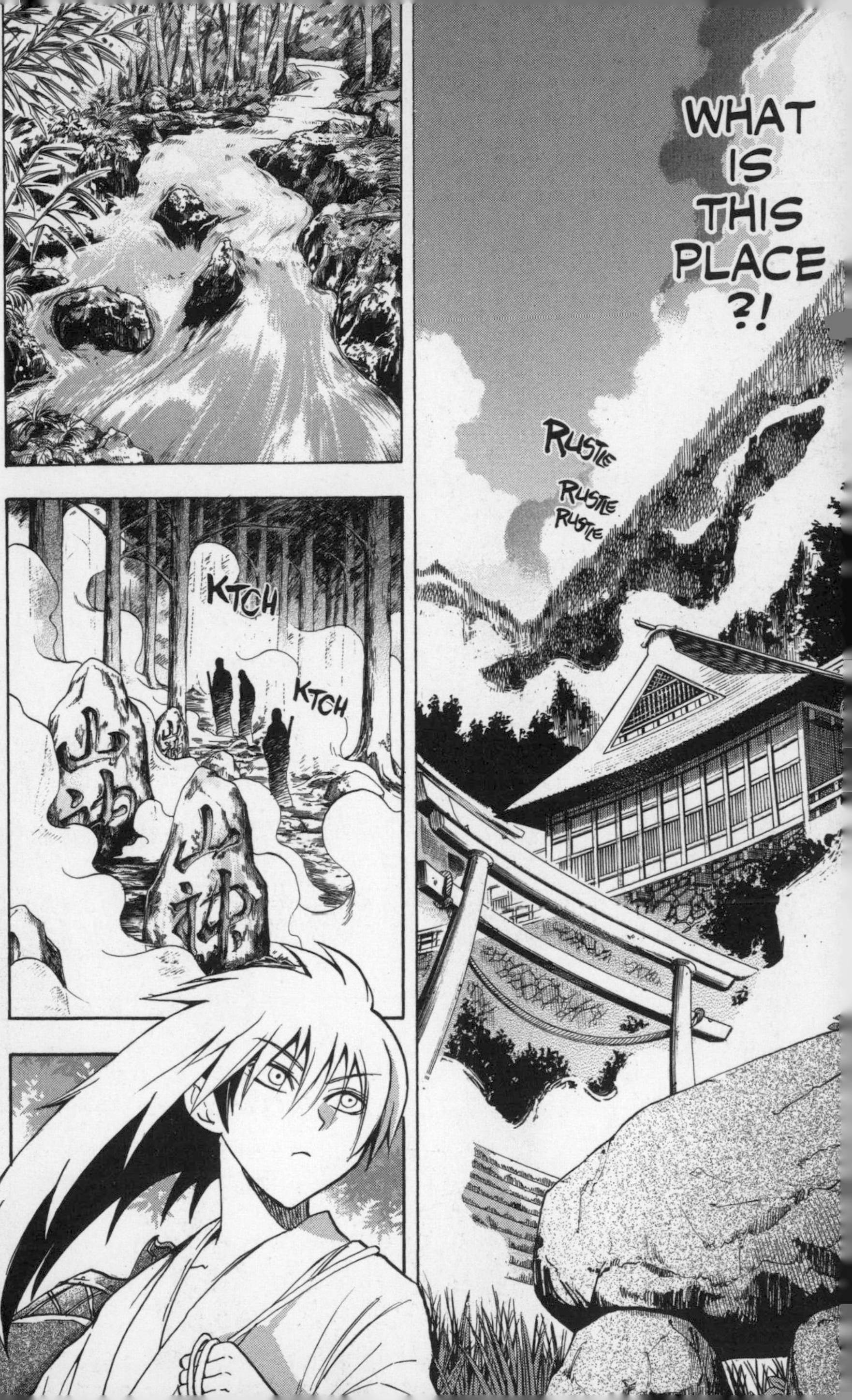
WHAT IS THIS PLACE ?!
RUSTLE
RUSTLE
RUSTLE
KTCH
KTCH
山神
山神
山神

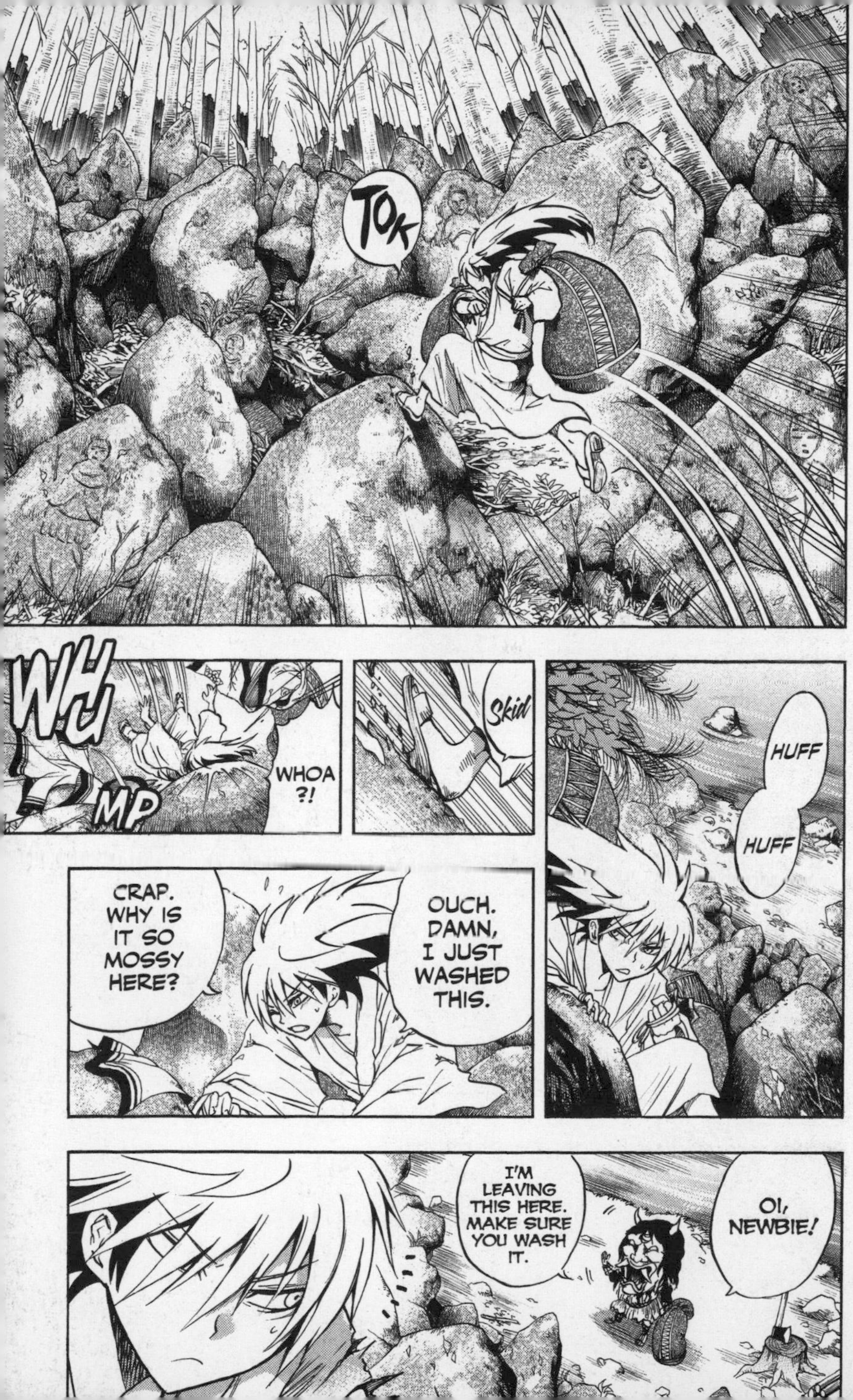

TOK
HUFF
HUFF
Skid
WHUMP
WHOA ?!
OUCH. DAMN, I JUST WASHED THIS.
CRAP. WHY IS IT SO MOSSY HERE?
OI, NEWBIE!
I'M LEAVING THIS HERE. MAKE SURE YOU WASH IT.
...

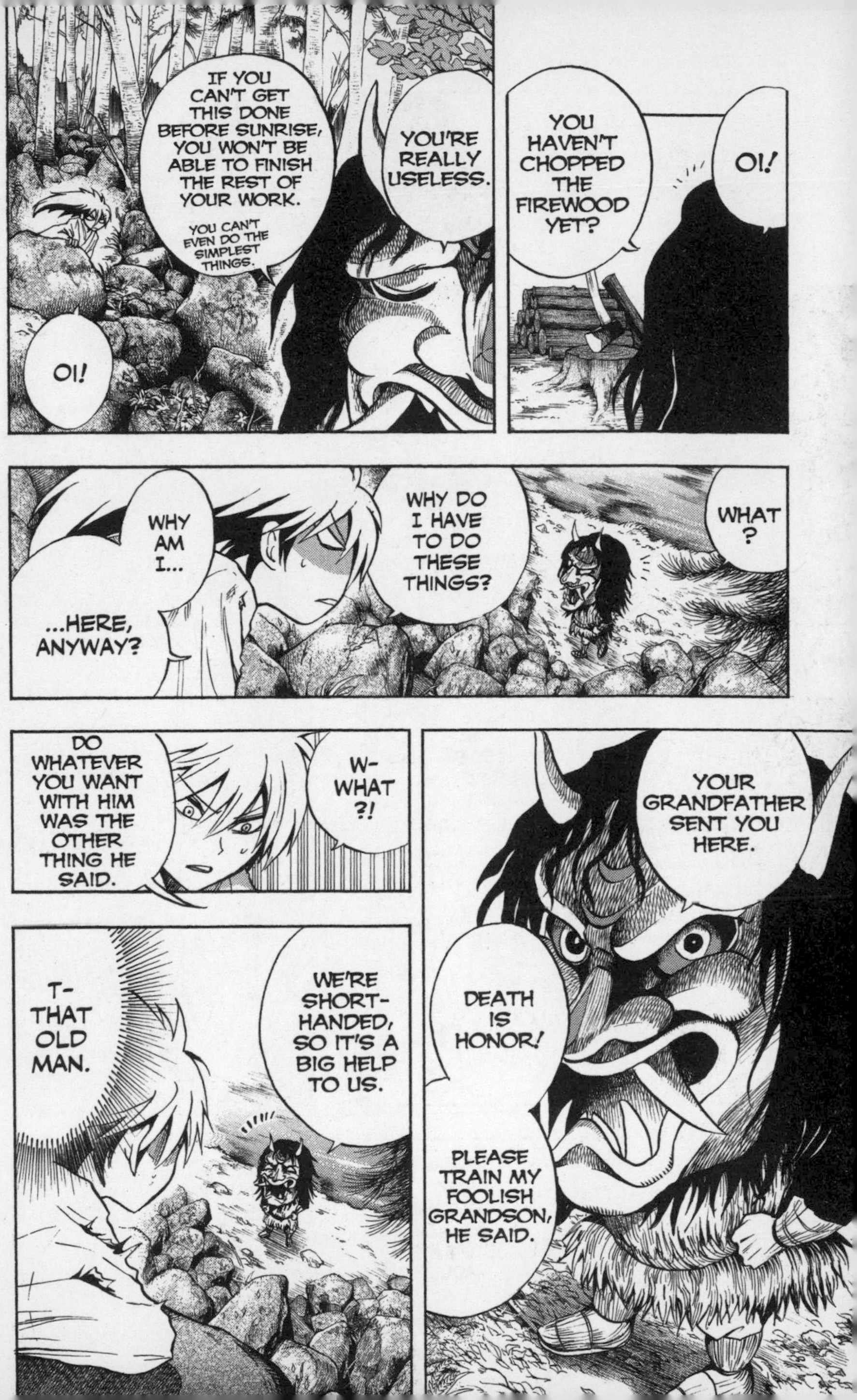
OI!
YOU HAVEN'T CHOPPED THE FIREWOOD YET?
YOU'RE REALLY USELESS.
IF YOU CAN'T GET THIS DONE BEFORE SUNRISE, YOU WON'T BE ABLE TO FINISH THE REST OF YOUR WORK.
YOU CAN'T EVEN DO THE SIMPLEST THINGS.
OI!
WHAT ?
WHY DO I HAVE TO DO THESE THINGS?
WHY AM I...
...HERE, ANYWAY?
YOUR GRANDFATHER SENT YOU HERE.
DEATH IS HONOR!
PLEASE TRAIN MY FOOLISH GRANDSON, HE SAID.
W-WHAT ?!
DO WHATEVER YOU WANT WITH HIM WAS THE OTHER THING HE SAID.
WE'RE SHORT-HANDED, SO IT'S A BIG HELP TO US.
T-THAT OLD MAN.

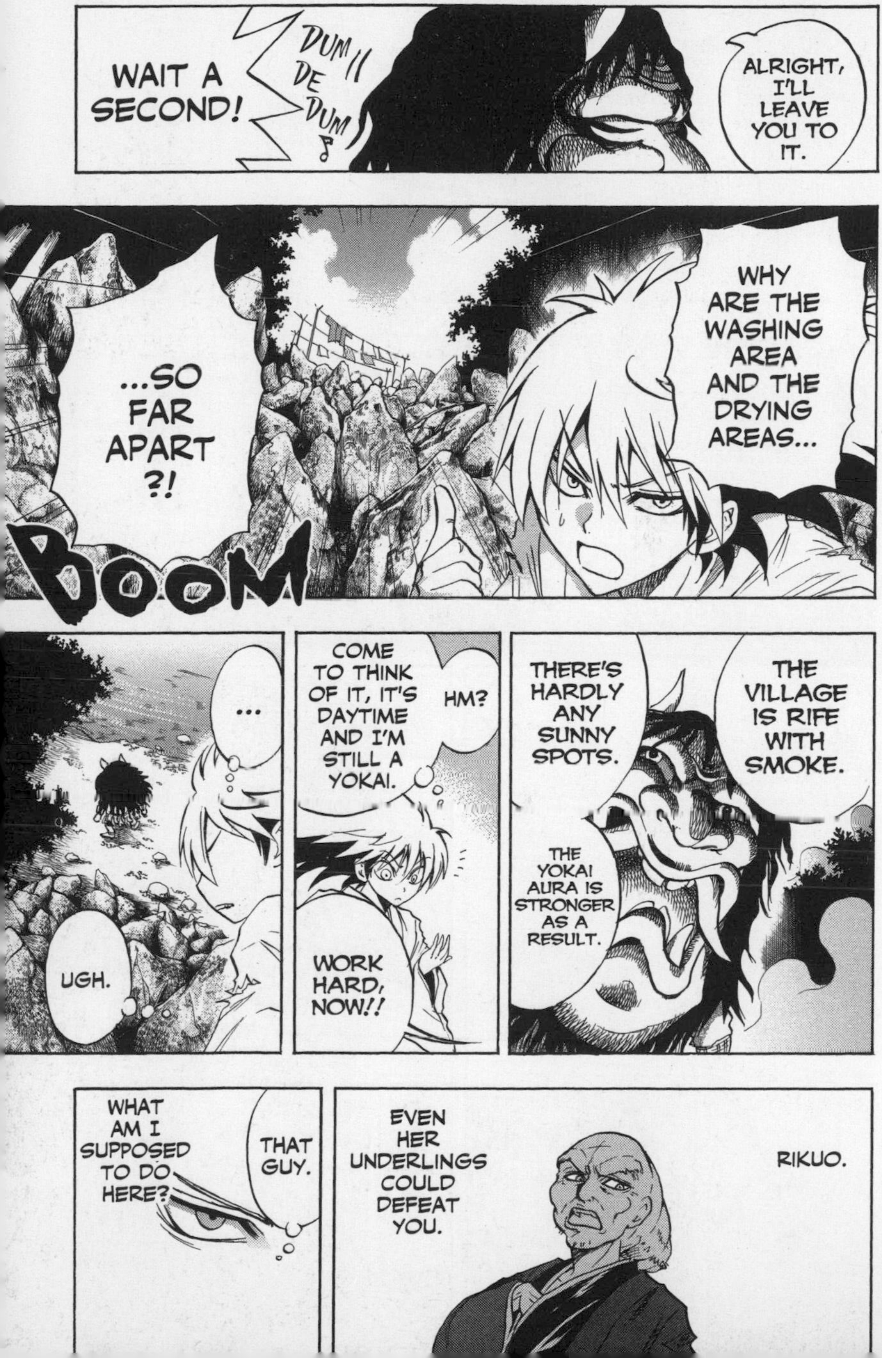
ALRIGHT, I'LL LEAVE YOU TO IT.
DUM DE DUM
WAIT A SECOND!
WHY ARE THE WASHING AREA AND THE DRYING AREAS...
...SO FAR APART?!
BOOM
THE VILLAGE IS RIFE WITH SMOKE.
THERE'S HARDLY ANY SUNNY SPOTS.
THE YOKAI AURA IS STRONGER AS A RESULT.
HM?
COME TO THINK OF IT, IT'S DAYTIME AND I'M STILL A YOKAI.
WORK HARD, NOW!!
...
UGH.
RIKUO.
EVEN HER UNDERLINGS COULD DEFEAT YOU.
THAT GUY.
WHAT AM I SUPPOSED TO DO HERE?

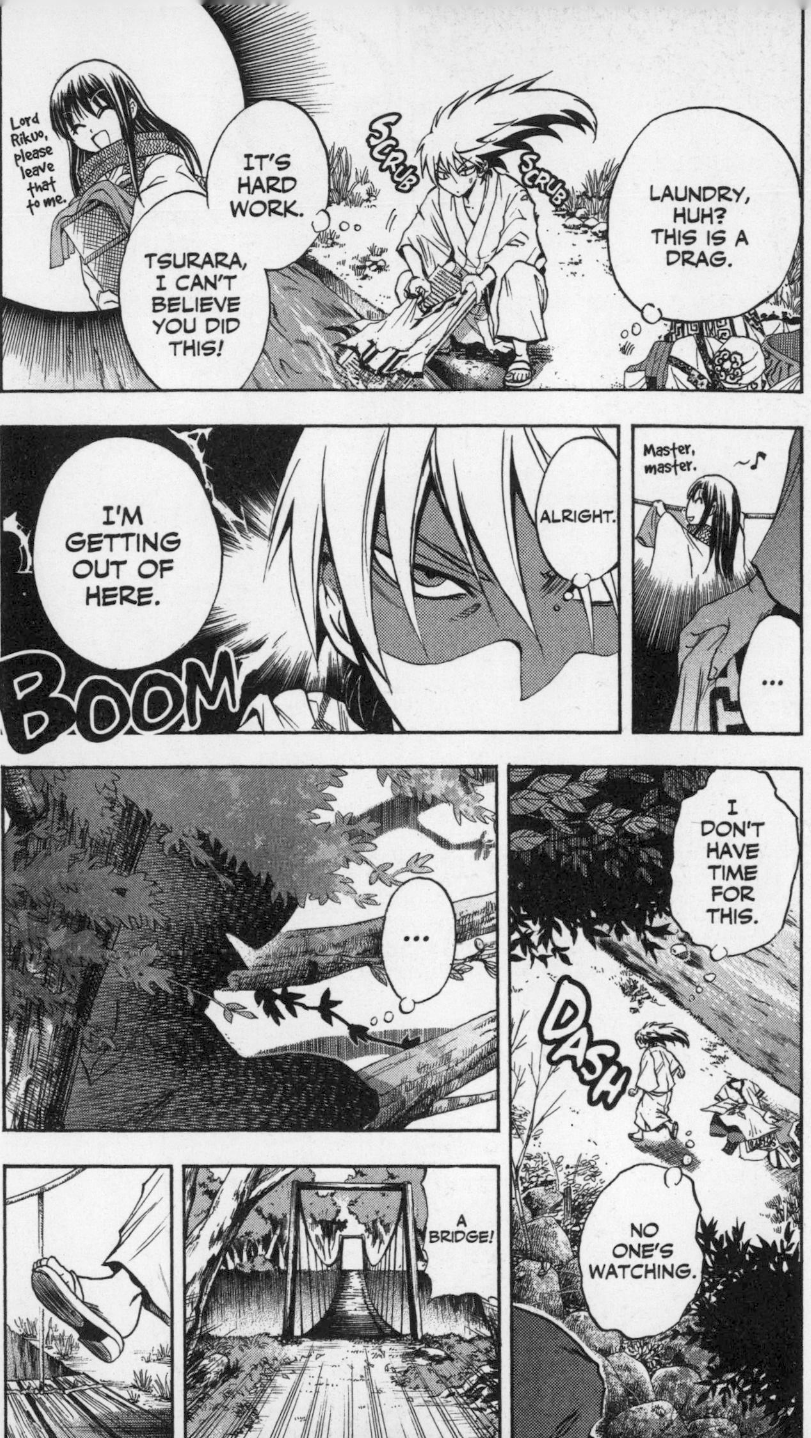
LAUNDRY, HUH? THIS IS A DRAG.
SCRUB
SCRUB
IT'S HARD WORK.
TSURARA, I CAN'T BELIEVE YOU DID THIS!
Lord Rikuo, please leave that to me.
Master, master.
~♪
...
ALRIGHT.
I'M GETTING OUT OF HERE.
BOOM
I DON'T HAVE TIME FOR THIS.
DASH
NO ONE'S WATCHING.
...
A BRIDGE!

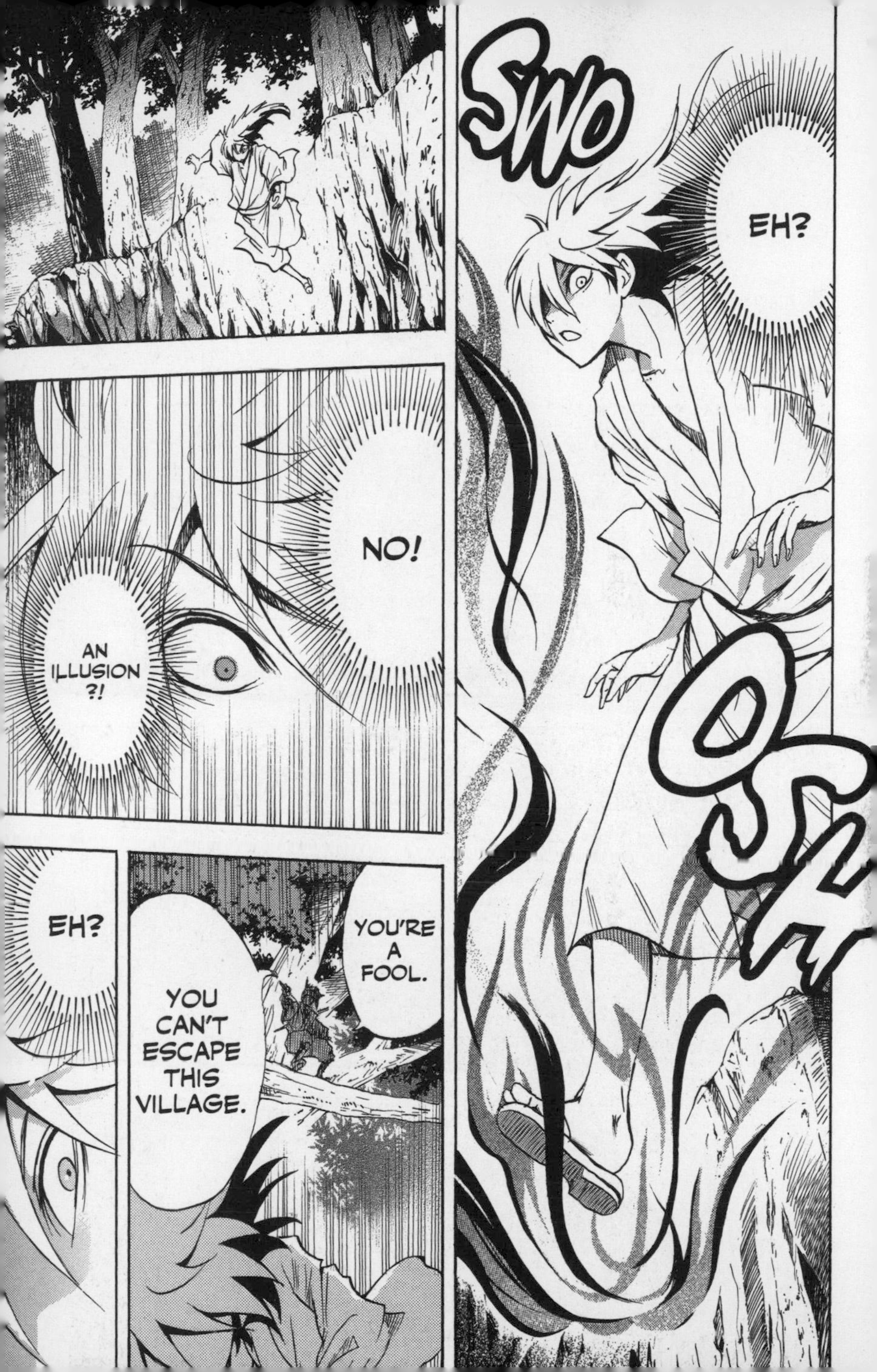
SWOOSH
EH?
NO!
AN ILLUSION ?!
YOU'RE A FOOL.
YOU CAN'T ESCAPE THIS VILLAGE.
EH?

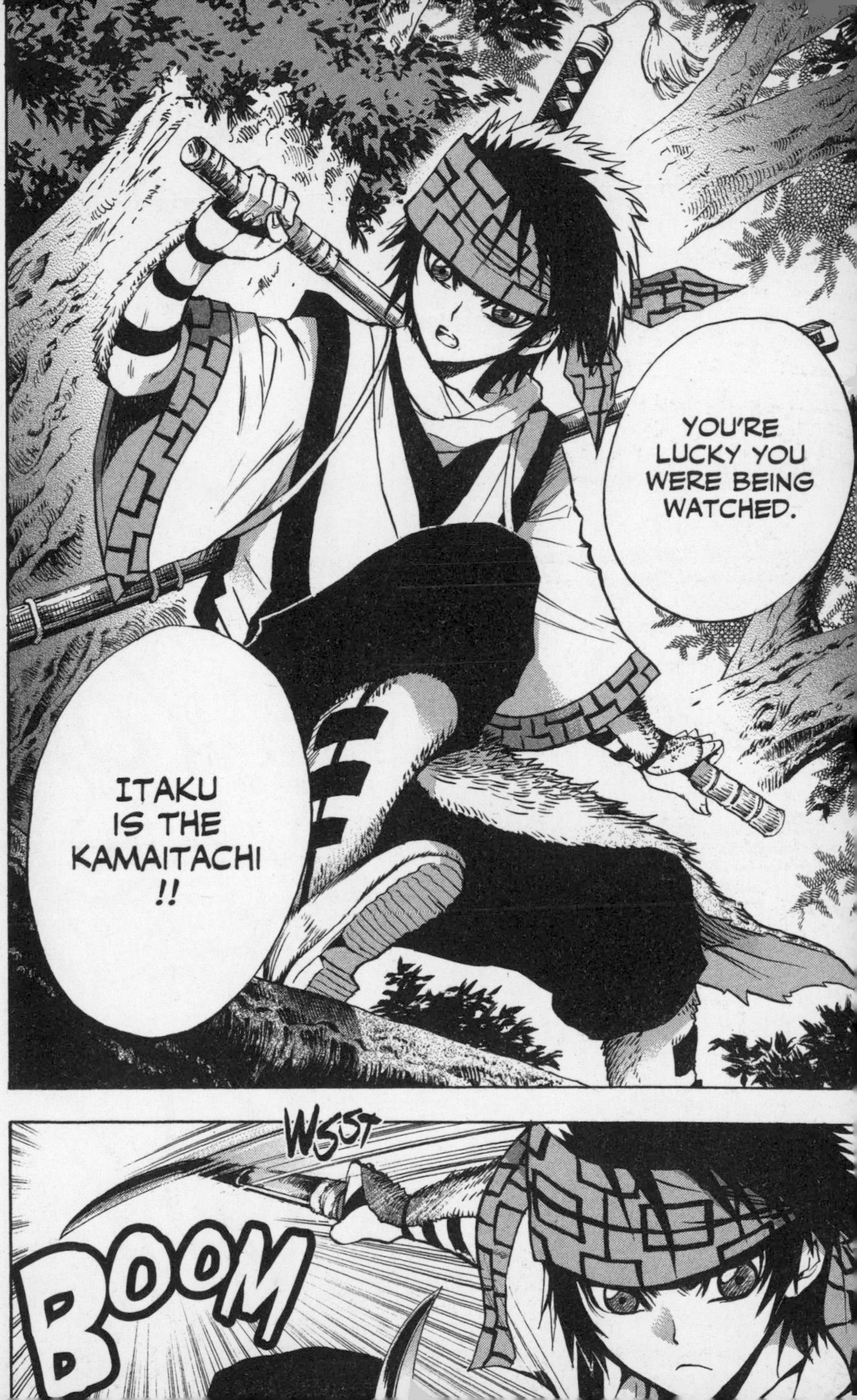
YOU'RE LUCKY YOU WERE BEING WATCHED.
ITAKU IS THE KAMAITACHI !!
WSST
BOOM

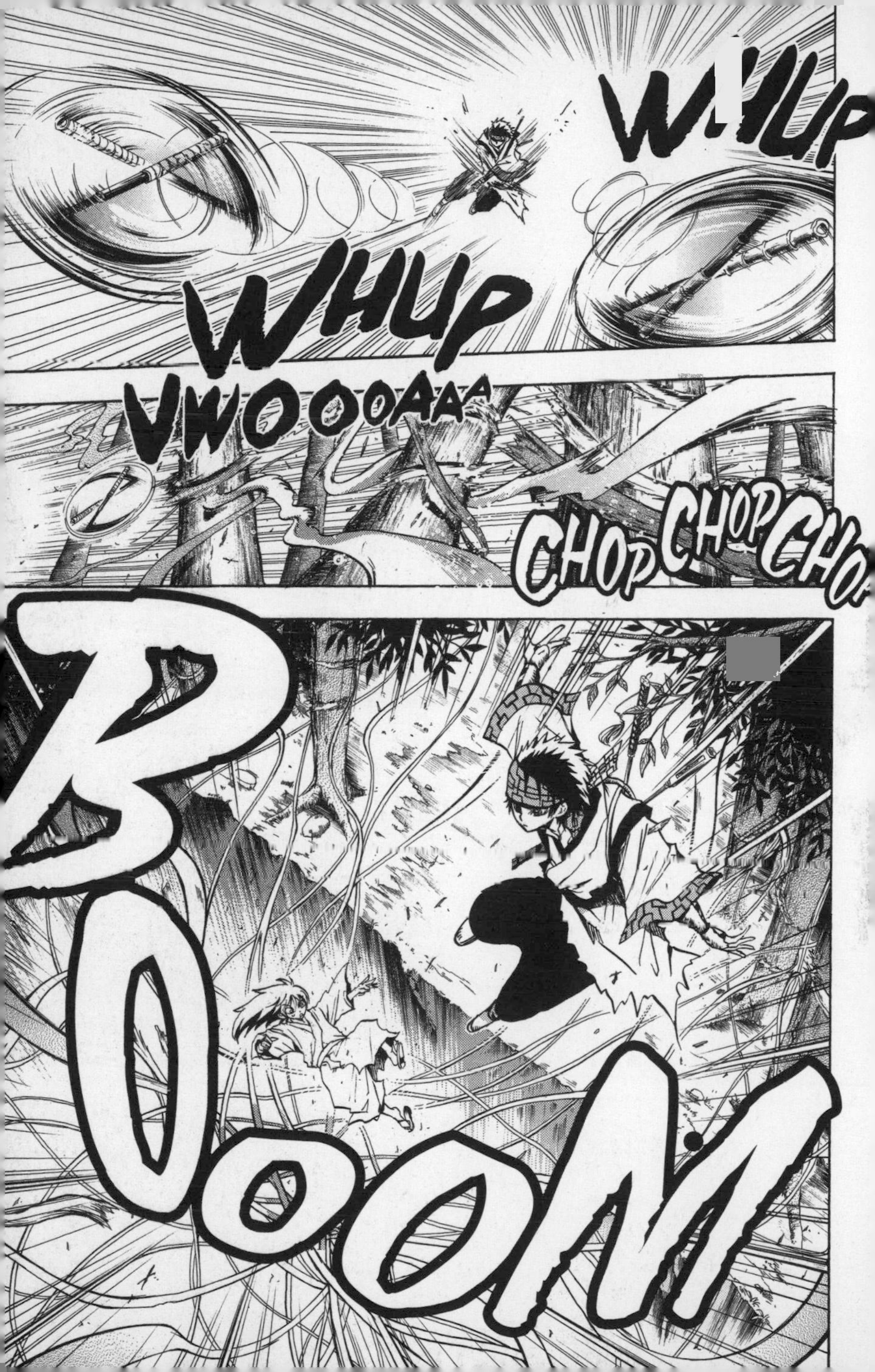
WHUP
WHUP
CHOP CHOP CHO
VWOOOAAA
BOOM

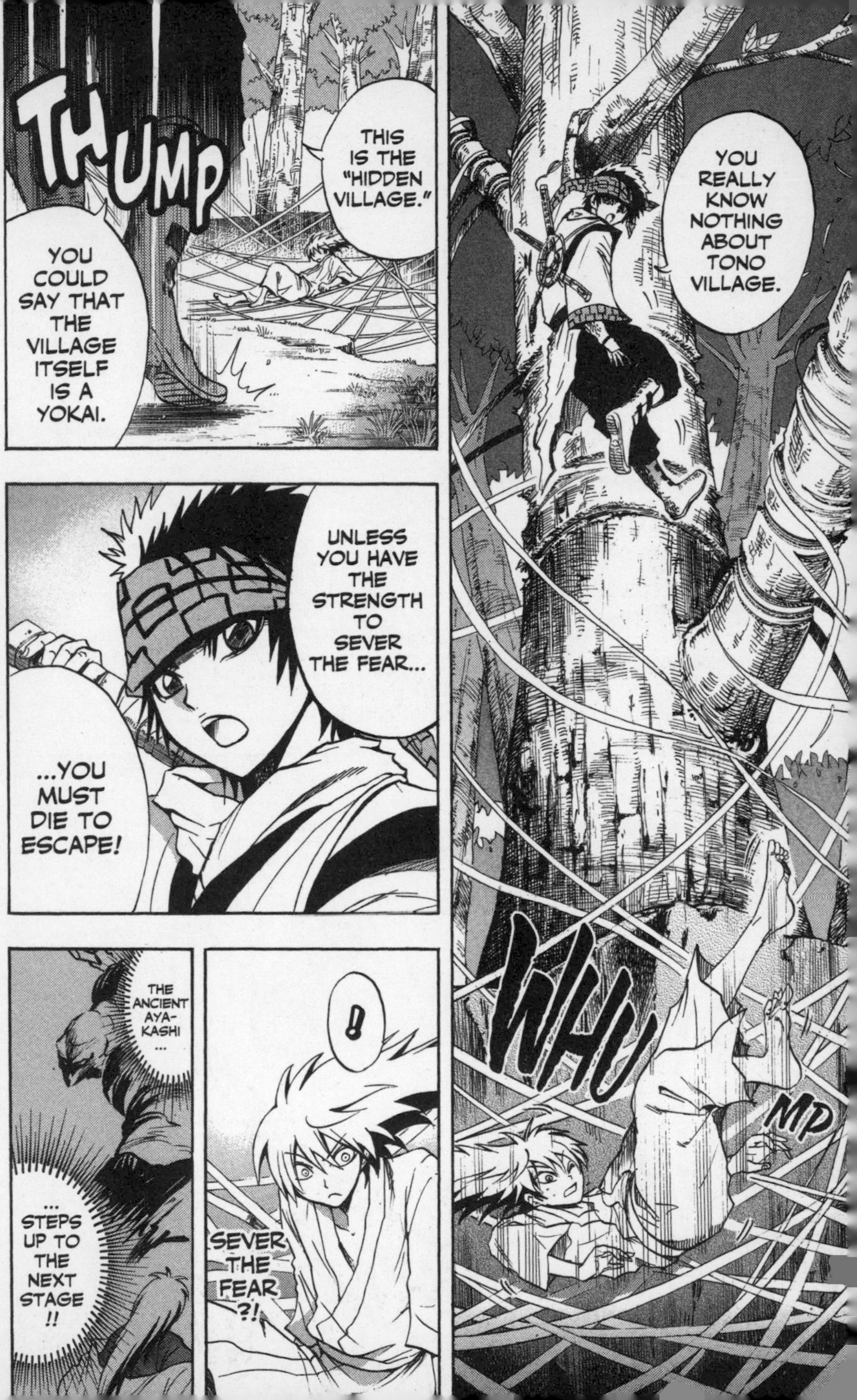
YOU REALLY KNOW NOTHING ABOUT TONO VILLAGE.
WHU
MP
THUMP
THIS IS THE "HIDDEN VILLAGE."
YOU COULD SAY THAT THE VILLAGE ITSELF IS A YOKAI.
UNLESS YOU HAVE THE STRENGTH TO SEVER THE FEAR...
...YOU MUST DIE TO ESCAPE!
!
SEVER THE FEAR ?!
THE ANCIENT AYA-KASHI ...
... STEPS UP TO THE NEXT STAGE !!

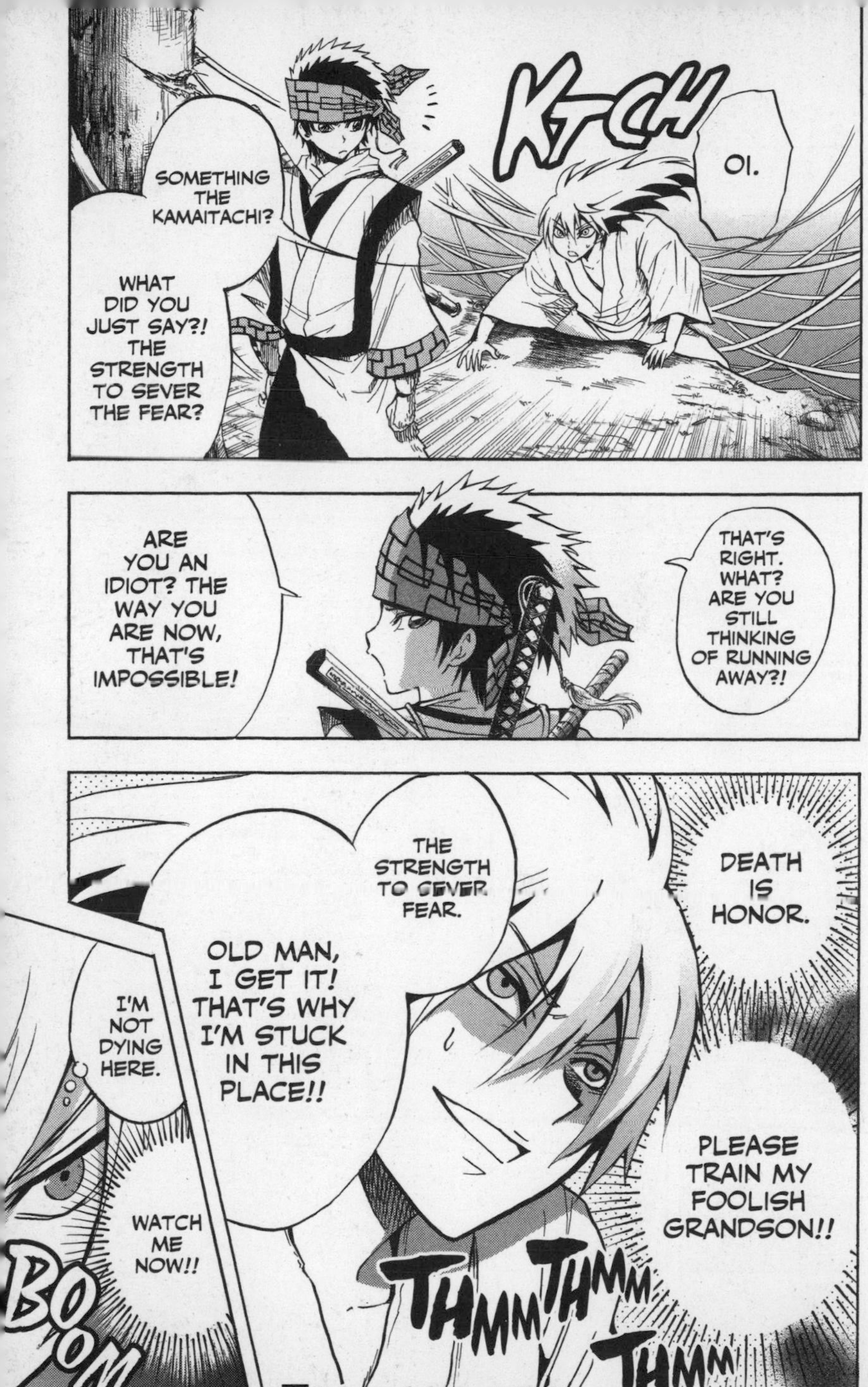
KTCH
OI.
SOMETHING THE KAMAITACHI?
WHAT DID YOU JUST SAY?! THE STRENGTH TO SEVER THE FEAR?
THAT'S RIGHT. WHAT? ARE YOU STILL THINKING OF RUNNING AWAY?!
ARE YOU AN IDIOT? THE WAY YOU ARE NOW, THAT'S IMPOSSIBLE!
DEATH IS HONOR.
THE STRENGTH TO SEVER FEAR.
PLEASE TRAIN MY FOOLISH GRANDSON!!
OLD MAN, I GET IT! THAT'S WHY I'M STUCK IN THIS PLACE!!
I'M NOT DYING HERE.
THMM THMM THMM THMM
WATCH ME NOW!!
BOOM

8 Echoes of the Past (End)

Bonus Story: Birthday Date

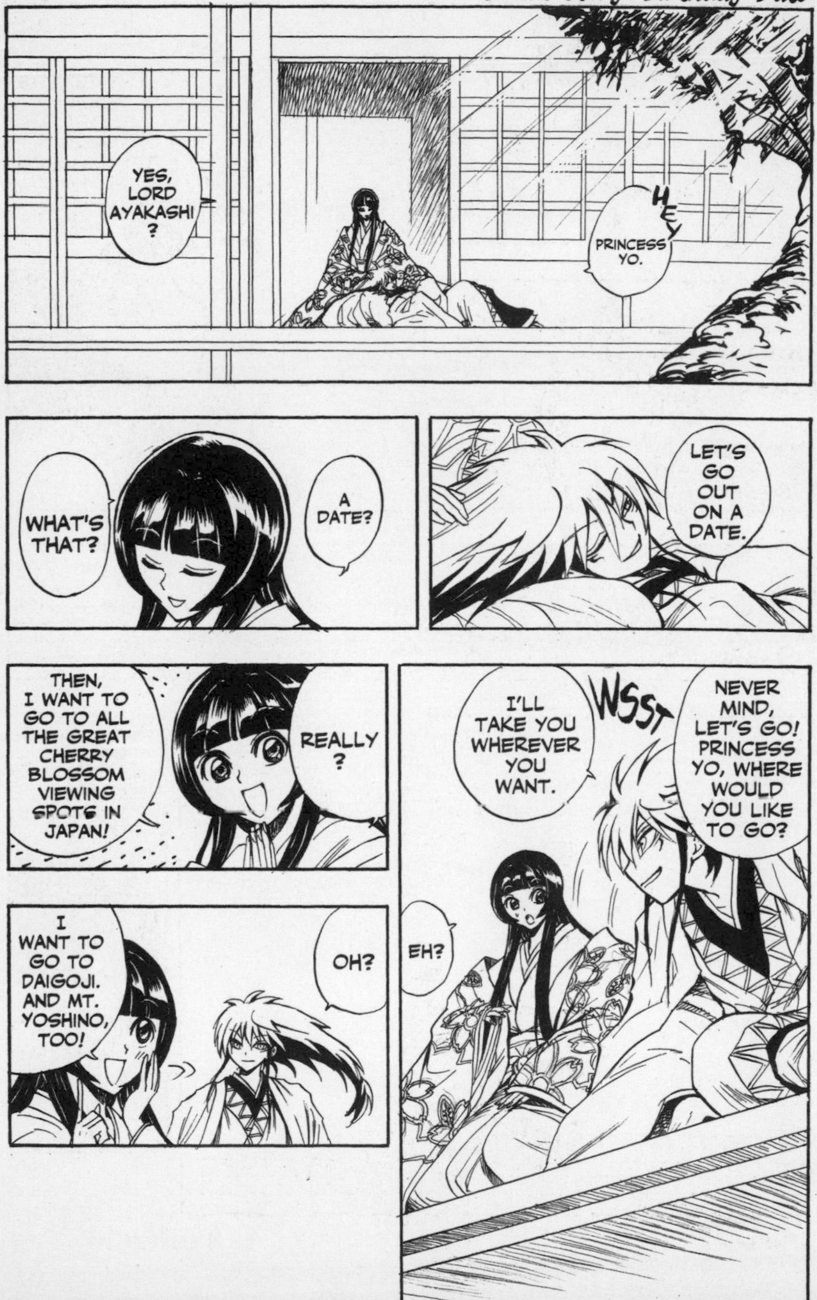
HEY
PRINCESS YO.
YES, LORD AYAKASHI?
LET'S GO OUT ON A DATE.
A DATE?
WHAT'S THAT?
NEVER MIND, LET'S GO! PRINCESS YO, WHERE WOULD YOU LIKE TO GO?
WSST
I'LL TAKE YOU WHEREVER YOU WANT.
EH?
REALLY?
THEN, I WANT TO GO TO ALL THE GREAT CHERRY BLOSSOM VIEWING SPOTS IN JAPAN!
OH?
I WANT TO GO TO DAIGOJI. AND MT. YOSHINO, TOO!

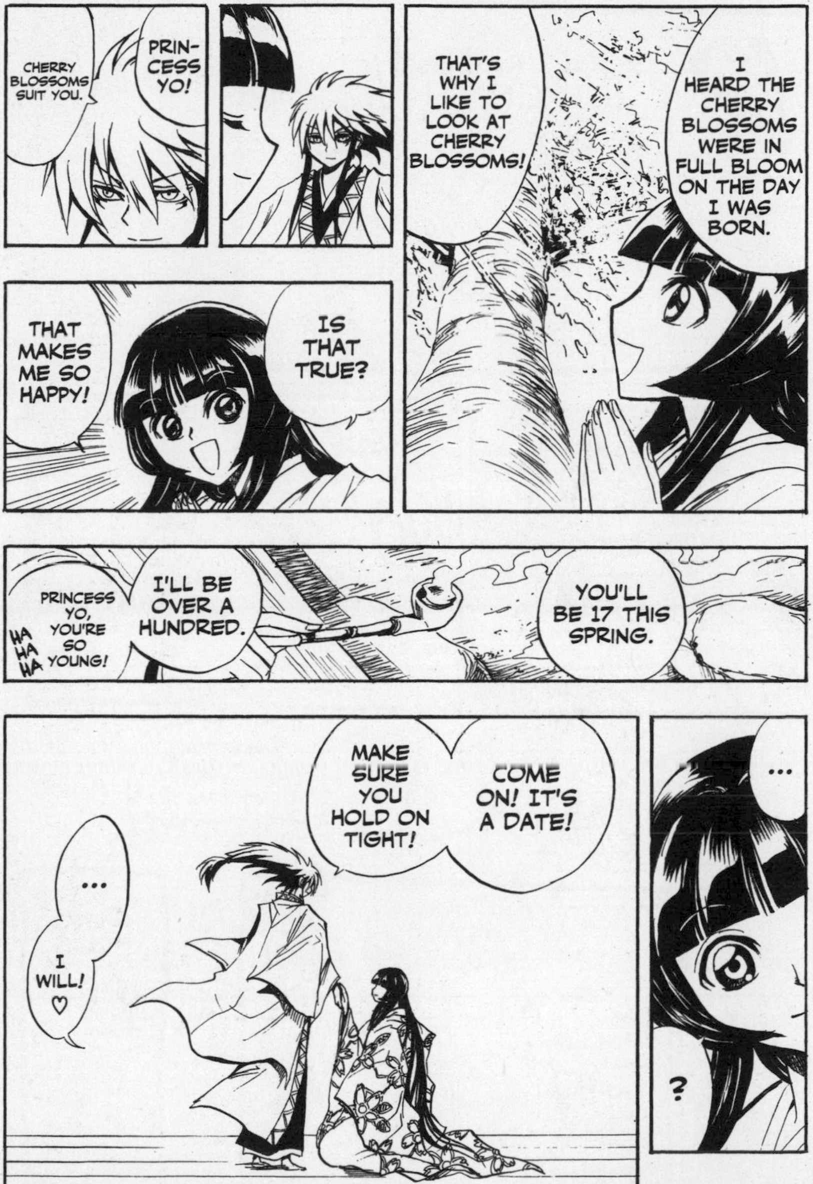
I HEARD THE CHERRY BLOSSOMS WERE IN FULL BLOOM ON THE DAY I WAS BORN.
THAT'S WHY I LIKE TO LOOK AT CHERRY BLOSSOMS!
PRINCESS YO!
CHERRY BLOSSOMS SUIT YOU.
IS THAT TRUE?
THAT MAKES ME SO HAPPY!
YOU'LL BE 17 THIS SPRING.
I'LL BE OVER A HUNDRED.
PRINCESS YO, YOU'RE SO YOUNG!
HA HA HA
...
?
COME ON! IT'S A DATE!
MAKE SURE YOU HOLD ON TIGHT!
...
I WILL! ♡

THE END

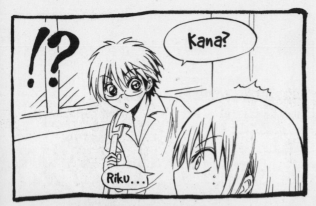

Kana?
!?
Riku...
OSH
Huh!?
WO
Why...!? I see him all the time, so why...!?
My... face is all red...!?
Ah...
Did...
Did he...? Did he see it??
I'm leaving now... do you want to walk home together?
Kana, there's no Kiyojuji Patrol today—
Oh, where's oikawa?
I think she left already.
...oh♪
I feel relieved, but...
...a bit disappointed, too...
...
Um... Rikuo... did you... see it?
Eh? See what?
N-nothing!
o-okay...

CONTINUES...AS NORMAL!

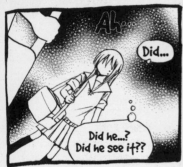

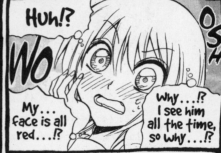

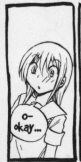

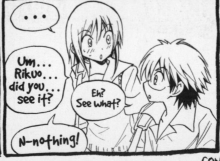

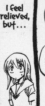

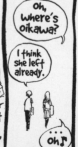

IN THE NEXT VOLUME...
TONO MONOGATARI

The yokai Hagoromo-Gitsune continues her attack to
break the eight seals of Hidemoto. If she succeeds,
the entire city of Kyoto will be under her full control.
To save the city, Rikuo and his newfound allies, other
trainee yokai that he's met in the city of Tono, will have
to harness all the power they've acquired and travel from
the safety of Tono toward the ensuing fray in Kyoto!

AVAILABLE JUNE 2012!

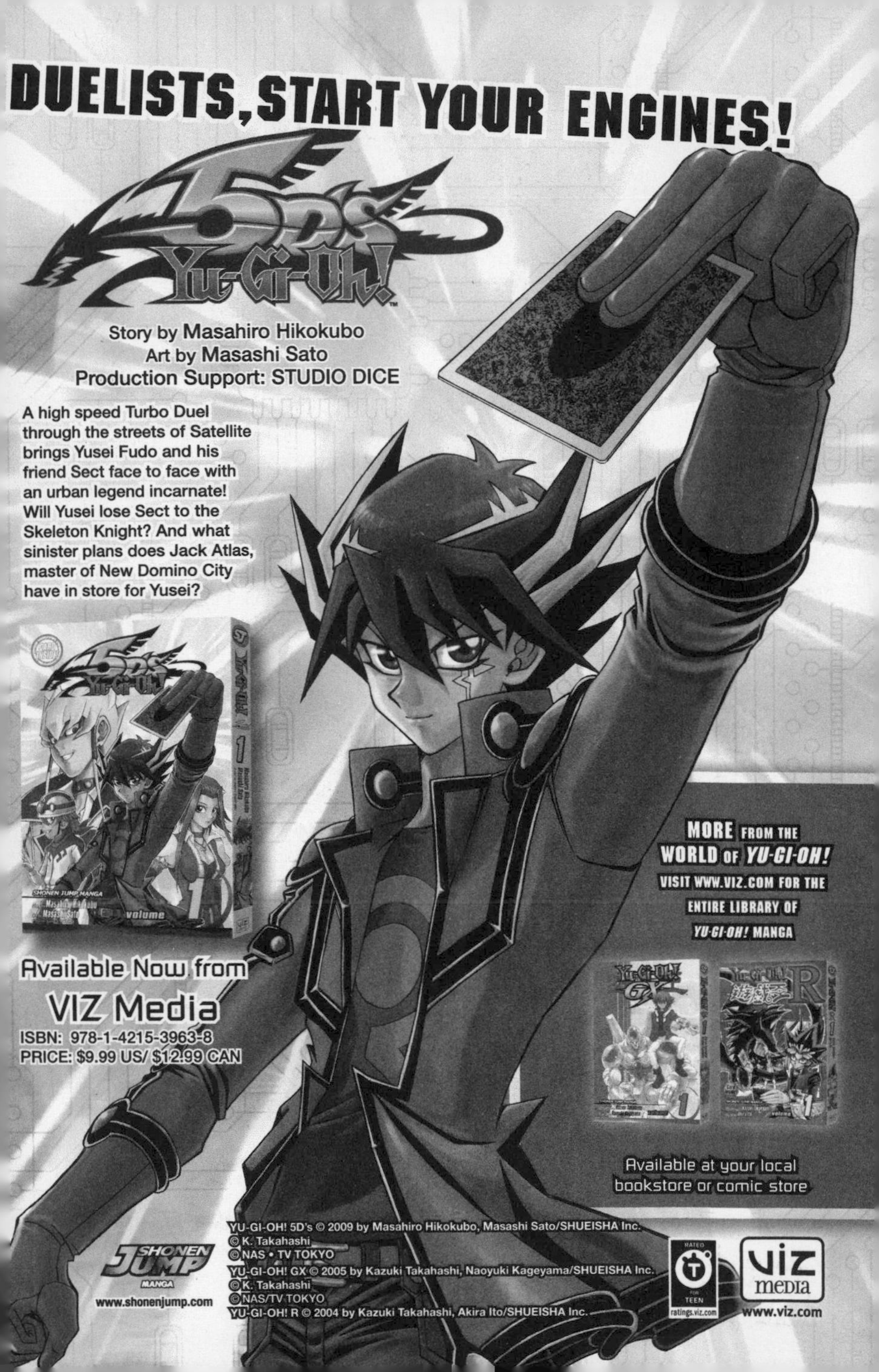

DUELISTS, START YOUR ENGINES!
5D's
YU-GI-OH!
Story by Masahiro Hikokubo
Art by Masashi Sato
Production Support: STUDIO DICE
A high speed Turbo Duel through the streets of Satellite brings Yusei Fudo and his friend Sect face to face with an urban legend incarnate! Will Yusei lose Sect to the Skeleton Knight? And what sinister plans does Jack Atlas, master of New Domino City have in store for Yusei?
Available Now from
VIZ Media
ISBN: 978-1-4215-3963-8
PRICE: $9.99 US/ $12.99 CAN
MORE FROM THE WORLD OF YU-GI-OH!
VISIT WWW.VIZ.COM FOR THE ENTIRE LIBRARY OF YU-GI-OH! MANGA
Available at your local bookstore or comic store
SHONEN JUMP MANGA
www.shonenjump.com
YU-GI-OH! 5D's © 2009 by Masahiro Hikokubo, Masashi Sato/SHUEISHA Inc.
© K. Takahashi
© NAS • TV TOKYO
YU-GI-OH! GX © 2005 by Kazuki Takahashi, Naoyuki Kageyama/SHUEISHA Inc.
© K. Takahashi
© NAS/TV TOKYO
YU-GI-OH! R © 2004 by Kazuki Takahashi, Akira Ito/SHUEISHA Inc.
RATED T FOR TEEN
ratings.viz.com
VIZ media
www.viz.com

By Tite Kubo, creator of ZOMBIEPOWDER.

THE SECRETS OF THE SOUL SOCIETY REVEALED!

Become an unofficial Soul Reaper with the official *BLEACH* character book containing 326 pages of:
- Character and storyline info from vol. 1-22
- The original *BLEACH* one shot
- Bonus manga
- An interview with series creator Tite Kubo

Plus, exclusive stickers and poster!

COMPLETE your *BLEACH* collection with the **BLEACH SOULs.** *Official Character Book*— **GET YOURS TODAY!**

On sale at **www.shonenjump.com**
Also available at your local bookstore and comic store.

bleach.viz.com

www.viz.com

BLEACH OFFICIAL CHARACTER BOOK SOULs. © 2005 by Tite Kubo/SHUEISHA Inc.